A Social History of Education in England

A Social

Methuen & Co Ltd, London

George Cruikshank

History of Education in England

John Lawson & Harold Silver

First published 1973 by Methuen & Co Ltd
11 New Fetter Lane, London EC4
© 1973 John Lawson and Harold Silver
Printed in Great Britain by
Butler & Tanner Ltd
Frome and London

SBN (hardbound) 416 08670 5
SBN (paperback) 416 08680 3

Distributed in the USA by
HARPER & ROW PUBLISHERS INC.
BARNES & NOBLE IMPORT DIVISION

To Muriel and Pam

Contents

Contents

Illustrations

Preface

Although the authors share responsibility for the planning and execution of the book as a whole, John Lawson has been mainly responsible for the first six chapters, and Harold Silver for the last five. In addition to suggestions for further reading at the end of the chapters, a general list has also been given, indicating some useful books covering aspects of education over a long span of time. Spelling and punctuation have for the most part been modernized.

The authors would like to thank Professor Kenneth Charlton, Dr S. H. Atkins and Mrs Judith Ryder for reading chapters of the manuscript and making valuable comments and suggestions. They are greatly indebted to the staff of Chelsea College library and the Brynmor Jones library and the Institute of Education library of the University of Hull. They are grateful to the headmaster and chairman of the management committee of St Mark's primary school, Kennington, for permission to use material in the possession of the school.

Lastly, and above all, they would like to thank their respective wives for their immeasurable help, patience and encouragement.

John Lawson, University of Hull
Harold Silver, Chelsea College, University of London

Acknowledgements

The authors and publishers wish to thank the following for permission to reproduce the illustrations appearing in this book (the numbers of the pictures can be found in the list of illustrations):

Aerofilms Ltd for No. 12
B. T. Batsford Ltd for No. 14
Bodleian Library for No. 3
British Museum for Nos. 4, 6, 15
Central Press Photos Ltd for No. 52
Fox Photos Ltd for Nos. 22, 45, 46
Girton College, Cambridge, for No. 37
Greater London Council for Nos. 24, 27, 28, 29, 39, 40, 41, 44, 47
Henry Grant for Nos. 50, 51, 53, 54
Guildhall Library and Art Galley for title page, Nos. 17, 20
Kensington Library for No. 32
Leicester Museum and Art Gallery for No. 21
Mansell Collection for Nos. 7, 19, 26, 31, 33, 36, 38, 42, 48
National Monuments Records for No. 2
Radio Times Hulton Picture Library for Nos. 5, 9, 10, 18, 23, 43, 49
Malcolm Seaborne for Nos. 13, 25, 30, 35
Sheffield City Libraries for No. 34
Alan Sorrell for No. 1
Victoria and Albert Museum for No. 11
Walters Gallery, Baltimore, for No. 8

Introduction

A 'social history of education' in the widest sense of the phrase would relate education to every possible aspect of changing social structures, relationships and ideals. Education seen as an activity in and of society concerns not only schools and universities, teachers and pupils, but also all those social institutions which have at different times shaped it, been influenced by it or become enmeshed in it. To be complete, such a history would have to take account of all the phases of educational development in their complex relationships with the church and the state, social and political movements of every kind, the changing patterns of social stratification and family and population structure, and the social needs and philosophies of all sorts and conditions of men. It would need to do all of this, and more, not only for educational institutions but also for the informal networks of learning and activity that can be called 'education' – from tribal systems of socialization to medieval forms of apprenticeship, from the moulding of the Renaissance courtier to that of the Victorian wife, from the distribution of the evangelical tract and the Chartist newspaper to the function of the television set.

This book does not attempt to offer such a total history of education and society over thirteen centuries. Such an attempt would be presumptuous and foolhardy, if only because enormous areas of these relationships remain unexplored or unexplorable: what detailed work has been done is normally confined to particular topics and relatively short periods of time. Evidence is all too often incomplete or perhaps does not exist. Before the nineteenth century statistical approaches are hardly possible, and much in our earlier chapters is necessarily based on non-quantitative, often literary, material that allows only speculations and impressions. The growing interest among historians and sociologists in the position of education in the history of social processes may make it possible in the near future to take a broader view with greater confidence. In the meantime, we believe, the 'social history of education in England' can be written only with a more limited aim.

The first concern of this book is the history of education itself – the questions of who, at different times, was being educated, by whom, how, and to what ends (as much a question of attitudes to children in general as of the classroom situation). The book seeks to explore consistently two themes which widen the context of discussion – first, changes in population structure and distribution, and secondly the extent and functions of literacy. The clues it is possible to offer to broader social explanations vary according to the period under discussion – at one point it is an examination of the structure of the church, at another shifts in secular philosophies; at one point it is the social position of girls, at another the emergence of new social class identities; at one point it is the monastery, at another the factory or local government. The scale of the book and the present state of the subject make it impossible to do detailed justice to all the events, agencies and institutions that would have merited such attention. The book, as the title emphasizes, deals with education in England, although much of the analysis could be applied to Wales (and less often to Scotland, with its very different educational history).

The persistent 'social' themes of this book are therefore, in the nature of things, restricted. The direction of interest also inevitably changes in different parts of the book, especially before and after the late eighteenth century, when a profound change took place in the dimensions, pattern and context of English education. There have been other historical periods in which education has undergone far-reaching changes, but none so sharply divides one picture of education from another as the so-called industrial revolution, with its industrial, urban and other transformations. The history of education up to the decades in which these developments occurred is concerned, broadly speaking, with processes and attitudes which altered only gradually. The educational system was relatively undiversified, and consisted of small institutions, moulded by the church, and set in rural or small urban communities subject only to slow changes in population structure and social composition. It catered for a society in which social mobility was slight and in which schooling and literacy served precisely defined ends.

After the late eighteenth century, however, the history of education is concerned with rapid changes. These related to the size and distribution of population, the decline in the traditional authority of the church and the disruption of settled ways of life, new social and political tensions, controversy about the provision and purposes of education, a new and increasing involvement of the state in education, and education as an element in social policy.

There were, of course, continuities and common features in society and education before and after the industrial revolution. Pre-industrial society was not without change, and nineteenth-century England was not entirely urban, industrial and socially or geographically mobile. In *Jude the Obscure*, for example, written at the end of the nineteenth century, Hardy describes how Jude as a boy in a small village asks a man the whereabouts of the town of Christminster (which turns out to be under twenty miles away and visible on a clear day). 'Christminster?' the man replies, 'O, well, out by there yonder; though I've never bin there – not I. I've never had any business at such a place.' If old ways of life were not entirely destroyed, neither were old ways of educating, as the history of the grammar schools in the nineteenth century indicates. There had been, nevertheless, enormous changes. In approaching the social history of education the historian finds that from the beginnings of industrial, mass society his attention moves to wider phenomena, new social relationships, new and influential ideas and social movements, and different sources of evidence.

There are, therefore, differences of emphasis between the chapters of this book which deal with pre-industrial society, and the later ones. Much that is central to the early chapters – for example the role of the church, study and life at Oxford and Cambridge, and the curriculum and pedagogy of the endowed schools – subsequently, and inevitably, recedes. In the later chapters the new phenomena of a more complex society – such as monitorial schools, the education of middle-class girls and the growth of the mass media – acquire importance and require explanation. It is hoped, however, that the varying emphasis and focus of interest will not mask the underlying themes which we consider central and unifying – the history of educational institutions and processes and their relationship to questions of population, literacy and the social philosophies and institutions which are predominant or influential at any given time.

CHAPTER I

Anglo-Saxon beginnings: education in the service of Christianity
600–1066

The diffusion of Roman civilization throughout the empire was achieved in part by a public educational system designed to train a native governing class for the imperial service. According to Tacitus, Agricola established schools in Britain in A.D. 78 in order to romanize the sons of native chieftains; further evidence is scanty and uncertain but it may be assumed that eventually Britain had much the same educational arrangements as other more developed Roman provinces. In the main administrative and commercial urban centres there would perhaps be state-paid and also private grammarians and rhetors providing an influential native minority with a Roman education, partly to fit them for public office. Latin was the only written language. Among the British population at large, knowledge of Latin would be confined to relatively small groups: tribal notables, officials, some craftsmen and traders in the towns, a few wealthy villa owners in the countryside, and, from the third century, the leaders of scattered, mainly urban, Christian communities. Largely unaffected by Roman ways, the great majority of country dwellers remained Celtic and illiterate.[1] Mass education of subject peoples was never contemplated by the Romans. The empire was ruled through an educated élite.

The post-Roman period of the English invasions and settlements between about 450 and 600 remains a historical dark age. Unlike other Germanic invaders of the empire, the Anglo-Saxon war bands who attacked Britain had no desire, even if they had

Anglo-Saxon village

possessed the means, to preserve the remnants of Roman civilization, and soon over most of the country only the roads and monuments remained. Knowledge of Latin and the tradition of letters
gradually died. Only in the Celtic west where organized
Christianity survived is there any trace of a continuing literary
culture. About 500 a school for missionaries was taught by the
semi-legendary St Illtud, abbot of a Celtic community at Llantwit
Major. The Latin prose of one who was perhaps his pupil, the
mid-sixth-century Welsh writer Gildas, describing the destruction
of Britain *(De Excidio Britanniae)*, suggests a thorough training
in Latin, but as a written rather than a spoken language. Ordered
centralized government, urban civilization and a high level of
material prosperity, the basic conditions of the Roman educational system, no longer existed.

The English invaders and colonists were pagans whose simple
culture knew nothing of reading and writing. They came in small
kin-groups of peasant warriors led by war-chiefs and settled in
scattered, self-contained hamlets and isolated farmsteads. Tribal
relationships and conquest soon led to the formation of petty
kingdoms. Their social organization recognized essentially three
grades of men, in proportions that are unknown: noblemen,
common freemen *(ceorls)* and slaves.[2] Noblemen, the king's companions and leaders in war, lived in their timber halls with their
retinues, supervised their estates and kept order among their
followers. Freemen, bound to a lord by obligations of service,
worked their own land as farmers and stockbreeders; some of
them later became the first specialist craftworkers – smiths,
wrights, tanners, millers. Slaves, perhaps native Britons or cap-
tives in intertribal wars among the invaders, were the property
of either noblemen or freemen; men slaves probably did heavy
labouring such as tree-felling, ploughing and ditching, women
slaves worked about the homestead. The earliest settlements
might have consisted of no more than a freeman and his family
and a few slaves. For generations they were frontier communities
where life was a struggle for survival against human enemies and
the natural wilderness of forest and scrub. Given these conditions,
we may conjecture that education was a matter for the family
group, and confined to the ancestral skills of farming and fighting, knowledge of the powers of nature, and oral folk traditions
about gods and heroes, demons and monsters.

A new era began when St Augustine and his missionary band

of monks arrived from Rome in 597 to convert King Ethelbert and the men of Kent to Christianity. The supposition is that he established at Canterbury not only a church but also a school to train native converts as priests, providing instruction in the Latin language, the Latin Scriptures and liturgy and the Roman chant – all essential for the priestly office. From Kent preachers and teachers moved into neighbouring English kingdoms, setting up schools alongside churches to form other centres of evangelism, first at Rochester and London, later at York, Dunwich and Dorchester-on-Thames. In each one, following the Roman tradition, the bishop would receive into his household suitable young boys to educate for the priesthood, and he would teach them himself or through a *scholasticus*, a cleric who combined teaching and secretarial duties. Meanwhile Christianity of the Celtic or Irish kind was spreading from Ireland and western Scotland into northern England and establishing monastic communities as centres of missionary and therefore educational endeavour. For Irish as for Roman evangelists in a heathen countryside, schools for the education of a native clergy were essential if Christianity was to survive.[3]

In the event, Christianity proved to be much more than a religion that chanced to survive. In a rude and barbarous society it was a moral code, a way of life, a civilizing agent. The church through which it was organized stood for order and stability. Eventually it became almost a separate entity inside the secular kingdom, with its own laws and government. It was a wealthy landowner. It was the principal patron of schools and learning, literature and the arts. To the callings of monk and priest it attracted men of both noble and common birth – men with a mission, men with scholarly interests, men of gentle disposition who recoiled from the harshness and violence of the world, and perhaps some who wanted only a relatively easy living. Gradually overcoming, if never wholly obliterating, pagan beliefs and practices, it became through its preaching and sacraments and social organization an all-pervading influence in the life of the English people.

After the arrival of the cultivated Byzantine Theodore of Tarsus as archbishop of Canterbury in 669, a new stimulus was given to evangelism and religious education. The country was still further divided into bishoprics, and the bishop's church and *familia*, whether composed of monks or of secular priests, was the focal point of apostolic and teaching activity. The school at Canterbury, touched now by the sophisticated learning of the Graeco-Roman world, became famous throughout England for the study of Latin and even Greek, for biblical exegesis, versification, astronomy, arithmetic and the Gregorian chant. In the kingdom of Wessex, where Irish missionary influence was strong, there were monastic schools at Malmesbury, Winchester and Glastonbury, but the most celebrated after Canterbury were in the kingdom of Northumbria, at Jarrow, Monkwearmouth, Hexham and York. Schools needed books and they were imported from the continent in great numbers. The monk Benedict Biscop, a Northumbrian nobleman who founded the monastery at Monkwearmouth, brought back from Rome some 200 or 300 books, which thus became available to his disciple Bede.[4] Bede, who was the first English historian, was dedicated to the religious life at Monkwearmouth at the age of seven and moved in 685 to Jarrow where he lived for fifty years 'observing monastic discipline and the daily care of singing in the church, and always delighting in learning, teaching and writing', as he himself tells us. The cathedral school at York was outstanding after 732 under Archbishop Egbert, one of Bede's pupils, and especially during the period when Æthelbert was *scholasticus*, followed by his disciple Alcuin. Alcuin left York in 782 to be master of the Frankish King Charlemagne's palace school at Aachen, where he became a leading figure in the Carolingian revival of learning. In a poem dedicated to the archbishop he later recalled the subjects and authors, classical and Christian, that were studied at York. What is remarkable about them is their great range – grammar and rhetoric, law and chant, astronomy, natural history, arithmetic, and above all scripture; but the programme he describes is probably ideal rather than actual.[5]

The curriculum inherited from the classical world, summarized and formulated by the sixth-century scholar-statesmen Boethius and Cassiodorus, consisted of the seven liberal arts. The trivium, or three basic subjects, comprised grammar, logic and rhetoric; the quadrivium, more advanced, comprised arithmetic, geometry, astronomy and music. The task of the church was to adapt these subjects to Christian use. Grammar was fundamental, for Latin was the essential key to the Scriptures, the Fathers and the service books of the church as well as to all the inherited wisdom of the ancients. Comparatively, logic and rhetoric received little attention from Anglo-Saxon scholars. Nor was the quadrivium much studied, save for some arithmetic and astronomy, mainly for calculating the date of Easter and the other movable feasts. Music — which meant the Roman chant — was important, but as a practical art rather than as a theoretical study. Notwithstanding the comprehensive erudition of a few eminent scholars, like Aldhelm at Malmesbury and Bede at Jarrow, Anglo-Saxon educators did not see themselves as inheriting and transmitting the classical tradition embodied in the liberal arts, but primarily as teachers of grammar to make possible the study of the 'sacred page'. Their motive was essentially religious.

In the country as a whole, the influence of this educational activity can have been only small. Some twenty or so episcopal and monastic schools are known from the eighth century and there can be no doubt that their sole purpose was to train monks and priests. Probably only a minority of churchmen, secular or monastic, had much Latin culture and they would be found in the important minsters and monasteries. Most of the ordinary clergy must have had little schooling and doubtless shared the illiteracy and rustic habits of the population at large. Among laymen, literacy would be confined to a few interested noblemen who had been brought up as youths in bishops' households or in monasteries, some of them active propagators of the faith as a result. Book knowledge and writing were irrelevant in a poor and primitive society, in which the vast majority of men, free and unfree alike, had to struggle ceaselessly to clear and work the land in order for their families to survive. Alongside this minority culture — written, Latin and Christian — there existed a popular, native English culture consisting of pagan folk tradition and heroic songs and poetry, preserved and transmitted not by the scribe but the minstrel. Among peasants, in spite of the spread of Christianity, heathen customs and superstitions remained ineradicable: rural isolation, mass ignorance and illiteracy nourished for nearly 1,000 years to come beliefs in magic and marvels, fairies and ogres, ghosts and witches.[6]

Mass illiteracy is not incompatible with a high degree of artistic culture, when this has the patronage of an educated or social élite. Between about 670 and 770 Anglo-Saxon civilization reached a peak, particularly in Northumbria, and monasteries and noblemen were its patrons. In scholarship, as we have seen, this was the age of Bede and Alcuin. It was also the age of the

Lindisfarne Gospels, the Franks Casket, *Beowulf* and the Bew-
castle and Ruthwell crosses. By the year 700 the Christian con-
version was complete, and after the Synod of Whitby in 664
Christianity meant the Roman, not the Celtic, church. In its
service calligraphers, jewellers, metalworkers, enamellers, stone
and ivory carvers produced illuminated gospel books, liturgical
and other religious objects of superlative design and workman-
ship. For aristocratic society, such as the poem *Beowulf* depicts,
craftsmen made weapons, armour and personal ornaments whose
artistic and technical excellence is seen at its best in the grave-
goods of the Sutton Hoo ship-burial. Books were copied and
illuminated by monks themselves in their *scriptoria*, but we know
nothing of the men who made these other things, whether monks
or laymen, literate or illiterate. Clearly, skills of this order must
have depended on long training, and presumably they could have
been gained and transmitted only through some kind of apprenticeship, either of son to father within a family of craftsmen, or
in permanent craft workshops attached to certain monasteries or
noble households.[7]

Civilization sustained by a united, organized and influential
church suffered a setback in the ninth century during the
colonizing invasions of the heathen Danes and then during the
long struggles to reconquer the Danelaw and unite England,
which were launched by Alfred, king of the West Saxons (871–
99). In two generations, monasticism and an educated clergy
disappeared. 'The first five hundred years of English history
cannot show more than three kings who were even probably
literate', says Professor Galbraith. King Alfred, the most educated
of these, lamented in 894 the decay of Latin learning, and in his
concern for England's recovery looked to the spread of vernacular
education among both laity and clergy. He planned to translate
into English such books as 'are most necessary for all men to
know', and to set freeborn youths of sufficient means to learn to
read English; those who wanted to become priests would learn
Latin afterwards. English had long been used for writing down
laws (and native poetry too) but it was now to serve a wider use
for vernacular prose literature and for teaching those who could
not read or who knew no Latin.[8]

The tenth-century renaissance of education, Latin scholarship, vernacular literature and the visual arts was the work of
the church inspired largely by Dunstan, abbot of Glastonbury

and later archbishop of Canterbury. Minsters – larger churches served by communities of secular priests – again became centres of pastoral work and teaching. However, the mainsprings of intellectual, literary and artistic activity were the restored monasteries, now observing the Rule of St Benedict. Although secular priests were better placed to train clergy for the parishes that were now taking shape, as local churches were built and endowed by bishops and lay patrons, there was a preference for cathedrals and other great churches to be served by monks. Monasteries were depositories of educational texts and liturgical, legal and theological writings, and they afforded economic security and therefore leisure for study. With few exceptions, the only learned men were now monks. From the mid-tenth century to the Norman conquest they furnished the great majority of bishops, and bishops were the king's closest advisers. St Benedict's rule assumed the monk's ability to read and imposed an obligation to study daily; each one had to choose a book from the library at the beginning of Lent for reading during the Lenten period.[9] Although the Rule makes no mention of monastic schools, each community was responsible for training its own recruits. These

*Religious instruction for the illiterate: 'The Ladder of Salvation',
wall painting in Chaldon church, Surrey, c. 1200*

were either oblates, boys dedicated to the religious life from infancy by their parents and brought up in the monastery under the childmaster, or postulants, grown men admitted from the secular world as novices and instructed by the novice master. For all professed monks some grammar and song would be indispensable for sharing in the divine office, and teaching these would be a task for each house. Monasteries for women were very few (at this period perhaps only six or seven in all); nuns were recruited from the daughters and widows of noble families and they provided education for girls of this class; some nuns evidently had considerable educational attainments, but rarely in Latin.

In certain monasteries, notably Winchester under Bishop Æthelwold, Glastonbury, Ramsey, Worcester and Evesham, scholarly activity reached a high level, not only in Latin but also in a remarkable flowering of the Anglo-Saxon vernacular. This was cultivated for the instruction of rustic clergy ignorant of Latin and was used for the writing of homilies, saints' lives, works on herbs, cures and charms, and translations of Latin treatises on the calendar and methods of calculating Easter. In government, too, written English gained added importance with the increasing use of the sealed charter and especially of the sealed royal writ addressed to the shire courts: a development which, if it had not been cut short by the Norman conquest, would no doubt have speeded the growth of a more literate lay society.

Apart from a small body of professional clerks in the king's service, writing in Latin and English was virtually a monopoly of the monks, copying books slowly and laboriously in the new Carolingian minuscule script for their own relatively affluent and leisured communities, and for such priests and privileged laymen as could read them and afford them. Some noblemen of this period were certainly literate and owned books. The best known is Æthelweard, an ealdorman of Wessex (about 950), who wrote a chronicle in very bad Latin. Outstanding among monastic teachers of the age was Æthelweard's protégé Ælfric, a pupil of Æthelwold at Winchester, later *scholasticus* at Cerne Abbas and finally abbot of Eynsham, a prolific writer of schoolbooks, sermons, pastoral letters and Bible commentaries. Byrhtferth, *scholasticus* at Ramsey, wrote Latin treatises and an English handbook of miscellaneous knowledge useful for young clerks. Whether the books were in Latin or English, the purpose was the same: to instruct monks and priests in the performance of their sacred office.

To what extent the monasteries of this period provided education for boys and youths other than monks is uncertain. Clearly it was the intention of Dunstan and other leaders of the English revival that monasteries should stimulate religious and educational vitality in the church as a whole. Books were written to serve students outside as well as inside the cloister. Occasionally boys who had no intention of becoming monks may have been admitted for education, but in the social and economic conditions of the time there can have been no general demand for this; the exceptional few would be the sons of men of influence in the neighbourhood, and perhaps most of these would be intended for the priesthood.[10] The famous *Colloquy* of Ælfric, written about 1000, consists of dialogues (in interlinear Latin and Anglo-Saxon) between a master, a young monk, and boys of both free and servile birth who represent certain common occupations — a ploughman, shepherd, cowherd, hunter, fisherman, seaman, shoemaker and so on. This has been taken to depict actual schools of the time and to show how socially comprehensive they were. But in all probability the *Colloquy* is no more than a Latin reader for the instruction of monastic oblates. There is no evidence, and no likelihood, that monks had any concern with teaching the general laity, and it is impossible to believe that ploughmen, shepherds and sailors went to school alongside young monks to learn Latin.[11]

Outside the monasteries, instruction might have been available from some relatively lettered priest, but individually and privately rather than in schools. Some laws of King Edgar about 960 suggest that teaching (religion and crafts are the subjects mentioned) was one of the pastoral duties commonly expected of priests, and other laws some thirty years later enjoined priests to keep schools in their villages and teach young boys without fee.[12] But almost certainly these were utopian aspirations rather than practical objectives. Most secular priests can have had little to offer save elementary religious instruction; in the remote countryside they were probably hardly less ignorant than their parishioners.

About the mid-eleventh century there was a movement for the foundation of collegiate churches of secular priests or canons, living a quasi-communal life according to Rule, and on the eve of the Norman conquest eleven of the fifteen English cathedrals were churches of this kind. There is evidence that some of these, like the college of the Holy Cross at Waltham founded by Earl Harold in 1060, maintained schools of grammar and chant for clerical recruits and the local clergy. But compared with the greater monasteries, churches of canons, including those that were cathedrals, were educationally obscure and unimportant until after the conquest. At this time there were some thirty-five monasteries, all following the Benedictine Rule but probably containing not as many as 1,000 monks altogether, and only nine nunneries. Nearly all of these, like the colleges of secular clerks, were to be found south of a line from Chester to Boston.[13] In a sparse, poverty-stricken peasant population totalling about $1\frac{1}{2}$ million their combined educational influence can only have been slight and local. Society as a whole must have been oral, customary, illiterate, semi-barbarous. It is hard to imagine the mentality of whole communities of people unable to read, knowing only what they had personally experienced or been told by word of mouth, who had never seen a map (because none existed) or travelled more than a few miles from the village where they were born.

Notes

1 JOAN LIVERSIDGE, *Britain in the Roman Empire* (London, 1968), pp. 305–22, considers the meagre British evidence against the background of Roman education. For the conjectural extent of literacy see SHEPPARD FRERE, *Britannia* (London, 1967), pp. 311–14.

2 D. WHITELOCK, *The Beginnings of English Society* (Harmondsworth, 1952), pp. 83–114.

3 P. HUNTER BLAIR, *An Introduction to Anglo-Saxon England* (Cambridge, 1959), pp. 116–31; M. DEANESLY, *Sidelights on the Anglo-Saxon Church* (London, 1962), pp. 3–7, 139.

4 W. LEVISON, *England and the Continent in the Eighth Century* (Oxford, 1946), pp. 139–48, for books and libraries.

5 A. F. LEACH (ed.), *Educational Charters and Documents* (Cambridge, 1911), pp. 11–17; R. R. BOLGAR, *The Classical Heritage and its Beneficiaries* (Cambridge, 1954), p. 105.

6 R. H. HODGKIN, *A History of the Anglo-Saxons* (Oxford, 1952), I pp. 230–44, for the mentality of Anglo-Saxon heathen society.

7 For a brief account and illustrations see C. THOMAS, *Britain and Ireland in Early Christian Times* (London, 1971), pp. 99–105, 126–34.

8 V. H. GALBRAITH, 'The literacy of the medieval English kings', *Proceedings of the British Academy*, XXI (1935), p. 12; LEACH, *Charters*, pp. 23–5.

9 J. MCCANN, *The Rule of St. Benedict* (London, 1950), pp. 314–15.

10 J. W. BALDWIN, *The Literacy of the Laity in the Middle Ages* (New York, 1960), pp. 116–20.

11 G. N. GARMONSWAY (ed.), *Ælfric's Colloquy*, 2nd ed. (London, 1947); D. KNOWLES, *The Monastic Order in England* (Cambridge, 1949), pp. 487–9.

12 LEACH, *Charters*, pp. 34–7.

13 F. BARLOW, *The English Church 1000–1066* (London, 1963), pp. 277–88, discusses the education of the pre-conquest clergy.

Further Reading

M. DEANESLY, *The Pre-Conquest Church in England* (London, 1961).

C. J. GODFREY, *The Church in Anglo-Saxon England* (Cambridge, 1962).

P. HUNTER BLAIR, *An Introduction to Anglo-Saxon England* (Cambridge, 1959).

D. KNOWLES, *The Monastic Order in England* (Cambridge, 1949).

P. RICHÉ, *Education et culture dans l'Occident barbare VIe–VIIIe siècles* (Paris, 1962), pp. 353–70, 419–49.

D. WHITELOCK, *The Beginnings of English Society* (Harmondsworth, 1952).

See also pp. 89–90, 471–3.

CHAPTER II

Early medieval: education a function of the church
1066–1300

The twelfth-century renaissance

Between 1050 and 1200 changes took place in England and Western Europe generally which opened a new era in intellectual life and education. A fundamental cause was the steady enlargement of knowledge by the spread from Moslem Spain and Sicily of ancient Greek and Arab learning in Latin translation. Most profound in its consequences was the impact made by the metaphysical and scientific works of Aristotle, knowledge of which flooded into the West after about 1120. Elements of Aristotle's logic had long been known in the translations of Boethius, but the 'new logic' based on the syllogism came as a revelation. Syllogistic reasoning became a certain guide to truth, able to reduce the chaos of the natural and political world to order and system. Scholars were fascinated by it. It was applied to all kinds of studies and eventually gave rise in the thirteenth century to a vast structure of scholastic thought which is as characteristic of the age as the Early English cathedrals. Aristotle became in Dante's phrase 'the master of those who know'.

If the twelfth century was excited by the discovery of new knowledge, it was no less concerned to organize and preserve old knowledge. The classical authors were sedulously studied and correct Latin cultivated. The scattered learning of the past was consolidated and systematized in compilations or *summae*, which became standard authorities in higher education, notably in canon law the *Decretum* of the monk Gratian of Bologna (c. 1140), and in theology the *Sentences* of Peter Lombard (c. 1150). The

Decretum gave canon law a new importance in ecclesiastical administration and made it one of the great and most lucrative branches of higher education. Also at Bologna, the law teacher Irnerius established the authoritative text of the great body of Roman civil law, which soon came to exert a profound influence on other legal systems and quickly established itself as another highly profitable subject of advanced professional study.

The stimulus of all this new knowledge and of disputation by the syllogism made the twelfth century one of epidemic scholastic excitement. Famous teachers at particular centres attracted disciples from a floating population of students eager to argue and learn. These teachers tended to gravitate to cathedrals where there were already schools and libraries. Northern France was the principal area of activity: especially celebrated were the cathedral schools at Chartres, Paris, Rheims, Laon and Orleans. Bologna and Salerno in Italy and Toledo in Spain were other cosmopolitan centres of learning. Of these, the schools at Paris and Bologna had a succession of teachers and students who soon after 1150 came to be organized as permanent, self-governing communities – gilds or universities.[1]

Although England was only on the edge of this movement, the Norman conquest brought English learning and higher education into the main current of European civilization as never before in Anglo-Saxon times. Schools multiplied as a result of the importation of books and masters from France.[2] In the post-conquest reorganization of the English church by the new Norman bishops, certain cathedrals had been attached to monasteries in the old Anglo-Saxon tradition, but others had been reconstituted on the continental pattern with chapters of secular canons.[3] In each of these normanized cathedrals a *scholasticus* was responsible for keeping a school, and at some of them, notably London, York, Lincoln and Exeter, there were in the second half of the twelfth century celebrated teachers of grammar, law and theology.[4] None of these schools, however, was to survive permanently save as a grammar school. Surprisingly, the schools of higher learning that were to prove permanent in England were not attached to any cathedral but located in Oxford. In this small but growing town – a road centre and river-crossing with a royal residence and two recently founded monasteries – schools had developed since before 1120 around the parish church of St Mary. Soon after 1200 Oxford was becoming, like Paris and Bologna, one of the great educational centres of Western Europe: a *studium generale* with an organized gild or *universitas* of masters and scholars.[5]

Being in minor orders if not actually priests, all these schoolmen were technically clergy and had received the tonsure. Thus, learning tended to become increasingly an activity of secular clerks (who were often ecclesiastics in little more than name) rather than of monks. Nevertheless, even in this new, turbulent, questing age the Benedictine tradition of study continued, not only in the larger older houses, some of which (like Canterbury, Winchester and Worcester) remained as cathedral priories in the reorganized Norman church, but also in several new Norman foundations such as Durham and Norwich (also cathedral priories), Chester and St Mary's abbey, York. The twelfth century was in many respects a Benedictine golden age of learning and literary activity, especially in the writing of history – to preserve and rehabilitate the Old English heritage. But the scholastic temper of the time – strenuous, inquisitive, disputatious – was alien to the quiet, contemplative and orderly mode of life of the black monks; they became old-fashioned and by the early thirteenth century their monasteries were intellectual backwaters.[6] Of the new monastic orders for men and women introduced into England during the twelfth-century religious revival the most important numerically were the Cistercian monks and the Augustinian canons. The latter had some concern with schools, but the Cistercians had none. Intellectual and educational hegemony thus passed from the monasteries; not, however, to the cathedral schools, which during the thirteenth century tended to become mainly schools of grammar, but to Oxford and also, as the century advanced, to Oxford's offspring, the smaller and less prominent university at Cambridge.

Grammar schools and song schools

The ancient responsibility of each bishop to provide for the education of his clergy gradually passed to the chapter of his cathedral. This became part of church law in 1179 when the Third Lateran Council ordered that in every cathedral there should be a schoolmaster to teach 'the clerks of that church and poor scholars freely'. This obligation was repeated and extended in 1215 by the Fourth Lateran Council. Thereafter, not only

every cathedral but also every other church of adequate means
was to support a grammar master, and every metropolitan church
a theology lecturer as well. In England this seems to have been
a usual practice since soon after the conquest.[7] In the nine
secular cathedrals the grammar school was the responsibility
of the *scholasticus*, one of the four dignitaries in the chapter, but
sometime between about 1150 and 1200, as his legal and
secretarial duties increased, the *scholasticus* assumed the grander
title of chancellor and appointed as his deputy a *scholasticus* or
magister scholarum to teach the school. The chancellor paid the
schoolmaster a salary (since he had no prebend) and granted
him a licence which carried with it a monopoly of grammar
teaching in the city. Presumably this was to maximize his living
from the fee-paying pupils whom he admitted, but it must sometimes have operated against the educational interests of the area.
However, with the bishop's permission the chancellor had the
right, at his discretion, to license other schoolmasters in the city
and outside it, whether in the whole diocese or only in parts of it.
The Lincoln chancellor, for instance, made appointments to all
schools in the city and county, except those on prebendal estates.
From the thirteenth century, cathedral statutes show that the
schoolmaster, although never assigned a prebend as the Lateran
Councils had recommended, was nevertheless a person of some
importance. He had to be a master of arts (a rare qualification,
which meant some experience of university teaching), and he
deputized for the absent chancellor in the choir, usually occupying a stall below the canons but above their vicars choral – the
clerical assistants who performed choir duties, originally for those
canons who were absentees.

There can be no doubt that the purpose of the school was to
provide instruction in Latin, chiefly for the lesser clergy who
formed the cathedral's everyday working staff – the younger
vicars choral, minor clerks and choristers, some of them probably
aspirants for the priesthood; but it would provide also for the
local parish clergy, and almost certainly admitted fee-paying boys
from the neighbourhood who wanted to learn Latin but might
have no intention of becoming priests. The perpetual celebration
of divine worship in choir and at altar was the cathedral's primary
function and this depended on a supply of Latin-trained clerks
which it was the grammar school's main task to produce.

The eight monastic cathedrals had the same canon-law obligation to provide a grammar school, but its purpose was different because the maintenance of the daily services fell on the monks themselves, who had their own educational arrangements for sustaining them. The school therefore had no connection with the monastery but served the general needs of the city; responsibility for the school, including the appointment of the master, was the bishop's, since there was no chancellor.

In addition to a grammar school, most of the secular cathedrals at times maintained a school of theology and sometimes of canon law for the instruction of the clergy who lived near enough to attend or who were allowed by the bishop to be absent from their benefices in order to study. This was usually the chancellor's responsibility, like the grammar school. Although he was expected to lecture in person, more often he appointed and paid a deputy, being as a rule an absentee himself. How continuously, at what academic level, and with what numbers of students these theology schools functioned is uncertain. Strengthened by a migration of students from Oxford in 1238, the cathedral schools at Salisbury remained an active centre of the liberal arts and theology until well into the fourteenth century, forming a nascent third university; but no other cathedral schools had this potential after the growth of Oxford and Cambridge.[8]

Another type of school which cathedrals maintained was the song school. The Gregorian chant was as important a part of the service as the Latin Scriptures and the liturgy – and therefore a song school was as necessary to the establishment as a grammar school. Whilst the grammar and theology schools were the chancellor's province, the song school was the precentor's. Like the chancellor, the precentor in time appointed deputies – a succentor in the choir and a songmaster in the school; and he had a similar control over other songmasters in the city and, in some cathedrals, in the diocese or parts of it. In the song school, choristers and younger clergy would learn the liturgical chants and how to read the Latin texts – if not to understand them grammatically, though some would attend the grammar school as well. At first the boys seem to have lived with the canons in their houses, receiving board and lodging in return for domestic service, but from the later thirteenth century separate boarding foundations were provided for them, as in 1264 at Lincoln, where the bishop assigned an income to support a common residence for twelve boys with a canon as warden.[9]

If these educational provisions had been confined to the nine secular cathedrals their impact on the country as a whole would have been small indeed. But song and grammar schools were sometimes appendages of other collegiate churches, of which there were perhaps over fifty by 1300. Some of these churches were small and may not have kept schools continuously, if ever; but the larger ones, like Beverley, Ripon and Southwell in the diocese of York, were constituted like minor cathedrals, and there can be little doubt that they supported masters of song and grammar more or less regularly. During the religious excitement of the twelfth century when benefactions were showered on the new monastic orders, some schools together with churches and mills were conveyed with the land they stood on to newly established monasteries, especially of Austin canons, who thus became the school's patrons and governors. A few Benedictine abbeys also had charge of schools which had passed to them along with the borough, and which continued to serve the town's educational needs under the trusteeship of the abbot or convent, as at Bury St Edmunds and St Albans.[10]

The kinds of schools so far described were not by any means the only ones, though being in the care of ecclesiastical corporations they may have been the most securely established and permanent. How much schooling was available it is impossible to know, but almost certainly there was far more in the twelfth and thirteenth centuries than ever before. London, pre-eminent in wealth and power among English cities, had three 'famous schools' about 1180 when William FitzStephen wrote his account of it. They were connected, he says, with the three principal churches, and other evidence shows these to have been St Paul's cathedral, the nearby collegiate church of St Martin-le-Grand and the church of St Mary-le-Bow (or 'the Arches'), seat of the archbishop of Canterbury's provincial court.[11] FitzStephen vaguely refers to other schools, specially allowed because of the reputations of their teachers – presumably private schoolmasters unattached to any particular churches.

In the country at large most of the teaching obtainable was probably provided by individuals, not by permanently established institutions, and was therefore casual, sporadic and unorganized. Parish priests, if themselves sufficiently literate, may have undertaken the task of teaching, as they were enjoined to do by numerous ancient canons. In 1200 they were ordered by a synod at Westminster 'to keep schools in their towns and teach little boys gratis'.[12] Soon afterwards the prior of Canons Ashby in Northamptonshire observed that in his youth 'there were scarcely any masters . . . whose teaching was not mercenary . . . But now . . . there are many who teach without a fee. Many are the founts . . . ever open to those wishing to draw from them.'[13] Samson, later abbot of Bury St Edmunds, received his early education 'freely and in charity' in the school of William of Diss in Norfolk, and after studying at Paris became a schoolmaster himself in the same county, whence – 'well known and approved' – he moved to teach the school at Bury St Edmunds, and eventually entered the cloister there about 1165.[14] For some masters, teaching may have been occasionally a work of charity; for most it was almost certainly a means of livelihood. There must always have been unbeneficed clerks ready to make a living by teaching individuals or random collections of boys and youths for a fee. No town of any size or importance could have managed without a school to supply it with Latin-reading and Latin-writing clerks, and lacking a great church to maintain one, the burgesses themselves in some towns came in time to assume the responsibility, perhaps by contracting with a master to come and live among them.

Schools grew in number in these various ways during the twelfth and thirteenth centuries. We know little about them, and even less about their pupils. In a poor peasant society, book learning was only for a favoured few and those who attended schools can be assumed to have come mainly from families of moderate fortune – lawyers, well-beneficed clergy, small landholders, merchants. Most of them were probably intended for an ecclesiastical career (some of the older students would already be ordained and perhaps beneficed), but a growing number during this period must have had in mind secular occupations that were open to men with the necessary skills in Latin, notably in law and the administrative services of boroughs, great households, officials and merchants.

The growth of education is amply evidenced by the abundance of written records of many kinds after the mid-twelfth century – local manorial court rolls, accounts, rentals and deeds in all parts of the country, no less than the vast body of records accumulated by the king's government at Westminster, all systematically kept in serviceable Latin. These plainly point to the existence of competent scribes with a methodical training in grammar and writing.

The development of a sophisticated machinery of royal administration dependent on the use of written documents was an outstanding feature of the twelfth and thirteenth centuries and it could scarcely have taken place without a significant increase in schooling.[15] Writing in Latin ceased to be an amateur skill possessed by monks. During these two centuries there emerged a numerous, if ill-defined, body of professional writers of varying degrees of expertise, some expensively copying Bibles and service books – masterpieces of calligraphy in the new gothic 'book hand', others writing letters and keeping records in the new cursive 'court hand', for great men from the king down to bishops, barons and manorial lords.[16] Where and by whom they were trained in writing is far from clear. Some no doubt were laymen, but during this period most were probably clerks in the ecclesiastical as well as the technical sense, though only in minor orders. Numbers of them must have taught their skills for fees to pupils and apprentices, who presumably already possessed some knowledge of Latin.

Notwithstanding this expansion of educational opportunity, in most towns (with populations counted in hundreds) permanent schools of any kind must have been few. In the deep country, where the vast majority of the peasant population lived in small lonely villages and farmsteads, the teaching of Latin or writing, even if anybody had wanted it, must have been either fortuitous or nonexistent.

The rise of the universities

The university that had emerged at Oxford by about 1200 was essentially a community of masters and scholars, and it remained no more than that for over 100 years.[17] The fees which each student paid to the master who taught him were its financial basis. It had no property of its own. Books were hired from copyists; for assemblies and disputations the church of St Mary was used; and for schools or lecture halls the masters rented rooms in houses in the neighbouring streets and lanes. Students lived at first with townspeople or in boarding houses (*hospicia* or halls) managed by graduate principals who rented houses for this purpose.[18] Living at close quarters with the burgesses, masters and scholars found unending grounds for friction – rents, prices, debts, disputed rights and immunities. Teaching and learning went on amidst quarrels and brawls. Unencumbered by material possessions, the university could easily migrate or threaten to migrate to some other place. An exodus in 1209 led to the foundation of the university at Cambridge, of which town and region some of the leading Oxford migrants happened to be natives. Another dispersal in 1238 failed only by accident to plant other permanent *studia* at Northampton and Salisbury. As the university at Oxford developed into the country's principal source of learning and higher education it was able increasingly to depend on the support of the king in any quarrel with the town, and every reference of a dispute to the Crown invariably ended in the confirmation and extension of the university's privileges and the humiliation of the burgesses.

At the base of the university's developing educational system were the seven liberal arts, the scheme of subjects which had come down from the Roman world. These provided a general foundation course, partly vocational, partly humane, that had to be mastered before a start could be made on the more specialized professional disciplines of canon or civil law, medicine or theology, 'the divine mother of all the sciences'. Of the trivium, grammar became predominantly the school subject; perhaps the main centre in the country for its study and teaching was Oxford, and the grammar masters there were licensed and supervised by the university, not by the diocesan chancellor at Lincoln.[19] After grammar, the essential tool of all the arts was logic, and this formed the main part of the university course, with rhetoric a relatively unimportant ancillary. Then followed the quadrivium – arithmetic, astronomy, geometry and music; but as the recovery and assimilation of Aristotle proceeded, these subjects, whilst still remaining, were completely overshadowed by the three Aristotelian philosophies – natural, moral and metaphysical. All these were expounded in lectures and proved in disputations, using Latin and a highly technical dialectic founded on the syllogism; each master taught the whole course. When a student had become a master of arts he received the *ius ubique docendi* – in theory the right to teach the arts in any other *studium generale* and to be admitted there to the same degree.

By command of Henry III in 1231 all students at Oxford and Cambridge had to have their names entered on the roll *(matricula)* of a particular regent master (one officially lecturing in the schools) for the purpose of instruction and supervision – a measure to eliminate impostors. As the regent masters grew in corporate consciousness, unwritten customs governing the academic community, originally influenced by those of Paris, the senior university in Christendom, were formulated into written statutes. The earliest ones known, only recently discovered and published, relate to Cambridge and date from about 1250 and they show the university already possessing a defined constitution.[20] But custom continued for some time longer to regulate periods of study, syllabuses and set books and the sequence of dialectical exercises for degrees in each faculty.

Medical instruction, c. 1298

In the arts faculty after four years of lectures and exercises on the prescribed texts the student 'determined', i.e. engaged in a series of formal disputations, and if approved by four regents he was made a 'bachelor', thereafter giving 'cursory' or less formal lectures in his master's school. Three years later, after more lectures and disputations he 'incepted' and became a master of arts, and then he was obliged to lecture in the schools himself as a 'necessary regent' for two years. Teaching and administration were thus largely in the hands of a succession of relatively young, recently graduated masters. When a master had discharged this obligation he might stay on as a regent, making a living out of his students' fees, but most left the university as soon as they found other employment and so become non-regents. A few, given sufficient fortitude and financial resources, would enter one of the superior faculties to study for a higher professional qualification. At Oxford four more years led to the bachelor's degree in civil law, six to the doctor's degree in medicine, seven to the bachelor's degree in theology, and after that two more to the doctorate. Not surprisingly, these degrees were relatively rare. For them, as for the master's, there was no formal examination: the candidate swore before the chancellor that he had studied the prescribed books and a number of regents in the faculty testified, from personal knowledge or belief, to his sufficiency for the degree.[21]

The faculty of arts was the dominant body in the constitutional arrangements that took shape during the thirteenth century. At Oxford, its members, both masters and scholars, formed two 'nations' divided, Dr Emden conjectures, by the river Nene (not the Trent, as Rashdall supposed): 'northerners' included the Scots, and 'southerners' included the Welsh, the Irish and all other foreigners. The two principal assemblies were the congregation of regents from all four faculties (which elected the chancellor) – though the arts regents later had their own 'black congregation' – and the much rarer great congregation of all regents and non-regents. Although academically more prestigious, the three higher faculties of law, medicine and theology had no separate organizations of their own. From the arts faculty were elected the pairs of annual officers, one from each nation, who carried on the routine administration of the university under the chancellor, chief among them being the proctors.[22] The chancellor, who was elected from the doctors of canon law or theology, was the chief executive and judicial officer but was removable by the great congregation. It was a democratic community in which all full members had equal rights of participation. Broadly speaking, the Cambridge constitution was similar, but gave no official recognition to the two nations.

Intellectually, the great task of the thirteenth-century universities was the assimilation of the newly discovered body of Graeco-Arabic science, medicine and philosophy, and in particular the integrating and harmonizing of the new Aristotelian metaphysics with the revealed truths of Christianity. The process went on unevenly and eclectically and in a fervour of controversy. Aristotelianism found its stronghold in the arts faculty, where reason and logic sometimes went beyond what theology allowed and led to ecclesiastical intervention and censure.

The principal role in this movement was played by the new orders of mendicant friars which arrived on the university scene in the 1220s.[23] The Dominicans from the start were an intellectual order, austerely dedicated to combating ignorance and error through study and preaching. In contrast, the Franciscans were evangelists seeking a spiritual rebirth through apostolic poverty and self-denial, initially rejecting learning as inconsistent with their purpose. Both orders, however, soon needed theologians to train their recruits, and their convents at Oxford and Cambridge were a powerful attraction to masters who wanted economic security for prolonged study. The Franciscans early admitted to their Oxford friary a number of celebrated regent masters, outstanding among them Robert Grosseteste, one of the great creative minds of the age; and Franciscans soon dominated the Oxford schools. It was Aristotle's natural philosophy that stimulated the speculative research of Grosseteste and his chief disciple, Roger Bacon, into mathematics and optics, which made Oxford a leading centre of thirteenth-century science. At Cambridge, too, the friars predominated, especially in theology.

Taking the whole of Christendom for their parish, the friars helped to preserve the international character of higher education. There was coming and going between the English and the continental universities throughout the later middle ages, but much less than in this early formative period, when the friars were most active and ubiquitous. Furthermore, at a time when secular masters and scholars lived dispersed among the townspeople in lodgings and halls, the friars' convents set the example of a corporate life of study and it was perhaps this that prompted the foundation of the first secular colleges.

A college was an endowed and therefore financially self-supporting and self-governing society of mainly graduate scholars or fellows living and studying together, and praying for their founder in return for his benefaction. Its usual purpose was to provide lodging and financial security for a privileged minority of men who were already either advanced in arts and studying to become masters or masters who wished to continue in the higher faculties. It was generally not for undergraduates and provided no instruction. Originally small, unimportant and hardly noticeable in the university as a whole, the colleges later became paramount. The earliest to have a corporate existence was Merton College at Oxford, founded in 1264 by a future bishop of Rochester for twenty scholars, preferably his kinsmen. This was followed about 1280 by University College, originally for only four masters studying theology, and in 1282 by Balliol College, which at first was to support sixteen scholars through the arts course. At Cambridge, the earliest college was Peterhouse, founded by the bishop of Ely in 1284.[24]

By 1300 both universities were well established and playing a nationally important role. Oxford had then some 1,500 students, almost as large a body as the townspeople. Cambridge, much smaller until the mid-fifteenth century, had perhaps about 500. The vast majority would be taking the arts course. Most would be boys aged from fourteen or fifteen, with some preliminary grounding in grammar. They were mainly, says Rashdall, 'sons of knights and yeomen, merchants, tradesmen or thrifty artisans, nephews of successful ecclesiastics, or promising lads who had attracted the notice of a neighbouring abbot or archdeacon'.[25] All would need financial support from family or patrons to pay for their lodging and master's fees. Through lack of means or aptitude many of them left without getting as far as a degree. Some older ones would be rectors of parishes with the bishop's licence to be absent from their livings in order to study; these licences greatly increased in number after 1300. Others would be friars living in their own convents and a few were monks, for the monks were just beginning to show interest in university study.

Although the universities did not have a monopoly of learning, for it was still cultivated in some cathedral schools, monasteries and friaries, they had by 1300 a practical monopoly of higher education. Their function was both ideological and professional: they set themselves to interpret and defend Catholic doctrine, and also to train men for the service of church and state in its widest sense. The men they produced were in great demand. Already in the thirteenth century university graduates – the *magistri* – dominated the ecclesiastical hierarchy. Of 78 bishops between 1215 and 1272 no fewer than 40 were *magistri*.[26] From this time until the early sixteenth century secular as well as ecclesiastical administration was largely in the hands of an intellectual and managerial élite of graduate clerics, rigorously trained in arts and often in law or theology: it was perhaps as training grounds for government service that the universities exerted their greatest influence on society.

Thus the early universities did not aim to provide general academic culture for a social élite; they were centres of professional training — equipping men for careers as teachers, preachers, civil and canon lawyers, officials and administrators. Nor did they exist to pursue knowledge for its own sake or to prosecute research in any modern sense. Society generally and students individually could not afford these intellectual luxuries. In any case, in orthodox medieval thought the truth was not to be discovered by free inquiry and experiment: it existed in the Scriptures, the Fathers, Aristotle and other texts of unimpeachable authority, and it had to be extracted and interpreted by logic and reason in lectures, questionings and disputations. However, this could not have been all the education that the universities afforded. They were centres of vigorous adolescent life as well as of teaching and learning. Subject to hardly any official restraints in this early period, these young clerks must have been shaped not only by prayers and sermons and the methodical procedures of the schools, but also by their friendships and love affairs, by talk, contention and violence in the streets, lodging-houses and taverns of the town.

Monks and friars

From all this scholastic and intellectual ferment the monks were detached and isolated. Among the Benedictines a six-centuries-old monopoly of learning had come to an end in the twelfth century. They were no longer the only teachers and educated men. Their distinctive literary culture had become out of date. With the gradual passing of child oblation (the dedication of young boys to the religious life) monasteries had only postulants for recruits – older men educated in the outside world and perhaps already priests or experienced in other occupations. For these no more than a year's novitiate was required. Although one or two of the older and larger communities, notably St Albans, maintained the tradition of ordered study, book copying and history writing, the educational role of the black monks for a time ceased as compared to their splendid past. It became confined in practice to some vocational training of the novices in the customs of the house and in the liturgical texts and ceremonies by a novice master who was not very highly rated in the conventual hierarchy. In the way of life of the Cistercians, the largest of the new orders, learning had no place. They had no writing of books, their novices were not admitted under the age of sixteen, and their houses were too remote to have external schools.[27]

More directly concerned with external education were the Augustinian canons. Unlike the monks, whom they resembled in all other respects, they were allowed by their Rule to serve the parishes of their appropriated churches, which in their earlier history gave them more contact with the outside world. Their houses not only were sometimes custodians of schools that had been acquired with estates conveyed by twelfth-century bene-factors, but often seem of their own accord to have provided schools for local children. Furthermore, houses of canons appear to have made a practice of boarding the sons of the gentry for education. These activities might be carried on to the detriment of the religious life, in the opinion of a strict diocesan. After visiting Guisborough priory in North Yorkshire in 1280, the archbishop of York forbade 'for the future burdensome schools of rich and influential scholars, and even of poor scholars, unless our chancellor of York shall approve them as fruitful and useful to the monastery'.[28] Nunneries increased greatly in number during the religious revival of the twelfth century, and nuns, even more upper-class in their social origins than monks, often boarded the daughters of aristocratic and gentle families for education, but without having schools in any sense of the word.

Before the mid-thirteenth century, religious and intellectual life and higher education had been revitalized by the friars, and their academic eminence no less than their popular evangelism emphasized the isolation of the monks. It was at the universities where they made their sharpest impact, as we have seen. There in their own convents they had the great advantage of a regulated community life dedicated to study. But in the country at large each order developed its own self-contained educational system for the training of its members, the earlier Dominican one serving as a model for the Franciscans. Novices were expected already to have some knowledge of grammar. For their vocational train-ing in biblical knowledge and preaching each Dominican friary according to the constitutions of the order had to have a school with a doctor of divinity as rector. At certain provincial houses there were more advanced schools for arts (mainly logic) or philosophy or theology. After passing through these, promising friars might be sent to the convents at Oxford or Cambridge, which stood at the apex of the system, to read for degrees in theology. A generally similar organization was developed by the Franciscans.[29] Because of the arts teaching in their own schools, the friars eventually won dispensation from the university rule that no one could proceed to degrees in theology without first taking the arts course, but this was achieved only after a long struggle against the opposition of the secular masters. Although their schools were all internal, there is some evidence that in the thirteenth century the local ones might have been attended by parish clergy. However, they were certainly never intended for the instruction of the laity, though popular religious instruction no doubt gained from the preaching of better-educated friars.

Late in the thirteenth century, conscious of their isolation from the intellectual trends of the age, of the scholastic prestige of the mendicants and of the rising importance in the church of university-trained administrators, the monks turned their eyes to Oxford, and a new era in monastic education began. The first move was made by the Cistercians, surprisingly in view of their original ideal, and in 1281 they founded Rewley abbey just outside Oxford to accommodate their student monks. The Benedictines followed in 1283 with Gloucester College, a common house of study financed by the provincial chapter of the order and the individual abbeys that contributed students. About 1289 the cathedral priory of Durham started sending monks to Oxford and took steps to establish a college for them. Monks were rarer at Cambridge, but a Benedictine incepted there as a doctor of canon law in 1297. In the next century these developments led not only to the appearance of a new kind of monk, the university scholar and graduate, but also to more systematic teaching of the novices and young monks in the cloister, so as to fit them for the university later.[30]

The extent of literacy

A late-thirteenth-century manuscript in the British Museum depicts in an illuminated capital the three estates into which feudal society was theoretically divided — the tonsured clerk, the

Clerk, knight and labourer, c. 1280

armoured knight and the peasant with his mattock: three groups
each with a specialized function – those who prayed, those who
fought and those who worked. How far was literacy spread among
these social groups by about 1300?

Literacy is an imprecise concept. Until the nineteenth century,
writing – usually one's name – is really the only test applicable
and this does not necessarily imply ability to write much else,
though it is assumed to imply ability to read at some level. Until
the advent of universal education, there must have been many
who could read, if only indifferently, without being able to write
at all. Even for ability to write one's name statistical evidence is
incomplete and hardly allows generalization until after 1754.
For the early middle ages it is nonexistent, and only guesses can
be made from the very slight circumstantial evidence.

The development of the vernacular, a feature of late Anglo-
Saxon England, was set back by the Norman conquest, which
restored Latin as the language of government and administration.
Thus whether literacy is confined to reading or includes writing
as well, it must be understood to mean Latin for most of the
period before 1300. Nearly everything that was written down and
therefore existed to be read was in Latin. This being so, the
illiteracy of the great mass of the population – those who worked
– is not in question.[31] Peasants spoke English in one or other of
many dialects. English was seldom written down until the early
thirteenth century, and then mainly in the form of sermons and

devotional works for reading to uneducated audiences. With some exceptions, the native poetry of this period, originally transmitted orally, was rough and raw, like the common people for whose entertainment it came into being. Religious story and symbolism, folk custom and village experience, not the written word, formed the basis of peasant education.[32]

But if Latin is to be taken as the index of literacy, most of the Anglo-Norman barons and knights – those who fought – were hardly more literate than the peasantry. To the feudal magnate, reading and writing were of little account, merely technical skills possessed by clerks whom he kept in his service to read and write for him, just as modern commercial magnates employ lawyers and accountants. In an age in which the written word had no meaning for the vast majority, the great man's seal was the visual proof of authenticity, not his signature. Evidence shows, however, that some barons were literate and had had a training in letters, but the little that is known about their education hardly justifies confident conclusions about 'the universality of education among the highborn and well-to-do'.[33] From the conquest until the fourteenth century the vernacular of the court and aristocracy was French, though perhaps the lesser knightly families from the mid-twelfth century acquired some familiarity with spoken English through intermarriage and from their closer contact with the land. French thus became the language of polite literature – the romance and the *chanson de geste* written to be read aloud in courtly circles. From the mid-thirteenth century it was also used along with Latin by the judges and lawyers in the king's courts (perhaps because of the inadequacy of their Latin) and so became the language of the English common law. French not English was the vernacular used in writing by the more educated laity who had imperfect or nonexistent Latin.[34]

To what extent the nobility understood Latin we do not know. The first two Norman kings were illiterate, but Henry II was the most educated king since Alfred; from his time onwards kings were probably more or less literate, though how good their Latin was is uncertain. Kings and some barons were perhaps technically literate only in the sense of being able to write their names, to half understand Latin when it was spoken or read aloud and to recognize biblical and liturgical phrases and sentences. Even this may have declined as their vernacular French came to be used as a written medium during the thirteenth century. Of course, illiteracy in Latin or even in the vernacular is not necessarily to be equated with ignorance, especially in a relatively bookless age. Rich men and poor men had their own cultures made up of traditional, vocational knowledge and skills, legend in vernacular song and recited verse, visual symbol, spectacle and ceremony. Among those who had no need to read and write, literacy conferred no status and lack of it no stigma.

Latin was the professional expertise and largely the monopoly of the clergy — those who prayed. It was the language not only of all the church services but also of ecclesiastical and secular administration, so that wherever documents had to be written and records kept clerks were to be found. So rare was literacy among the laity that the ability to read and write Latin came to be the definition of a clerk, and it was their literacy rather than their holy orders that gave these men their privilege of 'benefit of clergy'. By ancient custom felonious clergy could be tried only in the church courts; Henry II in 1164 had failed in an attempt to make them subject like laymen to the ordinary criminal law of the land. An accused clerk, however, had first to prove his clergy in the king's courts, and the test of this was his ability to read Latin. In dress and mode of life many clerks in minor orders were barely distinguishable from laymen. Benefit of clergy thus became the privilege of large numbers of men who were only nominally clerics, some of them really laymen whose knowledge of Latin qualified them for ordination. In effect, the doctrine was that any man who could read was a clerk, and therefore immune from much of the ordinary common law.[35]

This exclusive use of Latin by the clergy was the greatest obstacle to the spread of literacy outside the ranks of the clergy. As Professor Galbraith observes, 'so long and so far as literacy was identified with the knowledge of Latin, lay society remained virtually illiterate.'[36] However, even among the clergy literacy was very unevenly spread. The higher learning of cathedral schools and universities soon created a gulf between the clerical aristocracy of bishops, canons and well-to-do rectors, and the clerical proletariat of stipendiary curates and chaplains who were the casual work force of the church, recruited mainly from the peasantry. The most educated clergy were probably trilingual, speaking French and their native English as well as Latin. Abbot Samson, who was educated as a secular, was eloquent — says his biographer Jocelin of Brakelond — in Latin and French and also in English, 'in the speech of Norfolk, where he was born and bred'.[37] About the low educational standard of the lesser clergy there can be no doubt. Among the more learned, like Giraldus Cambrensis writing about 1200, it was a subject for jokes. The bishops' registers of the thirteenth century often show clerks with little or no Latin. Candidates for ordination or induction into a benefice were sometimes ordered to attend the schools to study the Scriptures or song. Sometimes they were rejected outright. Grosseteste, bishop of Lincoln from 1235 to 1254, refused even an influential candidate on the grounds that he was 'insufficiently literate, not to say almost utterly illiterate'. Some others, he complained, were mere 'ABC boys' (*pueri abcdarii*).[38]

Because of the ignorance of the lower clergy the instruction of the faithful suffered, as bishops frequently reiterated. Apart from visual symbols like wall-paintings, statues and religious drama, nearly all that the mass of the population knew about religion came from the priest's vernacular sermons. To assist him in instructing his flock, the decretals of Pope Gregory IX in 1234 ordered that each parish priest should have a clerk who was to help in the singing and reading of the services and also to keep a school to which the parishioners were to be admonished to send their sons.[39] For the practical guidance of their parish clergy, bishops issued constitutions setting out among other things what they should know and teach – the ten commandments, the creed, the seven works of mercy, the seven deadly sins and so on. Every incumbent was supposed to have his copy. The most authoritative syllabus of religious instruction of this kind was prescribed in the provincial constitutions of Archbishop Pecham in 1281. In a section beginning *Ignorantia sacerdotum* specified articles of belief were ordered to be expounded to the people in the vernacular four times each year, and this, says Dr Pantin, 'became henceforth the standard legislation on the subject'.[40] Episcopal visitations, however, often found priests themselves ignorant of what they were supposed to teach.

The educational deficiencies of the parish clergy are not to be wondered at. Many of them were by birth unfree peasants, for ordination was one of the few lawful ways of escaping from the soil. Until 1406 a bondsman could send his son to school (with the lord's permission and on payment of compensation) only if he intended to become a priest; according to the lawyers, if he failed to become a priest his serfdom revived. Opportunities for schooling would be rare if he lived in the countryside, and if he attained sufficient literacy to become a priest, books would be beyond his means, and his rustic surroundings would offer few incentives for continued self-improvement.[41]

This traditional (mainly theoretical and over-simplified) division of feudal society into clergy, knights and peasants omits the townsmen – those who manufactured, bought and sold. Although only a tiny minority of the population as a whole, their importance grew during this period as society became more commercialized and economic specialization increased. Long before 1300 there were merchants and moneylenders in London (and perhaps in a few other important trading cities such as York, Bristol and Norwich) who could read and write in the vernacular, whether French or English, and possibly even in Latin, and who did not leave all their writing and accounting to hired clerks. Illiteracy would be incompatible with financial dealings on any large scale.[42] The common lawyers, emerging during the thirteenth century as the earliest learned lay profession, must have been more or less trilingual. Other small groups of laymen must be presumed to have been literate in English and French and to some extent in Latin: book copiers and illuminators, eminent jewellers, metalworkers, tomb-makers and similar highly skilled craftsmen, not least the master masons, who designed such technical masterpieces as Salisbury cathedral and Edward I's Welsh castles, and also organized the labour and materials for these enormous undertakings. After 1300 it is increasingly unwise to make a distinction between illiterate laymen and literate clergy: there were still many illiterate or semi-literate clergy but growing numbers of literate laymen, in the widening sense of the term literate.

About 1300, when the population of England was some 3 million, there were perhaps 30,000 ordained clergy from acolyte upwards, some 15,000 monks, canons and friars, and 7,000 nuns.[43] How many of these were literate in Latin, French or English it is impossible to know. Probably not many of the nuns were literate at all. Even if all the clergy and religious were literate in one or other language – an unlikely assumption – they accounted for only about 1·5 per cent of the population. If we add lay civil servants, lay judges and common lawyers and at least some of the magnates, knights and leading burgesses, merchants and craftsmen (a relatively small minority altogether) it would

hardly bring the total to as much as 3 per cent. This would be
very unevenly spread, the heaviest concentrations being in
London and a few other towns, and in colleges of priests, friaries
and monasteries. None the less, over the past two centuries
literacy and education had certainly grown in extent and also
become more secularized: England was far more civilized as a
result. The vast rural majority, however, still passed their lives in
mental confinement, limited by their own experiences in a small
circumscribed world ruled by village custom and popularized
religion. Hence their inertia, their credulity and fear-ridden
superstitions, which to a large extent explain the slow pace of
social change.

Notes

1 R. W. SOUTHERN, *The Making of the Middle Ages* (London, 1953),
pp. 162–208; A. L. POOLE. *From Doomsday Book to Magna Carta*
(Oxford, 1951), chapter 8.

2 R. W. SOUTHERN, 'England in the twelfth-century renaissance',
Medieval Humanism (Oxford, 1970), pp. 162–4.

3 The monastic cathedrals were Canterbury, Carlisle, Durham, Ely,
Norwich, Rochester, Winchester and Worcester. The secular cathedrals
were Chichester, Exeter, Hereford, Lichfield, Lincoln, London,
Salisbury, Wells and York.

4 R. W. HUNT, 'English learning in the late twelfth century', *Transactions of the Royal Historical Society*, XIX (1936), pp. 19–42.

5 G. LEFF, *Paris and Oxford Universities in the Thirteenth and Fourteenth
Centuries* (New York, 1968), pp. 76–8.

6 D. KNOWLES, *The Religious Orders in England*, 1 (Cambridge, 1948),
p. 291.

7 K. EDWARDS, *The English Secular Cathedrals in the Middle Ages*
(Manchester, 1949), pp. 195–200.

8 Ibid., pp. 200–8; K. EDWARDS, 'The College of De Vaux', *Victoria
County History Wilts.*, III, pp. 369–85.

9 EDWARDS, *Secular Cathedrals*, pp. 168–71, 313 ff.

10 KNOWLES, *Monastic Order*, pp. 491–2.

11 A. F. LEACH, *The Schools of Medieval England* (London, 1915), pp.
138–43. SIR FRANK STENTON, 'Norman London' in G. BARRACLOUGH (ed.), *Social Life in Early England* (London, 1960), pp. 203–4,
takes the third of FitzStephen's 'three principal churches' which had
'famous schools' to be the Austin priory of Holy Trinity, Aldgate, not
St Mary-le-Bow.

12 LEACH, *Charters*, pp. 139–41.
13 HUNT, 'English learning', p. 20. The reference here is to teachers of theology.
14 H. E. BUTLER (ed.), *The Chronicle of Jocelin of Brakelond* (London, 1949), pp. 33, 44.
15 H. G. RICHARDSON and G. O. SAYLES, *The Governance of Medieval England* (Edinburgh, 1963), pp. 265–83, for the new class of literate lay civil servants.
16 V. H. GALBRAITH, 'Handwriting', in A. L. POOLE (ed.), *Medieval England* (Oxford, 1958), II, pp. 552–4.
17 H. RASHDALL, *Universities of Europe in the Middle Ages*, ed. F. M. POWICKE and A. B. EMDEN (Oxford, 1936), III, is the standard authority. LEFF, *Paris and Oxford Universities*, is shorter and incorporates recent research.
18 A. B. EMDEN, *An Oxford Hall in Medieval Times* (Oxford, 1924), pp. 7–59.
19 R. W. HUNT, 'Oxford grammar masters in the Middle Ages', *Oxford Studies presented to Daniel Callus* (Oxford Historical Society, 1964), pp. 163, 185–7.
20 M. B. HACKETT, *The Original Statutes of Cambridge University* (Cambridge, 1970), p. 64; for Cambridge origins, pp. 43–6.
21 RASHDALL, *Universities of Europe*, III, pp. 141–4, 153–9.
22 A. B. EMDEN, 'Northerners and southerners in the organization of the University', *Oxford Studies presented to Daniel Callus*, pp. 1–16.
23 For the friars see R. W. SOUTHERN, *Western Society and the Church in the Middle Ages* (London, 1970), pp. 272–99.
24 *Victoria County History Oxon.*, III (1954), and *Victoria County History Camb.*, III (1959), contain concise recent accounts of college histories.
25 RASHDALL, *Universities of Europe*, III, p. 408.
26 W. A. PANTIN, *The English Church in the Fourteenth Century* (Cambridge, 1955), p. 10.
27 KNOWLES, *Monastic Order*, pp. 421–3, 503–5, 634–6.
28 W. BROWN (ed.), *The Guisborough Chartulary* (Surtees Society, 1891), II, p. 360.
29 A. G. LITTLE, 'The educational organization of the mendicant friars in England', *Transactions of the Royal Historical Society*, VIII (1895), pp. 49–70; D. KNOWLES, *Religious Orders*, I, pp. 151–2, 212–13.
30 Ibid., pp. 25–7.
31 BALDWIN, *Literacy of the Laity*, pp. 166–82.
32 For traditional bookless education in rural society see JOAN SIMON, *The Social Origins of English Education* (London, 1971), especially pp. 60–77, and H. S. BENNETT, *Life on the English Manor* (Cambridge, 1937), pp. 27–37, 259–74.
33 RICHARDSON and SAYLES, *Governance of Medieval England*, p. 272. The earl of Warwick in 1305 gave twenty-seven books to Bordesley abbey (Worcs.), which suggests educated interests.

34 R. M. WILSON, 'English and French in England 1100–1300', *History*, XXVIII (1943), pp. 37–60.
35 On this see L. C. GABEL, *Benefit of Clergy in the Later Middle Ages* (Northampton, USA, 1929).
36 GALBRAITH, 'Literacy of the medieval English kings', p. 27.
37 BUTLER (ed.), *Chronicle of Jocelin of Brakelond*, p. 40.
38 J. R. H. MOORMAN, *Church Life in England in the Thirteenth Century* (Cambridge, 1946), p. 91.
39 *Liber Decretalium Gregorii IX*, III, i, 3, quoted RASHDALL, *Universities of Europe*, III, p. 350, note 1.
40 PANTIN, *The English Church*, pp. 193–4.
41 BENNETT, *Life on the English Manor*, pp. 288–90.
42 RICHARDSON and SAYLES, *Governance of Medieval England*, p. 282.
43 SIR MAURICE POWICKE, *The Thirteenth Century, 1216–1307* (Oxford, 1953), pp. 445–6.

Further reading, see pp. 89–90.

CHAPTER III

Later medieval: education within and without the church

1300–1530

Grammar schools

Throughout this period the cathedrals and other great churches remained in varying degrees important educational centres, more active at some times than others. Their chapters were usually composed of university-trained scholars, and if the chancellor or his deputy lectured on theology or canon law only inter- mittently there is some reason to suppose that their grammar and song schools existed more or less continuously. At Beverley minster grammar school, which may be taken as representative in the early fourteenth century, the master was appointed and paid by the chancellor, in the first instance for a term of three years. Five successive masters were all *magistri* and the one appointed in 1306 had just completed his necessary regency at Cambridge and came with a written testimonial granted by the university in full congregation. Within the liberty of the minster, which extended far over the surrounding countryside, he had a monopoly which the chancellor defended against unlicensed competitors, even to the extent of excommunication. The clerks, deacons and choris- ters of the church were taught free but others, the master's private pupils, paid fees. By ancient custom some of the older scholars – perhaps those who were already priests or deacons – were created 'bachelors', and as such may have assisted the master in the school, in the university manner.[1]

Some instruction in grammar was also obtainable during this period in the almonry schools which certain houses of Benedictine monks and regular canons maintained out of charity or for payment. Although the almonry school's primary purpose was to serve the liturgical needs of the convent, it afforded much the same educational opportunity to boys in the area as the schools of the great secular churches.[2]

The Black Death of 1348–9 and its recurrent outbreaks reduced the population, it is estimated, by over a quarter and perhaps by as much as a third. Mortality among the clergy was especially high, and there is evidence of a shortage of schoolmasters lasting well into the next century. It became rare for masters of arts to teach in schools. The custom of making appointments for only three years at a time lapsed, as the York chapter explained in 1368, 'because of the brevity of life and the scarcity of masters of arts since the pestilence'. To make good the shortage of clergy, new grammar schools came into being. Invariably they were connected with some ecclesiastical institution or other in order to ensure their permanence, for in turbulent and lawless times only the church seemed safe.

An unascertainable number of schools in this period – probably never as many as 100 – were maintained by new types of colleges of secular priests, the foundation of which was a characteristic of the late fourteenth and early fifteenth centuries.[3] Some of these were parish churches which were made collegiate, others were extraparochial and independent. In either csse they usually consisted of a varied number of priest chaplains with a complement of clerks and choristers, and sometimes a schoolmaster to instruct these and a few boys of the neighbourhood in grammar and song. One of the twelve priests of the college at Fotheringhay (1411) was to teach grammar, and another, song.[4] The college at Tattershall, Lincs. (1440), hired a schoolmaster, allowing him his board, clothing and an annual stipend of 4 marks (a mark was equal to 13s. 4d.); he was to teach grammar to the choristers and 'to all sons of tenants of the lordship of Tattershall and of the college without charge'.[5] Colleges of this kind may well have supported schools, regularly or intermittently, even when none are recorded.

More schools were attached to chantries. Chantries – foundations designed to maintain services of intercession for the dead – had become common in the thirteenth century. Their attraction increased after the mortality of the plague years and in this later period they were sometimes associated with schools. Chantry priests had no parochial responsibilities and so founders might require them to teach in addition simply to celebrating a daily mass. The provision of a school was clearly a primary object of the chantry founded by Lady Katharine Berkeley at Wotton-under-Edge in Gloucestershire in 1384.[6] But individual chaplains even when not obliged to teach might do so voluntarily in order to occupy their time and supplement their pay. Where colleges of several chantry chaplains were founded they differed little from other colleges of secular priests, and like them often served an educational as well as a religious purpose. Colleges at Oxford and Cambridge were really chantry foundations, pledged to learning as well as praying for their founders. Like other medieval schools those connected with chantries are an unknown quantity, for where teaching was done voluntarily no evidence exists, and where it was an obligatory part of the foundation there is no certain proof of continuity. Once established, however, most chantries seem to have survived until their suppression in 1548.

Another feature of social and religious life after 1350 was the proliferation of gilds or fraternities devoted to honouring particular saints or festivals, coupled with the performance of different kinds of good works. These sometimes included the support of a school, perhaps one taught by the chaplain who was paid to celebrate at the gild's altar in the parish church. From 1388 the gild of the Assumption of the Virgin in the church at Maldon in Essex kept a chaplain-schoolmaster.[7] In the same way schools were founded in association with hospitals or almshouses, sharing the same endowment and premises. In 1422 Archbishop Chichele established a college at Higham Ferrers, his birthplace in Northamptonshire, and incorporated in it an almshouse and an existing grammar school.[8] One of the biggest of all hospitals, St Leonard's at York, included on its establishment two schoolmasters.[9]

A landmark was raised in 1382 when William of Wykeham, a pluralist bishop of enormous wealth, founded a college and grammar school in his cathedral city of Winchester.[10] Whereas other schools were adjuncts of ecclesiastical institutions of some sort, this was planned to exist in its own right, though in organic connection with a college of priests. The whole society consisted of a college of ten fellows under a warden, a school of seventy boys taught by a master and usher (these last relatively minor persons in the hierarchy), and a chapel staff of chaplains, lay clerks and choristers. They were supplied with a complete set of buildings carefully designed to meet all their needs, and with rich endowments to ensure their corporate perpetuity. It was a closely knit, self-contained, quasi-monastic community of boys and men dedicated to education and prayer. The scholars, aged eight upwards, were to learn grammar and be prepared for entry to the bishop's sister foundation, New College at Oxford. In their selection for the school, preference was to be given first to the founder's kin, next to boys from the Winchester diocese, and then to those from parishes where the society owned property. They were all to be, in the common formula of the time, 'poor and needy' *(pauperes et indigentes)*, which the statutes defined as possessing no more than 5 marks (£3. 6s. 8d.) a year; this was the maximum allowed at New College, too, except for founder's kin. Besides the seventy scholars, ten non-foundationers – sons of noblemen and other worthy persons – were to be allowed as fee-paying boarders, and the sixteen choristers were to be taught free in return for singing in the chapel and performing menial service in the college. Commoners were soon admitted even though not mentioned in the statutes; they were the master's private fee-paying pupils, boarding outside the college and coming in daily to school. As their numbers grew, supervision by master

Young noblemen at school, c. 1340

and usher diminished and a code of boy-made law and order evolved – the origin of the prefect system.

In towns where no school was provided by the church or by benefaction, the burgesses collectively might support a schoolmaster by guaranteeing him a salary and a rentfree schoolroom. In 1364 the parishioners of Kingston-upon-Thames contracted with the almonry schoolmaster at Canterbury that he should come and teach their public school (*scolae publicae*).[11] Other towns were served by private schoolmasters who hired rooms and waited for pupils, just as the tradesman waited for customers. Because of the difficulties of travel, boarding must have been usual. To Simon, schoolmaster of Newark, Archbishop Melton of York in the 1330s sent his two fatherless nephews at 2s. 5d. a week (roughly a skilled craftsman's weekly wage) with a valet as their private tutor and guardian.[12] About 1380 Sir Edmund Stonor had a son living with a married schoolmaster at Ewelme, near Oxford.[13] Boys seem often to have been boarded with clerics who were not professional schoolmasters but who hired a teacher for them. Two London boys living with the vicar of Croydon in the 1390s paid 1s. each week for board and about 3d. for the master's fee.[14] In 1432 the treasurer of York minster had several young gentlemen residing with him for education.[15] Informal, non-institutional teaching of this kind, however casual and impermanent, must have accounted for much of the education that was available.

In the countryside, opportunities would have been much rarer, though they did exist in some places at some times. Two unlicensed masters silenced by the Beverley chancellor in 1306 were teaching in isolated villages, and 'masters of rural schools and teachers of rude boys' are mentioned as a possible source for book collectors by Richard de Bury, the bibliophile bishop of Durham, about 1345. Chantry schools were as likely to be in villages as in towns. Where no school existed, sons of country gentlemen were taught at home by a chaplain or tutor. In 1412 Sir William de Roos, lord of Helmsley, endowed a chantry of ten chaplains to pray for his soul for a term of eight years after his death, and the best-qualified was to instruct his sons *in disciplina et grammatica*.[16]

Endemic plague, depopulation, labour scarcity, diminished internal trade – these conditions helped to produce an educational depression which lasted from the mid-fourteenth to the mid-fifteenth century. Moreover, the preoccupation of the universities with logic and philosophy now led to the neglect of grammar, so depleting still further the supply of competent schoolmasters. Cries were raised of the decay of grammar teaching. William Byngham, a London rector, claimed in 1439 to know of seventy schools east of a line 'from Hampton to Coventry and so forth no farther north than Ripon' that were moribund for want of teachers.[17] In 1447 a petition in Parliament for more schools in London recalled 'the great number of grammar schools that sometime were in divers parts of this realm besides those that were in London and how few be in these days'.[18] The school which the corporation sponsored at Hull at this time was intermittently without a master. Only one was in business at Oxford in 1464 and the university complained that 'grammar, the basis of all education, had gone into exile and deserted this realm'. These conditions led Byngham, with Henry VI's encouragement, to found God's-house at Cambridge in 1439 – a college specifically for the study of grammar and the production of qualified schoolmasters. After taking their degrees, its members were obliged to accept any grammar-school appointment offered them at a sufficient salary.[19]

It was at this time of slump that England's premier school was founded. Eton, created by the young Henry VI in 1440, was a close copy of Winchester but on an even grander scale. In its final form it consisted of a college of ten fellows and a provost, all priests and at least masters of arts, a grammar school of seventy scholars with a master and usher, and a chapel establishment of ten chaplains, ten lay clerks and sixteen choristers. The scholars were to be drawn in the first place from parishes where the college had estates, choristers having preference, and they were to be 'poor and indigent' (having an income of no more than 5 marks a year, as at Winchester). Additionally, twenty noblemen's sons might be admitted as fee-payers, and thirteen 'poor scholars' taught free in return for domestic service. When sufficiently advanced in grammar, the scholars were eligible to proceed to King's College, the sister foundation at Cambridge, which was closed to all but Etonians. Disaster faced both colleges when Henry VI was deposed by the Yorkists in 1461 and recovery of the founder's endowment, or most of it, was delayed until the coming of the Tudors. Eton then formed with King's College the most privileged and splendid academic society in the country.[20]

The social and educational background of medieval school-masters is obscure, like that of the parish clergy whom perhaps they most resembled. Their knowledge of Latin must have been acquired in much the same way, at established schools or from private teachers, and the better-qualified among them would have studied at the university, if seldom long enough to graduate. Those who were masters of arts would be exceptional, probably being found only in the larger and more reputable schools. All of them technically belonged to the clerical order but without necessarily being priests. At all periods, married schoolmasters seem to have existed and these were presumably in minor orders, which afforded them benefit of clergy but otherwise made them hardly different from laymen.

Boys who attended grammar schools could scarcely have been poor. Whilst at school they had to be maintained at the expense of parents or guardians, and the master had to be paid by fees or gifts. Probably they were mainly the sons of freeholders, trades-men, officials and gentlemen, often lodging away from home in order to be near a school. Bequests in wills for boarding and schooling are frequent. Some grammar scholars would be intended for the university, some for the priesthood more directly through informal apprenticeship to a local incumbent, others for indentured apprenticeship to masters of various trades in which some competence in Latin was necessary, for example apothe-caries, copyists, notaries, scriveners, stationers and suchlike.

Latin was the staple of the curriculum, learnt as a written and spoken language in daily use for most official and professional purposes and therefore more as a vocational skill than as part of a liberal education. Notwithstanding the practical objective, the grammar was formal, complex and technical, and the teaching methods archaic. The standard authorities were two fifth-century Roman grammarians – Donatus for beginners and Priscian for the more advanced, the last supplemented from about 1200 by the *Doctrinale puerorum* of Alexander of Villedieu, a school-master in Brittany. Because of the scarcity of books and writing materials, teaching was entirely oral and learning depended on dictation, repetition and feats of memory. French was the vernacular used in the schoolroom until the second half of the fourteenth century, when English outgrew the prejudice against it and the English of the East Midlands and London gradually replaced French as the vernacular of educated people. 'The advantage', wrote John of Trevisa about 1385, 'is that they learn their grammar in less time . . . the disadvantage is that now children at grammar school know no more French than does their left heel.'[21] By the early fifteenth century English had entirely superseded French in national usage.[22]

Seven was the usual age for starting school, and since boys went to the university at about fourteen, seven years must have been the time considered necessary to become proficient in grammar. However, boys no doubt left earlier or stayed longer according to their needs; some grammar scholars might be older than this – deacons or priests, and some married men. All were taught together in the same schoolroom, irrespective of age or attainment. Older scholars were different from younger ones only in the stage they had reached, not in what they were studying, because all were learning Latin. In a Yorkshire inquisition taken in 1304, a witness deposed that he was at school at Clitheroe in 1283 and had to leave because he was so badly beaten, yet apparently he was nineteen or twenty years old then.[23] This mixing of children and adults was characteristic of medieval society. When clocks and calendars were rare, time was uncertain and of small account; people were hardly conscious of age. Death came early to all, but mortality was especially high among young children. Childhood as such was scarcely recognized. Children were seen not as individuals with natural rights and needs, but as imperfect adults, merely pieces of property of the father or extensions of the larger family group. Only those under seven were deemed at common law to be exempt from criminal liability on account of age. From seven upwards they were treated like adults, at work and play, and before the law.

Life at school was rough, crude and violent as life outside, and pain and physical punishment (amply justified by biblical authority) were regarded as indispensable for guiding the young to virtue. Something of the educational theory of the time is seen in a sermon composed probably by Bishop Alcock of Ely about 1490 for declamation by the Boy Bishop of St Paul's school.[24] In accordance with Aristotle's teaching, the infant mind is seen as disposed to neither virtue nor vice, but 'like a blank tablet on which nothing is written'.[25] Human knowledge is the result of reason operating on sense experience, but divine knowledge – following Aquinas – depends on grace, and without this man cannot attain his proper end. Thus, lacking reason and cognition, the infant needs God's special help and so when he is newly set to school he begins his ABC by first learning to read 'Christ's cross be my speed'. (This was usually the first line on the horn book.) At seven infancy gives way to adolescence, 'in the which age is the breaking of every child to goodness or to lewdness'. Stern correction is now added to instruction. The master teaches the boy his Donatus and:

> giveth commandments to the child in his growing age. And he break them he is sharply corrected. There is no fault that he doth but he is punished. Sometime he wringeth him by the ears. Sometime he giveth him a stripe on the hand with the ferule. Sometime beateth him sharply with the rod. And so with commandments and sharp correction he giveth him full instruction in the lower science.[26]

A succession of good harvests in the 1490s and 1520s, rising estate profits, the spread of affluence among the merchant class, more settled political conditions, a growing population – these made the period from about 1480 to 1530 one of expansion and rising investment in education through private philanthropy. Conscious of the value of education, successful merchants as well as churchmen founded or endowed schools in their native towns, usually still in connection with chantries or gilds. Sometimes these were new schools, sometimes existing schools which became free since the endowment provided the master's stipend. By establishing a chantry whose chaplain was to act as the town's schoolmaster, Bishop Alcock in 1479 endowed the grammar school at Hull which the corporation had previously supported; later he founded Jesus College at Cambridge.[27] It was perhaps an already existing school at Manchester that a local wool merchant endowed in association with a chantry of his foundation in the collegiate church there in 1508, and that another native, Hugh Oldham, bishop of Exeter, more ambitiously endowed in 1515. Bishop Waynflete of Winchester, having added a grammar school to his Magdalen College at Oxford in 1480, founded another at Wainfleet, his Lincolnshire birthplace, in 1484. Another bishop of Winchester, Richard Fox, who had already founded Corpus Christi College, Oxford, rebuilt and endowed an existing grammar school at Grantham in 1528.[28] London merchants munificently founded schools in their native towns, at, for example, Stockport, Macclesfield, Cromer, Wolverhampton, Cuckfield and Horsham. Other schools were endowed or newly established by the parishioners themselves, in the form of either a chantry (as at East Retford in 1519) or a gild (as at Berkhamsted in 1523). The last great educational scheme of the middle ages was conceived in the 1520s by the last great ecclesiastical statesman, Cardinal Wolsey. After his fall in 1529, his Cardinal College at Oxford was reprieved by Henry VIII but the school in his native Ipswich which was to have fed the college with scholars was vindictively suppressed.[29]

This expansion of educational provision after 1480 affected the universities as well as the schools and was the product of new needs as well as new forces. The growing literacy of the laity created a wider interest in education, and in the minds of the bishops made an educated clergy all the more necessary. New standards were set by the humanists, and new possibilities opened up by the relatively cheap printed book. There is some evidence of higher qualifications among schoolmasters and of educational innovation. Some schools at least were touched by the new learning which made rhetoric and elegant Latinity their aim rather than the old-fashioned scientific grammar. Novel methods of teaching Latin by the use of the vernacular and of conversational phrasebooks gained ground, pioneered by Magdalen College school. Dealing often with schoolboy situations, these *vulgaria* throw vivid light on school conditions at the time – the boredom and coarseness, the high spirits and grim humour, most of all the fear and flogging. Only Latin was taught, and manners and morals incidentally through grammatical examples.[30]

Oxford and Cambridge

The fourteenth century saw the consolidation of both universities. The last migration from Oxford took place in 1334 when some aggrieved northern masters and scholars seceded to Stamford. They were ordered to return by the king, who again confirmed and enlarged the university's franchises at the town's expense. In 1355 came the most decisive explosion of violence between town and gown at Oxford: there were looting and burning and a number of deaths. As in earlier outbreaks, the Crown took the side of the scholars: their privileges were extended and the town's ultimate humiliation was kept fresh by an annual penance of the mayor, bailiffs and sixty burgesses in the university church. The university's ascendancy was complete and lasted with mutual ill will until the nineteenth century. At Cambridge too the university gradually built up an economic and judicial system which rivalled the borough's. Constant friction and spasmodic violence culminated in the great riot of 1381, during which some of the university's records were burned. Until Victorian times, town and gown cohabited with no more affection than at Oxford.

Oxford University's first building was a small congregation house and library added to St Mary's church in 1320, an investment so small that it hardly committed the masters and scholars to staying in the town permanently. What helped to give each university a lasting footing was the growing number of colleges. These were a major development of the first half of the century. No fewer than ten were founded in the space of thirty-six years: three at Oxford – Exeter (1316), Oriel (1324) and Queen's (1341); and seven at Cambridge – King's Hall (1317), Michaelhouse (1324), Clare (1326), Pembroke (1347), Gonville (1347), Trinity Hall (1350) and Corpus Christi College (1352).[31]

Like their late-thirteenth-century prototypes, these were small, self-perpetuating communities of about a dozen scholars or fellows, who constituted a permanent corporate body ruled by one of their own number whom they chose themselves, all sharing a common life of study and prayer supported by the income from property given by the founder. Thus, Exeter College was for a rector and twelve scholars studying arts, Oriel for a provost and ten masters of arts reading theology or law, and Queen's for a provost and twelve masters studying theology. At Cambridge, Trinity Hall was for a master and twenty canonists or civilians. King's Hall was exceptional in several ways: it was first financially supported by Edward II and then endowed by Edward III as a training ground for the public service; its thirty-two scholars – an unusually large number, most of them undergraduates – were nominated by the Crown and drawn from the boys of the Chapel Royal and sons of court and household officials.[32] With these royal and aristocratic connections, King's Hall must have added considerably to the prestige of Cambridge. The general purpose of founders – very often bishops or other wealthy ecclesiastics – was to increase the supply of highly educated clergy, frequently for the benefit of some particular part of the country with which the founder had connections – Exeter diocese in the case of Exeter College, Cumberland and Westmorland in the case of

Queen's College, Norfolk in the case of Trinity Hall. King's Hall apart, all suffered poverty in their early years. Like the un-endowed halls, they occupied ordinary houses at first and used a neighbouring church as a chapel. Specially designed buildings of their own came later as resources and property accumulated. Even then the earliest planned buildings furnished only rough comfort. At Corpus Christi College, where the first enclosed

University lecture, early fifteenth century

college court was built in the years after 1352, 'the outside wall had no buttresses or parapets; the inside ones were bare of plaster; the windows were largely unglazed; and the ground floors were of clay, and the first-floor rooms open to the roof.'[33] For long, poverty curtailed statutory establishments. About 1360 the six Oxford colleges numbered about seventy fellows altogether, the eight Cambridge colleges perhaps eighty. They were small exclusive communities external to the university.

Nevertheless, their advantages made the colleges an attraction to able men, and their corporate attitudes and interests could carry weight in academic controversy. The dominant group of Oxford scholars between 1320 and 1360 were members of Merton

College, foremost among them Thomas Bradwardine, later arch-bishop of Canterbury, one of many bishops produced by the college in the fourteenth century. It was this group that carried on the Grosseteste tradition of hypothesis, experiment and induction, and made Merton famous for its contributions to astronomy and mathematical physics. However, the number of secular masters provided for in colleges was much smaller than the number of friars living securely in their convents, and the friars collectively remained a powerful force, enhancing the university's international reputation, claiming and receiving exemptions and privileges, and dominating the theology faculty. The most radical intellectual influence of the age was the Oxford Franciscan William of Ockham who, by applying the inductive method, divorced theology from philosophy and so diminished the number of Christian doctrines demonstrable by natural reason that eventually he left faith without any rational foundation.

During the fourteenth century the universities came to make an increasingly important contribution to national life. They stood at the apex of the educational system, such as it was, and although learning still flourished in other places, like the cathedrals and some greater monasteries, it was the universities that nourished it. University-trained men came to hold the highest offices in the administration of church and state. Some two-thirds of the bishops were graduates; a diminishing number of them were scholars appointed for their intellectual distinction and a growing number were professional administrators made bishops in return for their government service. Graduates, especially in canon or civil law, largely staffed the royal chancery, exchequer and diplomatic service and were remunerated not with salaries but with canonries or rectories, where paid deputies did the work. Others served bishops as auditors of causes, officials and registrars and were similarly rewarded with benefices in the bishop's gift. It was in the expectation of lucrative promotion of this kind that scholars persevered with their lengthy studies for higher degrees, and it was to help them stay the course that colleges were founded.[34]

From the mid-century the universities suffered a period of depression. The Black Death led to depleted numbers. Perhaps it was the plague mortality that prompted Bishop Bateman's foundation of Trinity Hall in 1350 and the establishment of Corpus Christi College by two of the town gilds of Cambridge in 1352. These were the last Cambridge colleges for nearly ninety years; in a similar period only one new college for seculars was founded at Oxford. The long wars with France probably attracted students from the schools to military service. Complaints of the shortage of educated clerks became frequent. The period was one of social malaise and discontent. One expression of this unrest was a wave of anti-clericalism which denounced ecclesiastical property and even questioned the church's authority and some of its doctrines. Intellectual leadership of this protest came from Oxford in the person of John Wyclif, whose teaching made the university's orthodoxy suspect for a generation.

Apart from two small monastic colleges which the cathedral priories of Canterbury and Durham instituted for their student monks, the only additional foundation of this period at Oxford was New College, established in 1379 by William of Wykeham, the civil-servant bishop *par excellence*. His declared object was to help 'cure that general disease of the clerical army . . . grievously wounded owing to the fewness of the clergy, arising from pestilences, wars and other miseries of the world'. No less than his school, his college was a striking innovation. Providing for a warden and seventy fellows, recruited exclusively from the school at Winchester, together with a chapel staff of chaplains, clerks and choristers to sing daily the seven canonical offices and seven masses, it was easily the largest college in either university. Its primary and unusual purpose was to support undergraduates through the arts course, though they could stay on in the higher faculties after graduating as masters if they so wished. Besides attending the university schools, the juniors were to be taught in their first two years by their college seniors. Three or four shared a common sleeping room, but each had his own partitioned study in a corner. The buildings, with chapel, hall and chambers forming an enclosed quadrangle, were the first complete purpose-designed college buildings and they became a model not only for later colleges, but also for the older ones when they eventually erected permanent buildings.[35]

Although New College doubled the numbers residing in colleges at Oxford, the total was still hardly a tenth of the members of the university as a whole. A minority of scholars perhaps for reasons of economy still lived in private lodgings; these were the 'chamberdeacons' whose freedom from supervision made for rowdyism and indiscipline: witness the bawdy escapades in the

Oxford carpenter's house where the 'poor scholar' Nicholas was a lodger in Chaucer's *Miller's Tale*. For such reasons, lodging in private houses was repeatedly forbidden and most students came to live under surveillance in halls or at Cambridge in hostels. These became the normal places of residence for undergraduates. Some seventy of them existed at one time at Oxford; the usual number at Cambridge was from twenty to thirty. They differed essentially from colleges in that they were unendowed and thus financially dependent on their members' payments. They occupied ordinary houses on the street front or above shops, and might consist of six or eight rooms, each accommodating two or three students, with a common room for meals, lectures and disputations. Each was conducted by a principal, who was usually a regent master, duly approved and regulated by the university. He leased the house (often from monastic or college landlords), charged his students a room rent and paid a manciple or steward to do the catering. Instruction was also provided for a fee, supplementing the public lectures in the schools. Most halls were for 'artists', others for canonists or civilians, and a few were grammar halls – private grammar schools for boys, which were important adjuncts to the university system and which the university supervised. However, any hall might change its character with its principal.[36]

Students began at the university when they were about fourteen, some younger, some older. Newly arrived perhaps with letters of recommendation they would seek admission to a hall, providing the principal with financial surety and promising to obey the rules of the society, and also enrol in a regent master's school. All would have received the first tonsure which made them technically clerics and most of them would be intent on a clerical career, though from the fifteenth century there was a well-born minority who apparently had no serious vocational motive and were there for only a year or two in order to finish off their education. With the enforcement of residence, discipline became stricter, the colleges setting the example. Common prohibitions were the keeping of dogs or hawks, sword-and-buckler play, dice, draughts and chess, wrestling or dancing in hall and ball games in chapel. Latin was to be spoken always. For undergraduates, fines and flogging were usual sanctions. Violence between the 'nations', or rival halls, or against the townsmen was common. An Oxford statute in 1432 fixed an elaborate tariff

New College and its 100 clerks

of fines in an attempt to curb brawling and fighting, but lawlessness was endemic and incurable – the normal state of society.
As late as 1506 a battle between northerners and southerners
outside the university church led to the deaths of a college
fellow, the principal of a hall and two undergraduates.[37]

During the arts course, students were usually financed by
parents or patrons, sometimes by means of legacies made expressly for their maintenance in the schools for a period of years –
four, or more rarely seven – commonly at 5 marks a year. In any
financial emergency there were loan chests from which sums
might be borrowed according to the student's academic status and
on deposit of a suitable pledge (usually a book).[38] Poor scholars
were allowed to beg by Act of Parliament if they carried the chancellor's licence, and this might be necessary on the long walk
home and back in the summer vacation. Sir Thomas More, talking to his children in poverty, says in jest that they all may have
to 'descend to Oxford fare' and 'with bags and wallets go a
begging together, and . . . at every man's door . . . sing *Salve
Regina*'.[39] Insufficient means forced many students to leave
without graduating.

For a more advanced scholar's education the most coveted
support was a benefice (or preferably two) with a dispensation
from the bishop to be absent for the purpose of study for a maximum of seven years. Presentation to a benefice might be sought
from the king, a bishop, a lay patron, or by papal provision. By
the late fourteenth century, however, the expansion of royal and
episcopal administration staffed by clerks maintained by benefices had drastically curtailed the amount of preferment available for scholars, and a crisis of student maintenance and
graduate employment faced the universities. The scramble for
benefices became intense. Petitions in Parliament and convocation
brought little relief. Student numbers declined; more left without
degrees – perhaps as many as two-thirds – leaving behind no
record of their presence; the higher faculties were especially
attenuated. By about 1400, numbers at Oxford had fallen to an
estimated 1,200, of whom some 150 were in colleges and 900 in
lodgings or halls, the remaining 150 being monks, canons and
friars in their own *studia*.[40] Still relatively small, Cambridge
was perhaps a third of this size.

To ease the problem of maintenance and for reasons of piety
and philanthropy or calculated self-interest King Henry VI and
several prelates and other clerics were prompted to found new

colleges. Lincoln College at Oxford (1427) was followed by five more within ten years: two at Oxford – All Souls (1438) and Magdalen (1448); and three at Cambridge – God's-house (1439), King's (1441) and Queens' (1447). Helped by benefactors, older colleges added to their buildings, acquired property (including interests in adjacent academic halls – a process which tended in time to lead to annexation), and accumulated libraries. (Peter-house had a library of 380 books in 1418.) Perhaps to increase revenue, some colleges now admitted a few outsiders as paying guests (*commensales* or commoners), either regent masters or undergraduates, and sometimes also one or two 'poor scholars' who fed on the fellows' leavings and acted as their personal servants in return for board or tuition. Commoners up to twenty in number were allowed by the statutes of Magdalen College issued in 1480 – an important innovation pointing to future developments.[41]

Meanwhile, the universities as such attracted few benefactions and were chronically poor, owning little or no corporate property. Lecture rooms ('schools') were still rented, and churches and friaries used for meetings and ceremonies. However, at Oxford a divinity school was built with an upper room to house the library which Duke Humphrey of Gloucester gave between 1435 and 1447, though poverty delayed its completion for half a century. At Cambridge a schools' quadrangle with a regent house and library (containing in 1474 some 330 books) gradually took shape during the century. Collectively, even individually, the colleges were far wealthier than the university of which they formed only a part. King's College, Cambridge, had a revenue of over £1,000 in 1460, when the annual income of Oxford University averaged about £58. The university's standing in relation to its colleges was eventually bound to suffer.

Studies were still dominated by the arts faculty, where the course had officially changed little since the thirteenth century; the seven liberal arts and the three philosophies of Aristotle remained the staple. To encourage the study and teaching of grammar in view of its decline, a master's degree in the subject was awarded, apparently from the late fourteenth century, and it was with this same object that God's-house was instituted at Cambridge in 1439. But grammar had relatively little prestige: it had only a quasi-faculty status and its masters did not sit in the congregation of regents.[42] Logic too was losing some of its old attractions and scholasticism was running to seed. Its elaborate and subtle refinements impeded constructive thought and led to a revulsion against it. Nevertheless, in the course of three centuries logic had contributed enormously to the progress of civilization, elevating intellectual discipline, reason, order and system, if also fostering a spirit of contentiousness, a preference for abstractions and merely verbal formulas divorced from life, nature and history.

Interest in logic declined as interest in humanism grew, and it was humanism that helped to restore the study of grammar, but grammar with a literary rather than a linguistic emphasis. Classical literature, stimulated by the recovery and critical study of ancient texts, attracted increasing attention, even though it formed no part of the official curriculum. By the 1480s humanism had reached both universities, and its devotees were enthusiastic for rhetoric and pure Latinity based on the imitation of the best models. Soon after 1500 'polite letters' included Greek as well as Latin. About the mid-century another subject within the arts faculty – music – was given separate degrees, both bachelor's and doctor's, but, like grammar, music was not highly esteemed academically and produced few graduates.

Of the superior faculties, civil and canon law attracted most candidates because law offered the best prospects not only of a benefice to support study but also of profitable advancement afterwards. Theology attracted mainly monks and friars, for whom maintenance was no problem. Medicine, always the smallest and least regarded of the faculties, was sometimes without regents at all, though a few colleges provided for one or two fellows to study in the faculty. In 1421 Parliament was petitioned by university physicians to prevent non-graduates from practising medicine, but only a minority of medical men can ever have had degrees: the majority were trained no doubt by apprenticeship, some study of standard authorities, and practice.[43] Falling numbers and the lack of any separate constitutional organization threatened the higher faculties with extinction. Even the few men who studied in them easily gained dispensation from the statutory requirements which made the courses so long and arduous. 'When a candidate thought he had studied sufficiently to have earned his degree, he presented his *supplicat*, stating the number of terms which he had kept, the exercises he had performed, and asking for the degree.'[44]

The universities benefited no less than the grammar schools from the upsurge of educational philanthropy and endowment between about 1480 and 1530. At Cambridge, St Catharine's College (1473) was followed by Jesus College (1496), Christ's College, an enlargement of God's-house (1508), and St John's (1511). To the Oxford colleges were added Brasenose (1509), Corpus Christi College (1517) and – in intention the most magnificent of all – Cardinal College (1525). All these last six were founded by prelates, except Christ's and St John's which were both nominally established by the Lady Margaret Beaufort, though at the prompting of her confessor, Bishop John Fisher. All had the same object of increasing the supply of educated clergy. By 1530 Cambridge was drawing nearer to Oxford in numbers and had fourteen colleges compared to Oxford's thirteen.

The role of the colleges was now changing. Undergraduates came to be admitted, as they had been from the beginning at King's Hall and New College. At Magdalen College, Oxford, the statutes of 1480 recognized two kinds of foundationers – fellows (graduate seniors) and demies (undergraduate juniors) – and also permitted a limited number of fee-paying commoners.[45] This set the pattern for the early sixteenth-century colleges. Corpus Christi College, Oxford, was to consist of a president, twenty fellows (BAs at least) and twenty undergraduate scholars (*discipuli*) not under twelve years old. St John's College, Cambridge, comprised a master, twenty-eight fellows (at least BAs) and twenty-two scholars. Some older colleges, like Balliol in 1507, now received new statutes dividing foundation members into fellows and scholars.[46] For the scholars, discipline became much more rigorous, reducing them to the level of schoolboys. The admission of a few commoners ('perendinants', later 'pensioners' at Cambridge) also now became usual.

Moreover, following precedents at New College, King's Hall and some of the unendowed halls, colleges began to take on some of the teaching hitherto the preserve of regents in the university schools. In some colleges not only did the seniors become academic and moral mentors of the juniors (one fellow and one or two scholars sharing a room) but also college lecturers were appointed for both juniors and seniors, and readers or professors were engaged to give public lectures to all comers. Corpus Christi College had public lecturers in Greek as well as Latin – the first official recognition of the new humanism – and at Cardinal College Wolsey intended to have public professors of theology, canon and civil law, philosophy, medicine and *literae humaniores*. The colleges were on their way both to becoming undergraduate communities and to taking over the teaching functions of the university.

The religious orders and education

The contribution of the religious to education between 1300 and their dissolution was unspectacular but not inconsiderable. In two different ways some monasteries – by no means all – assisted lay education. From the early fourteenth century some of the larger Benedictine houses provided a song school and a grammar school, separately or conjointly, partly as a work of charity, partly to serve the interests of the monastery. Both types of school came into being as a result first of the abolition of child oblation, secondly of the multiplication of private masses and the new veneration of the Virgin Mary, which led to the building of additional chapels and so increased the need for serving boys and choristers. The schools were supplied by local children and thus contributed to the educational provisions of the neighbourhood. In the song school they were taught the chant and doubtless reading by a hired master, perhaps a layman, who was sometimes organist as well. In the grammar or almonry school, which was supervised by the almoner and located near his chequer by the great gate, the boys were boarded and taught Latin by a secular master. Contrary to venerable belief, monks themselves were not schoolmasters. No doubt some of the boys eventually became monks, the majority perhaps became secular clergy. Where a grammar school existed in the town, the monastery might simply board the boys and put them out to school, as did St Mary's abbey at York. Almonry schools, like all medieval schools, were small – perhaps ten or twenty boys, sons of well-to-do tradesmen or yeomen of the area, giving personal service in and about the house in part payment for their education. At the other end of the social scale, particularly in the fifteenth century, some abbots and priors, especially of canons' houses, received as paying boarders in their households the sons of neighbouring gentlemen and gave them some book learning and training in 'courtesy', perhaps through a chaplain or hired schoolmaster.[47]

However, the main educational concern of monasteries was with the training of their own novices and young monks. For the most part these tended to be drawn from the younger sons of local gentry and lesser landholders. New standards for their education were set by Pope Benedict XII in 1335–6. Each house was to have a cloister school where the novices and juniors – seldom more than five or six all told, perhaps – were to be taught 'the primitive sciences', i.e. grammar, logic and philosophy, by a master who was usually an older monk but later often a hired secular or even a layman. It was for this school that monastic libraries frequently contained the standard texts of the arts course in addition to books on the canon law and the great works of patristic and scholastic theology. Moreover, each house was to send a fixed quota of its members, one in twenty and so *pro rata*, to study theology or canon law at the university. Visitation records show that neither obligation was regularly observed, perhaps because smaller houses could not afford the expense. Nevertheless, several of the greater Benedictine houses – notably St Albans, Westminster, Norwich, Bury St Edmunds, Peterborough and Worcester – sent a steady flow of monks to their joint house of study, Gloucester College at Oxford, the number varying perhaps according to each convent's financial resources and the interest of its prior. There, monks from the same house lived in common in their own set of chambers, the senior one acting as a moral tutor, but all were ruled by a *prior studentium*. In 1361 the cathedral priory of Canterbury founded Canterbury College for its own student monks at Oxford, and in 1380 the house which the Durham monks had maintained in Oxford was endowed as Durham College. Both of these later admitted monks from other monasteries of the order. The Austin canons had no *studium* of their own until 1435, when St Mary's College was founded for them; nor the Cistercians until St Bernard's was established in 1437, Rewley abbey having ceased to serve this purpose. At Cambridge the monks of Ely had a small hostel from 1321, and a general house of study for black monks was started in 1428 as Buckingham College under the control of Croyland abbey.[48]

On the strength of their claustral studies in the 'primitive sciences', the monks, like the friars, were privileged to take degrees in theology and canon law without first graduating in arts. Only a few, however, stayed long enough to take degrees.

A father presents his son to a monastery for education

Of these, one or two would stay on as perpetual students; the majority, with or without degrees, returned to their houses where they were promoted to posts of administrative responsibility and worked, like leaven in the convent at large, as preachers or claustral lecturers in theology or canon law. In the university as a whole their strength was fairly small – at Oxford about fifty monks and up to forty canons in 1400 was Professor Jacob's estimate. There was a considerable increase in the early sixteenth century when the total number of religious in the country was probably larger than at any time since the Black Death, and when some monasteries were actively interested in university learning and the new humanism.[49]

To the education of the laity the friars contributed little save through their popular preaching. But in the intellectual and religious life of the country they remained a force throughout the fourteenth century, prominent in theological controversy, in the art of the sermon, the writing of mystical verse and hymns, and in classical scholarship. In these activities the Franciscans and Dominicans were now joined by the lesser orders of Carmelite and Austin friars who were comparative latecomers to the academic field. These orders also had provincial convents designated for the higher education of their members, some of them widely celebrated. The Austin friary at York had a notable library, while the Carmelite friary at Norwich produced a succession of eminent scholars and confessors. All four orders regularly sent student friars to their convents at Oxford or Cambridge, mainly to read theology. At Oxford in the 1370s the friars perhaps accounted for as many as one in six of the total university population. After the mid-fifteenth century their academic reputation was undistinguished. An average of only three or four graduated annually at each university. With the growth in the number of colleges, the secular masters predominated, and the friars became relatively insignificant.[50]

Perhaps the chief contribution of the religious to lay education during this period was made by the nuns, though at a comparatively low academic level. Like every monastery, each nunnery was expected to educate its own novices, and for this purpose the larger ones might have a *magistra noviciarum*, though this was a duty often neglected, as visitation records show. However, many nunneries appear to have boarded and educated children, small boys as well as girls, no doubt in order to ease the convent's finances. This was a practice frowned on by the bishops, because of the disruption of the religious life caused by the presence of young children, but it was one that they came to accept. Later, when nuns had apartments of their own, they took in private pupils. Numbers of convent children seem to have been small — an average of ten would perhaps be too large an estimate — and no doubt they came, like the nuns themselves, from the well-to-do families of the neighbourhood. What the nuns offered would be conditioned by their own educational attainments and these were not very high. They consisted of

> reading and singing the services of the church, sometimes but not always writing, Latin very rarely after the thirteenth century, French very rarely after the fourteenth century; needlework and embroidery; and perhaps that elementary knowledge of physic, which was the possession of most ladies of their class. It was, in fact, very little more than the education possessed by laywomen of the same social rank outside.[51]

Manners, religious knowledge and household skills formed the content of most girls' education in this social class for centuries to come. Some ladies of rank apparently could read, but perhaps not write; the status of women in general was low and book education was not considered important for them.

The education of the parish clergy

Apart from the university-educated philosophers, jurists and theologians who provided the administrators and executives of church and state, the largest occupational group for whom some education in the schools was obviously necessary were the parish clergy. For them Latin was vocationally essential, if only because the Scriptures and the liturgy which were their everyday concern were all in Latin. It was for this reason that candidates for ordination, and also for presentation to a benefice, were supposed to be examined as to their literary competence, though bishops absent on the king's business were often too busy to take this duty seriously.

About the educational background of the ordinary clergy, as about their social background, there is much obscurity. Educationally and socially they defy generalization.[52] The more prosperous rectors or parsons came from good families and had been at the university, often long enough to graduate. To promote the education of the parochial clergy, fourteenth-century bishops frequently granted study leave involving non-residence, usually for periods of one, two or three years.[53] Judged by their wills, rectors were frequently scholarly men with considerable collections of books. But because they were graduates, these were the clergy likely to be absentees in the administrative service of some bishop or other great man. The mass of unbeneficed clergy – curates and chaplains who were the effective parish priests, working as the hired hacks of non-resident incumbents – were largely of peasant stock. For most of them, university study was an impossible luxury. Below the level of the university there was no organized system of professional training for the clergy, and even a university education provided no specific training in parochial work. Educational opportunities for the would-be cleric were haphazard. Some Latin might be picked up at an established school or privately from a local parson or some freelance master who happened to be living in the district. Liturgically, more would be learned from informal apprenticeship to an experienced priest (helping his routine ministrations as doorkeeper, lector, exorcist and acolyte) and, given sufficient literacy, from the various manuals compiled for the instruction and encouragement of the parish clergy. The pioneer of these was the *Oculus Sacerdotis*, written about 1325 by William of Pagula; John Myrc's

Manuale Sacerdotis, much of it in vernacular verse, was a common one in the fifteenth century.[54]

Thus, the educational standards reached by the rank-and-file parish priests are uncertain. No doubt they varied from area to area and from time to time, depending on local opportunities. Some priests were barely literate in English let alone in Latin, like the candidates for ordination whom Bishop Grosseteste had rejected as mere ABC boys. Although bishops still sometimes refused to ordain or induct candidates who fell short of the desired standard, more often they accepted them on condition that they studied further and submitted themselves for re-examination, usually after a year. Ill-educated and ill-paid, of peasant origin themselves and living among peasants in the deep country, it was all too easy for rural parish priests to display the same rude and earthy interests as their parishioners. On the other hand, there were some unbeneficed clergy who had evidently received a fair measure of education. Clergy themselves, wishing to improve educational standards in their profession, often made bequests to encourage boys to attend school with the priesthood in mind. A canon of Lincoln in 1438 left a kinsman £10 to learn grammar, the sooner to become a priest; more modestly, a York chaplain in 1466 willed his nephew a grammar book, several service books and a hymn book together with 3s. 4d. to support him at school.[55] Bequests were likewise made to maintain clerks at the university, and an unknown number of ordinary parish priests must have studied at Oxford or Cambridge without taking a degree. Their failure to graduate may be reasonably attributed to lack of means, not necessarily to lack of ability. Theology lectures, revived from time to time at some of the secular cathedrals, provided educational opportunities for clergy who lived within reach. Among non-graduate parish priests there were in the later fifteenth century considerable numbers who owned books. If graduates were almost unknown among the stipendiary chaplains and curates who were the working parish priests, there were some chantry chaplains who had degrees, for a chantry might be as profitable and secure as a benefice. Bishop Alcock's chantry which supported Hull grammar school was a benefice: the chaplain had control of his own endowments like any rector and with an income of £10 was much better off than many rectors.[56]

Complaints of clerical ignorance had long been common but

they were particularly frequent in the decades before the Reformation. The evidence is contradictory. The latest research, however, tends to suggest that in this period of increasing numbers of schools and printed books, and with a rising proportion of resident graduate incumbents, educational standards at the parish level were improving, even if, in an age of intellectual transition, they fell short of the new humanist ideals of their more scholarly critics.[57] Another century was to pass before the parish clergy could measure up to these ideals and pass for scholars and gentlemen.

Changes in popular education

On the literacy of the parish clergy depended to a large extent the only instruction that was available to the mass of ordinary people. In theory, it was the priest's competence to instruct his flock in accordance with the ancient canonical obligation that was examined when he was admitted to his benefice. But it was a programme of exclusively religious knowledge that he was required to give, along the lines laid down in Archbishop Pecham's constitution *Ignorantia sacerdotum* of 1281, reissued several times until as late as 1518.[58] Moreover it was intended to be expounded in sermons from the pulpit, not in lessons in a school. To this end, collections of English sermons suitable for all feasts and seasons were available – like the well-known *Festial* of John Myrc. If parish priests taught a school it was probably not so much a regular institution as an occasional gathering of children for religious instruction in the church porch, rather like a modern Sunday school. But many priests in country districts would be too unlettered to have much to offer, save to the most ignorant flocks.

Where the incumbent had a clerk, as the canon law required, one of his duties was to keep a school.[59] The primary purpose of this was to teach boys to sing the choral parts of the liturgy in order to help out the parish services, but to do this some reading would have to be taught as well, if with little understanding, since the texts were in Latin. In town churches, teaching song may have been a normal function of the parish clerk, as it was of the precentor or his deputy, the songmaster, in cathedrals and similar great churches. In 1305 all the parish clerks in the city of Lincoln (which then had some forty-six parishes) were said to be teaching song schools without the cathedral songmaster's permission, and his right to license them was upheld by the chapter. In 1439, however, the precentor was forbidden by the bishop to interfere with song schools in the county 'which certain curates hold for their own parishioners or which are held by parish clerks in the same'.[60] Evidently song schools were fairly common. It was a song school that Chaucer's 'litel clergeon' attended in the *Prioress's Tale*, learning

> Swich maner doctrine as men used there,
> This is to seyn, to singen and to rede,
> As smale children doon in hir childhede.

The 'litel book' he used was the primer though he also knew some of the *Alma redemptoris* by heart through hearing other boys singing it as they learned the antiphonal, but

> Noght wiste he what this Latin was to seye,
> For he so yong and tendre was of age.

An older boy in the school whom he asks to explain the anthem has only a vague idea, but tells what he knows,

> I can no more expounde in this matere;
> I learn song, I can but smal grammere.

For several more centuries the parish clerk was often the only available source of village education. John Foxe, the martyrologist, tells us that Thomas Cranmer went to Cambridge (in 1503 at the age of fourteen) from the Nottinghamshire village of Aslockton where he had 'learned his grammar of a rude parish clerk'.[61]

From the late fourteenth century educational opportunities for the general population were enlarged by the increase of chantry foundations, for chantry priests probably gave popular religious instruction and with it the rudiments of English reading more often than they taught grammar, not necessarily as a statutory duty but either as a work of charity or to make money out of fees. Private or unofficial teaching of this kind is likely to have gone unrecorded. It seems to have been common in the fifteenth century. By the early sixteenth century teaching children to read English had evidently become a duty ordinarily expected of chantry priests as of parish priests. Canterbury convocation in 1529 ordered 'all those having cures, rectors, vicars and chantry priests' to employ themselves outside the time of divine service 'teaching boys the alphabet, reading, singing or grammar'.[62]

Throughout the middle ages, Latin grammar was the predominant subject of formal schooling, and schools were mainly the concern of clerks. With the growing use of the English vernacular, however, other types of school came into existence. Who conducted these schools is not clear, but it seems certain that there were lay as well as clerical teachers. ABC schools taught young children (*parvuli* or 'petties') the elements of spelling and reading from the horn book and the primer, a manual of simple devotions for lay people, containing graces, prayers and psalms. The most elementary scholars were therefore 'abcdarians' or 'primerians' – girls as well as boys – and what they learned was often summed up as 'the alphabets and graces'. More advanced, the reading school used the psalter to teach reading (*lectura*) in Latin, presumably as an extension of the song school, though some English was probably taught as well, if only incidentally. It is hard to see the educational value of learning to read Latin without grammar, but even when reading was taught by the grammar master it was apparently taught quite separately and for a lower fee.

Writing was certainly a much rarer accomplishment than reading, but opportunities for learning to write were increasing. Since the thirteenth century, writing had tended to be the expert craft of professionals. Some were 'book hand' writers, either self-employed copiers of books, or engaged by stationers, the entrepreneurs of the manuscript book trade before the age of printing. Others, writers of 'court hand', were employed as clerks and secretaries to keep the records of barons or merchants, town corporations or gilds. From the fourteenth century there were also public writers of court hand (scriveners) who composed letters, drafted bonds and wills and kept accounts for a fee, and transmitted their art in all its technicalities to their apprentices in the scriveners' gild. Some scriveners kept private writing schools, teaching not only the everyday cursive hand of the time but also business methods, forms of correspondence and accounts – a kind of commercial training, using French until the early fifteenth century. About this time, the replacement of parchment by paper – a much cheaper writing material – probably increased the demand for writing skills among traders and craftsmen and the lesser clergy. Since most official documents

Grammar school, c. 1500

were still written in Latin, some previous instruction in grammar must be assumed. But French and English were being increasingly used in the later fourteenth century for official as well as for commercial and private transactions. To meet the needs of businessmen no less than those of students, teachers of French and writing operated at Oxford subject to regulations made by the university.[63]

During the fifteenth century, writing skills became much more widely diffused among the urban laity. Other teachers of writing appeared besides the scriveners; for example chantry priests sometimes taught writing along with reading or grammar. One of the three priests serving the chantry which was founded about 1480 by the bishop of Bath and Wells at Acaster, his birthplace near Selby in the West Riding, was required 'to teach to write and all such thing as belonged to scrivener craft'. Archbishop Thomas Rotherham of York, establishing a chantry college of three schoolmaster chaplains in Rotherham in 1483, similarly provided for one of them to teach grammar, a second song, and the third to be 'skilled in the art of writing and keeping accounts'. For, the archbishop observed, the district produced many intelligent youths who did not aspire to the priesthood and for whom these 'mechanical arts' would be more appropriate. Significantly, the last royal injunctions concerning chantry priests (in 1547) ordered them to 'exercise themselves in teaching youth to read and write'.[64]

How widely these expanding educational facilities were spread it is impossible to know. It seems safe to assume, however, that they were confined mainly to towns, and that the greater part of the population, living in poverty in out-of-the-way villages, were little touched by them.

Craft apprenticeship

It would be altogether wrong to think of medieval education mainly in terms of schools and universities. Formal institutional education was exceptional and confined to a small minority of the population − to clerks in the widest sense. They were the only men for whom education meant storing up knowledge before they applied it in one or other of the professions that were included within the church. Most people were educated by employment: by living and working with experienced practitioners in some sort of apprenticeship, formal or informal. Personal service was the cement that bound medieval society together – most men owed service to a superior in return for a consideration of some sort, and apprenticeship meant personal service in return for instruction. In a sense all medieval education was technical and vocational, directed to some particular occupation or function, and apprenticeship was the form it normally took. This generalization applies even to the education of clerks, which was as much professional as academic. The university student was his master's apprentice, and in the later colleges the servitor was the apprentice or servant pupil of a fellow. The combination of learning and service was common with boys in monastic song and almonry schools.

Apprenticeship was ordinarily organized in gilds of one kind or another. A gild was a fellowship dedicated to a particular profession or vocation – ordering its own life, controlling its own membership, safeguarding its own standards of skill and conduct, transmitting them to future members through apprenticeship. All organized higher education in the middle ages was provided by gilds: universities, craft companies, Inns of Court, the orders of chivalry – all were to some extent species of the same genus.[65]

Until the nineteenth century the only organized form of industrial training which England knew was the apprenticeship system of the trade gilds. This originated in private arrangements between individual master craftsmen and parents, stipulating a premium or a stated period of unpaid service by a boy in return for instruction and initiation in the mysteries of the craft. As the different trades developed a gild organization between about 1250 and 1450, so they adopted apprenticeship as the means of training new members. Responsibility for this work was delegated to each master who contracted to lodge, board, clothe, discipline and instruct his apprentices under the general control of the gild, which supervised standards of work, regulated apprentices' dress and behaviour, and heard appeals against ill-treatment. By 1450 this was the usual method of entry into the skilled trades.

Although at first the period of training varied, seven years from the age of fourteen to twenty-one became the general rule in London and this was followed elsewhere. The age of entry implies some previous schooling, and this is indicated also by testamentary bequests for the binding of sons, kinsmen or wards following a period at school. 'That my youngest son George, after he be expedited sufficiently in his grammar after the mind of my executors, be bound apprentice to a merchant of the Staple' was the will of Sir Richard Basset, a Nottinghamshire knight, in 1522.[66] In certain trades – scriveners and stationers, obviously – literacy would be technically indispensable, and some of the more prestigious gilds, like the London goldsmiths, forbade masters to take apprentices unless they could read and write. But above the lowliest level, all craftsmen in the ordinary course of business would have to write letters and keep a day-book recording purchases, sales and orders and this would necessarily form part of the apprentice's training. To this end, a master sometimes bound himself to pay for an apprentice's schooling. Some gilds maintained schools by employing a chaplain who not only celebrated in the gild chapel but also taught members' children, and perhaps their apprentices too, when need arose. The spread of apprenticeship may have been an incentive for the reading and writing schools which became numerous in towns during the fifteenth century.[67]

It is impossible to estimate the extent or the effectiveness of this system of education. Obviously, more than technical training was involved, for in the master's family and in the corporate life of the gild, its worship, moots, feasts, plays and pageants, adolescent apprentices must have gained much of their moral and social education. Equally obviously, its effectiveness would depend on individual masters, and there is evidence to show that whilst some were conscientious and kind, others were neglectful and brutal. Its extent was perhaps more limited than is sometimes supposed. Apprenticeship hardly existed outside the towns, and in most towns it must have been rare because of the small populations.[68] It did not apply to unskilled trades and hence to the vast majority of labouring men. Some gilds specifically excluded villeins' sons, but in any case until 1406 they could no more be apprenticed than sent to school without the lord's permission. And after 1406 a man had to own land worth 20s. a year before he could apprentice his son or daughter – for girls were apprenticed as well as boys, though more rarely. In effect, apprenticeship was probably limited to the more profitable trades in London and other large towns. There, high fees and expenses confined it to the relatively well-to-do: city merchants, yeomen,

the younger sons and bastards of gentlemen. In 1515 Sir Ralph
Bigod of Settrington in Yorkshire made provision in his will for
apprenticing two bastard sons in London.[69] Two contrary ten-
dencies in the later fifteenth century further reduced its effectiveness. In the wealthier gilds, the number of apprentices was kept
small in order to restrict membership in a spirit of monopoly;
in humbler gilds they were admitted in excessive numbers and
exploited as cheap labour.

The common lawyers

Legal training, like industrial training, developed along practical
lines within a broadly similar gild and apprenticeship system.
From the thirteenth century, the growth of a body of common
law based on unwritten custom supplemented by statute and
administered in the king's courts gradually gave rise to the first
profession of learned laymen – the common lawyers of England,
from whom the king's judges were appointed. To the doctrines of
civil and canon law which the universities taught, the common
law owed little. Its proceedings were in English and French, its
writs and statutes in French or Latin, whereas civil and canon
law used Latin exclusively; and whilst both these were to a large
extent scholastic and theoretical, built on standard codes and
commentaries on them, common law was essentially unacademic,
practical, empirical, constantly being shaped by experience and
actual needs.

Working in and about the king's courts in Westminster, the
common lawyers gradually came to live as corporate societies
in inns or *hospicia* situated between Westminster and the City.
Four of these existed by about 1400 – Lincoln's Inn, Gray's Inn,
the Middle Temple and the Inner Temple. Rather like the craft
gilds, they developed a hierarchical structure and admitted and
trained their own recruits. Each consisted of fully qualified
members ('utter barristers') and juniors or apprentices of the
law ('inner barristers'); each was governed by its senior members
or benchers, who nominated readers to teach the juniors. From
the readers the Crown appointed the serjeants-at-law, the
highest-ranking barristers, who formed a small select gild with
their own Inn in Fleet Street, and from these the king's judges
were chosen.[70]

At much the same time and in the same area similar Inns or

hostels came into being to accommodate the chancery clerks and their pupils learning the doctrines and procedures peculiar to the equity jurisdiction of chancery. In the course of the fifteenth century these chancery Inns (there were ten of them – Clement's, Clifford's, Furnival's, Staple Inn and the rest) became associated with and finally subordinated to the Inns of Court, as chancery itself began to hear common-law cases and as knowledge of equity procedures became useful to the common lawyers.

Because the training was long and expensive, common lawyers came mainly from the gentry and official class. Proficiency in Latin was essential, so intending apprentices of the law would first spend some years learning grammar. This might be followed by a period at Oxford or Cambridge, either in the arts faculty learning more grammar and logic, or in one of the inns or halls for canonists or civilians, learning something of the principles of the two rival legal systems. Private teaching of common-law subjects and of such necessary ancillaries as writing and French was also available there. The student began his real legal education by spending one or two years on the rudiments in one of the chancery Inns before being admitted as an 'inner barrister' at one of the Inns of Court. Here he studied the plea rolls and year books, listened to the readings, took part in learning exercises – case-puttings, bolts and moots – and during the law terms attended the sittings of the great courts in Westminster Hall. So after seven years – the same period required for the MA at the university – he became eligible to be called as an 'utter barrister'. The training was tough, technical and directly related to actual professional practice.

The earliest account of the Inns and their educational system dates from about 1470 and is given by Sir John Fortescue, a member of Lincoln's Inn, serjeant-at-law and chief justice of the king's bench, in his treatise *De Laudibus Legum Angliae*. Already by his time the training function of the Inns had been extended and diluted. During the later fourteenth century the justices of the peace had developed as an important element in the judicial system, and the landowning knights and gentry from whom these unpaid amateurs were appointed soon found some legal knowledge useful both for the discharge of their official duties and for the protection of their private landed interests in a violent and litigious age. Accordingly they started sending their sons to study for a time at one or other of the Inns, with no intention of qualifying for the practice of the law but simply to gain some general knowledge of it, and also to take advantage of the opportunities which London offered for acquiring courtly accomplishments. In all the Inns, writes Fortescue:

> there is besides a school of law, a kind of academy of all the manners that the nobles learn. There they learn to sing and to exercise themselves in every kind of harmonies. They are also taught there to practise dancing and all games proper for nobles, as those brought up in the king's household are accustomed to practise. In the vacations most of them apply themselves to the study of legal science, and at festivals to the reading, after the divine services, of holy scriptures and of chronicles. . . . So for the sake of the acquisition of virtue . . . knights, barons, and also other magnates . . . place their sons in these Inns, although they do not desire them to be trained in the science of the laws, nor to live by its practice, but only by their patrimonies.[71]

By the early sixteenth century, when the Inns of Court held about 180 students and the chancery Inns another 120, the common law had become more valuable than canon or civil law for a career in public service and administration.[72] The landowning gentry increasingly turned to it for professional training as well as for rounding off a general education. Bequests in wills illustrate this dual educational function of the Inns, which became progressively more marked. In 1497 a Yorkshire knight, Sir Thomas Markenfield, provided £15 a year for his heir to spend two years at Oxford and then three years at one of the Inns. Similarly in 1501 Robert Constable, a serjeant-at-law and member of a knightly family at Flamborough in Yorkshire, bequeathed £20 for his son to study at Cambridge for three years until he was fifteen, and then £24 to attend three years at one of the Inns of chancery. These were clearly providing for their sons a general education of a kind becoming fashionable for the gentry, one which combined study of the liberal arts with some study of the law. Three years seems to have been the normal period at the Inns for this. On the other hand, Sir Richard Basset of Nottinghamshire, whose will of 1522 we have already mentioned, wished his two sons to be kept at school until proficient in their grammar, and then the younger was to be apprenticed to the wool trade whilst the heir was to have £12 a year for

fourteen years in order to study the common law at Gray's Inn —
evidently for the full professional course.[73]

Until the mid-seventeenth century the Inns continued to fill
this dual function, providing a technical training for the practice
of the law whilst also serving, less seriously, as finishing schools
for country gentlemen.

Aristocratic education

The idea of the gild and of vocational training through apprenticeship and service was a marked feature of aristocratic education
during the middle ages. Chivalry was a European code of
manners and morals which developed first in France around the
feudal principle of service and was at its height between about
1150 and 1350. Institutionally, it expressed itself in the orders of
knighthood — the new feudal aristocracy of professional mounted
fighting-men, in the court of chivalry and the heralds and
heraldry. Ideologically, it meant the cultivation and exaltation
of the military virtues of courage, endurance, loyalty and physical
prowess, together with a romantic, quasi-religious devotion to
women and the protection of the poor and weak. No doubt a great
gulf always separated ideal and reality, and in decay chivalry
became a matter of rules and conventional good form — an exaggerated display of class manners.

Rather like the gild and the university, the knightly order
developed grades of fellowship — page, squire, bachelor and
banneret — with solemn rites of initiation, and the young aspirant
to membership learned his future vocation, like the apprentice
to trade or the law, by practice and service.

> It is fitting that a knight's son be subject to his lord [says a
> French book on chivalry], and to this end, every knight ought to
> put his son in the household of another knight, that he may learn
> in his youth to carve at table and to serve, and to arm and
> attire a knight. Thus, as it is fitting for a man that would learn
> to be a tailor or carpenter, that he have a master that is a tailor
> or a carpenter, even so is it meet that any gentleman that loveth
> the order of chivalry and desireth to become and be a good
> knight should have first of all a master that is a knight.[74]

From Anglo-Norman times the custom of noble families was
to send their sons, or at least their eldest sons, to be brought up

in the household of some great lord as companions or henchmen of his own sons, there to learn the knightly arts and the profession of arms. The greatest men would hope to have their sons reared in the king's own household. From personal attendance on lord or lady the young damoiseau of seven or eight years upwards learned 'chivalry' or 'courtesy' as a page. A chaplain or secretary taught him to read, and perhaps write, French; he picked up some religious knowledge and book learning (from romances and chronicles); he learned to sing and dance, play chess and backgammon, carve and wait at table, and to know the rules of heraldry and degrees of rank. Meanwhile, with men-at-arms he developed physical skills – riding, swimming, hawking, hunting and use of weapons, learned the rules of tournaments and war, and how to arm and array a knight. At fourteen or fifteen he was ready to serve as a squire, a knight's personal aide in the castle and in the field. Chaucer, who had started his career in the household of the duchess of Clarence in 1357, gives a vivid picture of the complete squire in the Prologue to the *Canterbury Tales*. At twenty-one the squire was ready to assume the dignity of knighthood. Elder sons with patrimonies became full knights, and besides their military obligations performed unpaid public service in their shires as tax collectors, commissioners, coroners and amateur judges – in time this civil function became as important as the military. Landless younger sons, unable to meet the obligations and expenses of knighthood, found employment in the service of a lord as 'bachelors'. In the fifteenth century these were the *generosi* and *armigeri* who formed the indentured retinues of great magnates, pledging fealty and service in peace and war in return for patronage and protection.

The ideal exemplars of aristocratic education are to be found in the romances – stories in French, either verse or prose, for reading aloud in courtly circles, telling with much heavy moralizing of the deeds and loves of knights and their ladies. Their heroes are the perfect page and squire – from Jehan de Dammartin, the earl of Oxford's squire in the thirteenth century, to le Petit Jehan de Saintré in the fifteenth. More expressly didactic are the fifteenth-century courtesy books – manuals of deportment and polite manners, often rhymed for easy memorizing – which tell the page how to conduct himself in his lord's presence and at table.[75] The ordinances of noble households often contained provisions for the training of henchmen or pages and other boys.

The Chapel Royal in the king's household had a songmaster and grammar master, who taught not only the singing boys and almonry clerks but also the king's pages and squires and other sons of gentlemen and noblemen at court. A 'master of the henchmen' supervised their training in 'urbanity' and 'nurture', taught them 'sundry languages and other learnings virtuous' – how to ride and joust and wear their harness, how to speak and behave with courtesy, observing the rules of precedence, how to harp, pipe, sing and dance; and he sat with them at table to watch their manners and conversation.[76] Instructions issued in 1473 for the education of the prince of Wales in his own establishment at Ludlow Castle, with Bishop Alcock as his tutor, ordered 'the sons of nobles, lords and gentlemen' in his household 'to rise at a convenient hour and hear their mass and be virtuously brought up; and taught in grammar, music and other cunning, and exercises of humanity, according to their births and after their ages'.[77] *The Northumberland Household Book*, drawn up in 1512 for the Percy manors at Wressle and Leconfield in East Yorkshire, shows regular provision made for a master of grammar, an assistant usher and a songmaster for the children of the chapel.[78]

To the socially ambitious this was the kind of education most likely to advance family fortunes, so it was especially appropriate for an eldest son. Thus in 1478 Sir John Pilkington, a prominent northern Yorkist, relying on the duke of Gloucester's patronage, planned to have his son brought up in the household of Lord Hastings, the lord chamberlain, until the age of sixteen.[79] However, the household was not the only type of education chosen by the gentry. In the fifteenth century the university and the Inns of Court opened other doors to acceptable careers, and these were sometimes combined with an earlier household upbringing. During the more peaceful sixteenth century, when knighthood became merely a title of honour among the landed gentry, unconnected with military expertise, and chivalry an empty convention, the patron's household continued to play an important but diminishing role in aristocratic education.

The diffusion of literacy

From the late fourteenth century, English gained social respectability with the gradual recognition of its suitability for business and literature, and its use in writing rapidly became general, completely displacing French by about the 1420s. Thus an educated laity could develop in a way that was impossible so long as literacy meant familiarity with Latin.

As late as Tudor times there were men of the magnate class who despised book learning as fit only for weaklings and inferiors like clerks and secretaries and felt no deprivation because they could neither read nor write. Nevertheless throughout the fifteenth century literacy in English and even knowledge of Latin was spreading among the nobility and gentry. More of their sons received a clerkly type of education in grammar, perhaps from a household chaplain or tutor, and then went on to the university, with or without an ecclesiastical career in mind. King's Hall at Cambridge had long attracted students of this kind. Scions of some of the greatest families – Neville, de la Pole, Grey, Courtenay, Scrope – attended Oxford or Cambridge if only nominally and for a year or two, taking over an inn for themselves and their servants, or lodging in a college as *commensales*. Henry V (who was educated as an earl's son, not as a future king) may have resided briefly at Oxford as a *commensalis* of Queen's College in 1398 when his uncle and tutor, Henry Beaufort, was university chancellor. However suspect this tradition, Henry V was certainly well educated; he read, wrote and spoke both Latin and French (but encouraged the use of the English vernacular) and had a considerable collection of scholarly books. His younger brothers also had educated interests: John, duke of Bedford, bought the library of the French king, Charles VI, and provided a lecture fund at Oxford; Humphrey, duke of Gloucester, gave the university the nucleus of its library.[80] No doubt this was an exceptionally well-educated noble family, but there were other fifteenth-century magnates whose education had included some academic training, notably John Tiptoft, earl of Worcester, who had studied at Oxford about 1440 and later at Padua and Verona. About this time married students occasionally appear at the universities: presumably these were young gentlemen without either clerical or academic ambitions. 'One of the silent revolutions of the later middle ages', writes Professor Denys Hay, 'is the way the old fabric of ecclesiastical education . . . housed a new lay clientele with no intentions of pursuing the traditional curriculum to its logical end.'[81] If not at the university, other sons of gentle families might spend several years at one of the Inns of Court either to become common lawyers and perhaps eventually judges or merely to round off a general education.

Wills, at first usually written in French if not in Latin, indicate the rising standard of literacy and literary interest within this social group. Among their bequests are not only primers, missals and psalters but also chronicles, courtesy books, law books, works on husbandry, hunting and heraldry. During the late fifteenth century wills in English became more common, and peers and gentlemen sometimes state specifically that they are writing their wills in their own hand.[82] Anthony Fitzherbert's *Book of Husbandry* (1523) shows that writing materials were an ordinary part of a gentleman's baggage when he travelled. 'Pen, paper, ink, parchment, red wax, pumice, books' were among the items his servant had to remember to pack.[83]

The correspondence of the Pastons, an aspiring family of Norfolk gentry in the fifteenth century, reveals a remarkably high level of vernacular literacy not only among the men of the family but also among their agents and bailiffs. Their wives and daughters, though apparently able to read, for the most part did not actually write their own letters but called in clerical help. The men's careers show the kind of education which the gentry received at the time. All of them perhaps had their earliest instruction at home from a clerk or chaplain. Of the four sons of Chief Justice William Paston, founder of the family fortunes, the eldest, John Paston, went to Cambridge and then to the Inner Temple; another was at Clifford's Inn; two others were at Cambridge, one of them afterwards having a tutor in London. Of John Paston's sons, his heir was brought up in Edward IV's household, the second son in the duke of Norfolk's, a third after a time at Staple Inn joined the indentured retinue of the duke of Gloucester, another was at Oxford, and after leaving Eton the youngest entered the service of the earl of Oxford.[84]

Among the more prosperous trading class, literacy in English became commonplace in the fifteenth century. Some of the opulent merchants of London, York, Bristol and Norwich had long shared much the same social and educational standards as the gentry. As early as the 1350s Chaucer, a London vintner's son, was schooled in grammar, perhaps at St Paul's, learned 'courtesy' as a page in the duchess of Clarence's household, and at a later stage was perhaps a member of the Inner Temple. The London Brewers' Company resolved in 1422 to keep their records in English instead of Latin or French as previously, because many of their members 'have the knowledge of writing and reading in ... English ... but ... Latin and French ... they do not in any wise understand'.[85] Even so, London merchants who founded grammar schools in their native towns later in the fifteenth century can be assumed to have had at least some interest in Latin and perhaps some knowledge of it, if only at a utilitarian level. Certainly, rich wholesalers trading overseas on a large scale can be assumed to have possessed a standard of English literacy no less than that of their clerks and factors.[86] Similarly, master masons or architects responsible for great building operations, and capitalist entrepreneurs in industries like woollen-cloth production, ship-building and iron-founding, controlling considerable wage-earning labour forces, must at least have been able to read, write and calculate. A high standard of English education among merchants in the late fifteenth century is indicated by the family and business correspondence of the Celys, a firm of wool exporters of Aveley in Essex.

There are clear indications too of growing literacy among lower social groups. The stimulus and the opportunity sprang from the break-up of the old seignorial estate based on customary tenure and labour services and the substitution of an economy based on leases, rents and wages – a change which presented able and enterprising peasants with new prospects of social mobility. An attempt to check this in the interests of the governing landlord class was made in 1391 when the Commons petitioned the king in Parliament 'to ordain ... that no serf or villein henceforth put his children to school in order to procure their advancement by clergy'. The petition was unsuccessful but in 1406 a statute allowed bondsmen's children to be sent to school without impediment.[87] Following these changes, the fifteenth century saw an increased demand for schooling by ambitious peasants who had left the land for the towns. Towns, schools and literacy were directly linked phenomena. Many of the English-writing clerks, bailiffs and stewards of the fifteenth century must have been the sons or grandsons of peasants. A rising standard of literacy must be assumed also among ordinary skilled artisans like weavers, glaziers, smiths, carpenters and masons. The will of a Beverley mason in about 1450 mentions among a medley of household effects 'six English books worth ten shillings'.[88] The agents of this spreading literacy were the reading and writing schools kept by parish clerks, chantry chaplains, scriveners and other teachers, either freelance or sponsored by town authorities.

Latin culture also was increasingly reaching the laity as more boys attended grammar schools with no intention of becoming priests. The church's influence even in this traditionally ecclesiastical field of education was lessening. Laymen as well as churchmen founded grammar schools. When William Sevenoaks, a London grocer, established one in his native town in 1432, he stipulated that the master should be a BA but 'by no means in holy orders'.[89] Lay masters appear elsewhere, not only in town grammar schools, as at Hull, but even in the schools of cathedral and collegiate churches, as at York and Beverley. More significantly, when Dean Colet reconstituted St Paul's school after 1508 he made the Mercers' Company trustees, not the dean and chapter of the cathedral. Knowledge of Latin and concern with education were no longer confined to clerks. One result of the narrowing educational gap between churchmen and laymen was Henry VII's restriction of benefit of clergy to clerks in major orders in 1512, so as to curtail mounting abuse of a now anomalous privilege.

Statistical calculations in this arithmetically primitive age are notoriously unreliable. Even so, it is remarkable that in 1533 Sir Thomas More, lately lord chancellor, could estimate that over 50 per cent of the population could read English. Even if he meant only the population of London, his estimate still seems improbably high. The dissemination of literacy at this period cannot possibly be quantified, but the circumstantial evidence for it is clear. A wide reading public is indicated by the rising output of vernacular works of general appeal – books of manners (some obviously intended for the lesser tradesman class), romances and chronicles, religious and secular lyrics, popular songs and ballads, not to mention the works of Chaucer and his fifteenth-century imitators. For all that, the high cost of books must always have acted as a discouragement to self-education. Printing, introduced into London in 1476 by William Caxton, a mercer, was an epochmaking event. By 1500 the age of the manuscript book-copier had gone. The mass production of relatively cheap and handy texts of both old and new works, in Latin and in English, afforded access to an unprecedented range of knowledge and ideas.[90] Above the humblest level of the common labouring man, the incentive to literacy must have been sharpened, and the reading public enormously enlarged, with portentous results. By the 1520s unorthodox ideas were being circulated by printed vernacular books, to the alarm of the bishops. Perhaps it was with some rhetorical exaggeration that the bishop of London in 1536 denounced that 'other word of God . . . which every souter and cobbler doth read in his mother tongue'.[91] But when access to the authorized English Great Bible was restricted by Act of Parliament in 1543, on a class basis so as to safeguard orthodoxy from promiscuous Bible study, those specifically forbidden to read it were women, artificers, journeymen, serving men under the degree of yeomen, husbandmen and labourers.[92]

Clearly, long before 1500 education had ceased to be the effective monopoly of churchmen, purveyed and controlled by them. Literacy implied ability to read and write in English rather than Latin, and it was the possession of all sections of the lay public, in towns at least, though to an extent that cannot be measured. Here, in the existence of an enlarged English-reading (and therefore more openminded and critical) laity, we have one of the conditions that contributed to the causes of the Reformation.

Notes

1 A. F. LEACH, *Early Yorkshire Schools* (Yorkshire Archaeological Society, 1899), I, pp. 80–100.
2 See below, p. 62.
3 D. KNOWLES and R. N. HADCOCK, *Medieval Religious Houses* (London, 1953), pp. 325–46, for a list of secular colleges.
4 *Victoria County History Northants.*, II, p. 171.
5 Statutes (c. 1460) in Historical MSS. Commission, *Report on the MSS. of Lord de L'Isle and Dudley*, I (1925), p. 182. For comparison, 12 marks was decreed the minimum for a vicar or chaplain in 1437.
6 LEACH, *Charters*, pp. 321 ff., prints the statutes.
7 *Victoria County History Essex*, II, p. 516.
8 *Victoria County History Northants.*, II, p. 177.
9 *Victoria County History Yorks.*, III, p. 343.
10 A. F. LEACH, *A History of Winchester College* (London, 1899), pp. 60–76, 88–103.
11 LEACH, *Charters*, p. 319.

12 L. H. BUTLER, 'Archbishop Melton, his neighbours and kinsmen', *Journal of Ecclesiastical History*, II (1951), p. 66.
13 C. L. KINGSFORD, *Prejudice and Promise in the Fifteenth Century* (Oxford, 1925), p. 39.
14 E. RICKERT (ed.), *Chaucer's World* (London, 1948), pp. 112–14.
15 *Testamenta Eboracensia* (6 volumes, Surtees Society, 1836–1902), III, p. 92.
16 E. F. JACOB (ed.), *Register of Archbishop Chichele*, II (Oxford, 1937), pp. 23–4.
17 LEACH, *Charters*, pp. 402–3. Hampton may have been Hampton-on-Thames (as Leach assumed) or Southampton (as Coulton supposed).
18 KINGSFORD, *Prejudice and Promise*, pp. 36–9, for schools in London at this time.
19 *Victoria County History Camb.*, III, p. 429. See also below, p. 59.
20 H. C. MAXWELLL LYTE, *A History of Eton College* (London, 1889), Appendix III, gives a digest of the statutes; *Victoria County History Camb.*, III, pp. 376–9.
21 LEACH, *Charters*, pp. 341–3.
22 HELEN SUGGETT, 'The use of French in England in the later Middle Ages', *Transactions of the Royal Historical Society*, XXVIII (1946), pp. 61–80.
23 W. BROWN (ed.), *Yorkshire Inquisitions*, IV (Yorkshire Archaeological Society, 1906), p. 92.
24 J. G. NICHOLS (ed.), 'Two sermons preached by the Boy Bishop', *Camden Miscellany*, VII (1875), pp. 1–13.
25 'As the Philosopher saith, *Tanquam tabula nuda in qua nichil depingitur.*' Ibid., p. 2.
26 Ibid., p. 7.
27 J. LAWSON, *A Town Grammar School through Six Centuries* (London, 1963), pp. 22 ff.
28 *Victoria County History Lincs.*, II, p. 479.
29 LEACH, *Schools of Medieval England*, pp. 270–310.
30 B. WHITE (ed.), *The Vulgaria of John Stanbridge and the Vulgaria of Robert Whittinton* (Early English Text Society, 1932); W. NELSON (ed.), *A Fifteenth-Century Schoolbook* (Oxford, 1956).
31 Details in *Victoria County History*.
32 A. B. COBBAN, *The King's Hall within the University of Cambridge* (Cambridge, 1969), pp. 9–85.
33 *Victoria County History Camb.*, III, p. 373.
34 For careers of graduates see A. B. EMDEN, *A Biographical Register of the University of Oxford to 1500* (3 volumes, Oxford, 1957–9), and *A Biographical Register of the University of Cambridge to 1500* (Cambridge, 1963).
35 *Victoria County History Oxon.*, III, pp. 144–5, 154 ff.
36 W. A. PANTIN, 'The halls and schools of medieval Oxford', *Oxford Studies presented to Daniel Callus*, pp. 31–100; H. P. STOKES, 'The

medieval hostels of the University of Cambridge', *Cambridge Antiquarian Society*, XLIX (1924).

37 A. B. EMDEN, 'Northerners and southerners', p. 10.

38 G. POLLARD, 'Medieval loan chests at Cambridge', *Bulletin of the Institute of Historical Research*, XVII (1939–40), pp. 113–29.

39 E. V. HITCHCOCK (ed.), *The Life of Sir Thomas More . . . by William Roper* (Early English Text Society, 1935), pp. 53–4.

40 E. F. JACOB, 'English university clerks in the later Middle Ages', *Essays in the Conciliar Epoch* (Manchester, 1953), p. 215.

41 COBBAN, *King's Hall*, pp. 194–207, for collegiate life.

42 RASHDALL, *Universities of Europe*, III, pp. 346–8. The first master in grammar at Cambridge incepted about 1385.

43 C. H. TALBOT and E. A. HAMMOND, *The Medical Practitioners in Medieval England* (London, 1965). Many surgeons, especially in rural areas, were really only barbers.

44 RASHDALL, *Universities of Europe*, III, p. 149.

45 *Victoria County History Oxon.*, III, p. 195.

46 H. W. C. DAVIS, revised R. H. C. DAVIS and R. HUNT, *A History of Balliol College* (Oxford, 1963), p. 58.

47 KNOWLES, *Religious Orders*, II, pp. 294–7. G. BASKERVILLE, *English Monks and the Suppression of the Monasteries* (London, 1937), pp. 36–41, gives a less sympathetic view.

48 KNOWLES, *Religious Orders*, II, pp. 14–28.

49 JACOB, 'English university clerks', p. 215; H. AVELING and W. A. PANTIN (eds.), *The Letter Books of Robert Joseph* (Oxford Historical Society, 1967), especially Dr Pantin's introduction.

50 KNOWLES, *Religious Orders*, II, pp. 155–6, 259–60; PANTIN, *The English Church*, pp. 119, 140–50.

51 E. E. POWER, *Medieval English Nunneries* (Cambridge, 1922), p. 260.

52 PANTIN, *The English Church*, pp. 27–9; for clerical learning generally see PETER HEATH, *English Parish Clergy on the Eve of the Reformation* (London, 1969), chapter 5.

53 L. E. BOYLE, 'The constitution "Cum ex eo" of Boniface VIII: education of parish clergy', *Medieval Studies*, XXIV (1962), pp. 263–302.

54 PANTIN, *The English Church*, pp. 189–219.

55 E. F. JACOB, *Chichele Register*, II, p. 563; *Testamenta Eboracensia*, II, p. 275.

56 LAWSON, *Town Grammar School*, p. 39.

57 On this point Heath's conclusions agree with those of M. BOWKER, *The Secular Clergy in the Diocese of Lincoln 1495–1520* (Cambridge, 1968), pp. 41–57.

58 See above, p. 37.

59 For the clerk's duties see HEATH, *Parish Clergy*, pp. 19–20, 84–5.

60 A. HAMILTON THOMPSON, *Song Schools in the Middle Ages* (Church Music Society, 1942).

61 J. G. NICHOLS (ed.), *Narratives of the . . . Reformation* (Camden Society, 1859), pp. 218, 238–9.

62 LEACH, *Charters*, pp. 445–7. For what a chantry priest was expected to teach, see Leach's account of the chantry school founded at Childrey in 1526, *Victoria Country History Berks.*, II, pp. 275–6.

63 H. G. RICHARDSON, 'Business training in medieval Oxford', *American Historical Review*, XLVI (1941), pp. 259–80.

64 LEACH, *Schools of Medieval England*, pp. 274–5; *Charters*, p. 472.

65 G. UNWIN, 'Mediaeval gilds and education', *Studies in Economic History* (1958), pp. 93–4.

66 *Testamenta Eboracensia*, V, p. 149.

67 S. THRUPP, *The Merchant Class of Medieval London* (Chicago, 1949), pp. 155–60, for London apprentices' schooling.

68 For an exceptional craft see L. R. SHELBY, 'The education of medieval master masons', *Medieval Studies*, XXXII (1970), pp. 1–26.

69 *Testamenta Eboracensia*, V, p. 56.

70 K. CHARLTON, *Education in Renaissance England* (London, 1965), pp. 169–77.

71 S. B. CHRIMES (ed.), *Sir John Fortescue De Laudibus Legum Angliae* (Cambridge, 1942), pp. 118–19.

72 E. W. IVES, 'The common lawyers in pre-Reformation England', *Transactions of the Royal Historical Society*, XVIII (1966), pp. 147 note 1, 160.

73 *Testamenta Eboracensia*, IV, pp. 125, 196; V, p. 148.

74 ANTOINE DE LA SALE, *Little John of Saintré*, trans. I. Gray (London, 1931), pp. 18–19.

75 See 'The Babees Book', 'The Book of Nurture' and 'Urbanitas' in F. J. FURNIVAL (ed.), *Early English Meals and Manners* (Early English Text Society, 1868).

76 A. R. MYERS, *The Household of Edward IV* (Manchester, 1959), pp. 126–7, 136–8.

77 *Ordinances . . . for the . . . Royal Household* (Society of Antiquaries, London, 1790), p. 29.

78 BISHOP PERCY (ed.), *The Northumberland Household Book* (1905 ed.), pp. 47, 323, 330.

79 *Testamenta Eboracensia*, III, p. 240.

80 K. B. MCFARLANE, *Lancastrian Kings and Lollard Knights* (Oxford, 1972), pp. 115–19; and, for Henry V's books, pp. 233–8.

81 DENYS HAY, 'The early Renaissance in England', in C. H. CARTER (ed.), *From the Renaissance to the Counter Reformation* (London, 1966), p. 99.

82 *Testamenta Eboracensia*, III, p. 310; IV, pp. 16, 74, 128.

83 W. W. SKEAT (ed.), *The Boke of Husbandry* (English Dialect Society, 1882), p. 93.

84 NORMAN DAVIS (ed.), *Paston Letters and Papers of the Fifteenth Century* (Oxford, 1971), pp. lii ff.

85 R. W. CHAMBERS and M. DAUNT (eds.), *A Book of London English 1384–1425* (Oxford, 1931), p. 139.
86 THRUPP, *Merchant Class of Medieval London*, pp. 156–8, for literacy among London laity.
87 G. G. COULTON, *Social Life in Britain from the Conquest to the Reformation* (Cambridge, 1918), pp. 57–8.
88 *Testamenta Eboracensia*, III, p. 98.
89 His will is printed by LEACH, *Charters*, pp. 399–403.
90 H. S. BENNETT, 'The production and dissemination of vernacular manuscripts in the fifteenth century', *Library*, 5th series, I (1947), pp. 167–78; *English Books and Readers 1475–1557* (Cambridge, 1952), pp. 19–29.
91 Quoted N. WOOD, *The Reformation and English Education* (London, 1931), p. 4.
92 A. G. DICKENS, *The English Reformation* (London, 1964), pp. 189–90.

Further Reading

J. W. ADAMSON, 'Medieval education' and 'Literacy in England in the fifteenth and sixteenth centuries', in *The Illiterate Anglo-Saxon and Other Essays* (Cambridge, 1946).
G. G. COULTON, *Social Life in Britain from the Conquest to the Reformation* (Cambridge, 1918), pp. 45–99.
M. DEANESLY, 'Medieval schools to 1300', *Cambridge Medieval History*, V (1926), chapter 22.
K. EDWARDS, *The English Secular Cathedrals in the Middle Ages* (Manchester, 1949).
A. B. EMDEN, 'Learning and education', in A. L. POOLE (ed.), *Medieval England* (2 volumes, Oxford, 1958), II, pp. 515–40.
V. H. GALBRAITH, 'The literacy of the medieval English kings', *Proceedings of the British Academy*, XXI (1935).
E. F. JACOB, 'English university clerks in the later Middle Ages', *Essays in the Conciliar Movement* (Manchester, 1953).
E. F. JACOB, 'Founders and foundations in the later Middle Ages', *Essays in Later Medieval History* (Manchester, 1968).
D. KNOWLES, *The Religious Orders in England* (3 volumes, Cambridge, 1948, 1955, 1959).
J. LAWSON, *Medieval Education and the Reformation* (London, 1967).
A. F. LEACH, *The Schools of Medieval England* (London, 1915).
G. LEFF, *Paris and Oxford Universities in the Thirteenth and Fourteenth Centuries* (New York, 1968).
J. N. MINER, 'Schools and literacy in later medieval England', *British Journal of Educational Studies*, XI (1962), pp. 16–27.

J. R. H. MOORMAN, *Church Life in England in the Thirteenth Century* (Cambridge, 1946), chapter 8.

W. A. PANTIN, 'The halls and schools of medieval Oxford', *Oxford Studies presented to Daniel Callus* (Oxford Historical Society, 1964), pp. 31–100.

G. R. POTTER, 'Education in the fourteenth and fifteenth centuries', *Cambridge Medieval History*, VIII (1936), chapter 23.

H. RASHDALL (ed. F. M. POWICKE and A. B. EMDEN), *The Universities of Europe in the Middle Ages* (3 volumes, Oxford, 1936).

E. RICKERT (ed.), *Chaucer's World* (London, 1948), pp. 101–47.

H. E. SALTER, *Medieval Oxford* (Oxford Historical Society, 1936), chapter 5.

See also pp. 150–1, 471–3.

CHAPTER IV

Social change and educational expansion
1530–1640

Religious and social developments bearing on education

Society is never static and all periods are periods of social transition. Nevertheless, if we consider the lives of the great mass of common people – perhaps 95 per cent of the population – the change that took place in the centuries before industrialization was small. Change did occur, but slowly, and it affected the dominant minority rather than the obscure and inarticulate masses. However, men born in the 1530s lived through a period of transition more radical than any since the Norman conquest, and change on this scale inevitably had its impact on education.

Between 1530 and 1560 most English people voluntarily renounced Roman Catholicism and espoused protestantism. Lutheran doctrines nourished by heretical books smuggled in from the continent had infiltrated south-eastern England in the 1520s and found adherents among a few young Cambridge divines and small groups of literate weavers and clothworkers. Reformation as an act of state began in 1534 when Henry VIII, in order to obtain a divorce, severed all legal ties with the papacy and had himself made supreme head of the church in England. Then between 1536 and 1540, mainly for financial reasons, came the dissolution of all the religious orders and the wholesale nationalization of their property. Monks, regular canons, friars and nuns disappeared into the secular, lay world, some with pensions, others without. Even more drastic were the changes made between 1547 and 1553 under Edward VI. Protestant doctrines and ceremonies replaced Catholic ones; the Book of

Common Prayer in English supplanted the old Latin service books; chantries, collegiate churches and religious gilds were suppressed and expropriated. Five years of Catholic reaction under Queen Mary followed: papal authority was restored, some of the monks reinstated, protestant recalcitrants exiled or burnt alive.

Elizabeth's urgent task on her accession in 1558 was to find a solution to a very dangerous religious situation. The Church of England, created by the Acts of Uniformity and Supremacy of 1559, was the result. A temporary, makeshift affair, it was designed to meet the pressing needs of the time. Its doctrine (summarized in the Thirty-nine Articles of 1563) was part Catholic and part protestant; it preserved the old institutional framework but with the queen as 'supreme governor'; all her subjects were theoretically members and had to attend its public services on pain of fine for each non-attendance. Many Catholics accepted the compromise only outwardly. Puritans of diverse beliefs and groupings looked for more radical protestant reforms to come. But the nation as a whole – perhaps with relief or indifference – soon accepted the new state church and its form of worship as set out in the Common Prayer Book.[1]

Thus, the Reformation subordinated the church to the sovereign and greatly reduced its former privileges and powers, as well as cutting its international ties. Religion became a pillar of the political and social establishment. The clergy were no longer a separate order, and society at large, and education with it, tended to become more lay and secular, less clerical and ecclesiastical. In two generations the transition – 'a remarkable act of national amnesia' – was complete.

Humanism, the intellectual fashion of the time stemming from the princely courts of Renaissance Italy, reinforced this transition by extolling the ideal of human excellence on the one hand and the vision of an ideal, essentially civil community (*patria* or 'common weal') on the other. Its educational exemplar, delineated by Baldassare Castiglione in *The Book of the Courtier* (1528), was not the celibate, tonsured clerk learned in Aristotelian philosophy or canon law but the accomplished noble-minded scholar-statesman trained for the disinterested service of the prince and the common weal. Educationally, humanism meant the cultivation of classical Latinity, the study of Greek, the rejection of scholasticism in favour of literature, history and antiquity, and the development of the whole man – for life in this world rather than the next. Influential exponents of this new outlook in England were Sir Thomas Elyot, a royal secretary and author of the *The Book named the Governor* (1531), and Roger Ascham, Cambridge don, sometime tutor to Princess Elizabeth and Latin secretary to Queen Mary, whose book *The Schoolmaster* appeared posthumously in 1570.[2]

If humanism changed the aims and emphasis of education, at least so far as polite society was concerned, the new printing trade enormously enlarged its scope and potential so far as literate society in general was concerned. Teachers, their pupils and the reading public at large had access to a much greater range of books – on history, law, science, travel and religion, both English and in English translations – and not least to practical instructional manuals on writing, cyphering, and vocational skills like pedagogy, husbandry, navigation, metallurgy and architecture. Informal self-education became possible as never before. The educated classes became book readers and new ideas and new knowledge were disseminated on a scale previously unknown, shaping public attitudes to problems of government, religion and society.[3]

The rise of the gentry is not a specifically Tudor phenomenon, though it is often treated as such. From the fourteenth century at least, prosperous yeomen and merchants had been rising into the ranks of the landowning class. However, greatly increased opportunities for the socially aspiring were created after 1540 when the Crown released onto the land market the vast estates confiscated from monasteries and chantries. By investing in land, exchanging land and leasing land, ambitious and successful yeomen, merchants and lawyers thrust upwards in two or three generations into the armigerous gentry. Rising agricultural rents and the profits of sheep-farming added to the wealth and importance of the landed classes, and by the reign of Elizabeth old and new gentry were barely distinguishable from the peerage. Sir Thomas Smith, writing in 1565, divided the nobility into the greater nobility, who included all the peers, and the lesser, consisting of knights, esquires and gentlemen. The test of social status which he applied was a man's part in government, and the nobility as a whole (comprising some 2 or 3 per cent of the population) formed the nation's ruling class. The lesser nobility or gentry became the Crown's indispensable agents in local government, notably as deputy lieutenants, justices of the peace and officers in the county militia; they also dominated the House of Commons as members for the shires or for the new parliamentary boroughs. Obsessed as they were with status and pedigree, their overriding concern was to preserve and advance their family interest by marriage and primogeniture, and they wanted an education commensurate with their social aspirations.[4]

Not least among the changes of the Tudor age which bore on education was the growth of population. The increase had started in the later fifteenth century and its causes are uncertain. Poverty, dirt, malnutrition, epidemics, capital punishment, the perils of childbirth — these no doubt kept the mortality rate as high as ever, so the likeliest explanation is a rising birthrate. Parish registers, wills, church monuments, family portraits all suggest a land full of children after about 1560. From under 3 million in 1530 the population rose to over 4 million in 1600. Not only did the population increase, but also there was some internal migration, especially of wage-earning families. Everywhere the old educational provisions fell short of new needs and called out to be supplemented and extended. Market towns in rural industrial areas became more important, though still often only large villages in size. London may have increased fourfold, exceeding 200,000 about 1600 and doubling again by about 1650. Few other cities surpassed 10,000; perhaps 80 per cent of the population still lived in isolated villages of only a few hundred inhabitants.[5]

This expanding population was probably the hidden cause of the chronic mass poverty of the age. No doubt Henry VIII's debasement of the coinage and the influx of silver from Spanish America contributed, but the root cause of the galloping inflation which set in around 1530 was the pressure of population on scarce means of subsistence. The worst decades were the 1540s and 1550s, though prices rose fivefold before 1640. The decline of real wages and a large surplus of labour led to pauperism and vagrancy, twin threats to public order and constant problems for Tudor government. Perhaps one-third of the population lived below the poverty line, another third on it or just above it, depending on the state of the harvest.[6]

It was these religious, economic and social changes and tensions that actuated the massive private charity of the age. This has been minutely studied by Professor W. K. Jordan of Harvard who analysed charitable donations made for public welfare of all kinds, including education, in ten counties between 1480 and 1660. Allowing for the fall in money values – which Jordan disregards, holding that a general price index cannot be established for the period – the greatest giving seems to have occurred just before the Reformation, between about 1510 and 1530. (Even this may not have surpassed the munificence which established Eton and also five colleges at the universities between 1430 and 1450.) A recession marked the years of religious and economic upheaval from 1530 to 1550, after which the tide of benefactions mounted again. Whatever the motives behind it, philanthropy changed the pattern of education in England after 1560.[7]

The Reformation and education

The first impact of the Reformation on education came with the declaration of the royal supremacy over the church in 1534. To ensure the compliance of the two universities, the church's highest educational organs, they were visited in 1535 by the commissioners of Thomas Cromwell, the king's vicar-general, and royal injunctions followed. All their members had to acknowledge the royal supremacy. The extinction of papal authority having now made Roman canon law obsolete in England, all teaching and degrees in the subject were prohibited. Thus, at a stroke, one of the superior faculties was terminated and a whole profession abolished – one that had for centuries furnished church and state with much of its administrative élite. To mark the end of the old order, the modish new learning was introduced: Greek had to be taught (it was already much cultivated at Cambridge), biblical theology replaced scholastic theology, and libraries were purged of the discredited writings of generations of schoolmen. At Oxford their dismembered folios were observed strewn about the quadrangle of New College, and reported to be made 'a common servant to every man, fast nailed up upon posts in all common houses of easement'. So – ignominiously – began the universities' submission to the Tudor state and their use as instruments of royal policy.[8]

Inevitably, the destruction of English monasticism had educational repercussions at both school and university levels. Song schools and almonry grammar schools which some houses had maintained came to an end. No reliable evidence exists about their number and it is impossible to assess the loss which education suffered. Loss there must have been, but it cannot have been as calamitous as used to be imagined. Some almonry schools and some other schools for which certain monasteries had been trustees were continued with a rent charge on former monastic lands, or with the financial support of town authorities. In one way or another most of the damage was probably made good within a few years. Moreover all the eight ex-monastic cathedrals were reconstituted in 1540–2 as secular cathedrals with deans and chapters of canons, and each (Winchester excepted) was obliged by its new statutes to maintain a grammar school with a master and usher and a specified number of foundation scholars. These 'King's Schools' were continuations of the schools previously maintained by the bishops of these cathedral priories for the clergy and boys of the city; in some cases the same master and usher continued in office, as at the King's school, Canterbury. Furthermore, six former monastic churches – Bristol, Chester, Gloucester, Oxford, Peterborough and Westminster – were elevated into cathedrals and each of their chapters (with the exception of Oxford) was required by statute to establish a grammar school out of the common fund. These schools went some way towards compensating for the loss of others. Unfortunately, nothing was done to make good the loss of the nunneries in the education of girls.[9]

The end of the religious orders automatically meant the end of the monastic colleges and convents of friars which had been a feature of the universities for nearly three centuries. For some time the friars had been of minor importance academically, but the number of student monks seems to have risen during the early sixteenth century. Gloucester College, the oldest and perhaps largest monastic house of study, consisted in 1537 of a prior and twenty-nine other monks drawn from six different abbeys, five of them BDs.[10] The total membership of the universities, already in decline, would certainly be depleted by the abolition of the religious, especially at Oxford where they had always been more numerous than at Cambridge. Even so, monks and friars were only a fraction of the total, and the loss was more than made up two or three decades later by rising student numbers. Nevertheless, their extinction must have tended to modify the ecclesiastical climate of university life.

Compared to the dissolution of the monasteries, the suppression of the secular academic colleges would have been a small matter, but the king had no designs on them. Their number indeed was increased from the spoils of the dissolution; new colleges compensated for the abolition of the monastic *studia* and it was not long before all the former monastic buildings at the universities were restored to academic use. Taking over the premises of the recently defunct Buckingham College, Lord Audley, Henry VIII's chancellor, founded Magdalene College, Cambridge, in 1542. The king himself handsomely endowed both universities out of the proceeds of monastic expropriations. To each he gave its richest college, making the head a royal nominee. After Wolsey's fall, the king had refounded Cardinal College as King Henry VIII College, and this he reconstituted in 1546 as Christ Church in conjunction with his new Oxford bishopric, cathedral and college having the same dean as head. As Wolsey had originally intended, its size and splendour made this college pre-eminent in Oxford. Also in 1546 the king suppressed the two adjacent, fourteenth-century societies of King's Hall and Michaelhouse in Cambridge in order to establish Trinity College, which he further endowed with estates and advowsons – rights of presentation to benefices – recently confiscated from religous houses.[11] Furthermore, at Cambridge in 1540 and Oxford in 1546 he founded five Regius professorships of divinity, Greek, Hebrew, medicine and civil law, and considerably added to royal influence in university affairs by making these crown appointments too. Although one may deplore Henry VIII's failure to invest more of his monastic appropriations in schools and colleges and other good works, nevertheless what he did contribute was on a scale which makes him outstanding among royal benefactors of education, however questionable the way in which he acquired his resources.

The Reformation carried out by the boy king Edward VI's ministers laid a much heavier hand on education, though here again the damage has been exaggerated.[12] The suppression in 1548 of all chantries, religious gilds and colleges of priests (with some exceptions like Eton and Winchester) put in jeopardy the schools which many of these foundations supported. However, the Chantries Act of 1547 which authorized this second great nationalization of church property provided that schools forming a statutory and obligatory part of any of these institutions should be preserved, restoring the lands of the foundation in perpetuity to support a schoolmaster. Unfortunately, near-bankruptcy forced the government to sell the lands it acquired; all that was actually granted was an annual crown stipend for the schoolmaster equal to the net income of the foundation at the time of suppression. Thus, many chantry schools were continued – those at Hull and Rotherham, for example – but on a fixed allowance which rapidly shrank in value as the sixteenth-century price revolution advanced.

Where schools were not officially continued in this way it was usually because they had been maintained by the parent foundation voluntarily, or under the old canon law which was no longer recognized. Obviously, the loss of a school was a serious matter for any self-respecting local community. About 1552 when the government's worst financial troubles were over, certain towns successfully petitioned the Crown for a grant of some parcel of recently nationalized local church property with which to support a school, as at Birmingham and Shrewsbury. These were usually known as King Edward VI grammar schools, and owning land they tended to be much better off than the schools with depreciating fixed annual stipends. Some towns received no such grants but were licensed to acquire lands in order to preserve or establish a school. This was so at Bedford, where a private benefactor, a native who had become a wealthy London merchant taylor, soon endowed the school. Numerous other boroughs voluntarily supported the local school rather than see it die out, as did Beverley when the burgesses' petition for a grant of land was rejected.

Edward VI's government carried further the process of subjecting the universities to royal control. Protestantism was now forced on them. To propagate the new doctrines, distinguished scholars of the continental Reformation were introduced. The Italian Peter Martyr, made Regius professor of divinity at Oxford in 1548, was installed at Christ Church with his wife, a former nun. Martin Bucer, a German ex-Dominican appointed Regius professor at Cambridge, made that university the intellectual focus of English protestantism. Royal visitations in 1549 again reformed the universities. Catholics were expelled, libraries despoiled of popish books, college chapels of superstitious ornaments. New statutes promulgated by the visitors further reshaped the curriculum on humanist lines. Greek was re-emphasized. Latin grammar as a subject was excluded as more appropriate for

schools; consequently degrees in grammar ceased to be awarded –
the last was at Oxford in 1569. Undergraduate studies included
mathematics (arithmetic, geometry, astronomy and cosmography)
and dialectic, rhetoric and philosophy, mainly in Latin authors.
Along with philosophy and astronomy, Greek was an important
subject in the course for the MA. Canon law having been ex-
tinguished, the commissioners now tried to encourage the study
of civil law because of its use to the Crown in administration and
diplomacy.

This renewed insistence on 'polite learning' reflected the
changes that were taking place in the social function of the
universities. With the end of the monks and canon law and with
the progressive repudiation of Catholicism, the universities were
becoming much less clerical and professional. Although many of
their members were still intended for ordination, they were not
tonsured clerks but belonged as undergraduates to the secular lay
world. Moreover, students were increasingly being drawn from
the gentry, and their interests were more mundane than godly.
None the less, even if the universities were losing their former
ecclesiastical complexion, religion was still the predominant
influence: most of the senior resident members were clergy, and
theology and Hebrew were the statutory studies for masters of
arts.

Religious tensions, political uncertainties, economic disorder –
these made the middle years of the century a low-water mark for
the universities. As numbers declined, unendowed halls died out
and poorer colleges admitted more fee-paying commoners in order
to make ends meet, thus further changing the composition and
role of the colleges. A census taken at Oxford in 1552 showed
1,021 members (including 659 undergraduates) – 761 in thirteen
colleges, 260 in eight halls. About average in size, Corpus Christi
College consisted of the president and vice-president, eight
masters, eight bachelors and thirty-six undergraduates.[13]
Numbers were perhaps rather higher at Cambridge; there the last
surviving hostel came to an end in the late 1550s.

In Mary's reign schools and universities alike were made agents
of the Catholic restoration. The queen's injunctions to the
bishops in 1554 ordered them 'to examine all schoolmasters
and teachers of children and finding them suspect in any ways to
remove them and place Catholic men in their rooms'. Cardinal
Pole's constitutions in 1555 required all schoolmasters to be

examined and approved by the bishop before being allowed to teach. Thus, the old canon-law practice of the church was re-affirmed, but with the bishop now responsible for the licence to teach instead of the cathedral chancellor. Hereafter, school-masters were important agents of the state as propagators of the official religion.[14]

Catholicism was reinstated at the universities by still more royal visitations. This time protestant dons were expelled, hereti-cal books destroyed, all graduands required to subscribe to Catholic doctrines, and the authority of college heads was increased to strengthen order and discipline. The Marian reaction met with some success at the universities and the reign saw an improvement in their condition. Numbers began to rise, and Catholic piety established the last colleges of the old religion. At Oxford in 1555 Trinity College was founded by Sir Thomas Pope, a royal official, in the former buildings of Durham College; and the derelict Cistercian college of St Bernard was used to house St John's College which Sir Thomas White, London alderman and merchant taylor, founded – as his statutes proclaim – in order to 'strengthen the orthodox faith . . . weakened by the damage of time and the malice of men'. White also re-established Gloucester College as an academic hall and made it part of the endowment of St John's. In 1557 Gonville Hall at Cambridge was refounded and much enlarged as Gonville and Caius College by one of its former fellows, Dr John Caius, an eminent London physician.[15]

After 1559 education was much more rigorously manipulated to secure adoption of Queen Elizabeth's new national church. Her royal injunctions of 1559 ordered that no man was to teach unless he had been granted the bishop's licence after an examina-tion as to character and orthodoxy.[16] This rule became part of the canon law of the Church of England in 1571 and finally in 1604, when candidates for the licence, whether teaching publicly in school or privately in any gentleman's household, had to sub-scribe to the royal supremacy, the Thirty-nine Articles and the Book of Common Prayer. Parliament reinforced the canon law in 1581 and 1604 with statutes which imposed penalties of fine and imprisonment for unlicensed teaching. Furthermore, school-masters were obliged by the new canons to teach approved English or Latin catechisms, to hold daily prayers in school and to attend church with their scholars on sermon days, occupying

Elizabethan schoolroom

some part specially set aside for them.[17] The habit of religious conformity thus inculcated was strengthened by the standardization of schoolroom practice, notably by the compulsory and exclusive use of the same Latin grammar – the *Royal Grammar* authorized by Henry VIII about 1540 but compiled some thirty years earlier for St Paul's school by its first High Master, William Lily, with the co-operation of Erasmus and Dean Colet.

This control of schoolmasters was made the responsibility of the diocesan bishop not only because there was no other convenient authority to undertake the task, but also because education was still regarded as essentially a religious activity. After 1571 bishops and archdeacons in their visitations regularly inquired about schoolmasters and their observation of the canons, and schoolmasters were cited to appear and exhibit their licences along with the parish clergy.[18] On the other hand, although women teachers were clearly required to have ecclesiastical approval they do not seem to have been formally licensed and rarely appeared at visitations.[19] There is no doubt that the church's visitation machinery was not always effective in enforcing the law. Examination of schoolmasters was unsystematic. Unlicensed masters certainly operated, some of them religious dissentients, either puritans or secret papists.[20] But the rapid acceptance of the new Anglican settlement by the nation as a whole must be attributed at least partly to the cumulative teaching of orthodox schoolmasters approved and supervised by the bishops.

During Elizabeth's reign the universities were gradually converted into strongholds of the new state religion, notwithstanding the fact that they both harboured minorities of religious extremists, both Catholic and puritan. In 1559 they received yet another visitation, this time to reverse the changes of Mary's reign. This was the last royal visitation of the universities; hereafter political control was exercised by their statesman-chancellors – Leicester at Oxford, Cecil at Cambridge – and in the colleges by their respective visitors, when discipline was necessary. After 1563 all graduates were supposed to take the Oath of Supremacy, which was apparently then accepted as sufficient proof of religious orthodoxy. At Oxford other tests were soon imposed by the university: from 1576 all graduands, and from 1581 all undergraduates over the age of sixteen, were to subscribe to the Thirtynine Articles, so that in effect the university was closed to all but Anglicans. It was largely in the interests of religious discipline and uniformity that all students were finally made to reside in a college or hall and to be officially matriculated by the university. Cambridge – much more puritanical and critical of the new church than Oxford – introduced no subscriptions of this kind and here the Oath of Supremacy taken on graduation was the only test until 1616, when a royal mandate of James I demanded subscription to the royal supremacy, the Book of Common Prayer and the Thirty-nine Articles from all recipients of degrees at either university.[21] Religious tests restricting Oxford and Cambridge to members of the Church of England were not finally abolished until 1871.

Educational philanthropy

The pious endowment of education which had risen sharply just before the Reformation and then been temporarily checked flowed again after the 1550s, slackened in the famine-stricken 1590s and then burst into a flood which reached full spate about 1620. This outpouring of private charity for education and social welfare generally is one of the phenomena of the age. Professor Stone has claimed that it 'did more to alter the pattern of English life and thought than the whole of Tudor legislation put together'.[22]

All social groups above the great pauperized masses contributed – peers and gentry, higher and lower clergy, professional men, merchants and tradesmen, yeomen and husbandmen. Altruism and self-interest were probably mixed in their motives.[23] The gentry, stimulated by the new humanist concept of the ideal gentleman made fashionable by Elyot and Ascham and eager to acquire the general culture that would fit them for public or court office (and thus perhaps add to their family honours and estates), now took to book learning. Bishops were anxious to improve the low educational standards of their parish clergy in order to enable them to defend the new religious settlement against its adversaries. The clergy themselves were concerned to enlarge educational opportunities in their parishes so that the young might be brought up, as the royal injunctions of 1559 required, 'to love and do reverence to God's true religion now truly set forth by public authority' and as a group the clergy gave to education the largest proportion of their charitable donations. By far the greatest benefactors of education, however, were the merchants, especially the rich entrepreneurs and wholesalers of London, whose wealth, unlike the landed gentry's, was fluid and easily donatable to charity. Often self-made men, they were munificent founders of schools in their native towns, partly for reasons of status and prestige, partly to help deserving local boys on the way to fortune, and partly for practical business purposes – to supply literate apprentices for the growing range of skilled occupations on which commercial enterprise depended: book-keeping, surveying, cartography, navigation, ship-building and so on.

Much of this philanthropy was inspired by puritanism, which motivated many gentry, clergy and merchants alike. Puritans are not easily defined, but they were, as Dr Collinson says, the 'real and fervent protestants in a nominally protestant and largely indifferent environment'. Critical of the doctrine, the ornaments or the government of the new Elizabethan church, they wanted essentially a more simple, Scripture-based religion. They were concerned with education not only because spreading literacy and Bible-reading would promote private judgement and personal salvation, but also because they wished to increase the supply of godly ministers of the Word. Added to this was the puritan-capitalist ethic which extolled competition, thrift and hard work, and saw in education a means of self-improvement and advancement for the meritorious. On the other hand, another motive – present consciously or not – in the minds of more conservative educational founders and benefactors was a desire to indoctrinate the rising generation with respect for the political and social system at a time when it was being threatened by enthusiastic sectaries of all kinds. In content and method, education was essentially authoritarian and so a convenient instrument of stability and order. 'Grammar schools and universities with their scholastic classical bias were deliberately designed', asserts Professor Stone, 'to inculcate habits of discipline and obedience.'[24]

The chief object of educational charity during the period from 1560 to 1640 was the foundation of schools – petty schools for the children of the poor but especially grammar schools for the sons of the better off. Throughout the country schools were established in great numbers, usually in places with which their founders had personal ties. The essential act was the gift of land or an annual rent charge on land so as to provide a schoolmaster's stipend, and this was commonly a school's only certain revenue, though the foundation might also include a schoolhouse and a master's dwelling next to it. With the provision of an endowment went the nomination of trustees charged with responsibility for appointing the master, administering the property and generally watching over the school's interests. Some founders, but by no means all, formulated statutes regulating in some detail the curriculum and general conduct of the school.[25]

Additional opportunities were often provided at the petty-school level through the foundation of apprenticeship charities, and at the grammar-school level through university scholarships. For these also, property was conveyed to trustees in order to yield an annual income. Scholarships might be administered by a school's trustees for the benefit of boys at that school, or by an Oxford or Cambridge college solely for boys from a particular school or locality, or by independent trustees such as a town corporation or a dean and chapter.

University education profited rather less than grammar-school education from this flood of charity. However, three new colleges were founded at Oxford, and two at Cambridge; existing colleges had their establishment of fellows and scholars increased by benefaction, as well as receiving gifts to enlarge their lodging accommodation and their libraries. The universities as such benefited less than the colleges, but their libraries were restored and new chairs endowed by private donors.

Apart from providing for school, college and university libraries, philanthropy established the first libraries for public use, mainly in the period after 1600 and in sizeable towns like Coventry, Norwich, Ipswich, Bristol and Leicester. Some of these were housed in parish churches, some in town grammar schools. Henry Bury, a Lancashire clergyman who died in 1636, gave £10 for books towards forming a library in Manchester and later, besides founding a grammar school at Bury, bequeathed over 600 books together with globes, maps and pictures to set up a parish library there, 'for the use of . . . ministers and of schoolmasters and others that seek for learning and knowledge'.[26] Consisting usually of pious and scholarly works, these libraries were intended primarily for the local clergy and gentry and the more educated tradesmen, so their readers must have been very restricted in number.

Every part of the country attracted gifts and bequests for schools and scholarships.[27] In London Westminster school, the old almonry school of the abbey, was refounded in 1560 by Queen Elizabeth as part of her new collegiate church, and closely associated by patronage and scholarships with her father's two colleges, Christ Church at Oxford and Trinity College at Cambridge. This was followed in 1561 by the establishment of Merchant Taylors' school, for which Sir Thomas White, a leading member of the Company, reserved thirty-seven places at his new Oxford college, St John's. With St Paul's, these became the capital's foremost grammar schools. At Leicester, the borough grammar school was re-established in 1564 with the help of Henry Hastings, the puritan earl of Huntingdon, and he with sundry gentlemen and yeomen of the neighbourhood founded a new grammar school at Ashby-de-la-Zouch in 1567. In the 1580s the pious Mrs Jocosa Frankland, twice a widow and without heir, founded a school at Newport in Essex and endowed fellowships at two Oxford and two Cambridge colleges. John Frieston, a West Riding gentleman, contributed to a public subscription for the establishment of Wakefield grammar school in 1591, endowed the grammar school at Normanton in 1594, and gave scholarships to University College, Oxford, and Emmanuel College, Cambridge. Among the bequests of Thomas Cave, a Wakefield chapman who died in 1603, was £250 towards the foundation of a grammar school at Otley and sums for two scholarships at Clare College for boys from Wakefield school. To build a schoolhouse for the newly endowed grammar school at Sheffield, £103. 18s. 3d. was raised in 1606 by an assessment on 473 inhabitants, the levy ranging from 2d. to 40s.

Educational provision was especially lacking in remote and thinly populated regions like the vast moorland parishes of the Pennines. At Askrigg on the North Riding fells a grammar school was endowed in 1604 by Anthony Besson, a Star Chamber lawyer, the parish having 'many persons of good sort and quality' but 'a great and grievous want and defect of school-masters and men of learning well disposed and fit to train up and instruct the children of the inhabitants there in civil manners, good letters and other necessary and wholesome rudiments'. Most schools were set up in the more populous market towns. A wealthy self-made merchant clothier of Tiverton, Peter Blundell, left in his will in 1599 the sum of £2,400 to found a grammar school there, together with £2,000 to establish three scholar-ships at Oxford and three at Cambridge for boys from his school. His declared objects were twofold – to advance the careers of local youths and also add to the number of 'good and godly preachers of the Gospel'. At Cambridge a grammar school was founded in 1615 by Dr Stephen Perse, a physician, who also provided for six more fellows and six more scholars at Gonville and Caius College where he was a fellow. Grammar schools were established at Oakham and Uppingham by Robert Johnson, arch-deacon of Leicester, who died in 1626; he also gave four scholar-ships to each of four Cambridge colleges for boys from either school.

Schools were also established at a lower social level. In the

Cambridgeshire village of Willingham 102 inhabitants subscribed a total of £102. 7s. 8d. in 1593 to endow a school for contributors' children, with some poor children admitted free.[28] An 'English' school – one that taught reading, writing and arithmetic to a higher standard than the ordinary petty school – was founded in 1631 for forty-eight poor children of the Suffolk market town of Beccles by a native, Sir John Leman, merchant and sometime lord mayor of London. Whatever the impulse, private philanthropy enormously enlarged the country's educational resources between about 1560 and 1640.

Village and town: the social matrix of education

Notwithstanding the growth of manufactures and overseas trading, England remained throughout this period essentially an agricultural country.[29] The daily existence of the vast majority of people, however they made their living, was dominated by the land and the seasons. English society was still made up of small local communities – villages, hamlets and miniature market towns – with London the only big urban centre. Villages varied in size and type. In more populated areas they were relatively close together and each might form a separate parish; in the sparser regions of the north and west, parishes were large and might contain a number of villages and hamlets cut off from one another by miles of rough, empty countryside. The distances that separated them were all the greater because they had to be travelled on foot or horseback, and because the roads were bad and likely to disappear in winter.

A village of moderate size might consist of some forty or fifty households, say 200 to 300 inhabitants. These fell into a number of socio-economic groupings, though the proportions varied from area to area depending on the type of farming. The peasant aristocracy were the yeomen – a minority of freeholders who cultivated or grazed mainly their own land; the most prosperous of them lived near the point of transition between common men and gentlemen, and by adding to their acres and adopting the life style of gentlemen they might establish themselves as such. Lower in status than the yeoman but not sharply divided from the poorest of them were the husbandmen – smallholders who farmed on their own account but as tenants, any of whom might become yeomen by saving enough capital to buy land. In all but the smallest settlements there would be two or three craftsmen such as a smith, tailor, shoemaker, carpenter, making a poor living as semi-independent workers in their own cottages. The largest single group would be wage labourers, either hired yearly by an employer and living in his household (women and girls as domestic servants, men and boys as ploughmen, carters and shepherds) or - a much more precarious existence – hired and paid by the day. One family in every three or four might be either cottagers, making what living they could by casual day labour and self-employment in and about their hovels and crofts on the waste, or paupers subsisting on poor relief, begging and poaching. Perhaps half of all the families lived more or less constantly in want, and the prosperity of the others would depend on each year's harvest.

The great personage in the village, to whom all deference was due, was the squire. He was a gentleman of breeding, perhaps a knight or baronet, the chief landlord and employer of labour, and, if a justice of the peace, a power in the neighbourhood. Unless he chose to reside on one of his other estates, he lived in the manor house in some style, with a domestic establishment that might almost be the same as the village community, where this was a small one. If the manor house was unoccupied, the more important yeomen and husbandmen would dominate the village. Next in social consequence to the squire was the parson. His influence as the spiritual mentor of the little rustic community was potentially great. The church he served was the principal building and focal point of village life. Everybody met there for the Sunday service, whatever their secret convictions or doubts, and absentees were rebuked from the pulpit as roundly as were drunkards and fornicators. The parson's sermons linked a simple and unlettered congregation with the great world outside. Baptism, marriage and burial, the decisive events in everybody's life, took place in the church. Public meetings were held there and public notices were displayed in the porch. There, in the absence of any other suitable storeplace, the communal property of the village was to be found – the clock or sundial, the pieces of armour, the fire-fighting apparatus, the common coffin, the records in the parish chest. If there happened to be a school, that, too, was likely to be found there.

The communal affairs of the village were ordered by all the

ratepaying male householders meeting as the vestry. This elected the annual, unpaid parish officers – churchwardens, petty constable, surveyor of highways, overseers of the poor – who administered the rates that were levied on householders for certain purposes. If the manor court still functioned, this regulated the cultivation of the open fields and customary rights on the common, but in some villages these responsibilities had passed to the vestry. In addition the parish officers together with the incumbent might be trustees of any parochial charities given for poor relief or village education.

Throughout much of the country, rising prosperity for land-lords and yeomen (but not for wage labourers) led to a largescale rebuilding of villages and market towns, farmhouses and gentlemen's seats between about 1570 and 1640.[30] This was an expression not only of growing affluence but also of a desire for better standards of living among those of middling fortune. It was this affluence and this desire that prompted the growing demand for education and the endowment of schools and scholarships during this same period.

Life in the village was isolated and self-contained. There was no shop supplied from outside; whatever was needed was made by families themselves or by the village tradesmen, or was bought at neighbouring markets and fairs or at the door from pedlars and chapmen. Unless the village stood on a main road it probably had no inn, though there might be several alehouses – ordinary cottages licensed by the JPs. The nearest apothecary would live in the market town; in emergency the parson might dispense physic, the blacksmith draw teeth. There might be no school, or one that existed only intermittently. It was still an oral, largely illiterate society, ignorant (save for the customary lore of the land) and deeply superstitious. The gentlefolk excepted, heavy manual labour was everybody's daily lot – for children as well as adults; homemade recreations at traditional festivals offered the only relief from the monotony of work. Isolated and self-reliant, the community was also inbred, closely knit, introverted; the village lads were likely to stone any stranger they found in the street.

Perhaps only 20 or 25 per cent of the population lived in towns during this period. London was incomparably the largest and wealthiest city in the land; with some 400,000 inhabitants it may have accounted for one-tenth of the total population by the mid-seventeenth century. Norwich, Bristol, York, Newcastle and Exeter were large cities, but perhaps none of them exceeded 20,000. Most towns had populations of only 1,000 or 2,000 and were no more than swollen villages dignified by a weekly market; often they were as dependent on a landlord as the village was. In these towns small tradesmen made miscellaneous consumer goods for the local market; some of them were also local centres of more specialized domestic industry, producing mainly woollens or linens, lace, ribbons, felt hats, nails, pins, buttons and buckles, and so on.

In London and the other great towns the richer merchants, mostly importers and exporters by sea, formed the ruling oligarchy of aldermen. Their social position was ambiguous. Self-made men, they might be as rich as the gentry, and some of them became gentry by intermarriage or by buying country estates and assuming the gentry's mode of life. Nearest to them in social standing were the professional men – lawyers, physicians and clergy, though these were relatively a very small group. Roughly comparable to the rural yeomen were the master craftsmen-shopkeepers working on their own account, employing skilled journeymen (comparable to the rural husbandmen) and training two or three apprentices in home and workshop. A large but unknown proportion of the population of London and these large towns was made up of labourers, including domestic servants (living in their master's family) and a destitute proletariat of paupers, beggars, vagabonds and petty criminals.

As a generalization, villages and towns retained these traditional characteristics with little change until the later eighteenth century. It is in this social context that we have to see the educational assumptions and provisions of the time.

The 'petties' and their teachers

We know very little about children in this as in earlier periods – how they were brought up, what their place was in the family and in the local community. As in medieval times there seems to have been no conception of a child's world different from the adult's. Death in childbirth or infancy was a matter of course for both rich and poor. Family portraits and funeral effigies – admittedly representations of gentlefolk only – show boys and girls dressed much alike until the age of five or six; thereafter they are dressed like adults, the boys sometimes with swords. From about the age of seven children shared the world of their elders, mixing freely with them at home, at work and at recreation. At that age, if of poor peasant stock they might be at work in the fields – bird-scaring, sheep-minding, stone-clearing; if of more affluent family they might be boarded away from home, the boys at grammar school, the girls in some genteel household. At seven they could be espoused, or make a legal precontract of marriage, and there are cases of children being married even before this age.[31] At seven, too, the common law presumed them capable of criminal intent like adults: an 8-year-old boy was hanged in 1629 for burning two barns at Windsor; a 7-year-old boy and his 11-year-old sister were hanged at King's Lynn as late as 1708.[32]

Grinding poverty must have denied practically all schooling to the great mass of the rural population living on or near the subsistence level as servants, labourers, cottagers and paupers. They could neither afford school fees nor forgo their children's earnings or labour. In any case they had little incentive, for schooling offered few returns: the daily round of physical drudgery left no time or energy for reading, there was no occasion for writing, and small chance of self-advancement in a stratified and apparently changeless social order. In the countryside educational demand and supply must have varied from area to area, depending on the prosperity of the yeomen and husbandmen, the villagers most able to afford schooling for their children. In towns there was perhaps always more incentive and more opportunity for the poor as well as the prosperous to become literate.

As from time immemorial, most children probably received whatever education they had informally, at their mother's knee, playing together in the village street and watching and imitating their elders at work about the cottage and the fields. Those who went to school would start at the age of five or six and perhaps stay no more than one or two years, attending very irregularly, according to the family means and the distance to be walked from home. When so many children died young and the expectation of life for adults was little over thirty, any longer schooling was an investment only for the better off. Thus few of the boys and girls in the village school would come from the very poor families. Mostly their fathers would be yeomen, husbandmen or craftsmen, with more means and motives for literacy; but the sons and daughters of the squire and parson might be there as

Little girls aged four, 1590

well, unless they were taught privately in the hall or the rectory. Professor Hoskins tells us that 'The only formal schooling the great Duke of Buckingham (George Villiers) had was at the village school of Billesdon as the son of a Leicestershire squire'.[33]

The essential task of the petty school was to teach spelling and reading, whence it was still often known as the ABC school and the teacher as the 'abcdarian', though in some schools writing and counting would be taught as well.[34] The horn book and the absey book provided the basic reading material, followed by the primer and catechism. This seems to have been as far as ordinary petty schools went, and most children probably left once they had mastered the rudiments at this stage. If they stayed longer it was to practise their reading skill and extend their religious knowledge by working through the psalter and testaments and recent works of protestant piety and devotion, and also to learn how to write – if the master was competent to undertake this.

Whether taught by a man or a woman, most schools were private ventures conducted for fees, and a village with too few children to make a school viable would lack one altogether, or have one only intermittently. Some parishes benefited from the educational philanthropy of the age and boasted an endowed charity school, where the master received an annual salary for teaching a specified number of poor children free, but even he was usually dependent on fee-payers as well in order to make up his living. So precarious was the livelihood afforded by teaching that it was frequently combined with some other sedentary occupation that could be carried on as children stood or sat around.

To help teachers of the petties, some experienced schoolmasters wrote practical handbooks offering guidance and advice. One of these, Edmund Coote, addressed his book in 1596 to 'such men and women of trades (as tailors, weavers, shopkeepers, seamsters and such other) as have undertaken the charge of teaching others'.[35] Several writers of this kind suggest that 'grounding the little ones' was often part-time work taken up as a last resort. John Brinsley, master of Ashby-de-la-Zouch grammar school, explaining his method of teaching reading, assures the would-be petty teacher 'thus may any poor man or woman enter the little ones in a town together and make an honest poor living of it, or get somewhat towards helping the same'.[36] Charles Hoole was another of the experienced grammar masters of the time who deplored the inadequate grounding their entrants had received and wrote with the object of improving petty-school teaching. This was too important, he believed, to be 'left as a work for poor women, or others, whose necessities compel them to undertake it, as a meer shelter from beggary'.[37]

Clearly, teaching the elements was regarded as menial work – work which only the poor were expected to take up. Clearly, too, women as well as men made it their livelihood. School dames were perhaps usually widows or spinsters, but there are instances of schoolmasters' wives who taught. A man at Reculver in Kent, presented at the archdeacon's visitation in 1619 for teaching without licence, confessed 'that his wife, by the minister's consent, teacheth two or three children their hornbooks'.[38]

As in pre-Reformation times, teaching the parish children remained one of the duties expected of the parish clerk. 'That he endeavour himself to teach young children to read if he be able to do so' was a usual injunction of Elizabethan bishops. Visitation records show him acting as schoolmaster in some places, but insufficiently literate to do so in others. In Yorkshire the parish clerk was teaching the children at Filey in 1595 but at Sheriff Hutton he could 'not write nor scarce read'.[39] Often during this period, however, the role of schoolmaster was assumed by the incumbent, and this was a work encouraged by the bishops in order to spread religious uniformity through instruction in the catechism. The canons of 1571 ordered those clergy who were not preachers to teach the children to read and write. By the canons of 1604, in every parish without a public school the curate was to be given preference over other candidates for the bishop's licence if able and willing to teach 'for the better increase of his own living and training up of children in principles of true religion'. Hence, observed Richard Mulcaster, first headmaster of Merchant Taylors' school, 'every parish hath a minister, if none else in the parish, which can help writing and reading'.[40] After about 1640 teaching the village school tended to devolve on the parish clerk rather than the parson, as the latter's social status rose.

If the school was endowed, it might have its own small schoolhouse; otherwise an ordinary cottage would suffice. Lacking either of these, the school was usually to be found in the church, which also housed the other common property of the village as we have seen. In *Twelfth Night* (c. 1600) Malvolio appears to Maria 'like a pedant that keeps a school i' the church'. The antiquary John Aubrey tells us that Thomas Hobbes, the philosopher, went to school first in 1592 in Westport church, Malmesbury, learning to 'read well and number four figures' before he was eight.[41] In 1624 John Evelyn, not quite four, started school in the church porch at Wotton in Surrey, where his father was the squire.[42]

Towns offered more opportunities for instruction than existed in the countryside. Beyond the petty stage were specialized writing schools kept by scriveners teaching their skills to children and adults indiscriminately, and sometimes touring the neighbouring villages and hamlets to sell their services there. Cyphering schools taught arithmetic and the skills dependent on it, like mensuration, surveying and casting accounts, and these schools too catered for adults as well as children. These basic subjects came to be taught together in 'English' schools, where the age range tended to be more like the grammar school's. For instance, the master of Sir John Leman's English school at Beccles was to teach writing, cyphering and accounts; children had to be eight on admission and able to read, and they could attend for no more than four years.[43] At Berwick-on-Tweed in 1636 a private schoolmaster was allowed by the corporation to conduct an English school, charging burgesses' children 1d. a week for reading, 2d. for writing, and 4d. for both writing and cyphering.[44] Girls as well as boys attended these schools as they did the ordinary petty schools.

Children of 'the poorer sort', says Hoole, were taken away from the petty school as soon as they could read 'any whit well' and 'permitted to run wilding up and down without any control'.[45] Others not so poor might pass on to the English school, or visit the writing or cyphering master until they were ready to start work or be apprenticed. At seven or eight some better-off boys, able to read English but perhaps not yet write it, would leave the petty school and enter the grammar school. In country areas without a petty school, boys at this age would begin immediately at the grammar school and have to be taught the rudiments there, though the master might think it was demeaning himself to do this. On the other hand, the more educated village schoolmaster might try his hand at teaching Latin if required to do so in the absence of a grammar school. There was often no rigid division of function outside the towns.[46]

The grammar schools in their heyday

Between 1560 and 1640 the grammar schools, like the universities which they fed, expanded until they were probably educating more pupils than ever again until the late nineteenth century. Schools varied considerably in size. Large ones in towns might at their fullest consist of upwards of 100–150 boys, and the very biggest, like Merchant Taylors' and Shrewsbury, perhaps twice or even three times as many. Eton had some 112 boys about 1613. On the other hand, small country schools must have numbered no more than twenty or thirty boys. The usual teaching complement was one master, sometimes aided by an usher. Even in the same school numbers fluctuated strikingly, no doubt according to the master's reputation and local economic conditions. Most schools drew their pupils from the immediate neighbourhood, and those who lived beyond walking or pony-riding distance would perforce have to board – with the master, or with kinsfolk, or with other families in the town.

The names and family origins of the boys are difficult to discover except in the case of the minority who went on to Oxford or Cambridge, and these may not have been representative of the whole. The majority were probably a cross section of what we should call the middle classes: sons of yeomen, substantial

husbandmen, merchants, prosperous tradesmen and artisans, clergy, apothecaries, scriveners and lawyers. Eton and Winchester excepted, and Westminster after about 1640, there was no marked social hierarchy of schools, but those well enough endowed to attract able masters and amply supplied with university scholarships had obvious attractions over poorer ones. Any school might contain at the top of its social scale the sons of one or two baronets, knights or gentlemen of the county, and at the bottom the sons of small shopkeepers and craftsmen, the neediest of them − orphans perhaps − taught free as 'poor scholars'. For boys of plebeian origin the grammar school opened the way to the university and so to social advance through the church: Laud, archbishop of Canterbury, was a clothier's son; Harsnett, archbishop of York, a baker's; Corbet, bishop of Norwich, a gardener's. However, probably very few boys came from that half of the population made up of the labouring poor.

During this period the vocational purpose of the grammar school changed. With the triumph of the vernacular, Latin lost its professional utility (save to a diminishing extent for lawyers

Eton College

and physicians) and it became mainly an accomplishment for
scholars and cultivated gentlemen. Even for the clergy, Latin was
no longer vocationally essential, for the liturgy, the canons and
the theology of the new national church were all in English. The
grammar schools now supplied a liberal intellectual education
through Latin, to a lesser extent Greek and (more rarely)
Hebrew, primarily with the university in view, although only a
minority of boys would pass on there. Of those who did, most
were intended for ordination, and to this extent the grammar
schools, like the universities, carried on their essential medieval
role of providing clergy. Whatever their intended vocation, boys
were all taught the same curriculum — ideally not only how to
read and write the best classical Latin (through imitation of the
most esteemed ancient authors) but also how to speak it, even
though few spoke it now save university dons and scholars who
wished to communicate internationally on learned matters.
Grammar included some rhetoric, classical history, geography
and mythology, and this, together with religious knowledge
gained largely through Latin, was the sum of the curriculum in

most schools.[47] In practice, humanist ideals touched them hardly at all: what was offered was a narrow, arid, linguistic grind. Writing was taught by the grammar master unwillingly, as a task beneath his dignity. Ordinarily, boys in country schools learned to write during the annual visit of an itinerant writing master; boys in town schools attended a writing master after school hours. Number was even more neglected, so much so, says Brinsley in his practical guide for young schoolmasters, that 'you shall have scholars, almost ready to go to the university, who yet can hardly tell you the number of pages, sections, chapters, or other divisions in their books, to find what they should'.[48]

Seven or eight was the usual age for starting school and the course was planned to prepare 'the best witted children' for the university at fourteen or fifteen. Most children probably left long before the course was finished either to start work or to be apprenticed. All were taught together in the one schoolroom, but divided into forms sitting on benches ranged along the two long walls. The master sat enthroned on a dais at the top end teaching the older forms (the upper school), whilst the usher taught the younger forms (the lower school) at the end near the door, where he could observe their goings out and comings in.[49]

An almost unrelieved diet of Latin and Greek can have appealed to only a minority of boys. All of them were urged to it by fear and whipping. Teaching and beating were interchangeable terms. Even in an age when life for everybody was harsh, and pain and cruelty taken for granted, complaints of the brutality of schoolmasters were frequent. Remedies open to parents were to withdraw boys from the school, if another was available, or petition the bishop as the licensing officer, or seek redress in chancery. At Clitheroe an attempt was made in 1619 to get the master removed by chancery, alleging that he was 'of a hot stomach and beats men's children most cruelly', so that many had been taken away and sent elsewhere.[50] The school day everywhere was long — seven or eight working hours beginning at 6 a.m. in summer and 7 a.m. in winter (much the same hours as those laid down for apprentices and workmen by the 1563 Statute of Labour). Holidays amounted to some six weeks in the year, at Christmas, Easter and Whitsuntide. Other feast days were holidays also, but usually spent at church or the writing master's, and there were discretionary day or half-day holidays or 'remedies'. On these 'play days' the boys amused themselves in the school close according to age with balls, tops, battledores, archery, cock fighting, fighting one another or climbing on the roof of the church, to which the schoolhouse was usually adjacent.

The qualities which trustees were to look for when appointing the schoolmaster were often stipulated in the founder's statutes. He was commonly required to be a master of arts, competent in Latin and Greek, and in order to avert any neglect of the school he was sometimes forbidden to be married, or ordained, or to hold a cure, or practise physic. Religious orthodoxy and moral character were particularly important. At Chigwell school founded by Archbishop Harsnett of York in 1629 the master had to be 'of a sound religion, neither papist nor puritan, of a grave behaviour, of a sober and honest conversation, no tippler nor haunter of alehouses, no puffer of tobacco; and above all . . . apt to teach and severe in his government'.[51] The schoolmaster's office, like the parson's, was a freehold, and even if he proved idle or incompetent or excessively tyrannical it was difficult to get rid of him. The school's reputation was largely his to make or mar.

'There is scarce any profession in the commonwealth more necessary, which is so slightly performed', wrote Thomas Fuller of schoolmasters in 1642.[52] Then as always they covered a wide range of ability and aptitude. Some were dedicated men who made teaching their life's work, like Camden at Westminster or Mulcaster at Merchant Taylors' and later St Paul's. Others saw it as a temporary employment until some more gainful appointment (usually a benefice) came their way. Often a master divided his attention between teaching and a cure or preachership, to the school's detriment. Southampton corporation forced out the town schoolmaster in 1620 for neglecting his pupils and leaving them 'to the teaching of a stranger unexamined and unripe of years'. The financial rewards in some schools were so meagre that capable men were hard to find and keep, and here the master might be a young man straight from the university, perhaps without a degree, not old enough for deacon's orders or a curacy. The usher, whether on the foundation like the master or engaged and paid by him as his servant, was generally a young man waiting for ordination, or for promotion in the church or another school, and his stay tended to be short.

Originally, the fact that the master had a stipend provided by the foundation meant that the school was free, at least for local boys. But as prices rose and money values depreciated, 'entering pennies' and quarterly fees had to be imposed, either to allow the master a sufficient living or to raise a salary for an usher. Fees for local boys were usually then fixed by the trustees, whilst for 'foreigners' the master was permitted to get what he could by private treaty with the parents. At Hull the fees from 1579 to 1647 were 1s. a quarter for burgesses' sons and the proceeds all went to pay the usher, so that when numbers reached 100 as in the 1630s he made some £20 p.a. The master's income of £26, plus a rentfree house and garden next to the school, came from the endowment, and he usually supplemented this with an ecclesiastical appointment − a preachership or an almshouse chaplaincy.[53]

These 'public' or 'endowed' or 'free' schools were by no means the only providers of grammar education. There was also much private teaching by parsons, curates and lay graduates, sometimes in towns but more often in country districts that were ill-provided with endowed schools. Thomas Hobbes, until he went to Oxford at the age of fourteen, learnt his Latin from a young BA who kept a small school next to the blacksmith's in Westport, outside Malmesbury; a generation later, John Aubrey, a Wiltshire squire's son, started school with the same master, then rector of a nearby parish, and later, after a period of private teaching at home, went on to Blandford school in Dorset, where he suffered the usual brutalities.[54] These private schools come to light mainly in diocesan records and in certain Cambridge college admission registers, where university freshmen gave their schoolmaster's name. They probably consisted of a few boys from better-off local families being taught in the rectory or the schoolmaster's house. Sometimes they were no more than tutorships in particular gentlemen's households. Men were occasionally licensed specifically for this purpose − George Sarson BA was licensed by the archbishop of York in 1634 'to teach in Sir Hardolph Wasteney's house' at Headon in Nottinghamshire, where his employer later presented him to the vicarage.[55] Such schools must have been relatively informal, personal and transient. But in London and in other towns where demand was plentiful there were masters who made private schoolkeeping their profession in active competition with the endowed schools. In the 1640s and 1650s Charles Hoole, formerly master of

Rotherham grammar school, kept a private school in the City of London where 'the generality of the youth were instructed to a miracle', and where he wrote his well-known treatises on teaching and school management, believing that 'there is no calling more serviceable to church and commonwealth, than this of a schoolmaster'.

The education of girls

Sixteenth-century humanism changed medieval attitudes to women, or at least to women of the upper class. Some Tudor ladies of aristocratic family, brought up at court or in noble households, were highly educated, even learned, able not only to read Latin and Greek but also converse in French and Italian, as well as to sing and dance and play the lute and virginals. Pleas were made for the more liberal education of girls of less exalted rank. The early protestant controversialist Thomas Becon deplored the loss of the nuns' services as teachers and argued for the setting up of girls' schools by public authority, with 'honest, sage, wise, discreet, sober, grave and learned matrons made rulers and mistresses of the same [with] honest and liberal stipends'.[56] Richard Mulcaster, best known of Elizabethan schoolmasters, also urged the claims of girls to have school education.[57] But neither of these writers had in mind girls of the labouring class.

Although girls attended petty schools and English schools along with boys, most parents had perhaps less incentive to keep them there as long as their brothers. From grammar schools girls were excluded by custom, if not explicitly by statute (as they were at Harrow in 1591); though very exceptionally in country areas where other provision was scarce they may have attended for a limited period in order to learn to read and write English, as they were allowed to do by the statutes of Bunbury grammar school, Cheshire, in 1594. On occasion during the seventeenth century girls attended the grammar school at Rivington in Lancashire, but apparently only for a year or two and perhaps when they were young.[58]

Daughters of the gentry and of prosperous trading and professional families were educated at home by resident or visiting teachers to a level determined by their ability and interests and their parents' notions of what was suitable for a girl. Mrs Lucy

Hutchinson, born in 1620 the daughter of Sir Allen Apsley, lieutenant of the Tower and a Sussex gentleman, tells us that as soon as she was weaned she had a French nurse and so grew up speaking French and English together. At four she could read English, and at seven she had tutors for languages, music, dancing, writing and needlework. Latin was her great love, and she learnt this from her father's chaplain, outshining her brothers who were at school.[59] This particular tutor was 'a pitiful dull fellow', but young men of talent sometimes found employment and patronage this way. Andrew Marvell was resident tutor to the ex-parliamentary general Lord Fairfax's daughter from 1651 to 1653, during which time he wrote some of his greatest poetry.

From the early seventeenth century, private boarding schools for girls of good family were established in the rural villages on the London fringe, notably in Hackney, and girls from all parts of the country attended them, often accompanied by their maids.[60] These schools were both a substitute for and an addition to domestic education; they taught reading, writing, music, dancing, needlework, household skills, and perhaps some French and Latin (with visiting masters). Mrs Bathsua Makin, formerly tutor to Charles I's daughter Elizabeth, kept a girls' school first at Putney, later at Tottenham, and wrote a book to further her aims. She deplored the 'barbarous custom to breed women low' and wanted to restore the high standards of the past, extending to women the whole range of learning available to men. In her school she offered not only the ladylike graces and accomplishments but also Latin and French with optional Greek, Hebrew, Italian and Spanish, and for those who stayed longer astronomy, geography, history and arithmetic.[61] Certainly, highly educated women seem to have been rarer in the mid-seventeenth century than in the mid-sixteenth century, but perhaps middle-class women generally were educated to a higher level of literacy than was usual again until the late Victorian era.

Apprenticeship and technical training

Throughout this period craft apprenticeship remained an important part of the country's provision of technical and commercial training. In the leading trades in London and the larger towns a seven-year term was normal by early Tudor times, boys being accepted at fourteen or so on giving proofs of their literacy and paying premiums that varied according to the exclusiveness of the gild. Apprentices came from the middle social groups — substantial burgesses, yeomen, craftsmen and the younger sons of the gentry — and in London they were drawn from all parts of the country. They were fed, clothed, housed and taught by their master in his own house and workshop, and often they formed a noisy, boisterous and even turbulent element in urban society.[62]

In 1562 the Statute of Labour established a national system of apprenticeship with the intention partly of improving craft training at all levels, partly of coping with the growing problem of poverty and vagrancy. In all existing trades, the justices were empowered to enforce a seven-year apprenticeship, with a parental property qualification in the more skilled crafts, and they could bind any poor or workless child to any person legally qualified to accept apprentices. Following this Act, smaller miscellaneous crafts in particular towns tended to amalgamate and form one large company, which made enforcement easier. Thus, apprenticeship came to be extended to semi-skilled occupations that really required little or no technical training, and where the apprentice might be no more than an unpaid juvenile labourer. This was the kind of apprenticeship to which pauper children were bound after the Elizabethan Poor Law of 1598 in order to ease the burden on the rates; 'parish prentices' tended to be the defenceless, unpaid drudges of local small tradespeople. Poor children too young to be apprenticed might receive instruction, in or out of the workhouse, in simple handicrafts like spinning, weaving and lacemaking at the expense of the parish. From this time the endowment of apprenticeship schemes became a common act of private benevolence, sometimes in connection with a parish charity school, the children being bound to specified trades, or to any at the trustees' discretion, after a period of elementary schooling.[63]

Technical and vocational training through apprenticeship was supplemented, or its absence in some occupations remedied, partly by the printed book, partly by the private teacher.[64] For those desirous of secretarial skills there were obtainable after about 1570, besides the writing master's personal tuition, printed copybooks of scripts and letter-writing manuals in English produced by professional penmen. The first to be published in

England was *A Book Containing Divers Sorts of Hands* (1571) by John Baildon and John de Beauchesne, showing secretary Italian, Roman chancery and court hands. Many others followed, dictating handwriting fashions for their time.[65] Practical handbooks based on Italian models were also brought out describing methods of accounting, foreign monetary systems, forms of business and such like for the self-instruction of merchants, their apprentices, clerks and factors. The authors were often freelance teachers of these skills with actual experience of them in London. In the same way the needs of sea captains and shipowners, a group of increasing importance, were met by books on navigation, cartography, practical astronomy and geography. Anthony Ashley's *The Mariner's Mirror* (1588), translated from the Dutch, set a new standard in nautical instruction. Similarly, private teachers and their books provided opportunities for learning about gunnery, fortification, land-surveying, husbandry and estate management. Architecture, still practised mainly by master masons or carpenters with an apprentice training, was much influenced now by technical manuals and pattern books from abroad. Knowledge of classical and Renaissance styles was diffused in England by John Shute's *The First and Chief Grounds of Architecture* (1563), the first book on architecture in English, but printing also made available to English builders a vast repertory of plans and designs in numerous foreign treatises on the 'new fashion', most influential being that of the Italian Sebastiano Serlio.

The basis of many of these technical skills was arithmetic, and during this period arithmetic and mathematics had profound influence on the development of many kinds of knowledge, from humble crafts to intellectual speculation in which quantitative thinking married to experimentation began to revolutionize science by the mid-seventeenth century. Again, textbooks provided new opportunities for self-education. Robert Recorde's *The Ground of Arts* (1543) was the pioneer. He defends 'numbering' against the traditionalist's charge that it is 'contemptible and vile' and argues its practical value in all manner of studies and occupations: music, physic, law, commerce, government, military science — 'for numbering of the host, summing of their wages, provisions of victuals, viewing of artillery, with other armour; besides the cunningest point of all, for casting of ground for encamping of men, with such other like'.[66] Recorde's book was followed by Humphrey Baker's *The Well Spring of Sciences which teacheth the perfect work and practice of Arithmetic* (1546) and others. 'Mathematicians' became a general label for teachers of almost any of the arts which depended on calculation. In London a public mathematical lectureship was endowed in 1588, and Gresham College after 1596 provided public lectures in geometry and astronomy, with the emphasis on practical applications.[67]

Some of these mathematicians were university men, mainly from Cambridge, where the influence of the French anti-Aristotelian philosopher, Peter Ramus, was strong for a time and stimulated interest in practical mathematics. Henry Briggs, first professor of geometry at Gresham College, was from Cambridge. When William Bedwell, another Cambridge man, edited the geometry lectures of Ramus he commended them as 'necessary and useful for astronomers, geographers, land-meters, seamen, engineers, architects, painters, carvers etc'. Ordinarily, however, mathematics was little studied at the universities in the early seventeenth century, save by individual enthusiasts, it still being regarded as primarily utilitarian and therefore inappropriate for the studies of gentlemen. John Wallis, Savilian professor of geometry at Oxford, remembering in old age his Cambridge undergraduate days in the 1630s, recalls that:

> mathematics (at that time, with us) were scarce looked upon as academical studies, but rather mechanical; as the business of traders, merchants, seamen, carpenters, surveyors of lands, or the like; and perhaps some almanack-makers in London . . . For the study of mathematics was at that time more cultivated in London than in the universities.[68]

Outside these practical callings, gentlemen highly educated in the traditional learning of grammar school and university could remain arithmetically ignorant. Samuel Pepys, a product of St Paul's school and Cambridge and a highly placed civil servant at the Admiralty, in July 1662 had a course of mathematical lessons at home from the mate of the *Royal Charles* and recorded in his diary the trouble and pleasure he had in mastering his multiplication tables.[69]

Oxford and Cambridge in transition

In no field of education was change so marked as in the universities. Most important so far as English society was concerned was the spectacular growth of the university population and its changing social composition, but there were intellectual and constitutional changes as well. From the 1560s students flocked to the universities. Judged by student entries, Cambridge was the more attractive until the 1630s, just as it was perhaps the more influential, both politically and ecclesiastically. Numbers reached a peak about 1580 when both universities together had some 3,000 students. There was a recession, perhaps for economic reasons, in the 1590s. Another wave of expansion followed after 1610 and numbers reached their summit – well over 4,000 – in the 1630s: a total not exceeded until the 1860s.[70] Indeed, assuming a population of over 4 million in the 1630s university students in England and Wales did not attain the same relative proportion until after the First World War.

As residence became compulsory, the colleges filled to over-flowing. Foundation members – fellows and scholars – were out-numbered by fee-paying commoners or pensioners, who previously had been received only exceptionally as room-renting lodgers. St John's, the largest and most eminent college in Elizabethan Cambridge, had 287 members as early as 1565; Corpus Christi College, a small society, grew from 32 in 1564 to 91 in 1574 – 13 fellows, 20 scholars, 4 Bible clerks, and 54 pensioners.[71] At Oxford, Queen's College had 70 com-moners in 1581 and 183 in 1612.[72] To meet the rising demand for places, colleges extended their accommodation by annexing adjacent houses, by adding attic storeys to existing quadrangles, or by adding a second or 'back' quadrangle to the original one. Some old colleges – like Oriel – replaced their medieval buildings entirely on a larger and grander scale. Private philanthropy founded new colleges. In 1571 Jesus College – the first protestant college – was established for Welshmen at Oxford by the treasurer of St David's cathedral. Two colleges at Cambridge followed, both intended to train up godly preaching ministers: Emmanuel (1584) founded by a puritan chancellor of the ex-chequer, and Sidney Sussex (1596) by a pious noble widow, the countess of Sussex. At Oxford a Somerset squire in 1610 founded Wadham College, a resort mainly of West Countrymen, and in 1624 one of the few remaining medieval halls was trans-formed into Pembroke College with endowments given by an Abingdon grazier and a Berkshire parson.[73]

As in the past, the men who crowded the universities were

socially mixed, representing all ranks of society above the great mass of the poor. But rich and well-born students, growing in number since the fifteenth century, formed a much larger proportion from the 1560s. Matriculands, registered according to the social status of their father, fell into three main categories – gentry, clergy and plebeians. 'Gentry' included not only the great and important – peers, knights, esquires and gentlemen, but also those who claimed or aspired to gentility, like successful city merchants, lawyers and physicians. 'Plebeians' included urban shopkeepers, small farmers and lesser professional men such as apothecaries and attorneys. The largest single professional group of fathers were the clergy, though the higher clergy really counted as gentry. From incomplete and defective matriculation registers Professor Stone estimates that from 1575 to 1639 50 per cent of Oxford students were sons of gentry, 41 per cent sons of plebeians and 9 per cent sons of clergy.[74]

Most of these were admitted to colleges as commoners, forming the main element in college membership, but the wealthiest and most influential among them eventually came to be entered as fellow or gentlemen commoners, paying extra fees for special privileges such as eating at the fellows' table and bringing with them their own private tutors and servants. Class distinctions and social deference thus became marked features of college life. A German visitor to Oxford in 1598 observed that in college halls 'earls, barons, gentlemen, doctors and masters of arts, but very few of the latter' were admitted to the top table, 'masters of arts, bachelors, some gentlemen and eminent citizens' occupied a second table, whilst a third was for 'people of low condition'.[75]

Few of the rich and well connected had serious academic interests; entrance standards were nominal; many did not bother even to matriculate but moved on after a year or so to one of the Inns of Court. Their invasion of colleges originally intended for 'poor scholars' was a subject of comment and complaint. William Harrison, the topographer, who knew both universities, wrote in 1577:

> poor men's children are commonly shut out, and the richer sort received (who in time past thought it dishonour to live as it were upon alms), and yet, being placed, most of them study little other than histories, tables, dice, and trifles, as men that make not living by their study the end of their purposes. . . .

Besides this, being for the most part either gentlemen or rich men's sons, they oft bring the universities into much slander. For, standing upon their reputation and liberty, they ruffle and roister it out, exceeding in apparel and haunting riotous company . . . and for excuse, when they are charged with breach of all good order, think it sufficient to say that they be gentlemen.[76]

However, poor scholars were by no means excluded. Indeed, opportunities for them expanded as philanthropy founded scholarships at schools and colleges, and as the growing number of wealthy members increased the demand for servants. Many poor students were thus admitted as servitors (sizars at Cambridge) and as such earned their board and tuition by working as college porters, waiters in hall, Bible clerks in chapel, and servants of fellows and gentlemen commoners. Plebeians slightly outnumbered gentry in the Oxford admissions from 1610 to 1640. In the 1630s at St John's College, Cambridge, gentry and plebs each accounted for rather more than a third of the undergraduates, sons of clergy and other professional men for about a quarter; half of the total admissions were as sizars. Even so, only to a limited extent were the universities agents of social mobility. They helped the advancement of some 'poor' boys but they were not from the lowest levels of society and, as Professor Kearney says, 'The net result . . . was to accentuate the differences between the gentry and the rest.'[77]

This influx of boys from the age of fourteen or thereabouts went far to transform the colleges. Instead of being small exclusive societies of graduate fellows they became places of education for large bodies of adolescent boys: not at all what earlier founders had intended. As the medieval system of public lectures by regent masters became obsolete, it was replaced by the private tuition of college fellows. Tutorial instruction was introduced earlier in some colleges than in others, but it became general during the late sixteenth century and the college rule was that every commoner like every scholar must have a tutor. The tutor might have five or six pupils and his relationship with them could be very close. They shared his room or had rooms nearby on the same staircase. He prescribed their reading, coached them individually, watched over their health and morals, kept their allowances from home, paid their bills, and finally saw them through the necessary exercises for their degrees. Thus, in time the colleges almost entirely superseded the university as the source of instruction. They also became responsible for admitting students to the university, which simply matriculated those whom each college presented. And as the importance of the colleges grew, so did the importance of their heads, who collectively became a new force in university government.[78]

Recognition of this change was the most significant feature of the revised Cambridge statutes of 1570. The new code gave effective power to a small oligarchy of vice-chancellor and college heads, who had the chief voice in the election of the 'caput', a body of six members empowered to approve all legislative proposals submitted to the Senate, the convocation of regents and· non-regents. This was an attempt to limit academic democracy and strengthen the forces of conservatism at a time when extreme puritans among the younger regents wanted to subvert the recent Anglican settlement. Similarly at Oxford when the ancient statutes were revised and codified in 1636 during the chancellorship of Archbishop Laud, the Hebdomadal Board, a weekly meeting of vice-chancellor, proctors and college heads which had evolved since the 1560s, became the effective executive authority. Each university was in process of being subordinated to its component parts, the colleges.[79]

Classical and humane studies, both Latin and Greek, at first formed the substance of the undergraduate course, providing the kind of education advocated by Elyot and Ascham for the training of lay gentlemen for the public service. From the 1590s, however, scholasticism revived and Aristotelian logic and philosophy shared the curriculum with classical humanism. Neither can have met the needs of young gentlemen who lacked both scholarly interests and the desire to take a degree. For them, college tutors doubtless recommended more palatable reading outside the official curriculum; much of their time was probably spent at the vaulting or fencing master's, or playing the viol or flageolet, or simply revelling and roistering, as Sir Simonds D'Ewes found at Cambridge in 1620. As in the pre-Reformation universities, the majority of students, commoners and poor scholars alike, were intended for the church. Most of them duly graduated as BAs and went off to country livings; some completed the full MA course in seven years and were fellows before they obtained benefices. Thus, the universities continued their primary medieval function of furnishing the church with educated clergy, but whereas the medieval parish priest had been an indifferently educated peasant, the Anglican clergyman, even if born a pleb, passed for a gentleman by virtue of his university education, if not quite on the same social level as the squire, his patron.[80]

Of the higher faculties, theology was by far the most important and the main preoccupation of senior members in the decades after 1560. The controversies of Cambridge divines largely shaped the attitudes of the various puritan groups within the established church. Medicine attracted more attention than before, particularly at Cambridge, but graduates often completed their studies at more celebrated centres abroad, like Leyden, Padua or Montpellier. Civil law, the only kind studied after the abolition of canon law, was a declining discipline, but it survived in a small way (mainly at Trinity Hall, Cambridge), because of its continuing practice in the prerogative, ecclesiastical and admiralty courts.

When the old statutes were codified, many of those regulating periods of residence, courses of study, and exercises for the various degrees were retained with little change. Latin remained the official language and all degrees were awarded after stipulated terms of residence and the performance of public disputations in the traditional dialectical form. Aristotelian scholasticism was thus as firmly entrenched as ever. But as late-medieval experience had shown, the long periods of residence required for higher degrees were impossible for most graduates, and the statutory demands were gradually relaxed or evaded, first in the case of the MA. Postgraduate studies thus became comparatively rare and unimportant.

In spite of the growing predominance of the colleges, the universities as such were not wholly eclipsed. Philanthropy, in its preference for founding colleges, fellowships and scholarships, did not entirely neglect them. Oxford in particular was strengthened by munificent benefactions in the early seventeenth century. In 1602 Sir Thomas Bodley restored the university library, defunct since the 1550s, and subsequent gifts, including the right to receive a copy of every book newly printed in the country, soon made it the greatest library in the kingdom. The university press started in 1585 with the appointment of a private printer-bookseller as university printer. A schools (i.e. lecture rooms) quadrangle was completed, a botanic garden founded, and between 1619 and 1627 individual benefactors endowed no fewer than seven chairs or public lectureships – the first since Henry VIII's endowment – in geometry, astronomy, natural philosophy, moral philosophy, ancient history, anatomy and music, though these subjects had little relevance for undergraduate studies.[81]

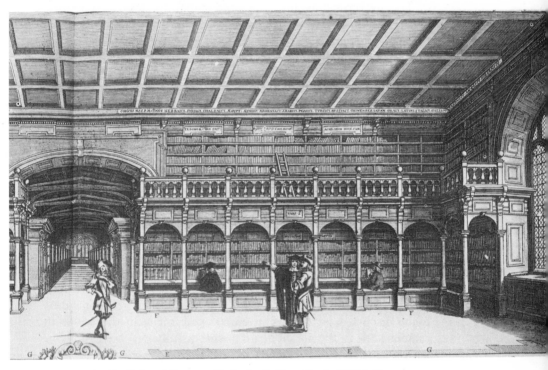

Bodleian Library, Oxford, Seldon End, 1634–7

Notwithstanding their use by the state as engines of Anglican uniformity, the universities nurtured religious dissentients of many kinds. Catholicism practically disappeared from Oxford after 1580, but there and at Cambridge various puritan groups worked for a godly reformation within the Church of England. 'Clerical puritanism . . . was created in the universities' as Dr Collinson says.[82] The most radical Cambridge sectaries rejected not only episcopacy and an ordained ministry but also the universities themselves. These they denounced as 'seminaries of anti-Christ': their élitist, classical, scholastic learning was a hindrance to revelation.[83] Puritan minorities survived in certain colleges in spite of the increasingly royalist and Erastian attitudes of the universities, and of the fact that by royal command after 1616 nobody could take a degree without giving proof of their Anglican orthodoxy. In 1604 – evidence of their new importance as pillars of the social establishment – the universities were granted the privilege of returning two members each to Parliament.

The overcrowding and the predominantly clerical, scholastic and ruling-class connections of Oxford and Cambridge suggested to some puritan critics the need for a third university, or for decentralized local colleges. The Inns of Court almost constituted a third university in London and were sometimes regarded as such, but they too were a gentlemen's monopoly. Gresham College, established in the City in 1596 under the will of the merchant financier Sir Thomas Gresham, had professors of divinity, law, physic, music, rhetoric, astronomy and geometry, and was intended to make university learning available to the merchants and tradesmen of London. In its early years through the teaching of mathematics it forged close links with the commercial and mercantile interests of the capital. But being academically dependent on Oxford and Cambridge, whose vested interests were involved, it had little chance of becoming much more than an extramural college.[84] To remedy the educational backwardness of the northern counties, schemes for a university in Ripon were promulgated in 1590, 1596 and 1604, but without success.[85] The need for a third university, however, continued to be discussed, and other attempts were made in the 1640s to establish one in the north, again unsuccessfully.

Aristocratic education

The aristocracy, who had lived mainly for hunting and war and scorned the book learning of clerks, became in the sixteenth century not only literate but educated. As we have seen, nobility and gentry descended on the grammar schools and universities to acquire that familiarity with classical literature, history and antiquities which fashion now decreed. There were other ingredients in aristocratic education, however, which these predominantly clerical and scholastic institutions could not supply. The Renaissance ideal re-emphasized the old skills of medieval courtly training – military exercise, riding the great horse, field sports, singing, dancing and musicmaking. Furthermore, some knowledge of the common law was now considered a necessary part of a gentleman's education, as was also, in the leading families, some first-hand acquaintance with foreign countries and their languages and cultures.[86]

Until the early seventeenth century the great household continued to be a training ground for the highborn, possibly supplemented by school and university. The most influential was that of the scholar-statesman Lord Burghley, Queen Elizabeth's secretary of state and chancellor of Cambridge University, who as master of the court of wards from 1561 was responsible for the rearing of orphaned young noblemen who were the royal wards. Other gentlemen's sons were brought up with them in the Burghley household. The studies which Burghley himself prescribed for them set a new standard in aristocratic education: the 12-year-old earl of Oxford in 1562 learnt dancing, French, Latin, writing, drawing and cosmography, with riding, shooting and more dancing on holidays.

As this system of household training died out, the private domestic tutor, who might also be secretary or chaplain, became a usual means of education in gentle and noble families. Gentlemen's sons were often sent to the local grammar school, however, and some noble as well as gentle families sent their sons to board at Eton. Among the commoners there in the early 1630s were eleven sons of peers as well as several knights' sons. Westminster became another fashionable school for the gentry after about 1640.

England had none of the celebrated courtly academies that existed in Italy and France, like that kept in Paris by M. de Pluvinel where the young French nobility learnt fencing, horsemanship, military science and the social graces. It was along these lines that Sir Humphrey Gilbert about 1570 planned an academy in London, where the queen's wards and other great men's sons might be given the ideal courtly training, through a curriculum consisting of ancient and modern languages, oratory, politics, natural philosophy, mathematics, cosmography and astronomy.[87] The nearest approach to an institution of this kind in England was Sir Francis Kynaston's shortlived *Museum Minervae*, opened with court patronage in 1635 in his house in Covent Garden. Fashionable private academies, however, became a feature of seventeenth-century London, but at first they were mainly grammar schools where opportunities existed to learn other subjects and accomplishments from visiting masters. One of the earliest and best-known, much patronized by wealthy families, was kept in the 1620s and 1630s by Thomas Farnaby, who though a schoolmaster was a complete man of the Renaissance: an Oxford scholar, he had studied with the Jesuits in Spain, soldiered in the Low Countries, sailed on Drake's last voyage, and was one of the most eminent classical scholars of his time.[88]

The mass invasion of the Inns of Court by the gentry was as much a phenomenon of the period as their invasion of the universities. Since the fifteenth century, young gentlemen had frequented the Inns with no intention of practising the law, but attendance became a matter of course from the 1560s onwards, especially for elder sons who would eventually inherit estates and responsibilities as justices and members of Parliament. The Inns became more socially exclusive than the universities, 'well over 80 per cent' of their entrants coming from the aristocracy and landed gentry. Sons followed fathers and uncles to the same Inn. Some went straight from school or private tutorage at home, but perhaps one in two had spent some time at Oxford or Cambridge. The peak years were from 1610 to 1640. In the 1630s, when the Inns were at their fullest, only about one in five of their members, it is estimated, was actually called to the bar.[89] Some of the others probably practised as attorneys or solicitors – humbler members of the legal profession. Many were there only to gain some general acquaintance with the law and to enjoy the social attractions – the masques and plays, the dancing and fencing schools in the City, the court life at Westminster. The result, however, was that knowledge of the law and of legal principles was more widely disseminated than ever before among the landed gentry, many of whom thus learnt to share the common lawyers' hatred of the prerogative courts and divine-right monarchy, and so were prepared to resist the king by force of arms in 1642.

In the leading families the education process was completed by foreign travel, but often only for the eldest son – for it was expensive. This became the fashion between the 1560s and 1630s, and it was revived after 1660. Motives were varied. Knowledge of foreign countries and their languages was important for government service; the most famous teachers of equestrianism and fencing were to be found abroad; the newest developments in military science were best studied in countries with more recent experience of war than England; while for the gentleman virtuoso Italy and France offered the latest fashions in painting, architecture and the decorative arts. Equipped with a safe conduct and letters of introduction, and accompanied by a travelling tutor and one or two servants with horses and baggage, the young man set off on a tour that might last two or three years, allowing for lengthy stays at the more celebrated academies and cultural centres. For his guidance travel books were written, one of the earliest being Robert Dallington's *Method for Travel* in 1598. About this time Francis Bacon in one of his essays offered sage practical advice on what to do, what to avoid, and what to see. Among things to see he mentions:

> the courts of princes, especially when they give audience to ambassadors; the courts of justice, while they sit and hear causes; and so of consistories ecclesiastic; the churches and monasteries, with the monuments which are therein extant; the walls and fortifications of cities and towns; and so the havens and harbours, antiquities and ruins, libraries, colleges, disputations, and lectures, where any are; shipping and navies; houses and gardens of state and pleasure, near great cities; armories, arsenals, magazines, exchanges, burses, warehouses, exercises of horsemanship, fencing, training of soldiers and the like. . . .[90]

'The wandering scholar of the new era', says Sir George Clark, 'was the travelling nobleman who wrote his name for a small fee in the matriculation book of Leyden or Padua, and ordered his horses to drive on next day to Amsterdam or Mestre.'[91]

Some illustrative educational careers

The educational system that developed during this period is well illustrated by the personal experience of particular individuals, recounted autobiographically.

How casual and haphazard schooling was in poor and backward regions at the beginning of the period is revealed by Sir John Savile, the Elizabethan judge, who was brought up in the Halifax area in the 1550s. He came of minor gentry stock in the chapelry of Elland and about the age of five started to learn the alphabet and English catechism with the curate and parish clerk

there, soon afterwards changing to another curate in Huddersfield. Altogether he mentions seven different teachers at various
places within four or five miles of his home, and he returned to
two of them a second time for short spells and to another three
times. At six he was learning his Latin accidence with one
teacher, at seven reading Aesop with a second, at eight the *Sacred
Dialogues* of Castellio with a third.[92] The longest period he
spent under any one master was nearly three years from twelve
to fourteen at Halifax, when he read Ovid, Virgil, Horace, Cicero
and the historian Eutropius – the complete humanist programme
of the time save for the absence of Greek. In 1561, just before he
was fifteen, he went up to Brasenose College, Oxford, taking
with him his 12-year-old brother Henry, but, the plague having
broken out, he left after two years without a degree and
returned home to read law with his father. At eighteen he
entered Clifford's Inn, moved after a year to the Middle Temple
and was admitted as an 'utter' barrister there at twenty-seven in
1573. In due course he became a serjeant-at-law and eventually
a baron of the exchequer. His brother Henry became an
eminent Oxford scholar, warden of Merton College and provost
of Eton.[93]

Another Elizabethan lawyer, Francis Bacon, member of a
prominent East Anglian family of lawyer-politicians and later
lord chancellor, was educated at home with his elder brother
up to the age of twelve, when the two of them went together
to Trinity College, Cambridge, as fellow commoners. He left
Cambridge without a degree after three years and entered Gray's
Inn – the family Inn – where he became an 'utter' barrister in
1582 when he was twenty-one, though his legal training had been
interrupted by three years spent travelling in France, learning
the language and the arts of diplomacy on the staff of the English
ambassador.

The royalist Edward Hyde, later earl of Clarendon, and the
parliamentary colonel and regicide John Hutchinson both
exemplify the typical early seventeenth-century gentleman's
education. Hyde's father, a Wiltshire squire, and three uncles had
all been at Oxford and the Middle Temple, two of the uncles
becoming prominent lawyers. He himself 'was always bred in his
father's house under the care of a schoolmaster, to whom his
father had given the vicarage of that parish'. Being a younger son
of a younger brother he had his own way to make in the world

and accordingly was sent to Oxford (at thirteen) with a career in the church in view. Through court influence – an uncle was the queen's attorney-general – he was recommended for election as a demy at Magdalen College by 'a special letter from King James'; the college by a pretence disregarded the royal mandate and was reprimanded for its disrespect by the secretary of state. Instead Hyde went to Magdalen Hall, then very fashionable, but having unexpectedly become his father's heir at sixteen he was given elder-son treatment and sent to the Middle Temple under the care of his uncle, later lord chief justice. There he became an 'utter' barrister in 1632 when he was twenty-three. In spite of his love of 'polite learning and history' he did not make the grand tour, though his father had rounded off his own education fifty years earlier by travelling in Germany and Italy, daringly visiting Rome in the late 1580s when the only Englishmen welcomed there were Catholic exiles.[94]

Colonel John Hutchinson, whose life was written by his highly educated and gifted wife Lucy, came from an ancient landed family at Owthorpe in Nottinghamshire, his father, Sir Thomas Hutchinson, being sometime MP for the county. With a younger brother he was sent first to Nottingham grammar school to board with the master; but on account of the master's idleness and negligence both boys were soon removed to Lincoln, where the grammar school was then much favoured by the county families.

> There being very many gentlemen's sons there, an old Low-Country soldier was entertained to train them in arms, and they all bought themselves weapons; and, instead of childish sports, when they were not at their books, they were exercised in all their military postures, and in assaults and defences; which instruction was not useless a few years after to some of them.

The master then was John Clarke, 'very famous for learning and piety', but 'such a supercilious pedant and so conceited of his own pedantic forms' that the two brothers hated him; the younger one developed a nervous illness and was taken home. The two had meanwhile lived in Lincoln with a relation, Sir Thomas Grantham, but on his death John Hutchinson was moved back to Nottingham school, boarding in the town. A new master at Nottingham 'advanced him more in one month than the other did in a year' and 'made him now begin to love that which the other's austerity made him loath'. After a year he was ready for Cambridge and in 1630, aged fifteen, he entered Peterhouse as a fellow commoner.

At Cambridge he spent five years and 'betook himself with such delight to his studies that he attained to a great height of learning, performed public exercises in his college with much applause, and upon their importunity took a degree in the university'. He did not neglect the social graces and 'for his exercise he practised tennis . . . for his diversion he chose music,

Elizabethan dame school

and . . . there were masters that taught to dance and vault, whom he practised with'. The college at this time was markedly royalist and Laudian, and the 'popish practices' of the chapel services, 'stretching superstition to idolatry', reinforced his puritan sympathies. From Cambridge he went to London and joined Lincoln's Inn. The law he found not to his liking, but 'for his diversion he exercised himself in those qualities he had not had such good opportunities for in the country, as dancing, fencing and music'. For a time he thought to travel in France but instead he went to live in Richmond, where the prince of Wales held court and in the smart society there he put the finishing touches to his education as a gentleman.[95]

What must be the fullest personal account of schooling at a lower social level during this period is given by the Lancashire presbyterian preacher, controversialist and schoolmaster Adam Martindale. His father seems to have been a mason or a carpenter. Helped by the more literate of his brothers and sisters, he learnt to read from the ABC and primer before he was six, when he started at the free school of St Helens in 1630, walking two miles there and back each day. From the outset he was unlucky in his teachers. The first was 'a young ingenious spark', the next 'an old humdrum curate, that had almost no scholars, nor deserved any, for he was both a simpleton and a tippler'. So his father soon transferred him to a dame school, where he 'did something better than quite lose . . . time, but not much'. Back he went therefore to St Helens free school which had meanwhile got another master − a competent scholar but as it turned out 'very silly and inconstant' and 'being a married man with a charge and very poor . . . open to impressions from such as could fee him well'. To escape ill usage here he was next sent to a private school at nearby Rainford, where the master was abler and more diligent, 'not only as to grammar learning but as to our profiting in the catechetical grounds of religion . . . His worst fault . . . was that he was humorous and passionate, and sometimes in these moods he would whip boys most unmercifully for small or no faults at all.' Soon this man was appointed to the free school at St Helens whither he was accompanied by his pupils, including young Martindale, and here he was thoroughly grounded in the classical curriculum of the time. But alas drink turned this master into a violent tyrant, 'so negligent and capricious that there was no abiding with him'. Fortunately a new master came to Rainford − 'a very civil man and a good teacher . . . eminently able and diligent . . . a man made for a schoolmaster'. So to Rainford Martindale was sent again, and he followed this master back to St Helens when he was later appointed there, remaining his scholar for three years until he finally left school at the age of sixteen in 1639. For a time he worked as secretary and tutor in a merchant's family and then became schoolmaster himself at Rainford before serving as clerk and quartermaster in a parliamentary regiment. Here we have evidence of some of the common complaints of the time: ineffective teaching methods, the arbitrariness and violence of masters and the frequent changes of school which seriously handicapped children's learning.[96]

Anthony Wood, the indefatigable and dedicated historian, antiquary and scandalmonger of Oxford, adds to this picture of school conditions in his autobiography. He was born in Oxford in 1632, his father a university man living comfortably in a large house opposite Merton College. When he was five 'he was put to school to learn to read the psalter'; at seven 'he was in his Bible and ready to go into his accidence'; so in 1640, aged eight, he was sent to a private grammar school kept by a schoolmaster preacher in a little cottage ('a poor thing God wot') near St Peter-le-Bailey. Next year he was moved to a school at New College where for three years he was taught by one of the fellows. Following his father's death, and because of the distractions of wartime Oxford, he was transferred in 1644, aged twelve, to the grammar school at Thame, sixteen miles away, which his three older brothers had previously attended. With him he took his 9-year-old brother and the two boys lodged with the vicar next door to the school, 'there to be educated till they were fit to be academians or apprentices'. In 1646, when he was fourteen, his widowed mother, unable to pay for him any longer as a boarder, had him brought home thinking to have him apprenticed to an 'attorney or solicitor' or 'some inferior mechanical trade'. But his love of learning made this distasteful, and an older brother, a young BA of Trinity College, coached him 'every afternoon in his chamber, which was a cockleloft over the common gate of that college', so that in 1647, just short of his fifteenth birthday, he entered Merton College as a postmaster. The university and its colleges and halls were then in process of godly reformation by the parliamentary visitors, but Merton was already decidedly puritan.[97]

Wood's exact contemporary Richard Kidder, a yeoman's son of East Grinstead in Sussex, who later became bishop of Bath and Wells, was fortunate in escaping so many changes of schooling:

> I was taught to read by a person of quality; a gentlewoman in the neighbourhood chose that employment, and would not suffer me to be sent to a school. This good lady taught me so effectually that I was very early fit for a grammar school. There was I placed when I was very young and continued under the same master till I was sent to the university.

This master was a young Dutch-born Cambridge puritan,

> a man of singular learning and extraordinary diligence, a great contemner of this world and of a generosity and beneficence that was very exemplary . . . he . . . bestowed all due pains both in teaching me the Latin and Greek tongues and more especially in instilling principles of religion and morality. This he did with as great care as if I had been his child, or son of his greatest benefactor; he did it without reward or hopes of it, till he thought me fit for the university.

Unable to go to the university through lack of means, he was apprenticed to an apothecary in Sevenoaks, but a subscription among wellwishers raised enough money to send him as a sizar to Emmanuel College in 1649 when he was sixteen.

Emmanuel had long been the most distinctively puritan college in Cambridge, and Kidder describes approvingly the zealous teaching and moral supervision its junior members received.

> The discipline was very strict and the examples which the young students had in the master and fellows were very conspicuous. . . . The tutors examined their pupils very often every night, before prayers, of the study of that day. They visited their chambers twice a week to see what hours they observed and what company they kept. There was strict notice taken of those who absented themselves from prayers and great encouragement given to those who were pious and studious. The young scholars were kept to their exercises and to the speaking the Latin tongue in the hall at their meals. Several of the fellows by that practice had attained to the greatest readiness and elegancy also.[98]

Social consequences of educational expansion

How did this expansion of educational provision affect the literacy of the country at large? Although the evidence is not so scarce as for previous centuries, it is still slight and fragmentary and an uncertain basis for generalization.[99] Original wills and written depositions in the church courts provide evidence from signatures. Wills suggest (what one would expect) that whilst yeomen were often literate, labourers were generally illiterate; but exceptions occur — for instance, among the effects of a labourer who died at Yardley in 1614 were 'certain small books' and 'one pen and ink horn'.[100] Professor Stone has studied other evidence and drawn tentative conclusions. Between 1612 and 1614 the Middlesex justices sentenced 204 men to death for a first offence; 95 of these (47 per cent) successfully pleaded the archaic privilege of benefit of clergy by reading the 'neck verse' and so escaped with branding instead of hanging (the 'neck verse' was the Latin verse – usually Ps. 1i,i – by reading which a person claimed benefit of clergy and so might save his neck). 'This', Stone suggests, 'implies a literacy rate among the total male population of the City which was at least as great [as], and probably greater' than 47 per cent.[101] In 1642 Parliament demanded an oath of loyalty to be taken of the general male population and such returns as were made and survive, bearing holograph signatures or marks, afford further evidence of popular literacy. In eighteen rural parishes of the two Surrey hundreds of Reigate and Tandridge 1,265 males took the oath, of whom one-third (417) signed and two-thirds made their mark. Returns from mainly rural parishes in fourteen scattered counties suggest (again, what one would expect) that literacy was higher in towns than in the countryside and that there it varied considerably from parish to parish, perhaps depending on the presence of a schoolmaster or a puritan minister preaching salvation from reading the Bible. On this evidence, Stone hazards the guess that in about 1640 'the average male literacy rate . . . was probably not less than 30 per cent, varying from 15 to 20 per cent in the rural north and west to up to 40 per cent in the countryside near London; and . . . in some of the larger towns of the south was as high as 60 per cent'.[102] The evidence for women scarcely exists.

Historically, of course, what matters is the level of literacy, and there is no means of measuring this. A safe assumption is that a man who could write his name would be able to read, but the limits of his reading skill are hidden from us – whether a few simple and familiar sentences in the Bible, or a popular political broadsheet, or the learned prose of Hooker and Hobbes. On the other hand, the spread of new ideas did not necessarily depend on a high general level of literacy. Religious and political attitudes must often have been influenced by one literate person reading aloud to groups of less literate neighbours in private homes, alehouses or workshops. Certainly, the diffusion of literacy did not mean the triumph of reason over ignorance and ancestral superstition. Prophecies, ghosts and fairies remained part of folk belief; old women were drowned or burnt as witches; until the age of Newton and Locke even highly educated men accepted astrology.

Literacy levels must very largely have depended on social and economic status and on the material prosperity of the area. By 1640 certain relatively small social groups can be assumed to have been fully literate – the nobility and gentry, the professional men, the merchants and master tradesmen in the towns. Similarly, the illiteracy of most of the lower half of the population can be taken for granted – the domestic servants, shepherds, carters, plough-men, drovers, labourers, paupers, beggars, rogues and vagabonds who made up the common people. Among intermediate groups – yeomen and husbandmen in the countryside, small tradesmen and artificers in the towns – literacy probably varied a good deal, and it may be that some urban working men like cobblers and weavers were more lettered than some rustic yeomen. Nevertheless, generally speaking, educational opportunity and literacy depended on a man's place in society. In the New Model Army of 1645 the majority of infantry privates (poor men by birth) could not write their names, but the troopers (who brought their own horses and tended to be of a higher social class) were often men of some education. Being literate, the cavalry men were the more articulate and politically conscious and so took the lead in the army's intervention in religion and politics after 1647.[103]

The general consequences of these rising educational standards between 1560 and 1640 are inextricably bound up with wider changes in English society during the period. Puritanism, which had been a major influence in extending educational facilities in order to spread Bible reading and scriptural belief, must in its turn have been strengthened and propagated by the spread of literacy. The records of dissenting congregations in Cambridge-shire during the Commonwealth suggest widespread reading ability.[104] Literacy undoubtedly aided the diffusion of revolu-tionary ideas after 1640, providing a reading public of urban artisans and small shopkeepers for the radical pamphleteers. And more generally the dissemination of reading ability among lower social groups must partly explain the change in English prose, from the sophistication and allusiveness of the Elizabethans to the direct, simple, unadorned style of Bunyan and Defoe.

At a higher social level, the new educational attainments of the nobility and gentry helped to fit them for their new role in the modern state.[105] Before the Reformation, kings drew their professional counsellors and civil servants from ecclesiastics trained in canon and civil law and rewarded them with bishoprics and canonries. Cardinal Wolsey, who died in 1531, was England's last great statesman-prelate. After the Reformation the monarchy was served by lay peers and gentlemen, amateur scholars from the universities and the Inns of Court, who were rewarded with hereditary titles and honours. The richest prizes were to be had at court or in the government, and these fell chiefly to the greater nobility and other eminent families; the ordinary gentry tended to live on their rural estates, carrying out the routine administration of the country in their shires as JPs – all things considered, perhaps the most important group of men in England. Bishops had been the great builders and patrons of the arts in the middle ages. Relatively impoverished by the Reformation, they were supplanted in this role by cultivated aristocrats. The monuments of Renaissance England were not cathedrals but palaces like Hatfield, Burghley, Hardwick, Longleat and Wilton. It was to noblemen not bishops that young writers and scholars dedicated their work in hope of place and patronage. Nine Oxford colleges were founded by bishops before the Reformation; none afterwards.

If bishops with some exceptions played a much less prominent part in national affairs than their medieval predecessors, the status of the parish clergy undoubtedly rose. More of them like the gentry were liberally educated products of the grammar schools and universities, though the proportion of graduates varied from diocese to diocese. Oxford and Ely were particularly favoured, as might be expected. In Worcester diocese, only 19 per cent of the clergy were graduates in 1560, 23 per cent in 1580, 52 per cent in 1620 and 84 per cent in 1640.[106] Some clergy came from gentle families; others who lacked gentility by birth came to be accepted as gentry because of their university degrees and their office.

'All the people which be in our country be either gentlemen or of the commonalty' wrote Mulcaster in 1581.[107] This was the fundamental cleavage in Elizabethan and Stuart society – between those who were gentry and those who were not, a difference not only of birth and family but also of deference and privilege. The division was now accentuated by the changes in grammar-school and university education. At all times the gentry

were an ill-defined group, especially at the lower end. Wealth
from land and a coat of arms were the usual criteria, but there
were others, for example gentlemen did not work with their
hands; now they all had the same sort of classical education and
common ties with the same few educational institutions imparting
the same élitist social values. The dichotomy between liberal and
mechanical arts became the most striking feature of the educational system: Latin and Greek were subjects for gentlemen,
merely useful or practical subjects were for tradesmen and
artificers. As Kearney says, 'A classical education . . . served to
mark off the ruling élite from those below it. The classical tag
was a class shibboleth of unerring simplicity.'[108]

*Schoolmaster and
scholar with hornbook,
1622*

By the early seventeenth century, some observers believed that
the vastly expanded grammar schools and universities were producing more educated men than society could absorb. Mulcaster
had pointed this out as early as 1581.[109] In 1611 Francis
Bacon as solicitor-general opposed the foundation of the London
Charterhouse, a combined almshouse and grammar school, on
the grounds that too many grammar schools existed already,
drawing youths from trade and husbandry so that there were
'more scholars bred than the state can prefer and employ'.[110]
The consequent disaffection was seen by some as a potential
threat to public order. Many malcontents were younger sons,
gentry by birth, but denied hope of an inheritance by the growing

custom of primogeniture, which the landed class applied in order to preserve and transmit family estates intact. Well-educated but otherwise unprovided for, some younger sons became clergy (though the church lost some of its attraction for them as the value of livings declined during the century); others as in the past took to trade through apprenticeship; others turned to soldiering, or looked for a wealthy widow. Younger sons of younger sons easily slipped into the tradesman or shopkeeper class, discontented and resentful.[111] Educated men of lowlier origins for whom the church had held out prospects of social advancement found that there were not enough benefices to go round. These 'alienated intellectuals', both gentry and plebeian, easily became critics of the social and political establishment. Many of them espoused puritanism, the religion of dissentients. The clergy among them often became town preachers or schoolmasters (sometimes both), declaring men's equality before God, denouncing tithes, episcopacy and Laudianism; their social and political as well as their religious radicalism helped to prepare the way for the revolution of 1640.[112]

Notes

1 DICKENS, *The English Reformation*, is the standard account and has many references to education.
2 CHARLTON, *Education in Renaissance England*, pp. 41–85.
3 H. S. BENNETT, *English Books and Readers 1558–1603* (Cambridge, 1965). Titles of books published in Elizabeth's reign total 7,130, but the size of imprints is unknown.
4 L. STONE, *The Crisis of the Aristocracy 1558–1641* (Oxford, 1965), pp. 36–53. D. C. COLEMAN reviews the literature of the rise of the gentry to 1966 in *History*, L (1966), pp. 165–78.
5 C. HILL, *Reformation to Industrial Revolution* (Harmondsworth, 1967), pp. 44–7.
6 Ibid., pp. 82–4.
7 W. K. JORDAN, *Philanthropy in England 1480–1660* (London, 1959). For criticism of Jordan's methodology and its effects on his conclusions see *Economic History Review*, XIII (1961), pp. 113–15.
8 JOAN SIMON, *Education and Society in Tudor England* (Cambridge, 1966), pp. 197–214.
9 Ibid., pp. 179–96.
10 AVELING and PANTIN, *Letter Book of Robert Joseph*, p. 265.

11 *Victoria County History Camb.*, III, pp. 450, 462; *Victoria County History Oxon.*, III, p. 231.
12 SIMON, *Education and Society*, pp. 223–67, for the Edwardian Reformation and education.
13 C. W. BOASE, *Register of the University of Oxford* (Oxford Historical Society, 1884), I, pp. xxi–xxv.
14 WOOD, *Reformation and English Education*, pp. 53–6.
15 *Victoria County History Oxon.*, III, pp. 238, 251, 298; *Victoria County History Camb.*, III, p. 358.
16 For examples of the examination of schoolmasters in the diocese of York in 1563–4 see J. S. PURVIS, *Tudor Parish Documents of the Diocese of York* (Cambridge, 1948), pp. 103 ff.
17 WOOD, *Reformation and English Education*, pp. 56–79, 165–76.
18 See Bishop Bancroft's Articles of 1601 for London diocese in W. P. M. KENNEDY, *Elizabethan Episcopal Administration*, III (London, 1924), pp. 343–4.
19 At Bishop Redman's visitation of Norwich diocese in 1597 some eighty schoolmasters were presented but no school dames. J. F. WILLIAMS (ed.), *Bishop Redman's Visitation 1597* (Norfolk Record Society, 1946).
20 A. C. F. BEALES, *Education under Penalty* (London, 1962), pp. 72–87, for clandestine Catholic educational activity.
21 MALLET, *Oxford*, II, pp. 121–3, 240; *Victoria County History Camb.*, III, pp. 192–3.
22 *History*, XLIV (1959), p. 258.
23 Professor Jordan (*Philanthropy*, pp. 142 ff.) seems to attribute too much to religious idealism.
24 P. COLLINSON, *The Elizabethan Puritan Movement* (London, 1967), p. 375; L. STONE, 'The educational revolution in England 1560–1640', *Past and Present*, XXVIII (1964), p. 77.
25 For examples see N. CARLISLE, *Endowed Grammar schools* (2 volumes, London, 1818), I, pp. 129, 152, 221, 508, 616.
26 R. C. CHRISTIE, *The Old Church and School Libraries of Lancashire and Cheshire* (Chetham Society, 1885), pp. 5, 139.
27 References for the examples that follow are too numerous to give. See generally CARLISLE, *Endowed Grammar Schools*, and P. J. WALLIS, *Histories of Old Schools: a revised list for England and Wales* (Newcastle, 1966). Other regional examples in W. K. JORDAN, *The Charities of Rural England* (London, 1961), pp. 52–60, 150–72, 299–360.
28 MARGARET SPUFFORD, 'The schooling of the peasantry in Cambridgeshire 1575–1700', in JOAN THIRSK (ed.), *Land, Church, and People* (British Agricultural History Society, 1970), pp. 131–3.
29 On what follows see PETER LASLETT, *The World We have Lost* (London, 1965), especially chapters 1 and 2.
30 W. G. HOSKINS, 'The rebuilding of rural England 1570–1640', *Past and Present*, IV (1953), pp. 44–59.

31 I. PINCHBECK and M. HEWITT, *Children in English Society from Tudor Times to the Eighteenth Century* (London, 1969), pp. 44 ff.

32 C. S. KENNY, *Outlines of Criminal Law*, 17th ed. by J. W. C. Turner (Cambridge, 1958), p. 74.

33 W. G. HOSKINS, *Midland England* (London, 1949), p. 88.

34 For a general account see T. W. BALDWIN, *William Shakspere's Petty School* (Urbana, USA, 1943).

35 *The English Schoolmaster* (London, 1596; Scolar Press facs., 1968), A.3.

36 *Ludus Literarius* (1612; ed. E. T. Campagnac, Liverpool, 1917), p. 20.

37 *A New Discovery of the Old Art of Teaching School* (1660; ed. E. T. Campagnac, Liverpool, 1913), p. 28.

38 A. HUSSEY (ed.), 'Visitations of the archdeaconry of Canterbury', *Archaeologia Cantiana*, XXV (1902), p. 49.

39 PURVIS, *Tudor Parish Documents*, pp. 190, 193, 194.

40 *Positions* (1581; ed. R. H. Quick, London, 1888), p. 139.

41 A. CLARK (ed.), *Aubrey's Brief Lives* (2 volumes, Oxford, 1898), I, p. 328.

42 E. S. DE BEER (ed.), *The Diary of John Evelyn* (6 volumes, Oxford, 1955), II, p. 6.

43 *Reports of . . . Commissioners . . . concerning Charities*, XXII (1829), p. 230.

44 JANET D. COWE, 'The development of education in Berwick on Tweed' (Durham MEd Thesis, 1969), II, p. 81.

45 *A New Discovery*, p. 25.

46 Mrs Spufford finds that in Cambridgeshire villages about a third of the men licensed to teach the elementary subjects between 1574 and 1604 were graduates and therefore competent to teach grammar. 'The schooling of the peasantry in Cambridgeshire', p. 129.

47 F. WATSON, *The English Grammar Schools to 1660: their curriculum and practice* (Cambridge, 1908), collects together much information.

48 *Ludus Literarius*, p. 25.

49 For grammar-school organization see *A New Discovery*, pp. 213–309.

50 C. W. STOKES, *Queen Mary's Grammar School Clitheroe* (Chetham Society, 1934), p. 61.

51 CARLISLE, *Endowed Grammar Schools*, I, p. 418.

52 'The good schoolmaster', *The Holy and Profane State* (1642), p. 98.

53 Lawson, *Town Grammar School*, p. 80.

54 *Aubrey's Brief Lives*, I, pp. 17, 35–6, 328.

55 York, Borthwick Institute of Historical Research, R.IV.B.c.2, fo. 15ᵛ.

56 J. AYRE (ed.), *The Catechism of Thomas Becon* (Parker Society, Cambridge, 1844), pp. 376–7.

57 *Positions*, pp. 161 ff.

58 M. KAY, *History of Rivington and Blackrod Grammar School* (Manchester, 1931), pp. 71–2, 84.

59 C. H. FIRTH (ed.), *Memoirs of the Life of Colonel Hutchinson* (London, 1906), p. 13.
60 DOROTHY GARDINER, *English Girlhood at School* (London, 1929), pp. 206–26.
61 *An Essay to Revive the Ancient Education of Gentlewomen* (London, 1673), pp. 3, 42–3.
62 T. F. REDDAWAY, 'The Livery Companies of London', *History*, LI (1966), pp. 291–2.
63 O. J. DUNLOP and R. D. DENMAN, *English Apprenticeship and Child Labour* (London, 1912), pp. 60–71.
64 On what follows see CHARLTON, *Education in Renaissance England*, pp. 253–96.
65 AMBROSE HEAL, *The English Writing-Masters and their Copy Books, 1570–1800* (Cambridge, 1931).
66 *The Ground of Arts: teaching the Work and Practice of Arithmetic* (London, 1575), p. ciiii.
67 See below, p. 131.
68 Quoted G. N. CLARK, *Science and Social Welfare in the Age of Newton* (Oxford, 1949), p. 88, note.
69 R. C. LATHAM and W. MATTHEWS, *The Diary of Samuel Pepys*, III (London, 1970), pp. 131, 134, 135, 137.
70 The early matriculation books are imperfect and contemporary calculations usually include college servants. Stone's figures ('Educational revolution', pp. 47–51) are based on J. A. VENN, *Oxford and Cambridge Matriculations 1544–1906* (Cambridge, 1906), but include a conjectural percentage of students who never matriculated.
71 *Victoria County History Camb.*, III, pp. 440, 374.
72 *Victoria County History Oxon.*, III, p. 134.
73 Details in *Victoria County History*, volumes cited.
74 STONE, 'Educational revolution', p. 61. See also JOAN SIMON, 'The social origins of Cambridge students, 1603–1640', *Past and Present*, XXVI (1963), and DAVID CRESSY, 'The social composition of Caius College, Cambridge 1580–1640', *Past and Present*, XLVII (1970).
75 PAUL HENTZNER, quoted J. D. WILSON, *Life in Shakespeare's England* (Harmondsworth, 1968), p. 93.
76 Quoted ibid., p. 92.
77 H. KEARNEY, *Scholars and Gentlemen: universities and society . . . 1500–1700* (London, 1970), p. 71.
78 DAVIS, *Balliol College*, pp. 83–114, for typical changes of the period in one college.
79 *Victoria County History Camb.*, III, pp. 183–5; MALLET, *Oxford*, II, pp. 332–3.
80 KEARNEY, *Scholars and Gentlemen*, pp. 28–33, for 'the rise of the parish clergy'.
81 MALLET, *Oxford*, II, pp. 213–30, 244–6.
82 COLLINSON, *The Elizabethan Puritan Movement*, p. 127.

83 *Victoria County History Camb.*, III, pp. 185–7; KEARNEY, *Scholars and Gentlemen*, pp. 71–6.

84 F. R. JOHNSON, 'Gresham College: precursor of the Royal Society', *Journal of the History of Ideas*, I (1940), pp. 413–38.

85 F. BUSSBY, 'An Ecclesiastical Seminarie and College General . . . at Ripon', *Journal of Ecclesiastical History*, IV (1953), pp. 154–61.

86 On this see J. H. HEXTER, 'The education of the aristocracy during the Renaissance', in *Reappraisals in History* (London, 1961), and STONE, *Crisis of the Aristocracy*, chapter 12. J. T. CLIFFE, *The Yorkshire Gentry from the Reformation to the Civil War* (London, 1969), chapter 4, 'Education and the pursuit of a career', gives examples from one county.

87 F. J. FURNIVAL, 'Queen Elizabeth's Academy', *Early English Text Society* (1869), pp. 1–12.

88 For Farnaby see *Dictionary of National Biography*. In 1623 Sir Arthur Ingram of Temple Newsam, near Leeds, was paying him £20 p.a. for a younger son's 'tabling and teaching'. CLIFFE, *The Yorkshire Gentry*, p. 71.

89 W. PREST, 'Legal education of the gentry at the Inns of Court', *Past and Present*, XXXVIII (1967), pp. 20–39.

90 *Essays Civil and Moral* (Everyman edition, London, 1906), 'Of travel', p. 54. See also Bacon's 'Advice to the Earl of Rutland on his Travels' in JAMES SPEDDING (ed.), *Bacon's Letters and Life*, II (1890), pp. 3–20; and, for one particular tour, R. E. W. MADDISON, 'Studies in the life of Robert Boyle: VII, the grand tour', *Notes and Records of the Royal Society of London*, XX (1965), pp. 51–72.

91 *The Seventeenth Century* (Oxford, 1947), p. 305.

92 Sebastian Castellio (1515–63), Calvinist theologian, humanist and sometime schoolmaster at Geneva; his dialogues on biblical subjects were designed to teach religion and good Latin together. See F. WATSON, *The English Grammar Schools*, pp. 338–40.

93 J. W. CLAY and J. LISTER (eds.), 'The autobiography of Sir John Savile', *Yorkshire Archaeological Society*, XV (1900), pp. 421–3.

94 *Life of Edward, Earl of Clarendon . . . by himself*, I, (Oxford, 1759), pp. 6–9.

95 *Memoirs of Colonel Hutchinson*, pp. 39–47.

96 R. PARKINSON (ed.), *The Life of Adam Martindale* (Chetham Society, 1845), pp. 5–30.

97 A. CLARK, *The Life and Times of Antony Wood*, I (Oxford Historical Society, 1891), pp. 46–9, 107, 108, 129, 131–3.

98 A. E. ROBINSON (ed.), *The Life of Richard Kidder* (Somerset Record Society, 1922), pp. 1–4.

99 Literacy, gauged solely by ability to write one's name, is currently being investigated by the Cambridge Group for the History of Population and Social Structure. See R. S. SCHOFIELD, 'The measurement of literacy in pre-industrial England', in J. R. GOODY (ed.), *Literacy in Traditional Societies* (Cambridge, 1968), pp. 311–25.

100 V. H. T. SKIPP, 'Economic and social change in the Forest of Arden, 1530–1649', *Church, Land, and People*, pp. 110–11.
101 STONE, 'Educational revolution', pp. 43–4.
102 STONE, 'Literacy and education in England 1640–1900', *Past and Present*, XLII (1969), pp. 99–102.
103 C. H. FIRTH, *Cromwell's Army* (London, 1962), p. 40.
104 M. SPUFFORD, 'Schooling of the peasantry in Cambridgeshire', pp. 144–5.
105 STONE, *Crisis of the Aristocracy*, pp. 702–24.
106 C. HILL, *Economic Problems of the Church* (Oxford, 1956), p. 207, citing statistics in Miss D. M. Barratt's Oxford DPh thesis.
107 *Positions*, p. 197.
108 KEARNEY, *Scholars and Gentlemen*, p. 118.
109 *Positions*, pp. 135, 142 ff.
110 *Bacon's Letters and Life*, IV, pp. 252–3.
111 Joan Thirsk, 'Younger sons in the seventeenth century', *History*, LIV (1969), pp. 358–77.
112 Mark Curtis, 'The alienated intellectuals of early Stuart England', *Past and Present*, XXIII (1962), pp. 25–41.

Further Reading

T. W. BALDWIN, *William Shakespere's Petty School* (Urbana, 1943).
T. W. BALDWIN, *William Shakespere's Small Latine and Lesse Greeke* (2 volumes, Urbana, 1944).
K. CHARLTON, *Education in Renaissance England* (London, 1965).
K. CHARLTON, 'The professions in sixteenth-century England', *University of Birmingham Historical Journal*, XII, No. 1 (1969), pp. 20–41.
M. H. CURTIS, 'Education and apprenticeship', in ALLARDYCE NICOLL (ed.), *Shakespeare in His Own Age* (Cambridge, 1965).
M. H. CURTIS, *Oxford and Cambridge in Transition, 1558–1642* (Oxford, 1959).
A. J. FLETCHER, 'The expansion of education in Berkshire and Oxfordshire, 1500–1670', *British Journal of Educational Studies*, XV (1967).
W. K. JORDAN, *Philanthropy in England 1480–1660* (London, 1959).
W. K. JORDAN, 'Social institutions in Kent, 1480–1660', *Archaeologia Cantiana*, LXXV (1961).
W. K. JORDAN, *The Charities of London, 1480–1660* (London, 1960).
W. K. JORDAN, *The Charities of Rural England, 1480–1660* (London, 1961).
H. KEARNEY, *Scholars and Gentlemen: universities and society . . . 1500–1700* (London, 1970).

G. B. PARKS, 'Travel as education', in R. F. JONES, *The Seventeenth Century: studies in the History of English Thought* (Stanford, 1951).

I. PINCHBECK and M. HEWITT, *Children in English Society from Tudor Times to the Eighteenth Century* (London, 1969).

W. R. PREST, *The Inns of Court under Elizabeth I and the Early Stuarts* (London, 1972).

A. L. ROWSE, *The England of Elizabeth* (London, 1950), chapter 12.

JOAN SIMON, *Education and Society in Tudor England* (Cambridge, 1966).

MARGARET SPUFFORD, 'The schooling of the peasantry in Cambridgeshire, 1575–1700', in JOAN THIRSK (ed.), *Land, Church, and People* (British Agricultural History Society, 1970), pp. 112–47.

L. STONE, *The Crisis of the Aristocracy 1558–1641* (Oxford, 1965), chapter 12.

L. STONE, 'The educational revolution in England 1560–1640', *Past and Present*, XXVIII (1964), pp. 41–80.

L. STONE, 'Social mobility in England 1500–1700', *Past and Present*, XXXIII (1966).

A. M. STOWE, *English Grammar Schools in the Reign of Queen Elizabeth* (New York, 1908).

F. WATSON, *The Beginnings of the Teaching of Modern Subjects in England* (London, 1909).

F. WATSON, *The English Grammar Schools to 1660: their curriculum and practice* (Cambridge, 1908).

N. WOOD, *The Reformation and English Education* (London, 1931).

See also pp. 163, 471–3.

CHAPTER V

Education during the puritan revolution

1640–1660

As we have seen, puritans were earnestly convinced of the importance of education. The Bible had set all men free and when all could read and ponder it for themselves the truth would prevail and the Kingdom of God would be at hand. Hence much of the educational investment of the period from 1560 to 1640 was prompted by puritan-inspired charity. During the upheavals of the 1640s and 1650s, when militant puritanism swept away the monarchy, the House of Lords and the bishops, and the country was governed in turn by a puritan Parliament, army and Lord Protector, education (like religion and politics) was endlessly debated and reforming ideas circulated as never before.

This ferment of ideas found expression in a flood of pamphlets and tracts; these were the new organs of public controversy, encouraged partly by the abolition of the Court of Star Chamber in 1640 which freed men from fear of the consequences of propagating anti-establishment views. Much of the intellectual inspiration of the time stemmed from Francis Bacon. He had helped to undermine the respect paid to authority and custom by assailing traditional Aristotelian scholasticism and urging close observation of the actual world by experiment and induction; this was to serve not only the disinterested pursuit of science but also the needs of society – 'the relief of man's estate'. More specifically in education, reforming ideas were stimulated by a foreigner, the Czech Moravian pastor John Amos Comenius, a man internationally recognized as the leading educational thinker of the day, who visited England in 1641 at the invitation of a group of puritans and Baconians actively interested in reforming and extending education. The most influential member of this circle was the Polish-born Samuel Hartlib, a Baltic merchant turned philanthropist, who through his many writings and wide personal contacts was the chief disseminator of Comenian ideas in England.[1] In brief, Comenius believed that the end of education is the comprehension of all nature ('pansophia') through reason, the senses and revelation, and that education should be extended to everybody through a system of graded schools in all towns and villages, using reformed teaching methods and textbooks.

An outpouring of tracts and pamphlets between 1640 and 1660 voiced discontent with prevailing educational conditions and put forward proposals for reform. The most celebrated – and least original – is Milton's tractate *Of Education*, written at Hartlib's suggestion and published in 1644 in the belief that 'the reforming of education . . . be one of the greatest and noblest designs that can be thought on, and for the want whereof this nation perishes'. Although Hartlib and his closest collaborator John Dury had been educated partly on the continent, most of the reformers were products of the school and university system which they criticized, and some had further experience of it as schoolmasters or dons. Hartlib himself had once kept a private academy in Chichester. Milton for about seven years kept one in London. But among the more radical critics there were some who seem to have had little formal education, like Gerrard Winstanley, an ex-tradesman and leader of the 'Diggers', and Richard Overton and William Walwyn among the 'Levellers' – discontented younger sons of middle-class families whose schooling had ended with apprenticeship.[2]

Throughout this controversial literature the same proposals and denunciations recur, and often they are only parts of more ambitious schemes for the reformation of society as a whole. Most striking are the plans for a compulsory, free and universal, or near universal, state educational system. In one form or another these were advanced not only by utopian visionaries like Winstanley and extreme democrats like Overton, but also by Hartlib and Dury and their associates, influential and well-established men such as the London merchant Henry Robinson, William Dell, master of Caius College, and William Petty, the economist.

Petty would have none excluded from education because of poverty or parentage, 'for hereby it hath come to pass that many are now holding the plough, which might have been fit to steer the state'. In 1654 Dell urged the provision of elementary schools in all villages, grammar schools in larger towns, and in the greater towns and cities state-supported colleges or universities to break the monopoly of Oxford and Cambridge. The political theorist James Harrington in his *Oceana* (1656) saw the provision of schools as one of the state's first responsibilities, and Milton in 1659 urged the foundation of schools throughout the land in order to spread knowledge, civility and godliness to 'all extreme parts which now lie numb and neglected'. An anonymous pamphleteer in 1659 advocated an English school in every parish for all children from seven to fourteen, workhouse children attending two hours daily; in every market town a grammar school for scholarly boys from ten to fourteen (sixteen if intended for the university), and supplementary writing and music masters, all receiving fixed state salaries.[3]

The traditional curriculum and methodology of grammar schools and universities came under attack from many of these writers, echoing here the criticisms made earlier by the puritan sectaries of Elizabeth's reign as well as by Bacon and Comenius. Education, they complained, was too much concerned with mere words and knowledge of no practical value; they wanted it to deal with the external world, with the real things for which words are only symbols. Then, declared the schoolmaster George Snell, dedicating his book to Dury and Hartlib, 'Our English youths may no longer be taught to be empty nominalists and verbalists only and to have no knowledge of the necessary things and matters ... but ... be realists and materialists, to know the very things and matters themselves.'[4] On these grounds nearly all condemned the dominance of Latin grammar and Latin authors, and also the conventional memorizing methods of teaching them. The traditional learning contained in books, Winstanley declared, was 'no knowledge, but a show of knowledge, like a parrot who speaks words, but he knows not what he saith'. Others, like William Dell and John Webster, sometime master of Clitheroe grammar school, criticized university education for the same reasons and urged more mathematical and scientific studies using the experimental-inductive method. In the education of young children the importance of sensory perception instead of verbal learning by rote was emphasized by Comenius and his followers. 'Nothing comes into the understanding in a natural way but through the door of the senses' asserted Hezekiah Woodward, echoing Aristotle, in *A Child's Patrimony*. To help reform teaching on this principle, Comenius produced in 1658 the first illustrated school book, the *Orbis Sensualium Pictus*, an introductory Latin vocabulary and reader based on classified pictures of common objects, encyclopedic in range, with appropriate labels and descriptions in Latin and the vernacular. An English edition was brought out in 1659 by Charles Hoole, who also recommended game-like visual aids of various kinds for teaching reading in the petty school.[5]

Social utility and relevance were the criteria which all the reformers applied to the education of their time. They wanted it to be more practical and realistic, less formal and scholastic, and available to all, not just to a small privileged minority. John Dury's *Reformed School* (1650) clearly embodied the ideas of the Hartlib group.[6] Several schemes emphasized technical and vocational training for trades and agriculture. The most utilitarian programme was Winstanley's. Education must fit people to live in his egalitarian, communistic, co-operative society, and therefore what mattered was knowledge of the real world, civic virtues and practical training in basic trades, all directly related to the common good. The academic learning of the schools and universities, he believed, was fit to produce only social parasites like lawyers and clergymen. Religion too formed no part of his educational plan, for with certain other extreme sectaries he held that divine truth comes from mystical revelation independent of reason and knowledge and so is vouchsafed not only to the educated but also the 'despised, the unlearned, the poor, the nothings of this world'.[7]

The inhumanity of school discipline was another aspect of education denounced by the Comenians. Thomas Grantham, who kept a private school in Lothbury Gardens in the City of London, deplored 'the misery that youth groans under in common schools, their pains great, the severity of the master intolerable, schools more like Bridewell than seminaries of learning'.[8] 'Slavish correction with the whip', declared Snell, 'breedeth in the corrected a base and abject spirit, a foul Bridewell face, bitter passions, a dogged ungentle disposition, a very hatred against the school, the teacher, and against learning, which hatred being once rooted is seldom afterwards removed from the heart.' These complaints were sometimes linked with demands for better teachers, 'that the business of education be not, as now, committed to the worst and unworthiest of men; but that it be seriously studied and practised by the best and ablest persons', as William Petty advised Hartlib in 1648, 'Though the unworthiness of many presuming to teach hath cast some aspersion upon the profession', George Snell claimed, 'yet without doubt they who set the foundation stones of all godliness, morality, literature and language ought for estimation to hold the next place of dignity to the best ministers of the Divine Word.'[9]

In some respects these two decades were propitious for large-scale educational advance. The ancient forces of conservatism were temporarily driven underground and new ideas of democracy and equality flourished in an atmosphere of free discussion and debate. Before the king had been executed and the House of Lords abolished, theories of popular sovereignty were argued and demands made for parliamentary reform, including manhood suffrage, and the sweeping away of all manner of privileges. In the New Model Army of 1645 men of education could rise from the ranks to a commission, and promotion depended to some extent on merit and not on social class alone. Some expansion of educational opportunity might well have been expected in this new and unprecedented climate of liberal opinion. The Long Parliament – a remarkably well-educated body, to judge by the number of university men who sat in it – carried out drastic reforms of all kinds and showed many signs of concern for education.[10] But state action during these two decades, however well intentioned, lagged far behind the plans of the reformers. Indeed, it seems very likely that on balance education at the school level rather lost ground, when compared to the developments of the preceding period.

Inevitably in conditions of civil war the orderly, routine work of education suffered, and in those areas most affected the upheaval brought hardship and loss to some schools. There must have been many schoolmasters who went off to trail the pike, or join a troop of horse, or serve as regimental clerk or quartermaster (like Adam Martindale) or as surgeon or chaplain (like John Webster). Others – royalist sympathizers – were expelled from their schools in the years after 1643 by the county commissioners appointed to find out those 'of scandalous life and ill-affected to parliament'. Still more were removed after 1649 for refusing to take the Engagement acknowledging the new Commonwealth. Moreover, some school buildings suffered physical damage during siege operations, as at Ashby-de-la-Zouch and Pontefract, or even complete destruction, as at York and Scarborough; at Scarborough the school had to seek accommodation in part of the neighbouring parish church – a temporary arrangement that lasted until the mid-nineteenth century.

Economic conditions, too, were unfavourable to educational stability in the 1640s and early 1650s. Massive transfers of land, currency dislocation, depressed trade, some bad harvests together with the cost of the war – all these led to falling rents and high prices. Thus, school endowments declined in value, masters suffered poverty and some were driven to abandon teaching in favour of a benefice or town lectureship. In several places there is evidence of an acute shortage of candidates to fill school appointments. Schools suffered financially in other ways. Rent charges due to them on estates which had been sequestrated from royalist delinquents were often hard to recover from the county commissioners, and in the confused conditions of the time tenants of school estates sometimes withheld rents with impunity. Commissioners for charitable uses, appointed to safeguard trusts, endeavoured to protect school endowments by ordering and assisting trustees to sue for lost dues, but the relatively large number of proceedings initiated suggests an unusual amount of misappropriation and abuse. It was a mischance, too, that the abolition of episcopacy and the Church of England's system of administration deprived some schools of the patronage and supervision of the diocesan bishop, which had to some extent previously protected their interests. Political and economic insecurity naturally discouraged philanthropic investment in education.[11] This continued to fall in the 1640s, though there was some recovery of confidence and endowment under the Commonwealth.

In these difficult conditions the assistance provided by the state fell short of the reformers' hopes. However, after 1644 and throughout the Interregnum free schools and colleges were regularly exempted from rate assessment. More important, in 1643 crown lands and lands of delinquent royalists were sequestrated and their administration placed in the hands of county commissioners who were to use the rents to aid grammar schools, among other social and pious works. In 1646 bishops' estates and in 1649 the estates of deans and chapters were nationalized; under an Act of 1649 the expected proceeds of £20,000 a year were to be administered by trustees, £18,000 going to support schoolmasters and preaching ministers, £2,000 to support less well-endowed college heads at the universities. From these funds, grants were made to augment the salaries of particular schoolmasters. For instance, the master of the grammar school at Chester was awarded £36 p.a. and his usher £9; at Salisbury £20 p.a. was granted to the master and £10 to the usher, and a master at Sunderland was allowed £5. 6s. 8d. to teach children writing and arithmetic 'to fit them for the sea or other necessary callings'.[12] Wales profited considerably from these grants, some sixty free schools being set up there between 1651 and 1653. Similarly, awards were made towards augmenting the stipends of the heads of certain colleges at Oxford and Cambridge, but they were soon petitioning for arrears like some of the schoolmasters. How much financial aid was actually given to education is unknown – much less, certainly, than to preaching ministers whom the government was more anxious to sustain. In the end, most of the proceeds of the great confiscations probably went to pay for the new standing army and Cromwell's energetic foreign policy.

Like the schools, the universities suffered disturbance in the tumultuous 1640s. Entrants were only half as many as in the 1630s. The collapse was especially dramatic at Oxford, where admissions in 1645 were only a tenth of what they had been ten years earlier. From 1642 to 1646 Oxford housed the king's court, government and army headquarters. Education practically ceased. The colleges were commandeered. All under sixty, says Anthony Wood, 'were upon military duty', and the juniors who remained were 'debauched by bearing arms and doing the duties belonging to soldiers, as watching, warding, and sitting in tippling-houses for whole nights together'. Cambridge suffered less; predominantly royalist and Laudian at first, it was purged by Parliament in 1644 and presbyterianism then gained control. After the surrender of Oxford in 1646 university royalists there were ruthlessly evicted by parliamentary visitors and Cambridge puritans were imported to fill their places. In 1648–9 new appointments were made to some 200 vacated fellowships. At Wadham College the warden, nine out of thirteen fellows, nine out of fourteen scholars and eleven commoners were put out and replaced.[13]

Puritan attitudes towards Oxford and Cambridge varied. More educated and moderate puritans criticized them for their antiquated Aristotelianism and neglect of experimental science, but paid no great attention to them in their plans for educational reform. What interested Hartlib and his friends was the prospect of founding a universal college on pansophist, Comenian lines – a state-financed scientific research centre like the House of Solomon in Bacon's *New Atlantis*, to do what the universities were failing to do. It was partly to promote an institution of this kind that Comenius had been invited to England in 1641. Nothing came of this, but divers schemes for 'the advancement of universal learning' with government aid were put forward by Hartlib and his circle in London – the so-called 'Invisible College' – right up to the Restoration.[14] Their concern was for social improvement through education, scientific experiment and technology; in their meetings at Gresham College can be seen perhaps the main source of the Royal Society, which was incorporated in 1662.[15]

Among more extreme puritan groups, however, an anti-intellectual and anti-university tradition went back to the Elizabethan sectaries. After 1649 this was mainly represented by the Levellers and Diggers who spoke for the socially and educationally deprived and had strong urban support, especially in London. They hated university learning because of its inutility, its association with social privilege, its irrelevance to godly religion, which they believed had nothing to do with Latin, logic and rhetoric. To Winstanley the universities were 'standing ponds of stinking waters'. Radical groups of this kind were strong in Barebone's Parliament in 1653 and this for a time put the universities' very existence in danger. More moderate opinion prevailed, however, and thereafter the universities resumed their old role as pillars of the social establishment.[16]

Under the relatively conservative Protectorate, Oxford recovered very quickly, its entrants increasing to about 350 a year, which was the level of the 1620s. Matriculations at the two universities together were about the same as in the 1590s. Notwithstanding the visitations and purgings of 'malignants' puritanism gave academic life new vigour. At the undergraduate level, earnest study of the old classical and scholastic curriculum went hand in hand with strict religious observance and close supervision of students' morals, as Richard Kidder found at Cambridge. Anthony Wood testifies to a similar regime in puritan

Oxford: 'discipline, strict and severe; disputations and lectures often; catechising, frequent; prayers, in most tutors' chambers every night'.[17] Mathematical and scientific studies of the new kind attracted some dons. At Oxford, where Cromwell was chancellor from 1651 to 1657, the university 'yielded a harvest of extraordinary good and sound knowledge in all parts of learning', as even the royalist historian Clarendon later admitted. There, the most significant development for the future came from a small club of mathematicians and experimental scientists meeting in Wadham College under the leadership of the new parliamentary warden, John Wilkins, Cromwell's brother-in-law. The activities of this group were a practical demonstration of Bacon's philosophy and their informal gatherings formed a second source of the Royal Society and the scientific revolution of the later seventeenth century.[18]

Another anticipation of future, but more distant, developments were the plans for the extension and reformation of higher education. In 1641 there were petitions to Parliament for universities at Manchester and York to serve the northern counties, but like the earlier schemes for a university at Ripon they came to nothing. Numerous other ineffectual proposals were made for the diffusion of higher education through the founding of local colleges and also of a University of London, which was to consist of a reorganized Gresham College together with several other specialist colleges.[19] In 1651 the citizens of Durham and some of the northern gentry petitioned for a college to be established there in the residences of the expelled dean and canons, and Cromwell commended the plan as one likely to promote 'learning and piety in those poor, rude and ignorant parts'. A college was started in the close in 1657 on his initiative and financed out of the funds of the dissolved cathedral chapter. But it remained poor and small and was not empowered to grant degrees, perhaps because of warnings from Oxford of 'the dangers which threaten religion and learning by multiplying small and petty academies'. When the bishop and canons returned in 1660, with King Charles II and all the other forces of reaction, the college came to an end.[20]

Set against the copious programmes of educational reform put forward so hopefully by puritan progressives, the achievements of the Long Parliament and Protectorate amounted to very little. Socially and academically schools and universities changed hardly at all. Nevertheless, developments in education over the previous hundred years had been revolutionary in extent, and Professor Jordan may be right in claiming that 'in 1660 educational opportunities were more widespread and stronger than they had ever been before or than were ever to be again until well into the nineteenth century'.[21]

'Boyes-Sport' from Comenius, Orbis Sensualium Pictus *(1672)*

Notes

1 G. H. TURNBULL, *Hartlib, Dury and Comenius* (Liverpool, 1947), is the standard authority. For a short account and selected texts see C. WEBSTER, *Samuel Hartlib and the Advancement of Learning* (Cambridge, 1970).

2 R. L. GREAVES, 'Gerrard Winstanley and educational reform in puritan England', *British Journal of Educational Studies*, XVII (1969), pp. 166–76.

3 *Chaos: or, a discourse, wherein is presented . . . a frame of government by way of a Republic.* This particular utopia was to be achieved in daily stages, like the Creation; educational reform was part of the sixth day's work, pp. 51–3.

4 G. SNELL, *The Right Teaching of Useful Knowledge, to fit scholars for some honest profession* (1649).

5 J. A. COMENIUS, *Orbis Sensualium Pictus* (3rd London ed., 1672; facs. reprint, introduction by J. Bowen, Sydney, 1967).

6 *The Reformed School* is printed in WEBSTER, *Samuel Hartlib and the Advancement of Learning*, pp. 139–65.

7 G. H. SABINE (ed.), *The Works of Gerrard Winstanley* (New York, 1965), especially 'The Law of Freedom' (chapter 5), pp. 576 ff.

8 THOMAS GRANTHAM, *The Brain-breaker's Breaker* (London, 1644), A_2.
9 SNELL, *Right Teaching*, pp. 5, 19–20; W. PETTY, *The Advice of W.P. to Mr Samuel Hartlib* (1649), p. 3.
10 University-educated MPs rose from 35 per cent in 1593 to 57 per cent in 1640. STONE, *Crisis of the Aristocracy*, p. 688.
11 J. E. STEPHENS, 'Investment and intervention in education during the Interregnum', *British Journal of Educational Studies*, XV (1967), pp. 253–62.
12 C. H. FIRTH and R. S. RAIT (eds.), *Acts and Ordinances of the Interregnum 1642–1660*, I (London, 1911), p. 879; LEACH, *Charters*, pp. 536–8. For government intervention generally see W. A. L. VINCENT, *The State and School Education 1640–1660* (London, 1950), pp. 58–81, 94–108.
13 MALLET, *Oxford*, II, p. 263.
14 J. J. O'BRIEN, 'Commonwealth schemes for the advancement of learning', *British Journal of Educational Studies*, XVI (1968), pp. 30–42.
15 C. WEBSTER, 'The origins of the Royal Society', *History of Science*, VI (1967), pp. 106–28.
16 KEARNEY, *Scholars and Gentlemen*, pp. 110–28.
17 See above, p. 140; WOOD, *Life and Times*, I, p. 300.
18 B. J. SHAPIRO, *John Wilkins* (Berkeley, USA, 1969), pp. 118–47.
19 WEBSTER, *Samuel Hartlib and the Advancement of Learning*, pp. 59–60.
20 G. H. TURNBULL, 'Oliver Cromwell's college at Durham', *Durham Research Review*, III (1952), pp. 1–6.
21 *Philanthropy in England*, p. 48.

Further Reading

R. L. GREAVES, *The Puritan Revolution and Educational Thought* (New Brunswick, 1969).

M. JAMES, *Social Problems and Policy during the Puritan Revolution* (London, 1930).

C. D. ROGERS, 'Education in Lancashire and Cheshire 1640–1660', *Transactions of the Historic Society of Lancashire and Cheshire* (1972), pp. 39–56.

W. A. L. VINCENT, *The State and School Education 1640–1660* (London, 1950).

F. WATSON, 'The state and education during the Commonwealth', *English Historical Review*, XV (1900), pp. 58–72.

C. WEBSTER, *Samuel Hartlib and the Advancement of Learning* (Cambridge, 1970).

C. WEBSTER, 'Science and the challenge to the scholastic curriculum 1640–1660', in *The Changing Curriculum*, History of Education Society (London, 1971), pp. 21–35.

See also pp. 225, 471–3.

CHAPTER VI

Education and society in pre-industrial England
1660–1780

The Restoration and education

The restoration of the monarchy in 1660 meant the restoration also of the House of Lords, the bishops and the Church of England, and a union of clergy and gentry in defence of the establishment against a resurgence of militant puritanism and republicanism. The gentry who composed the Cavalier Parliament elected in 1661 were inspired after their deprivations by feelings of revenge and self-preservation, and the series of Acts known as the Clarendon Code was intended to purge church and government of all puritan dissidents.

In 1662 the Act of Uniformity required all clergy, dons, schoolmasters and tutors to subscribe to a declaration of conformity to the Church of England's liturgy and to repudiate any obligation to change the government in church or state. Furthermore schoolmasters were to have the bishop's licence, and the penalty for teaching unlicensed was imprisonment and fine. This was the first time that subscription was required specifically by statute for the licence: previous statutes in 1581 and 1604 had implied this, but the only form of subscription actually prescribed had been that demanded since 1604 by canon law. Some 1,760 clergy and 150 dons and schoolmasters are estimated to have been evicted as dissenters under the Uniformity Act. To penalize them further, the Five Mile Act of 1665 made it illegal for any nonconformist minister to come within five miles of a corporate town upon pain of fine, and no nonconformist might teach in any public or private school.

For more than two centuries social, religious and political life in England was profoundly influenced by this and other repressive legislation of the Cavalier Parliament. Since Elizabeth's reign the state church had included within its fold numerous minorities of puritan malcontents, but after the Restoration it could no longer be pretended that all men belonged to the Church of England. For the first time protestant nonconformists, like Roman Catholics, were cast out, isolated and persecuted, and community life in town and village was split as never before. England became a divided society, and nonconformists second-class citizens. Prevented from teaching, excluded from the universities and thus from those occupations which required a university education, and barred too from politics and public office, dissenters tended to turn to industry and commerce. In general, nonconformity came to be identified with the trading middle classes of the towns. Theological differences among them soon led to the emergence of separate denominations – Presbyterians (some tending to unitarianism), Congregationalists and Baptists being the chief ones. Political and social disabilities and hostility to the Church of England provided a common bond, however, and over the years they developed as a whole a characteristic nonconformist conscience and outlook – critical, serious, independent, hardworking, resentful. This division of English society into 'Church' and 'Chapel' has deeply affected the history of education.

During the thirty or forty years following the Act of Uniformity, episcopal licensing was enforced as never before, though its effectiveness at any time still varied from diocese to diocese, depending on the vigilance of particular bishops. Usually the candidate presented himself at the bishop's registry, furnished with nomination papers from the school trustees or patrons, or testimonials from parishioners in the case of a private teacher, and there before the bishop's officer he subscribed under the 77th canon of 1604 to the royal supremacy, the Book of Common Prayer and the Thirty-nine Articles, and also made the statutory declaration demanded by the Act of 1662 renouncing rebellion and accepting the Anglican liturgy.[1] Thus the diocesan subscription books are valuable evidence for the distribution and qualifications of schoolmasters at this period.

The nonconformists of 1662 were the more conscientious and uncompromising of the puritans of the revolutionary era. Until 1689 they lived in fear of gaol, fines and confiscations. Even so, in the face of their educational disabilities some of them defied the law by opening schools – for the dual purpose of providing a general education for nonconformist youth and a theological training for their own pastorate. The earliest were, not unnaturally, kept by dons or graduate clergy of the commonwealth period who had been evicted in 1662, and out of conviction or habit taught the traditional classical curriculum; but the reforming 'realistic' ideas of Hartlib's circle still had influence, and modern subjects, reminiscent of Dury's *Reformed School*, were soon introduced alongside the classics. Educationally, the nonconformist academies combined the functions of grammar school and university for those excluded by the law, but by the end of the century some of them were also educating Anglicans who preferred them to the traditional schools. Thus, though never very numerous, the academies became a feature of English education and, with considerable changes, they lasted until the end of the eighteenth century, strongly influencing other forms of education.[2]

To escape the penalties of the law, the early nonconformist academies avoided the towns, and sometimes migrated from one place to another when they had attracted the attention of the local justices. They were small, domestic, private establishments, perhaps a dozen or a score of boys and young men living with the tutor's family. Some twenty or more are recorded from this early period. Two that are well known because they produced some distinguished pupils were in Stoke Newington, in the country north of London outside the five-mile limit, each kept by an ex-Oxford tutor. At one of them Isaac Watts was educated, and at the other Samuel Wesley and Daniel Defoe, both of whom left some account of their training. Richard Frankland, a former Cambridge don and tutor at Cromwell's Durham College, evicted from Bishop Auckland, opened an academy at Rathmell in the remote fell country near Settle in 1668. In its thirty years' existence it moved six times, ending where it had started. At one time it had as many as eighty students and Frankland had two assistants. Besides the classics, the teaching included Hebrew and theology, philosophy and science. Most of the students were prepared for the Presbyterian ministry, but some went into other occupations, including medicine, after further training at Edinburgh, where, as at the other Scottish universities, there was no religious bar to admission.[3]

By the Toleration Act of 1689 protestant nonconformists – except unitarians – were granted freedom of worship (a reward for their support of William III in the Glorious Revolution of 1688), and the penalties against teaching, though unrepealed, became largely inoperative. Thus, the academies were able to function more openly, and they spread accordingly. The chief enemies of dissent were the Anglican clergy and the squirearchy, twin mainstays of Toryism, and there was a danger of renewed persecution as the Tory interest grew in Anne's reign. In 1702 the convocation of Canterbury noted with alarm 'how the numbers of non-licensed schools and seminaries are multiplied and the dangers arising from their daily increase'.[4] The Tory high-church parson Henry Sacheverell assailed the dissenters' academies with inflammatory violence in 1709 as 'illegal seminaries' planted up and down the kingdom like so many 'schismatical universities' in opposition to the established church. By the Schism Act of 1714 the new Tory ministry aimed to destroy the nonconformists' educational system and re-establish the Anglican monopoly by means of subscription and licensing, the only exceptions being for tutors in noblemen's families and for teachers of reading, writing, arithmetic or any part of mathematics relating to navigation (because this would plainly have operated against the nation's commercial interests).[5] Although the Act was not repealed until 1719 the Hanoverian succession and the return of the Whigs in 1715 made it a dead letter. Thereafter the licensing of schoolmasters became an empty and apparently optional formality, and nonconformists were able to teach their own schools unmolested. The Dissenting Schoolmasters Relief Act in 1779 merely legalized this *de facto* situation, though it excluded dissenters from teaching in endowed schools founded before 1689. Catholics were similarly relieved in 1790.[6]

The division of English society into Anglicans and underprivileged non-Anglicans makes the Restoration an event of obvious importance in the history of education. The Restoration has also been blamed for extinguishing the prospects of reform held out by the educational debate of the revolutionary era, and for producing an educational slump – a long period of stagnation after the vigorous expansion of the previous 100 years. Humanitarianism and social concern were certainly much less in evidence after 1660 but education as a whole suffered no immediate setback. What is remarkable is the educational continuity. When the slump came a generation later there were other reasons for it than the Restoration.

The Restoration universities

At the two universities entrants rose to a peak of about 850 in 1670, about as many as in the 1620s, and this was not to be surpassed until the mid-nineteenth century. True, soon after 1660 there were complaints by Commonwealth dons of the licence and frivolity of the new 'cavalier' students, who wasted their time at plays, taverns and coffee houses. Anthony Wood, chief reporter of the Oxford scene, sourly deplored the decay of learning and the new generation of scholars who lived like gentlemen, keeping dogs and horses and turning their rooms and coal-holes into places for storing bottles, though his experience did not go back as far as the pre-war years when students of this kind must have been common.[7] The intellectual standards of the universities were sustained by 'the interval men' as Wood called them – those who had reached academic maturity during the Interregnum, like Wren and Locke at Oxford. At the Restoration no drastic purge of dons occurred: the majority continued in their places unaffected by it. For some colleges this was a period of prosperity and academic distinction.

Undergraduate studies consisted as before of the Latin, and to a lesser extent the Greek, poets, orators and historians, with rhetoric and Aristotelian logic and philosophy, mainly from Latin commentators. For the continued predominance of Latin there were still sound reasons: it remained the international language of learning, necessary not only for scholars but also for gentlemen of culture, as Locke and others insisted. It lost something of its practical utility only as translations and writings in the vernacular became more common in the eighteenth century, making knowledge of European languages more important. This concentration on classical studies and scholastic philosophy attracted less criticism than the form of the degree exercises; Locke, like some others, condemned the disputations (but not apparently while he was still a tutor) on the ground that they 'lead not men so much into the discovery of truth, as into a captious and fallacious use of doubtful words'.[8] Gradual relaxation of the statutes regarding residence and exercises, especially for higher degrees, now began to make them much less stringent than was originally intended.

However, it is the universities' activity in scholarship and research outside the official studies that invalidates the accusation of decline. Some of the most erudite and productive scholars of the age, in both traditional and modern branches of learning, were to be found there. In two spheres particularly this was a most fruitful period. The interest in scientific experiment which had been so marked a feature of Cromwellian Oxford did not by any means cease at the Restoration. The Royal Society was a natural and uninterrupted continuation of the activities of scientists previously meeting in Oxford and London and some of its leading members continued to have Oxford connections. Robert Hooke left Oxford to become the society's professional experimenter, but Boyle lived there privately, John Wallis remained professor of geometry from 1649 to 1703, and Wren, one of the founder members, was professor of astronomy from 1661 to 1673 with interests in mechanics, medicine and anatomy before he took up architecture. The chief feature of the science of this period continued to be its concern with experimentation and practical application in the Baconian tradition, and this was present in the Royal Society's activities from the beginning.[9] Medical studies based on empirical observation attracted serious attention at Oxford with men like Richard Lower and Thomas Willis, both Fellows of the Royal Society. It was Locke's study and practice of medicine that led to his election as FRS in 1667, and thus to his close connection with the scientific movement and to his conviction of the importance of science in a liberal education.[10] To serve as a centre for experimental science the Ashmolean Museum of natural history was opened at Oxford in 1683.

Incomparably the greatest scientist of the age was Isaac Newton at Cambridge. Of relatively poor yeoman stock, he was educated at the local grammar school at Grantham and as a sizar at Trinity College, and this was his academic home from 1661 to 1696. His work on the binomial theorem and differential and integral calculus in his early twenties led to his election to the recently established Lucasian chair of mathematics in 1669 when he was twenty-seven. Although he at first experimented with optics and telescopes in the manner of the time, he soon turned to abstract mathematics and the explanation of the physical world by mathematical concepts. Through his influence mathematics became an important study at Cambridge and eventually dominated the arts course.[11] An unprecedented amount of scientific investigation and publication between 1660 and 1690 was the work mainly of university-educated scientists.

Hardly less remarkable was the universities' contribution to the study of history at this time. Scientific activity based on experiment and induction created an atmosphere favourable to the growth of a new kind of historical scholarship, one founded on the systematic collection and critical study of manuscript remains, and the Restoration era forms a landmark in the development of historical research. Although history formed no part of official university studies, the scholars who distinguish this period – men like Anthony Wood, George Hicks and Thomas Hearne, for example – were all university men, some of them dons or librarians; and it was from the university presses, both reorganized during this period, that their massive folios issued. 'The Restoration', writes Professor D. C. Douglas, 'began an epoch in English scholarship as surely as it marked a change in English politics'[12] and the universities' part in this activity further refutes charges of reaction and decadence.

Charity schools, grammar schools, academies and tutors

Nor does the evidence suggest stagnation at the school level. The chief source of information about the number and spread of schools in Restoration England are the bishops' subscription books kept after the Act of 1662. These contain the autograph signatures of masters teaching in all manner of schools, both public and private, and variously designated grammar, common, English, 'Reading, Writing and Arithmetic', ABC and petty. They show how widespread were schools of all kinds. Even so, the picture they present is incomplete, for many masters clearly eluded subscription and women, who probably supplied much of the more rudimentary schooling, hardly ever subscribed.[13]

At the elementary level this period saw a large increase in the foundation of endowed parish schools supplying the rudiments of literacy to the children of the poor, under the supervision of the vestry or *ad hoc* trustees. After about 1685 a new method of financing charity schools by subscription resulted in schools being established in numerous London city parishes, by dissenters as well as Anglicans, and managed by committees of subscribers. After 1699 this idea was taken up by the new Society for Promoting Christian Knowledge as the basis of its plan to spread charity schools throughout the land.[14] With the progressive decline of apprenticeship in humbler trades, the 1690s also saw new workhouses established in London and some of the larger towns, with industrial schools attached to give pauper children vocational training. In a report to the Board of Trade in 1697 Locke recommended the institution of workhouse schools of this kind in every parish for all poor children over three and under fourteen.[15]

Generalization is difficult but the indications are that taken as a whole the endowed grammar schools flourished as much during the twenty or thirty years after the Restoration as before. The most eminent grammar school in England at this time was Westminster under Dr Richard Busby, the outstanding schoolmaster of the age, whose pupils included Locke, Wren, Hooke, Dryden and some thirteen future bishops. A pioneer investigation of the grammar schools by questionnaire was undertaken in the 1670s by Christopher Wase, printer to Oxford University and himself a former headmaster, and the results were embodied in his book *Considerations concerning Free Schools* in 1678. Many of them were clearly as active and efficient as they had ever been, sending a succession of boys to the universities and supplying their local communities with merchants' clerks, scriveners, apothecaries, printers, attorneys and booksellers. However, in country areas some grammar schools were now becoming quasi-English or even petty schools, because of poor endowments and the lack of local demand for classical teaching. Others were meeting competition from small private grammar schools taught by country clergymen in their parsonages, or from academies kept by professional teachers in the towns. The Coventry schoolmaster, replying to Wase's inquiry in 1675, complained that in Warwickshire 'all our schools generally are as to the number of scholars lower than formerly they have been, for that many others about us take upon them to teach private schools to the great detriment of our public schools'.[16]

The view that the reactionary forces reinstated by the Restoration brought to an untimely end the movement for reforms in curriculum, teaching and discipline which had marked the puritan era is hardly supported by the evidence. If the criticisms of the old grammatical routine were less voluble they nevertheless continued to be made. In 1661 Abraham Cowley, poet, physician and FRS, deplored 'the loss which children make of their time at most schools, employing, or rather casting away six or seven years in the learning of words only, and that too very imperfectly'.[17] Other writers in the 1660s and 1670s criticized the schools' preoccupation with words and advocated study of the real world. Protests continued to be made, too, against the barbarity of school punishment, and an attempt was made in 1669 and again 1698 to check this by parliamentary action.[18]

Notwithstanding the progress made by science and the lively interest it aroused in the universities and academies, science made little or no impact on the grammar schools. It is true that in 1673 the London charity school, Christ's Hospital, established a subsidiary mathematical school to teach 'the art of navigation and the whole science of arithmetic', and that in 1701 a school of mathematics was founded at Rochester by Sir Joseph Williamson, an early FRS. In general, however, grammar schools remained firmly committed to the old classical curriculum and taught little else. This was not so with some of the increasingly fashionable private schools or academies mainly in or around London, which offered a much more varied course of studies with less emphasis on the classics. In 1657 the earl of Westmorland had two sons at a private school of this kind in Twickenham, paying £100 p.a. for their board and tuition and servants.[19] Another school at Tottenham in the 1670s claimed to teach Latin by an easier and shorter method than the common one, and also geometry, arithmetic, astronomy and geography, with gardening, dancing, singing and music. 'Ordinary persons' were admitted at '£20 per annum or under to learn what they please; gentlemen at £25 per annum; and persons of greater quality at £30'. The grandsons of the earl of Anglesey were said to be pupils at the school.[20]

The education of noblemen and gentlemen was a subject that attracted much attention at this time. Because of the great influence they exercised in society their proper training was regarded as a matter of national importance.[21] Some gentlemen themselves took a serious interest in the problem. The earl of Clarendon in exile in France about 1670 reflected on gentlemen's education at home and school, at the university and the Inns of Court and through travel abroad, discussing opposing views in dialogue form but revealing his own conservative, traditionalist sympathies.[22] About the same time James Boevey, a London merchant turned Gloucestershire squire, was committing his thoughts on the subject to writing, noting down ideas on the rearing of young children by nurse and parents, the subjects to be learned at home and school (not only grammar, logic and rhetoric but also arithmetic, accounts, geometry, geography and astronomy), the role of foreign travel, the tutor's duties and the choice of a profession. Some of his ideas clearly recall the child-centred, sense-perception theories of Comenius and his followers.[23]

More novel and remarkable is the design of John Aubrey, the friend of so many cultivated gentlemen of his time. In his *Idea of Education*, jotted down between 1669 and 1684, he rejected private education by domestic tutors in favour of public education, not in endowed schools but in certain aristocratic academies ('at once both school and university') of his own devising. There were to be at least seven of these, promoted by distinguished sponsors and distributed about England and Wales. Each was to be established in a fine house with a park, and to consist of at most sixty boys between nine and seventeen under a 'provost' and three well-paid ushers (these – remarkably – to come from Calvinist Scotland or Switzerland), all of them to be unmarried laymen. Aubrey was clearly influenced by Baconian–Comenian ideas, and particularly by the mathematician John Pell, once one of Hartlib's close associates. He was much impressed, too, by the new mathematical school of Christ's Hospital. Latin and Greek he believed to be essential (though they should be taught by a reformed method) and to these he added other traditional subjects – logic, rhetoric and ethics; but he attached especial importance to arithmetic and geometry, and also included in the curriculum civil law, politics and economics. When the course was completed, the young gentlemen were recommended to undertake a period of foreign travel or to study chemistry. Throughout, he was concerned that they should be trained in good manners and knowledge of the world as well as in book learning. Like the Comenians, to 'whipping, cuffing and brow-beating' he was firmly opposed – 'there should be nothing here of terror or gehenna to fright youths from the love of learning . . . no such thing as the turning up of bare buttocks for pedants to exercise their cruel lusts.'[24]

Among the nobility and gentry the private tutor was now a usual member of the household establishment where there were children. Samuel Taylor, a newly graduated MA from Cambridge, was engaged in 1662 to instruct the sons of Sir Roger Langley at Sheriff Hutton and was licensed to the appointment by the archbishop of York.[25] As in this instance, the tutor was often a young man fresh from the university, who was paid £20 or so a year, had his own room in the house, dined with the family, and provided intellectual conversation for his employer as well as tuition for his son. Some tutors of experience wrote about the 'breeding up' of gentlemen, advocating private education at home or in small boarding academies rather than public education in the endowed grammar schools. Obadiah Walker, a prominent Oxford don who had been a private tutor and travelling companion, wrote an influential book on the subject in 1673, recommending traditional rather than modern studies but attaching more importance to virtue, urbanity and good breeding than to learning: a gentleman needed to be well informed but not erudite.[26] Character formation, good manners and knowledge of the world were a main concern, too, of Jean Gailhard, who as 'tutor abroad to several of the nobility and gentry' strongly favoured private training; his book was dedicated to his patron, the earl of Huntingdon.[27] Both these writers accepted the principle that even gentlemen must be inured to hardship, and so approved of corporal punishment, though only as a last resort.

Locke on education

These ideas and trends of the time found their most influential exponent in John Locke. The son of a Somerset attorney, he was nominated to Westminster school by a gentleman of the county and from there passed to Cromwellian Oxford with a closed scholarship at Christ Church. After being a don there he became tutor to the future earl of Shaftesbury's son, and later travelling companion to the son of the financier baronet Sir John Banks. From 1684 he wrote a series of letters to a kinsman, Edward Clark, a Somerset squire, advising him on the upbringing of his eldest son and heir, and these formed the substance of *Some Thoughts concerning Education* published in 1693.[28] Locke is here concerned with the education only of gentlemen – the 3 or 4 per cent of the population who constituted the ruling class – for as he wrote elsewhere, mental culture was not for men of low condition, only for those with means and leisure, 'who by the industry and parts of their ancestors have been set free from a constant drudgery to their backs and their bellies'. In the conditions of the time it could hardly have occurred to him that all children should be educated, and certainly not educated along the same lines, as we now accept. Men were educated according to their social rank and even 'a prince, a nobleman and an ordinary gentleman's son should have different ways of breeding'. For Locke, education served a practical and vocational end. Although he admitted differences of natural endowment he believed that men of all social classes are born with a mind that is blank, and that 'nine parts of ten are what they are, good or evil, useful or not, by their education'.[29] And by education he meant mainly sense-impression and experience, not the formal training of natural faculties by drill and memory, which was the traditional view.

Obviously, Locke owed much to earlier writers, classical, Renaissance and modern, but his importance lies not so much in adapting these for his own age as in the new direction he gave to educational thought through his insight into human understanding. From this springs his respect for children and their natural rights, and his insistence on their special needs, interests and capabilities. From this, too, stems his conviction of the importance of the early years in the formation of character, and his view that education means less the acquisition of knowledge than the cultivation of mental and physical powers through habit, formed by precept and practice. Thus, for much of the learning gained in school and university – 'Latin, logic and quibbling' – he has no use. Nevertheless, he believes Latin is as 'absolutely necessary' to the gentleman as to the scholar, but that it should be taught by conversation and reading, not by grammar rules. Latin, however, is much less important than breeding, knowledge of the world, and some understanding of the new experimental science. To this end he recommends for gentlemen's sons not the public school but the private tutor, and the tutor 'should have something more in him than Latin, more than even a knowledge in the liberal sciences. He should be a person of eminent virtue and prudence, and with good sense have good humour, and the skill to carry himself with gravity, ease and kindness in a constant conversation with his pupils.'[30]

Utility is Locke's criterion of subjects for study: they should be those 'which will be of most and frequentest use'. Thus, besides reading and writing, he would have the young gentleman learn drawing, shorthand and French; later, geography, arithmetic, geometry, chronology, history, some law and natural philosophy; and certain social accomplishments such as dancing, riding the great horse, and painting, gardening and craftwork; but he is not enthusiastic about music (real proficiency demands too much time), or about fencing (skill in this leads to duelling). The finishing touches to his education are best provided, Locke advises, by the grand tour, when, accompanied by his tutor, the young man visits the various countries of Europe to improve his foreign languages and add to his 'wisdom and prudence by seeing men and conversing with people of tempers, customs and ways of living different from one another'. The usual age for this was from sixteen to twenty-one, but he would have it either earlier, when languages are more easily mastered, or later, when a tutor might not be necessary.[31]

Locke's advice on managing children, like his advice on what they should study, shows remarkably 'modern' insight. Children should be allowed to do without punishment whatever is natural for them to do at their age; their learning should be made easy and pleasurable and based on activity and curiosity rather than rule and rote, on discovery and experience rather than dictation and authority; and it should be inspired at all times by affection, not fear. Although he was concerned with the education of only a small social élite, 'nearly all the rules that he gives are universal' as his earliest French translator observed in 1695.[32]

Undoubtedly Locke had great influence. His book went through fifteen English editions by 1777 and made his ideas part of eighteenth-century educational thought. Private education at home and in the academies was much more influenced by him than public education in the grammar schools. One of his enthusiastic disciples in the early eighteenth century, John Clarke, master of Hull grammar school, devoted himself in his writings to persuading other public schoolmasters to follow his example and reform their teaching on Locke's principles. But generally Locke's impact on grammar schools was small: Latin with some Greek continued to predominate, formal training by drill and repetition persisted and fear of the rod and the master's displeasure remained the chief incentive for learning.[33]

Educational recession in the eighteenth century

If the Restoration was not immediately followed by reaction and depression, except in the case of the nonconformists' educational deprivation, something like a recession had set in by the end of the century. However, this was to affect mainly the public or endowed sectors; their relative inactivity and inefficiency stimulated the extension of educational opportunity by private enterprise.

In the 1680s Oxford and Cambridge began a decline which lasted 100 years. After 1685 both were disturbed by dissensions brought about by James II's attempts to romanize them, and then by the non-juror schism which followed the accession of William and Mary in 1689. Clerical and political feuds disrupted college and university life and dissipated intellectual energies, especially at Oxford. Numbers began to fall, markedly at Cambridge. Entrants to the two together are estimated to have averaged about 500 a year in the 1690s, compared to over 1,000 in the 1630s.[34] Simultaneously, a widening gap developed between the conservative, gentlemanly studies of the universities and the commercial and professional needs of the age. Obadiah Walker, later one of James II's Catholic converts at Oxford, put the traditionalists' case when he wrote in 1673: 'In these parts of the world, we seem to run after sciences, and think them to be all things; whereas the great and universal business of our life, especially active, is wisdom, prudence, nobleness and liberty of spirit. Sciences are necessary to . . . whom it concerns to know them; in other persons wisdom is the chiefest.'[35] By the end of the century, interest in science was on the wane. The Royal Society itself was much less active, and science was becoming a dilettante interest rather than a means of social improvement.

Admissions to the Inns of Court also fell in the 1690s, reaching the lowest point for 100 years. The Inns had ceased to be academies for gentlemen, and had ceased (since the Civil War) to provide instruction in the law for would-be lawyers. Residence requirements were relaxed in much the same way as for higher degrees at the universities; all that the intending barrister had to do was to keep terms by eating dinners in hall, and before being 'called' perform exercises as perfunctory and meaningless as those for university degrees were becoming. His real training came from private study and apprenticeship.

Considered as a whole, the grammar schools also began to decline, and this is the most significant feature of their eighteenth-century history: numbers attending them fell, and new foundations were rare.

Reasons for this prolonged depression in public education can only be conjectured. Wedded to the classical curriculum which no longer attracted the trading and farming middle class, the grammar schools lost ground to English schools and private academies which offered more 'useful' or vocational courses, and the more rural and poorly endowed among them tended to become village petty schools. At the universities the Anglican monopoly kept out all dissenters in an age when dissent was on the increase and identified with some of the most enterprising, industrious and resourceful sections of the community. Clerical conservatism also shut the door against science, and the universities' refusal to come to terms with the new economic interests of the country further limited them to the role of finishing schools for the nation's gentlemen and the clergy of the state church.

But there were other developments which no doubt contributed to the falling numbers at grammar schools and universities. With rising rents and more specialized agriculture, small freeholders and tenant farmers were poorer than they had been, and there was less surplus to pay for a son's extended education. Moreover, the church offered fewer material prospects for the socially uninfluential than it had earlier in the seventeenth century. In Hanoverian England, it was fashionable for the younger sons of the gentry to become clergy and inevitably they secured the choicest benefices and preferment appropriate to their family connections; the poorest livings, stipendiary curacies and chaplaincies were left for the more plebeian clergy, and for them pluralism became a condition of survival. In 1721 over half the benefices were worth under £50 a year, nearly a quarter under £30, one in eight under £20; and an unbeneficed curate or chaplain might expect no more than £5 a year.[36] This fall in the social status and prospects of the rank and file of the clergy must have discouraged many poorer men from seeking the sort of education which for most of them led only to ordination.

Other social changes affected demand for the traditional type of education designed for gentlemen of leisure. In the eighteenth century, as a result of strict primogeniture and the increase of entails, together with rising agricultural prosperity for the big capitalist investor, land ownership tended to become concentrated in a few very wealthy families of nobility and upper gentry at the expense of smaller gentry and freeholders.[37] Estates were preserved intact and transmitted undivided to the eldest son, so that younger sons looked for other careers and found them in trade or the professions, in the revenue services, the army or navy or the East India Company. The contraction of the land market also made it more difficult for successful city merchants and entrepreneurs to become gentlemen by buying country estates. Instead, they and their sons ploughed their capital back into foreign trade or invested in government funds, banking and insurance and later in manufacturing industry. For these activities there were more fitting kinds of education than the Latin and Greek classics and the remnants of scholastic philosophy. Not until the nineteenth century was there a new rising professional and commercial middle class buying land and a prestige education in order to gain the status of gentlemen, and this gave rise to the Victorian public school and brought numbers at Oxford and Cambridge once more to their early seventeenth-century level.

Among the ruling élite a view strongly held throughout the eighteenth century, and well into the nineteenth, was that too much literacy among the population at large was a danger to the established order. The social system, divinely ordained, depended on a plentiful supply of labourers and servants; to educate them above their station would make them dissatisfied with their lot and invite social disruption. The earl of Newcastle had advised the exiled Charles II in the 1650s that 'The Bible under every weaver and chambermaid's arm hath done us much hurt . . . the universities abound with too many scholars. . . . But that which hath done most hurt is the abundance of grammar schools and Inns of Court.'[38] This belief gained ground in the years following the Restoration when it came to be accepted that the tumults of the 1640s and 1650s had resulted from the earlier overproduction of educated men whom society could not absorb. Christopher Wase's inquiry in the 1670s 'whether the free grammar schools of England be so notoriously multiplied beyond their occasion' was undertaken because of the 'opinion commonly received that the scholars of England are over proportioned to the preferments for lettered persons', with consequent danger to the state.[39] The philosopher Thomas Hobbes in his *Behemoth*, published in 1679, blamed the universities for the rebellion: through their teaching of classical antiquity they had, he believed, imbued men with political ideas which identified liberty with republicanism and monarchy with despotism. Thus, the general attitude of the governing class was that liberal education should be confined to their own kind, and that elementary education for the poor should be minimal, designed to inculcate mainly practical religion, social obedience and low-level occupational skills. As a result society was probably much more static in the eighteenth century than it had been in the period from 1530 to 1660.

Religion, which had been a driving force for educational expansion in puritan England, became in the eighteenth century a prop of the establishment, and the Anglican hierarchy shared the unsympathetic and pessimistic attitude to popular education of the propertied class with which it was closely identified. Sectarian rivalry between Anglicans and dissenters certainly stimulated some educational activity, mainly at the humble level appropriate to the poor, but it was of small importance compared with the puritan-inspired educational philanthropy of a century earlier.

Lastly, in this search for possible explanations of the educational recession, one must remember the veneration paid in the eighteenth century to private property and the rights that went with it. Crimes against property were punished by the law as harshly as crimes against the person. Property owners enjoyed almost complete immunity from external interference and inquiry. Thus, endowed corporate institutions of all kinds – schools, colleges, universities, town corporations, the church – not being answerable to public opinion, conducted their affairs in secret and not always efficiently or honestly or with the public good in mind. A 'place' in government service, a college fellowship, a professorship, a grammar-school mastership, a benefice – these were regarded as pieces of freehold property which one enjoyed with no fear of accountability to stimulate a sense of duty. Hence the inertia and creeping paralysis that tended to characterize endowed places of education until the age of reform in the nineteenth century.

Schools for the poor

Such elementary education as was available for the mass of the population in the eighteenth century was provided as in the past by private enterprise, supplemented by philanthropy.

Private-venture schools covered a wide range of scope and competence from English and common schools in towns, some of which were hardly distinguishable from middle-class academies, to the lowliest kind of dame school, where some old woman looked after the village children in her parlour and taught them to read, knit and sew for whatever their parents could afford to pay each week. In larger villages and market towns common day schools which taught reading, writing and arithmetic were typical in a country still predominantly rural and agricultural, with a poor and sparse population. More substantial towns could support schools which aimed higher and prepared their pupils for apprenticeship to the skilled trades, like that advertised in 1740 by 'J. Jones, writing master and accomptant, in Small Street, Bristol': he included spelling, reading, writing, arithmetic and book-keeping, and made a special point of geography – an appropriate subject in a trading seaport.[40] Many villages and hamlets in the deep country had no school at all, because there were too few children to provide a teacher with a living.

Private-enterprise schools were probably small and unorganized; they were usually held in the teacher's own house, and they tended to have an uncertain and intermittent existence. When demand fell, as in times of extreme hardship, they would cease, temporarily or permanently: the teacher would find other work or move to some other place where the prospects for keeping a school seemed better.

During the eighteenth century these private-venture schools were supplemented throughout the country by charity schools founded by philanthropy, either from charitable impulse or ulterior motives. Charity schools to spread literacy and religion among the poor had been founded since before the Reformation, but in much smaller numbers than grammar schools. By the end of the seventeenth century this preference was reversed and educational benefaction was almost wholly directed towards the schooling of the poor, at a suitably elementary level. Being endowed, these charity schools had a more or less guaranteed income and so a more permanent existence than private-venture schools. The founder conveyed property to trustees – often the parish officers – and they paid the yield or a stipulated part of it as salary to a master. In return he was usually required to teach free a specified number of local children nominated by the trustees. Necessity almost always compelled him, however, to admit fee-paying pupils as well, and to that extent he was not easily distinguishable from the private-venture teacher. Indeed, most educational charities consisted of no more than a small annual sum which the trustees paid to a private teacher to give free tuition in his school to an agreed number of poor children.[41]

A well-endowed foundation, however, might provide not only a master's salary but also a schoolhouse, not only free tuition but also free clothing. In 1707 Richard Piggot, citizen and cutler of London, founded a charity school at Shinfield, his birthplace near Reading, endowing it with a farm and other property then worth £42 a year. The master was to have £15 a year and teach twenty poor children gratis with the right to admit others for fees. Reading, writing, accounts and psalmody were the subjects he had to teach. £1 was allowed him for coals to heat the school-room, £1 was payable to the vicar for an annual Founder's Day sermon, 10s. to the trustees for their annual meeting. Children on the foundation were to have an outfit of clothing for Founder's Day, and any surplus was to be devoted to apprenticing them on leaving.[42]

Schools of this kind were augmented in the course of the century by numbers of decayed country grammar schools of older foundation, many of them too impoverished to attract graduates capable of teaching Greek and Latin, for which in any event there might be little or no demand in a pauperized, rural community. Numbers of these in decline admitted girls as well as boys and were hardly different from the charity schools of the time.

Towards the end of the seventeenth century a number of charity schools had been opened in London by public subscription, and, as we have seen, this method of financing new schools was encouraged after 1699 by the Society for Promoting Christian Knowledge as part of its grand design to spread practical Christianity among the godless poor. The society's primary objective was to combat vice and profanity and propagate the gospel and Anglicanism at home and in the colonies: its educa-

As for me and my House, we will serve the Lord, Joshua 24. 15.

ORDERS Read and Given to the PARENTS on the Admittance of their CHILDREN into the CHARITY-SCHOOLS. To be set up in their Houses.

I. THAT the Parents take Care to send their Children to School at the School-Hours, and keep them at Home on no pretence whatsoever, except in Case of Sickness.

II. That they send their Children Clean, Wash'd and Comb'd.

III. That they Correct their Children for such Faults as they commit at Home, or inform their Master of them. Whereby the whole Behaviour of their Children may be the better ordered.

IV. That in regard the Subscribers to this School will take due Care that the Children shall suffer no Injuries by their Masters Correction, which is only designed for their Good; the Parents shall freely submit their Children to undergo the Discipline of the School when guilty of any Faults, and forbear coming thither on such Occasions. So that the Children may not be countenanced in their Faults, nor the Master discouraged in the performance of his Duty.

V. That they set them good Examples, and keep them in good Order when they are at Home.

VI. And that this School may not only serve for the Instruction and Benefit of the Children, but also of their Parents, particularly of such who cannot Read; They for their own sakes, as well as their Childrens, are frequently to call on them at Home to Repeat their Catechism, and to Read the Holy Scriptures, especially on the Lord's-Day, and to use Prayers Morning and Evening in their Families; so that all may the better be informed of their Duty, and by a constant and sincere Practice thereof, procure the Blessing of God upon them.

VII. If the Parents do not Observe the said Orders, their Children are to be dismist the School, and to forfeit their School Cloaths.

Ye Fathers provoke not your Children to Wrath ; but bring them up in the Nurture and Admonition of the Lord; having them in Subjection with all Gravity, Eph. 6. 4. 1 Tim. 3. 4.

Honour thy Father and thy Mother, that it may be well with thee, and thou mayest live long on the Earth, Eph. 6. 2, 3.

LONDON, Printed by *J. Downing* in *Bartholomew-Close* near *Smithfield,* 1708.

tional activities were always subsidiary to this. It did not invent subscription schools and did not establish any itself: it took up the subscription principle and stimulated local endeavours to promote schools for the poor financed in this way. With SPCK encouragement and advice local societies were formed to raise funds by weekly or quarterly subscriptions, and the schools they created were run on lines approved by the SPCK and managed by committees of subscribers, each with a corresponding secretary to keep in touch with the central co-ordinating body. Locally, the initiative usually came from well-disposed clergy, and the subscribers were tradesmen, merchants and local gentry. Inevitably, most of the schools thus established were in London and the larger towns, where contributions were more plentiful. Town corporations sometimes gave generous support, and in cathedral cities the bishop and chapter were prominent patrons. Other income came from church collections, particularly at the annual charity-school sermon, and from offertory boxes in churches and schools.[43]

Schools sponsored by the SPCK were intended for the very poorest children, and in some of the larger and better-supported town schools the children were given a uniform and boarded as well as taught, and often put out as apprentices when their schooling was finished. The curriculum was one considered appropriate for the poor: reading, writing and perhaps some accounts for the boys and sewing for the girls, but the essential object for all was moral and religious discipline and social subordination. In the hymns they sang, the prayers they recited and the sermons they had to listen to, the charity children were constantly reminded of their low estate and the duty and respect they owed their betters. Supporting schools of this kind suddenly became fashionable among the more benevolent well-to-do. Educationally, the poor were very much what the rich made them.[44]

At York two subscription charity schools – a Blue Coat school for forty boys and a Grey Coat school for twenty girls – were established in 1705 in association with the SPCK and with the patronage of the archbishop, the dean and chapter, and the lord mayor and corporation. The children were to be orphans or dependants of poor freemen with large families, and they received free board and tuition, an annual outfit of uniform and were eventually apprenticed to York tradesmen, the boys at fourteen, the girls at twelve.[45] In time some schools of this kind attracted endowments, which ensured their continuity. Some were converted into National schools in the nineteenth century: a few survived little changed into the twentieth, to be closed in the educational reorganization that followed the Act of 1944.

By 1730 the SPCK's activity in this field had largely spent itself. The fashion had passed. Its most successful work had been done in the early years, and its capture by the high church party during the Tory offensive against dissent late in Queen Anne's reign lost it much support and involved it in political and religious controversy that seriously damaged its appeal after the Hanoverian succession. Moreover, although some (like Joseph Addison) had seen these schools 'as the glory of the age we live in', others (like Bernard Mandeville) entertained fears of the social and economic risks of overeducating the poor. Perhaps the SPCK's chief importance was in establishing the tradition of a central body encouraging local effort in school provision – a tradition which was taken up a century later by the National Society and so largely determined the form that state intervention was eventually to take.

One remarkable enterprise inspired by the SPCK was the Welsh circulating-school movement devised about 1730 by Griffith Jones, rector of Llanddowror in Carmarthenshire. He raised, trained and organized a missionary band of unpaid itinerant teachers who travelled round the countryside conducting day and night schools in Welsh for young and old in church, chapel and farmhouse during the three or four months of the year when field work was slack. Religious instruction was the primary concern, and reading was simply a means to this. Soon after his death in 1761 there were 279 schools scattered throughout Wales, but the movement petered out after his successor died in 1779.[46]

If a village had no endowed school, or only a poor one, and if its population was too small or too impoverished to attract a private-venture teacher dependent on fees for a living, the parish officers or the inhabitants collectively might offer financial inducements. The parish might pay him a small salary out of the parish stock – the revenue from miscellaneous charities – or from the poor rate, or the church rate. Alternatively, or additionally, the villagers might make voluntary contributions in money or in kind towards his livelihood. Sometimes this took the form of a

'The Parson's School' by Samuel Wale c. 1740

customary levy, for example a number of sheaves at harvest, or a few pence a year on each oxgang, as at Rudston in East York-shire, or the householders in rotation might give him his dinner, as at nearby Garton-on-the-Wolds. There in 1743 he had fourteen scholars and 'his meat from house to house is most he gets for his instruction, he receives very small wages'. In places which were too poor to attract a master of any kind, teaching the children might fall to a mere boy, as at Hutton Bonville, a village of a dozen families near Northallerton, where in 1764 the curate reported Thomas Rowntree, 'of tender years', teaching 'a private school of ABCDarians'; or the work might be undertaken for nothing in the interests of religion by the curate himself, a man who was anyway hardly more exalted than the schoolmaster in the social hierarchy. Where support of some kind was given by the parish, the master was commonly the parish clerk. The school was then likely to be found as in centuries past in some part of the church — the choir, a former chantry chapel, an aisle boarded or bricked off, or the ringing chamber under the tower; the graffiti and mutilated monuments are often to this day a reminder of the school's presence.

When Bishop Nicolson of Carlisle held his primary visitation in 1703 he made particular note of the parish schools and school-masters in his diocese. School dames he seldom mentions — perhaps they were not worth considering. Occasionally it is the curate who teaches the village school; more often it is the parish clerk. Often in the poorer places the school is in the church, a fact which he deplores but takes for granted. 'I was glad', he notes at Westward, 'to find the curate . . . surrounded with so good a number of scholars; though I could have wished to have seen them elsewhere than in the chancel, and spoiling Mr Barwis's monument . . . with writing their copies upon it.' At Farlam he observes 'the teaching of children in the choir (a general practice) is a great inconvenience'; at Orton 'the church and choir . . . spoiled with the school boys'; at Long Marton 'the children were formerly taught in the vestry, with a door into the churchyard . . . but they now learn in . . . an aisle on the south side'; at Morland 'the south aisle . . . is deserted by the Lord Lonsdale . . . and therefore the parish . . . have turned it into a school'; at Crosby on Eden 'the schoolmaster . . . teaches . . . in the choir, where the boys and girls sit on good wainscot benches, and write on the Communion Table'.[47] In many places it was not until the 1830s or 1840s that the village school left the village church, when new schoolhouses were being built and churches put to less secular uses.

About 1700 half the population lived in poverty, a third of them on the subsistence level, and one family in five was receiving poor relief. Pauperism and the burden it imposed on the poor rate was a constant problem for parish authorities, and one of the eighteenth century's attempted solutions was the workhouse school. Every parish workhouse contained pauper children — dependants of destitute parents, foundlings, orphans, bastards — whose moral standards were shaped by the vagrants, thieves, drunks and prostitutes with whom they lived unsegregated in the house. The workhouse school, like the charity school, was primarily a means of inculcating moral and social discipline, providing semi-skilled industrial training, and — much less important — some instruction in the rudiments of literacy. A school of industry in every parish, as Locke had recommended, never came about, but after the General Workhouse Act of 1723 workhouses increased rapidly in towns and large parishes, and here the overseers often engaged a schoolmaster to teach the children reading, perhaps some writing, but mainly spinning, weaving or knitting. The hope was that 'the children of the poor instead of being bred up in ignorance and vice to an idle, beggarly and vagabond life, will have the fear of God before their eyes, get habits of virtue, be inured to labour and thus become useful to their country'.[48] Such parishes were relatively humane: there were others where the pauper children were 'apprenticed' as soon as they were old enough – to costermongers, chimneysweeps or pedlars, outside the parish wherever possible so as to prevent them from becoming permanently chargeable. In the last decades of the century they were 'apprenticed' in batches to northern factory masters where their notorious exploitation as cheap labour was an important factor in the textile revolution and England's early industrialization.

Following the workhouse example, many of the later charity schools, whether endowed by private philanthropy or financed by public subscription, took the form of schools of industry where reading and perhaps writing might be taught, but always subordinated to vocational training. Here the product of the children's labour was intended to supplement the trustees' income from endowments or subscriptions, just as in the workhouse schools it was intended to save the ratepayers' money. Some working charity schools for girls provided training in housecraft as well as the inevitable moral and religious discipline, and the scarcely concealed purpose of these was to supply the local tradesmen – often the subscribers – with obedient cheap domestic servants.

Teachers of the poor

Although perhaps more men than ever before devoted themselves to teaching, for most of them it remained, as it always had been, a casual, part-time occupation. In towns, where demand would be more plentiful and constant, some men (and perhaps some women too) spent their working lives as teachers and made a modest living out of it, but with no more qualifications or preparation than their own schooling and private reading, and perhaps some previous experience of other occupations. The majority of teachers, however, were countrymen, living in villages and teaching the children of ploughmen, shepherds and small farmers, and here the living to be made from schoolkeeping was exiguous and uncertain. Bishop Nicolson notes how rarely the schoolmasters in the diocese of Carlisle had regular incomes. At Crosby on Eden the master 'has no certain and fixed salary'; at Wigton, where he was also parish clerk, 'he has no standing salary more than the interest of £20 stock, but has a shilling in the quarter for each boy or girl'; at Shap 'no certain salary more than £6 which is a voluntary gift . . . of the Lord Wharton's'; at Rockcliffe he had 'contracted with the parishioners for a salary of £3 and his diet', with 10s. a year as parish clerk; at Warwick near Carlisle he was 'a poor cripple . . . who has no settled salary, only 12d. a quarter and his diet, and would be thankful for . . . the clerk's place, which . . . would bring him an addition of about 6s. p.a.'[49]

Few teachers managed without doing other work as well. As we have repeatedly seen, the village schoolmaster was often the parish clerk, keeping the registers of baptisms, marriages and burials, leading the psalms and responses in church, perhaps collecting the poor rate and church rate. But he might also be a husbandman, ploughing his own holding, or, later in the century, keeper of the village shop, if there was one. The most literate and knowledgeable person in the rustic community save for the curate (the parson and squire probably being absentees), he often served the village in numerous unofficial roles – writing or deciphering letters for his more illiterate neighbours, gauging the crops for the reapers' pay, surveying the fields at enclosure, reading out the news in the ale house, playing the fiddle at village assemblies. Essentially he was a peasant like the rest of the villagers; he had grown up among them or in some neighbouring village, spoke the same dialect, knew the land and the seasons as they did. The more dedicated ones, though largely self-taught, took to schoolkeeping through love and pride of knowledge and because literacy opened few other doors for men of peasant origin.

Oliver Goldsmith gives a well-known sketch of an actual or idealized country schoolmaster of this kind in *The Deserted Village* (1769).[50] Another example is John Day, schoolmaster of Sigglesthorne in the East Riding of Yorkshire, who reveals something of himself in his notebooks and poems. Born of illiterate, farm-worker parents at Withernwick in the ploughlands of Holderness, he started work as a hired labourer and in the slack winter months educated himself with the help and encouragement of two neighbouring village schoolmasters. At twenty-one he set up as schoolmaster himself and after two attempts settled at Sigglesthorne, a scattered parish of about 100 families, a few miles from his birthplace. Here he was schoolmaster for thirty-five years, except for a nine-year interval when poverty forced him to give up his school and work as a gardener and labourer. A simple, self-taught man, he was practical and versatile, without envy or ambition. His school was his main love but to eke out the living it provided he also worked at different times as parish clerk, sexton and rate collector. He kept the village mangle and sometimes acted as village barber, and he was called upon to draw up wills and indentures, to survey the fields and to settle village quarrels.[51] Teaching the children of the labouring poor was a humble occupation that might earn local respect but conferred no status: the financial rewards were meagre and the work was considered suitable only for the poor themselves to undertake. It is a tradition that has died hard.

Not all teachers were like this. Undoubtedly there were large numbers who took to schoolkeeping as a last resort, through personal misfortune or incapacity. The widow, the spinster, the failed tradesman, the discharged soldier, the cripple unfit for heavy work – all these were likely to turn to teaching as a temporary or permanent expedient. In 1762 the diarist James

Woodforde, son of the prosperous rector of Castle Cary in
Somerset, bred up at Winchester and Oxford, mentions with pain
his cousin James Lewis, whom ill fortune had reduced to keeping
'a little school at Nottingham . . . He was a private soldier in the
army, and being wounded in the leg rendered him unserviceable
. . . he has been rather wild in his time, which wildness has
brought him to this.'[52] It was these uncommitted, reluctant and
often bogus teachers who depressed the standing of all, and justified the common charge that teaching 'usually fell to the lot of
old women, or men of mean capacities'.

Episcopal control, which made possible at least some supervision of teachers' competence, weakened greatly during the
eighteenth century. Under the Uniformity Act of 1662 bishops
were still responsible for licensing schoolmasters, but a number
of judicial decisions early in the century established that at common law the church had no control over the reading and writing
and other non-grammar schools, and that although the bishops
had a statutory power to license teachers (and therefore a 'discretionary power of judging of the qualification of persons to be
licensed'), jurisdiction in the matter of unlicensed teaching
belonged to the temporal, not the ecclesiastical, courts.[53] Even
so, bishops still had a canon-law responsibility for schools in their
dioceses, and in their visitation articles one of the questions
requiring written answers from each incumbent invariably concerned the schools and teachers in his parish. Bishops continued
to grant licences to petty- as well as to grammar-school teachers
(but seldom to women, and perhaps only to men who requested
them) and sometimes their courts heard parents' complaints
against a master's violence or negligence. For example in 1729
the York consistory court investigated allegations that the master
at Knottingley had neglected his school since taking up work
as a part-time exciseman,[54] but such action seems to have
become rare as the century advanced.

About the distribution and continuity of schools there is un-
certainty. Evidence for the existence of schools over fairly wide
areas at particular times is supplied by episcopal visitation
returns, but few of these have yet been thoroughly explored.
Those for Archbishop Herring's primary visitation of the York
diocese in 1743 contain valuable information about education.[55]
The third of the eleven questions which he addressed to his clergy
for a written reply asked, 'Is there any public or charity school

endowed or otherwise maintained in your parish? What number of children are taught in it? And what care is taken to instruct them in the . . . Christian religion according to the . . . Church of England; and to bring them duly to church?'

Of the 645 returns from all Yorkshire, 379 (nearly 58 per cent) report a school of some sort, variously designated 'charity', 'free', 'endowed', 'public', 'private', 'English', 'petty'. In the East Riding 67 parishes and chapelries out of 168 (nearly 40 per cent) had a school. For comparison, the returns to Bishop Secker's visitation articles for Oxford diocese in 1738 show only 53 out of 179 parishes with a school (nearly 30 per cent).[56] Some of the larger East Riding parishes had two or three schools – North Cave with 123 families had two, 'wherein the most, if not all, of the children in the parish are taught'; but ten parishes, each with over 100 families, had none. Those without were mostly small remote communities where poverty and the small number of children had ruled out a school. Numbers attending, where they are mentioned, varied considerably, but suggest an average of about twenty. Attendance was irregular and uncertain, depending on the opportunities for children's labour in the fields. Some returns make it clear that schools existed intermittently – 'There is no . . . regular school . . . The clerk undertakes to teach such as come to him; but he is very oft without any scholars.' Attempts by parson or parishioners to start a school were sometimes defeated by failure to find a competent or willing teacher.

Other evidence suggests that in country districts where no choice existed schools continued socially unsegregated, and the gentry's sons might still be taught alongside the village children. In *Tom Jones* (1749) Fielding shows a neighbouring squire's two sons attending the village school, the elder at the age of seventeen learning the rudiments of Latin, the younger learning to read and write with seven boys of the parish. The master here was clerk and barber as well, and to his earnings the squire added an annuity of £10 every Christmas.

Popular literacy

After 1754 it becomes possible to assess rather more accurately the extent of popular literacy, to which these schools must largely have contributed. Lord Hardwicke's Marriage Act of 1753 required brides and grooms to sign their names, or make their marks, in a specially printed register. Although ability to write one's name is only with qualifications a reliable indication of literacy, this evidence is the best there is for the relative extent of elementary education in different places at different times. A sample in seventeen rural parishes and chapelries in the East Riding shows certain clear results.[57] Firstly, considerably more men than women were literate: the average in all the parishes together from 1754 to 1760 was 64 per cent for men and 39 per cent for women, an average of 51 per cent for both sexes. Secondly, literacy varied greatly from village to village, from 72 per cent in one to 30 per cent in another, taking men and women together. Thirdly, although the literacy rate improved considerably in some parishes between 1754 and the end of the century, it declined in others; over all the parishes the improvement was from 51 per cent in the 1750s to 57 per cent in the 1790s. Fourthly, the extent of literacy is not always explained by the presence or absence of a school: other factors must have operated.

At all times informal instruction by parents or friends or even by unaided self-help must have been almost as important as systematic instruction in schools. Since Tudor times popular literature in the form of ballads, broadsides and pamphlets had formed part of the stock-in-trade of the travelling bagman and furnished means of self-instruction. In the eighteenth century there was a great increase in the output of popular reading and didactic material intended primarily for juveniles, though also for their elders: spelling books, writing sheets, fairy stories, moral tales, fables, histories. Hack-written, crudely printed and illustrated, chapbooks of this kind were produced in great variety in numerous towns, and peddled round the fairs, villages and farms of the countryside by the 'travelling stationers'. The publisher John Newbery, who died in 1767, was the father of the children's book trade. Many intelligent but unschooled labourers and their children must have learned to read by puzzling their way through *The History of Tom Hickathrift, Jack the Giant Killer* or *Tommy Trip and his Dog Jowler*, bought at the door for a few pence.[58]

The parson poet George Crabbe in his poem *The Parish Register* reflects on the 'marks uncouth' made there by rustic grooms:

> how strange that men,
> Who guide the plough, should fail to guide the pen.
> For half a mile the furrows even lie;
> For half an inch the letters stand awry.

But the rural poor, who still comprised nearly half the population, had very little incentive to become literate. Literacy conferred no material benefits in a society where prospects depended on rank and family. Indeed, the ploughman who could read and write might be at a disadvantage if he worked for a farmer who could do neither. There was no question of education promoting social mobility for the poor; it was fear that it might do this that led many influential people to oppose it. Even if the labourer could read, incessant physical labour left him with no leisure for reading such books as he possessed or could borrow. If he could write, there was nobody to write to: everybody he knew lived in the village, or in the next one, and if he had anything to say he walked there and said it. On the few occasions when he needed to sign his name the law allowed him to make his mark instead, which was just as good. And if he sent his children to school he had not only to pay the schoolmaster but also manage without their earnings, which might mean hunger for all the family. Schooling was a risky investment for the poor, anyway, when perhaps only one child in two might survive to adulthood.[59]

The ploughman, the thatcher and the cowherd might still have little need of education, but a desire for literacy probably came after about 1750 from the growing numbers of countrymen whose livelihood necessitated such skills. Tenant farmers, village artisans, part-time manufacturing smallholders, cottage workers under the 'putting out' system, market town and village shopkeepers – all these must have been caught in what Professor Hobsbawm calls 'the meshes of the web of cash transactions' which spread over the countryside in the second half of the eighteenth century and which called for some knowledge of reading, writing and arithmetic.

In towns the literacy rate was higher than in rural areas, as one would expect, though here too there were variations. Between 1754 and 1762 adult male literacy indicated by town parish registers was 74 per cent in Oxford and Northampton, 66 per cent in Bristol, 62 per cent in King's Lynn, 61 per cent in Nottingham, and 60 per cent in Halifax.[60] Obviously, urban tradesmen would have greater need than rural labourers for reading, writing and calculating skills; more newspapers and books would be available, and opportunities would exist for informed discussion. The growth of the retail trade (and so of shopkeepers, commercial travellers and other middlemen), the multiplication of skilled crafts, the increasing need for clerks and copywriters as foreign trade and banking developed – all these must have stimulated urban demand for education in the later eighteenth century. Much of this, however, would be met less by the common schools for the poor than by the private academies for the more prosperous and 'middling sort' of people, who were now growing in number, relatively and absolutely.

Grammar schools

Above the level of schooling for the poor the grammar school continued to represent the conservative classical tradition of education, though boys entering at the age of seven or eight might still have to be taught reading and writing there in the absence of a petty school in the district. When William Wilberforce first went to school in Hull at the age of seven in 1766 it was to the grammar school that he was sent after some preliminary teaching at home. It is certainly true that on the whole the grammar schools prospered far less than in their early-seventeenth-century heyday. Their curriculum had less attraction for the growing commercial class, and they now encountered serious competition from private schools offering more modern courses of study. New foundations were few, and there was a general decline in numbers of pupils. Some schools survived by introducing more 'useful' non-classical subjects, some became petty schools (in this changed state admitting girls as well as boys), some died out.[61]

Most grammar schools, including the largest, continued to be conducted by one master or a master and an usher, and to occupy only a single room. As in the past, numbers fluctuated unpredictably. At Bedford school there were twenty-six boys in 1718, three in 1739, ten in 1769.[62] Thirty or forty might have been a good average for a grammar school. For the most part they were the sons of local farmers, clergy and professional men with some tradesmen's sons and occasionally one or two from the gentry of the area. Those who could not live at home would board with the master or with private families, as the two Wordsworth brothers from Cockermouth, thirty-eight miles away, boarded with Ann Tyson and her husband, when they were boys at Hawkeshead school.

Falling numbers exacerbated the poverty which in many

schools resulted from the dwindling yield of endowments. Impecunious masters everywhere were driven to much the same financial expedients. They sought benefices or curacies, in plurality if possible, which inevitably meant some neglect of the school. They introduced subjects like arithmetic and accounts to appeal to the local tradesmen and farmers, and had these taught by the usher or some hired teacher. The more ambitious tried to attract moneyed boarders from a distance as private pupils, which might mean in effect keeping a separate private school, to the detriment of the local free boys. On the other hand the better endowed the school the less was the master's incentive to attract pupils of any kind. However neglectful he might be, his freehold made it almost impossible to remove him.

Poverty and the master's divided attention apart, many schools suffered from the indifference of their governing bodies. By their default complete responsibility might pass to the master, and physical as well as academic deterioration result. Some schools existed in slum conditions. Long neglected by the dean and chapter, St Peter's at York occupied the chancel of a derelict town church (lately used as a brothel), the nave serving as a stable.[63]

However, if some schools stagnated and others perforce changed their role, there were many which, though small, continued to provide a sound if narrow classical education and send boys to the universities or equip them for apprenticeship to the professions and the more genteel trades. Much depended on the master's dedication and ability, and his independence of other employments.

Notwithstanding the criticisms of Locke and later educational theorists and practitioners, conviction as well as conservatism bound these grammar schools – especially those in close touch with the universities – to the ancient classical curriculum. Latin and Greek remained the staple fare and the more academically successful the school, the more narrowly classical the teaching tended to be. The neglect of mathematics, the fundamental tool of economic and technical progress in an age of growing commercial and industrial expansion, put such grammar schools increasingly behind the times. Able boys from good schools went up to Oxford and Cambridge in the mid-century well grounded in the classics but 'so little versed in common figures as to be obliged to have recourse to a master of a day school in the town for instruction in the four fundamental rules of arithmetic'.[64] Later in the

Academy for young gentlemen, 1739

century some of these schools were teaching a little of other subjects — arithmetic, accounts, English grammar, the globes. The trustees of a few well-endowed foundations, for instance Birmingham in 1751 and Bedford after 1764, went so far as to divert some of their income to set up separate writing and English schools, and these might admit girls as well as boys.[65]

Even in this age of privilege and rank, the grammar school and the closed scholarship continued to provide an avenue to the university for the poor, or relatively poor, boy. A scholarship was a school's valued possession, whether nomination to it belonged to the school itself, or to the college where it was tenable, or to some other body, such as a town corporation. An unusual multiple scholarship for a group of north-country schools was founded in 1739 by Lady Elizabeth Hastings of Ledsham near Leeds. She gave property in the West Riding to Queen's College, Oxford, to maintain five poor scholars each for five years, and the scholars were to be chosen from twelve specified schools — Beverley, Bradford, Leeds, Ripon, Sedbergh, Sherburn, Skipton and Wakefield in Yorkshire, Appleby and Haversham in Westmorland, Penrith and St Bees in Cumberland. Every fifth year on the Thursday in Whit week each school was to send its competitor to the best inn at Aberford on the Great North Road, where they would be examined in Latin and Greek by the parsons of seven prescribed churches in the area. The names of the ten best boys were then to be sent to Queen's College and the provost would choose five by lot. If a school decayed and failed to send candidates, the college would substitute another.[66]

Social mobility upwards could still be assisted by such means. Financed by a scholarship and a college servitorship or sizarship, the son of a tradesman or husbandman might rise to a college fellowship or a rectory and so pass for a gentleman. If he became tutor or chaplain in some family with government influence he might even hope for the sort of ecclesiastical preferment – a deanery or even a bishopric, if only in Wales or Ireland – which would put his gentility beyond question.

The 'great schools'

Among the grammar schools a few now began to be patronized by wealthy and aristocratic families and so gradually to stand apart from the rest, though there was as yet no attempt as in the more class-conscious nineteenth century to exclude boys because of their comparatively plebeian origins.

For a hundred years after the Restoration the most fashionable school in England was Westminster. It owed its attraction largely to its connection with Westminster abbey and its proximity to the court and government, which made it a convenient school for the sons of the clergy, lawyers, courtiers and officials who thronged the area, and for the nobility who had their town houses nearby. Closely linked by scholarships with both universities, the school was a nursery of aristocratic statesmen, bishops, scholars, men of letters, generals and admirals. The foundationers – the King's Scholars – lived within the college adjacent to the abbey, but these were now far outnumbered by the wealthy fee-payers, who lodged in dames' houses in the neighbourhood, until for their better supervision boarding houses were built near the school in Dean's Yard.[67]

Latin with some Greek formed the sum of the curriculum. As the classics became vocationally 'useless' so they increasingly became the symbol of the gentleman's education, for gentlemen by definition did not have to work for a living. Whatever training the meticulous study of Ovid and Horace might have afforded in mental and moral discipline, in taste and refinement, Westminster was notorious for its violence and lawlessness. Fighting among the boys and with outsiders was a traditional pastime. In 1679 a royal pardon had been granted to the scholars collectively for the murder of a bailiff. Whether boarded in college or in town houses, boys were herded together largely unsupervised; the young were exploited and bullied by the older boys, and when these sallied out to roam the streets after lock-up, drunk or sober, they struck terror into the neighbourhood. Rich, arrogant and unafraid, the young gentlemen of England were hard to control in these unprecedented concentrations.[68]

Notwithstanding Westminster's eminence, Eton was scarcely ever eclipsed as England's leading school. In the early eighteenth century it grew rapidly, and although numbers fluctuated as elsewhere it was easily the largest grammar school in the country. In 1720 there were 425 boys; in 1745 only 244; in 1766 as many as 483; in 1773 only 230. The aristocratic element became very marked during this period, though local tradesmen's sons were often to be found among the scholars. A school list in 1745 arranges the lower school without regard to rank, but the upper school shows noblemen first (designated 'Mr'), then baronets, followed by commoners. Of the 483 boys in 1766, 50 were noblemen, noblemen's sons, or baronets. After 1760 the school's growing attraction for the nobility and gentry owed much to the personal interest of George III, who was a frequent visitor from Windsor, where he preferred to live. Not only were peers and bishops thus stimulated to send their sons there, but so also were socially aspiring lesser families. In the second half of the century Eton supplanted Westminster as the training ground for Parliament and the state service.[69]

As the fee-payers rose in number and social standing they increasingly set the tone of the school, and the collegers or foundation scholars lost status. Although they all mixed in school, they were kept separate in other ways: the all-important commoners lived in the town in boarding houses kept by dames or dominies, the scholars lived in college, where the starvation diet and the barbarities of the Long Chamber became so notorious that the number often fell short of the statutory seventy.

Larger numbers forced the headmaster and usher, the only two teachers known to the statutes, to employ assistants and the school thus came to have a regular staff of masters: eight in 1718,

ten in 1766. These, however, had no official status, being merely
the hired servants of either the headmaster in the upper school
or the usher in the lower school, though almost always they were
Etonians and King's men. Every assistant taught his own class and
also acted as private tutor to a number of boys of varying ages –
a system peculiar to Eton though later copied elsewhere.[70]

Because of the school's prestige, the Eton curriculum, which
was entirely classical, had great influence on other schools. Latin
and to a lesser extent Greek grammar and literature (mainly
poetry), the composition of themes and orations, and – most
esteemed of all – Latin versification occupied all the time spent in
school. Out of school hours there was some writing and arithmetic for younger boys, algebra and geography for older ones,
and on half- or full-day holidays French, drawing, fencing and
dancing – all offered by visiting masters as 'extras' for those who
wanted them. It was a far less strenuous regime than in past
centuries, and the boys had much spare time for their own amuse-
ments – rudimentary and still largely unorganized cricket and
football, swimming, boating, bird-nesting, poaching and
fighting.[71]

By tradition Winchester was a somewhat inbred community,
living in a secluded private world which it shared with New
College; it was never so closely connected with the great world as
Eton and Westminster. However, Winchester developed along
much the same lines as these other 'great schools' in the
eighteenth century. The college came to be completely overshadowed by the rich commoners who lived at first with the
headmaster, the second master or individual fellows. Later, a
boarding house was specially built for them, and there the headmaster eventually went to reside, enjoying the high fees and
patrician associations and leaving the second master in charge of
the socially inferior collegers.[72] Winchester and Eton had little
of Westminster's lawlessness until later in the century. Discipline
was largely left to the older boys with little interference from
the masters, and as long as the headmaster had their goodwill
order was maintained. But as numbers increased, overcrowding
and understaffing led to a breakdown of personal relations and
this resulted in floggings and expulsions and occasionally –
when schoolboy opinion had been particularly outraged – open
rebellion.[73]

As Westminster's illustrious patronage declined, the way was

Harrow: the schoolroom, 1816

opened for the rise of Harrow. The grammar school there had been founded in 1571 by John Lyon, a yeoman of the parish, for the free education of local poor boys, though the statutes allowed the trustees at their discretion to admit fee-payers as well. After the mid-century a succession of three headmasters, all ex-Etonians, built up its aristocratic connections, with boarding houses and a tutorial system on the Eton model, and by the end of the century there were as many boys as at Eton, drawn from all over the country, among them the sons and heirs of great Whig noblemen, but no free boys at all from the parish. Thus, by deliberate policy, a local grammar school became one of the 'great schools', superseding Westminster and rivalling Eton but thereby subverting the founder's intentions to the educational deprivation of the neighbourhood.[74]

Another local grammar school transformed into a fashionable boarding school after 1780 was the free school at Rugby, founded in 1567 expressly for the benefit of local children by Lawrence Sheriff, a native of the town, who had grown rich as a grocer in London. Its rise in the social scale was the result of a sudden increase in the value of its property in London and of the appointment of an ambitious headmaster with experience at Eton. Later, the grammar school at Shrewsbury, long in decline after its Elizabethan heyday, started a similar ascent under a headmaster who had been at Rugby.[75]

Meanwhile, two London city charity schools, both associated with almshouses for the poor, were changing their social complexion. Christ's Hospital, founded in 1552, boarded, uniformed and educated in rather bleak austerity not the poorest children but the orphans of such lower clergy, officers and indigent gentlemen as could secure nomination by a member of the governing body. Charterhouse, dating from 1611, provided similarly for the needy gentry but admitted fee-payers as well.[76] Although these two schools lacked the others' aristocratic associations and pretensions, by the end of the eighteenth century they were included with them among the 'great schools', or, as they soon came to be known, the 'public schools' — a term which these few élite boarding establishments arrogated to themselves, although by custom it belonged to all endowed schools simply to distinguish them from private schools.

Private tutors and private academies

Throughout the eighteenth century, in noblemen's and gentlemen's families, a common alternative to the public schools was the private tutor, possibly because of the schools' narrow curricula, their unruliness or their social promiscuity. Some families had their sons tutored at home before sending them away to school; some employed tutors as a substitute for schooling, right up to university entrance; others, including some of the greatest political families, had their sons educated entirely at home, dispensing with both school and university. The cultural resources of many aristocratic houses, with their libraries and collections of paintings, sculptures and curiosities, would exceed those of any school and most colleges. Tutors were usually graduates and former dons, who might also be the domestic chaplain or incumbent of a family living, hopeful perhaps for future patronage and preferment. Some of them later gained considerable reputations in other spheres. Not all of them were university men, however. William Jones, a self-taught mathematician and FRS, was tutor in turn to the future earl of Hardwicke and the first and second earls of Macclesfield. The radical earl of Shelburne employed the unitarian theologian and scientist Joseph Priestley as librarian and tutor to his sons in the 1770s, allowing him a house near the family seat in Wiltshire, rooms in their town house in Berkeley Square and £250 a year.[77]

Instead of employing a resident tutor, well-to-do families in towns might engage private teachers to instruct boys daily at home, perhaps one for general subjects and individual specialists for languages, music, drawing and fencing. At a lower social level, professional men like clergy who could not afford the services of a tutor would educate their own sons, or perhaps send the eldest away to school and teach the others themselves: the second son of Goldsmith's Vicar of Wakefield being 'designed for business, received a sort of miscellaneous education at home'. It has been calculated that the proportion of boys educated privately at home was about one in four for the peerage, one in three for the gentry, one in four for the clergy and one in five for other professions.[78]

Among the more significant developments of the eighteenth century was the proliferation of middle-class private schools offering an alternative training to that of the grammar schools and based on an entirely different educational philosophy.[79] Private classical schools competing with the endowed grammar schools had been common in the seventeenth century, as had private teachers of more practical or vocational subjects like languages, mathematics and navigation, and of accomplishments like fencing and music. Throughout the eighteenth century, individual teachers of these and other subjects offered their services in the towns, visiting homes or giving private lessons in their own houses. The dissenting academies had early developed a more comprehensive curriculum, embracing modern and utilitarian subjects as well as the classics. Schools or academies of this kind with or without denominational attachments now became a marked feature of the educational system. They existed, in rivalry with one another, in most large towns but especially in London and the surrounding villages, where there was a growing middle-class trading population disenchanted with the grammar schools and the classics.

Whilst grammar schools everywhere showed a more or less uniform purpose and method, the academies were remarkable for their diversity. Many of them were kept by non-graduate laymen, perhaps largely self-taught but sometimes men of considerable talents; others by nonconformist ministers, themselves academy-educated; others by Anglican clergymen with a conventional grammar-school and university education. The smallest would be taught by the proprietor singlehanded or with the help of a paid usher, usually – in the literature of the time, at any rate – a downtrodden youth little better than a menial. In the largest, the principal might employ a permanent staff of several assistants and engage visiting instructors for particular subjects.

In the kind of courses they offered, the academies fall into no clearcut categories. Some confined themselves to the classics, and these were often kept by clergymen, perhaps former dons who had resigned a college fellowship in order to marry and take up a parsonage, where they sustained scholarly interests by teaching small groups of fee-paying boys as day or boarding pupils and perhaps prepared them for the university. The majority of the academies offered a general curriculum, including the classics and such subjects as English grammar, arithmetic, accounts, geography ('the globes'), history ('chronology'), elementary science ('natural' or 'experimental philosophy') with French, music and dancing taught by visiting masters. Others were more specifically vocational and provided professional courses in such subjects as commerce, surveying, navigation and military science as well as a general course of study. Heath Hall academy near Wakefield, established by Joseph Randall in 1740, offered separate courses designed for 'gentlemen', business, the army and navy, and the universities. At its largest there were some 170 students aged from eight to eighteen boarding in the hall and neighbouring village, and nine assistants. The library contained 1,400 books and the scientific apparatus included an orrery. When this academy failed financially in 1754 Randall opened another in York.[80] Whatever their bias or emphasis the academies claimed to avoid the rigid, authoritarian, book-centred approach of the grammar schools and to be more flexible, informal and practical. Several of them attracted attention by their educational innovations. At the long-lived school at Cheam in Surrey William Gilpin after 1752 practised new methods of teaching and moral training through self-government. David Williams, a dissenting minister turned deist and naturalist, ran an academy in Chelsea on Rousseauist principles in the 1770s.[81]

The smaller academies limited themselves to a dozen or so boys, who lived with the proprietor's family and were taught in his house alongside his own children, paying, in the 1770s, £30 or £40 a year for board and tuition. The worst of these were homes for unwanted children. Many others seem to have been unprincipled exploiters of parents' ignorance and credulity. Goldsmith, who had briefly been usher in an academy in Peckham in 1757, refers disparagingly to schools of this kind,

> Is any man unfit for any of the professions, he finds his last resource in setting up a school. Do any become bankrupts in trade, they still set up a boarding school, and drive a trade this way, when all others fail; nay, I have been told of butchers and barbers, who have turned schoolmasters, and more surprising still made fortunes in their new profession.[82]

But successful speculators of this kind must have been rare, for, whether good or bad, most academies tended to be shortlived.

Some won high reputations, however, and were passed on in the same family or from one proprietor to another across the century. The school at Cheam was one of these. Hackney academy, in the country to the north-east of London, lasted from the 1680s to 1820 and was almost as aristocratic in clientele as Eton and Westminster, sending a steady stream of boys to the universities. Scholastically, the most reputable were the non-conformist academies providing not only superior school education but also teaching of university standard, and in modern subjects like mathematics, science and languages as well as classics, philosophy and theology. Outstanding examples were the academies at Hoxton in London, Northampton, Daventry and Warrington. After the mid-century these tended to be not so much private establishments as public institutions, financed by subscribers and managed by trustees of particular denominations. Warrington academy, founded in 1757 by a predominantly Presbyterian body, was particularly distinguished. Most of its students followed a three-year course designed for business careers; those who followed the full five-year course tended to go into one of the various dissenting ministries, law, medicine or the army. At its largest it had no more than thirty students, and normally three tutors. One of these in the 1760s was Joseph Priestley, an early student at Daventry, whose eminence as a scientist has obscured his importance in education. He was a conspicuous example of the type of radical, rationalist intellectual produced by the later dissenting academies, and his *Essay on a Course of Liberal Education for Civil and Active Life* (1765), based on his Warrington lectures, was a call for 'larger and more liberal views of education' than were necessary when 'none but the clergy were thought to have any occasion for learning'. By the last quarter of the century the nonconformist academies were either dying out because of the multiplication of other private academies, or being converted into denominational theological colleges. Warrington, increasingly unitarian in outlook, closed in 1783 and was dissolved in 1786.[83]

Taken altogether, private and nonconformist academies helped to change eighteenth-century society. They established modern subjects as an important part of middle-class education (though these were to lose ground to the classics in the nineteenth century). For some they provided an alternative route to the universities and the professions, and in so doing contributed to the depression of the grammar schools. And through their teaching of mathematics and experimental science they helped to diffuse an attitude of mind in which the industrial revolution could take place and also trained some of the clerks, mechanics, technical innovators and entrepreneurs who pioneered it.

'That famous question, whether the education at a public school, or under a private tutor, is to be preferred?' was discussed by the *Spectator* in 1712.[84] Locke had recently done much to rekindle the debate by his criticism of the grammar schools and his advocacy of the private tutor for gentlemen's sons. But it was the growth of the academies that extended the controversy, and a dialogue on the respective merits of 'private' as opposed to 'public' education runs through a good deal of eighteenth-century educational literature. By 'public' was meant the endowed grammar school and the ancient classical course; by 'private' was meant either the domestic tutor or the academy, and by implication the broad, modern curriculum.

Conservatives – the clerical, graduate grammar-school masters – argued what they claimed to be the incomparable merits of Greek and Latin, 'languages which contain all that is or can be valuable to mankind, either here or hereafter', as one of them alleged. In public schools boys had the stimulus of rivalry in their work and learned self-reliance and endurance, whereas in private education at home or in small academies emulation and competitive learning were lacking, boys were spoilt by indulgent tutors and interfering parents and so were ill prepared for life in the adult world. Moreover private teachers were often notoriously ill qualified for their work, so much so that academy keeping had become merely another petty trade, 'as much a species of haberdashery as the measuring of tape or the retailing of worsted'.[85]

Progressives — generally academy proprietors advertising their own establishments — used arguments as old as those of educational reformers of the 1640s and 1650s, and indeed older. The commonest censure of public schools was of their narrow classical curriculum. For most boys — so the accusation ran — this was a waste of time: not only was it irrelevant for careers in business, but also boys commonly left school ignorant even of Latin, the only subject they had studied, so unenlightened were the traditional methods of teaching it. For the great majority a more modern and 'useful' curriculum was obviously to be preferred. Furthermore, the 'common method' of teaching used in grammar schools gave boys none of the individual attention and encouragement that the academies afforded, and corporal punishment was all too often the only spur to learning. Besides, where large numbers were herded together without adequate supervision, vice and depravity flourished. 'It is well known', observed Joseph Priestley in 1778, 'that most of our public schools . . . are in such a situation, that a young person runs the greatest risk of having his morals corrupted in them.'[86] In short, because of their intentionally limited admissions, the teacher's individual instruction and supervision and the variety of subjects which they offered, the academies were able to prepare boys for life far more successfully than the public grammar schools were.

Whatever the respective merits and demerits of public and private education, the latter provided one service which the other certainly did not — it catered for girls, though only for girls from comfortable or affluent families. At the level of schooling for the poor, girls benefited with boys, but above that no systematic provision existed for their formal education. Perhaps most daughters in the middle and upper ranks of society received what instruction they got at home, either from governesses, who were treated little better than the servants, and visiting music and dancing masters; or from parents and private reading, where the father was parson, doctor or lawyer. The aim was not usually a high one. Mrs Primrose, the Vicar of Wakefield's wife, claimed that her 'two girls have had a pretty good education. . . . They can read, write, and cast accompts; they understand their needle, breadstitch, cross and change, and all manner of plain-work; they can pink, point and frill; and know something of music; they can do up small cloaths, work upon catgut; my eldest can cut paper, and my youngest has a very pretty manner of telling fortunes upon the cards.'[87]

From the later seventeenth century, however, private boarding schools for girls established themselves as a regular part of the educational system in London and the larger county towns where there was a ready clientele of landed, commercial and professional families. Aubrey in 1678 mentioned four or five in Oxford, where he thought they were a snare for 'young heirs and gentlemen commoners' at the university. On her northern tour in 1698 Celia Fiennes noted 'schools for young gentlewomen' at Shrewsbury ('for learning work and behaviour and music'), at Leeds and Manchester ('very fine . . . as good as any in London').[88] Schools of this kind were always fewer in number than the boys' academies; they tended also to be smaller and of shorter duration, more limited and less ambitious in their aims. A typical one might be kept by a widowed or maiden gentlewoman, who boarded in her ample house ten or twelve girls of mixed ages, superintended their manners and morals, taught them needlework and house-wifery, and engaged, at the cheapest rate, visiting masters to give lessons in French, writing, music and dancing. Some, with no higher aims, nevertheless gained some repute and lasted two or three decades, like the Abbey school at Reading which Jane Austen attended and which she describes as Mrs Goddard's school in *Emma*: 'a real, honest, old-fashioned boarding-school, where a reasonable quantity of accomplishments were sold at a reasonable price, and where girls might be sent to be out of the way and scramble themselves into a little education, without any danger of coming back prodigies'.[89]

The eighteenth century yielded a harvest of literature on female education: treatises aiming to improve it, both at home and at boarding school; books in letter form for the moral edification of young ladies; books in the form of dialogues and catechisms supplying them with scraps of 'polite knowledge'. They all show how heavily weighted in favour of moral training and genteel accomplishments, how lacking in intellectual content, girls' education was expected to be. The essential object was clearly a limited one – 'to increase a young lady's chance of a prize in the matrimonial lottery', as Maria Edgeworth wrote. Towards the end of the century this concept was strongly assailed, though with little practical result, by such middle-class blue-stockings as Maria Edgeworth, Mary Wollstonecraft and Hannah More.[90] The century certainly produced some remarkably erudite women, but it may well be – the evidence hardly exists – that for much of its course the average country gentlewoman was scarcely more literate than her kitchen maids.

Oxford and Cambridge

There is no doubt that as the eighteenth century advanced, as society and the economy were changing, the English universities dragged their feet. But in criticizing their record then it has to be remembered that many of the functions which universities now perform were not expected of them in those days. Whole areas of professional training lay outside their purview. They educated but did not 'train' the clergy of the Church of England and a few of the physicians and barristers; but the more plebeian apothecaries and surgeons (who carried out the bulk of medical practice) and attorneys (who conducted most of the country's routine legal business) were still trained by apprenticeship after a period of schooling, and most practitioners of the emerging professions of engineering and architecture had started as working mechanics or masons, or were gentlemen amateurs in the case of architecture.[91] Some Englishmen went to Edinburgh or Glasgow or to Leyden or Utrecht for professional training, mainly in medicine; others received training of quasi-university standard at dissenting academies. Nevertheless, as in previous centuries, most of the Englishmen who made any mark on their times had been at either Oxford or Cambridge, and their attitudes and assumptions must to some extent have been influenced by their experiences there.

The clerical monopoly and the exclusion of dissenters may help to explain the comparative inactivity of the universities; so too may the growing predominance of students who had little or no incentive to work. But the universities also reflected the conservatism and complacency of the governing class – its belief in the sanctity of traditional institutions and its preoccupation with the preservation of inherited rights and privileges, which made change of any kind seem dangerous.

Despite some institutional differences, and also some of outlook – for instance, until about 1760 Oxford was predominantly high Tory and Jacobite where Cambridge was Whig – the two universities were essentially similar. Oxford was the larger, with an average of about 250 matriculations a year over the century as a whole, compared with about 160 at Cambridge. Both slumped in numbers and intellectual vitality in the middle decades. Secluded and self-contained, both failed to respond to new national needs in an age of commercial and industrial change. At both, the lively new interests which had distinguished the Restoration period, notably in experimental science and medieval research, died out and classical and scholastic learning, long approved for the social and political training of gentlemen, reasserted their old predominance. However, at Cambridge the tradition of Sir Isaac Newton gradually made mathematics of primary importance, and this was perhaps the redeeming feature of the eighteenth-century universities.

Constitutional forms, studies, exercises and terms of residence for degrees were regulated by the codes of statutes of 1570 at Cambridge and 1636 at Oxford.[92] These were now long out of date, especially in the curriculum they prescribed, but they remained formally unchanged because of constitutional obstacles to reform, though where particular statutes were greatly inconvenient they might be modified in practice or quietly ignored. Executive control belonged to a small oligarchy in which the college heads predominated – at Oxford the Hebdomadal Board, at Cambridge the Caput Senatus. From the college heads the vice-chancellor, practically the sole administrative officer, was chosen annually. All the college heads tended to be elderly, conservative-minded men, unfriendly towards innovation. The legislative assemblies – Convocation at Oxford, Senate at Cambridge – consisted of the general body of full graduates, but they could only accept or reject proposals sent to them, and here too majority opinion tended to be strongly conservative. Reform was difficult, and had deliberately been made so.

The university's principal concern was the awarding of degrees; teaching had been the concern of the colleges since the mid-sixteenth century. The great majority of students read for the BA, for which residence for four academic years was required, and in practice this was the only degree for which instruction was provided. At Oxford the substance of the course was still Latin and Greek grammar and literature with some rhetoric, logic and scholastic philosophy; here, Aristotle reigned supreme until the mid-nineteenth century. At Cambridge the studies were broadly similar, though Aristotle was largely ousted by Locke and the emphasis became more mathematical after about 1750.[93]

Throughout the course there were statutory disputations in Latin using the scholastic method, and finally a public examination in this form, all before moderators. These 'hypothetical conjectures, confirmed by plausible arguments of wit and rhetoric, ordered in a syllogistical form' had long been ridiculed, but they survived unchanged. However, at Cambridge from 1763 these exercises were used only to group students for the final or Senate House examination which became the most important test of all. As the questions for this became more mathematical, English was substituted for Latin and the answers came to be written down – the beginnings of written as opposed to oral examinations. Moreover, to stimulate effort successful candidates were divided according to merit into lists as wranglers, senior optimes, junior optimes and passmen, and this is the origin of the Cambridge mathematical tripos, the oldest honours degree examination. By modern notions the pass standard was low: 'Two books of Euclid's geometry, simple and quadratic equations and the early parts of Paley's *Moral Philosophy* were deemed amply sufficient' by the end of the century. But for honours the examination embraced 'arithmetic, algebra, fluxions, the doctrine of infinitesimals and increments, geometry, trigonometry, mechanics, hydrostatics, optics, and astronomy in all their various gradations' and this was considered a very searching test.[94]

By comparison the Oxford examinations were meaningless outworn forms which nobody took seriously any longer – a ritual rather than a test. Vicesimus Knox, an advocate of examination reform, described them in 1778. The disputations performed during the course on points of grammar, rhetoric, logic and ethics had degenerated into a formal repetition of stereotyped syllogisms read out from 'strings' or lists, handed down from generation to generation of students. Left to themselves in the schools, the disputants usually passed away the statutory two hours carving their names on the desks or reading a novel. The final examination was conducted by three MAs of the candidate's own choice, and the questions and answers in Latin were got up beforehand out of 'skeletons' of stock examples. According to Knox, 'as neither the officer, nor anyone else, usually enters the room (for it is reckoned very ungenteel) the examiners and the candidates often converse on the last drinking bout, or on horses, or read the newspaper, or a novel, or divert themselves as well as they can in any manner, till the clock strikes eleven, when all parties descend, and the *testimonium* is signed by the masters.'[95] In effect, residence for four academic years was the only qualification for the Oxford BA.

Other first degrees in civil law and medicine were comparatively rare. Civil law offered diminishing professional opportunities and common law was not taught until Sir William Blackstone started his Oxford lectures in 1758. Medicine was not hospital-based and had little connection with actual practice. The standard for both degrees was notoriously low. For the MA and higher degrees in law, medicine and divinity, residence and accordingly lectures and disputations ceased to be obligatory, and such exercises as continued to be required after a period of years on the books were largely nominal, save perhaps for the BD at Cambridge. Advanced study and research had no official encouragement; they were pursued by dons as hobbies, if at all.

Outside the statutory degree studies were the lectures of the university professors, endowed to expound particular subjects. During the century the number of chairs increased considerably, in such diverse subjects as poetry, Anglo-Saxon, Arabic, chemistry, astronomy, botany and geology. A Regius chair of modern history was established at each university in 1724 by George I with a view to having men trained for the state service. But the traditional systems of study had become so ossified that no room could be found for these new subjects, and if professors started by giving lectures they soon stopped because nobody went to hear them. The first two Woodwardian professors of geology at Cambridge each gave an inaugural lecture and then continued silent, the second occupant of the chair throughout the twenty-eight years of his tenure.[96] Certainly there were professors who lectured, but they were exceptional and since their lectures had no connection with degree courses and exercises audiences were probably confined to the casually interested.

In time professorships became prizes for place hunters; no special knowledge or competence was required and few academic responsibilities were incurred, unless one happened to be exceptionally conscientious. An Oxford satirist scoffed in 1726: 'I have known a profligate debauchee chosen professor of moral philosophy, and a fellow who never looked upon the stars soberly in his life professor of astronomy.'[97] Thus, a man passed over for the chair in one subject might get one in another, if he could collect sufficient support, and if he had a conscience he would read the subject up afterwards. These freehold sinecures were often held in plurality with others in the church. Richard Watson, a progressive and enlightened man for his time, exchanged the chemistry chair at Cambridge for the Regius chair of divinity in 1771 and held this for thirty-four years in conjunction with the bishopric of Llandaff, living for much of the time neither in Cambridge nor Llandaff but on his private estate at Windermere.

Although the fact of the university's existence was made more evident by splendid new buildings, the predominance of the colleges was complete. Collectively, they were nine or ten times as wealthy as the university, and the college heads virtually ruled it. Two new ones were founded at Oxford: Worcester College (1714) was the ancient Gloucester Hall endowed by a Worcestershire baronet; Hertford College (1740) was the former Hart Hall transformed by its principal, Richard Newton. Despite great differences in size and wealth, the colleges were broadly similar. Each one tended to be self-centred and inbred, jealous of its autonomy and suspicious of the university. Many of them preserved ancient territorial associations and links with particular schools. New College was still confined to boys from Winchester, King's College to Etonians, and All Souls consisted entirely of fellows, many recruited from the founder's kin.[98]

The fellows, the permanent members of the college, in most cases elected their own head, usually from among their own number, whilst they themselves were chosen from the scholars, who were ordinarily appointed from the undergraduates. As a rule the fellows had to be unmarried clergymen, and they held office for life or until they resigned, which was generally when their turn came for a college benefice with its opportunity for matrimony. Mostly they were undistinguished and unambitious; they 'waited for their livings, went to them, published an assize sermon, sent their sons to the college, and died'.[99] But as some college rents rose, increasing stipends and standards of comfort made fellowships more attractive and fellows less willing to resign, and since there was no compulsion to study or write or teach, those without scholarly interests or college office might grow old in well-fed idleness, boredom and eccentricity. In a famous passage Edward Gibbon gibes at the 'fellows or monks' of Magdalen College, Oxford, as he knew them, 'steeped in port and privilege', in the 1750s:

> decent easy men, who supinely enjoyed the gifts of the founder; their days were filled by a series of uniform employments; the chapel and the hall, the coffee-house and the common room, till they retired, weary and well satisfied, to a long slumber. From the toil of reading, or thinking, or writing, they had absolved their conscience ... Their conversation stagnated in a round of college business, Tory politics, personal anecdotes, and private scandal: their dull and deep potations excused the brisk intemperance of youth.[100]

Gibbon's invective may well be suspected of some rhetorical licence, but his picture is borne out by the unconscious testimony of James Woodforde's diary. Woodforde was at New College as scholar and fellow from 1759 to 1776, when he left to take up a college rectory in Norfolk, and the prosaic and unimaginative chronicle of his daily doings presents a view of college and university life at its most somnolent, and it is unquestionably authentic. The college with its sister foundation at Winchester was a small closed society, and for a Winchester boy to become a scholar of New College and later a fellow was almost routine. Like Gibbon's 'monks of Magdalen', Woodforde's fellows enjoyed their founder's munificence with untroubled minds, passing their time in eating, drinking, conversation and amusement, with daily chapel services and occasional college meetings; their liveliest interest was the yield of the college rents and the disposal of vacant college livings.[101]

The tutors, two or three in each college, were the most important of the fellows, and it was they who provided all the undergraduate teaching and so made the university professors superfluous. Since Elizabethan times any of the fellows might act in a tutorial capacity by private arrangement with parents, and instruction was provided by other fellows as official college lecturers. But gradually in the eighteenth century college lectures tended to lapse and tutors became college officers, not only teachers but also guides and guardians of all the undergraduate members. The system depended on the tutors as individuals; if some were later criticized for their negligence and indolence by gifted and precocious pupils like Edward Gibbon and Jeremy Bentham, there were others who won reputations for zeal and

A FORM of a Subscription for a
CHARITY-SCHOOL.

Whereas Prophaneneſs *and* Debauchery *are greatly owing to a groſs Ignorance of the Chriſtian Religion, eſpecially among the poorer ſort: And whereas nothing is more likely to promote the Practice of* Chriſtianity *and* Virtue, *than an early and pious Education of Youth: And whereas many* **Poor** People *are deſirous of having their Children Taught, but are not able to afford them a Chriſtian and uſeful Education: We whoſe Names are underwritten, do hereby agree to pay Yearly, at Four equal Payments, (during Pleaſure) the ſeveral and reſpective Sums of Money overagainſt our Names reſpectively ſubſcribed, for the ſetting up of a* Charity-School *in the Pariſh of in the City of or in the County of for Teaching* [Poor Boys, or Poor Girls, or] **Poor Children** *to Read, and Inſtructing them in the Knowledge and Practice of the Chriſtian Religion, as profeſs'd and taught in the Church of* England; *and for Learning them ſuch other Things as are ſuitable to their Condition and Capacity. That is to ſay,*

	l.	*s.*	*d.*
I A. B. do Subſcribe	----	----	----

Subscription for a charity school

devotion to their pupils. Colleges and tutors no doubt varied in the standards they set and expected.

For the most part the students came from the landed gentry and the clergy, in rather larger proportions at Oxford than at Cambridge. Others came from families of farmers, merchants, tradesmen, doctors and lawyers. The majority were commoners or pensioners paying their own fees, but some of these were assisted by school exhibitions. Poor scholars were still admitted as servitors or sizars, acting as college servants in hall or chapel in return for reduced fees or special allowances, and many of these would be partly supported by school or other local awards. At Cambridge the sizars were about as numerous as the pensioners and not far removed in station; at Oxford the servitors were much fewer than the commoners and the social gulf between them was far wider. Heading the college undergraduate lists were the noblemen and gentlemen or fellow commoners – peers and baronets or their sons, sons of bishops and financial magnates – a tiny aristocratic minority of privileged students who dined at the high table, hired the cocklofts for their servants, were exempt from the vulgar scrutiny of college and university exercises, and received honorary MAs after a comparatively brief residence.

Their fortunes already assured, most of these gilded youths idled away their time with no intention of taking a degree. As at school, there were no organized games and those who were not given to reading amused themselves with their guns and dogs, riding, hunting, gambling, or with the women of the town. Commoners and pensioners, destined mainly for the church, had few incentives to work, unless ill provided for; many of these took life easily and did not bother to graduate. At New College, where all members were on the foundation, the undergraduate Woodforde has remarkably little to say about study. Periodically he is called upon to perform the statutory exercises in hall or chapel; he buys few books, and those he borrows from the bookseller are the fashionable light reading of the time; he has dancing lessons and hires a harpsichord; but what he mentions most is eating, drinking, smoking, cardplaying and other pastimes such as billiards, bowls, boating and cricket. Discipline was easy, save when drunken bouts and destructive violence compelled the intervention of authority, and then there would be written impositions, gating or fines, but corporal punishment was now a thing of the past.[102]

The servitors and sizars, with their own way to make in the world, were the hard-reading men, and from their ranks came the university's eminent scholars and some of the country's leading churchmen. The great antiquary Thomas Hearne, Anthony Wood's successor as historian and gossipmonger of Oxford, was a Wiltshire parish clerk's son who got to the university as a servitor through the benevolence of the local squire. George Whitefield, the Methodist preacher, son of an innkeeper, was an Oxford servitor. So was John Moore, a grazier's son, who started as tutor to the duke of Marlborough's family and rose to be archbishop of Canterbury. It was the richer students, however, who set the pace, and costs rose steadily as the century went on; towards the end, poorer ones were being squeezed out, especially at Oxford.

Although boys occasionally still matriculated at fourteen or fifteen (Jeremy Bentham was only twelve when he went from Westminster to Oxford in 1760), the age of entry tended to become somewhat later. Over the century as a whole the vast majority of students came from grammar schools of all kinds, a large proportion of them coming from the 'great schools', Eton and Westminster in particular; private schools and academies contributed a relatively small proportion, perhaps only about one in ten, but private tutors may have provided as many as one in four.[103] After the 1720s numbers sank; they reached their lowest level in the 1750s and 1760s. The largest Oxford college, Christ Church, had only eighty-three undergraduates in 1750 and smaller colleges might have only four, five or six admissions in a year.[104] Only three Cambridge colleges had fifty or more students in 1781, only seven had more than forty.[105] The universities had probably not been so small for over 200 years. Not only did entries fall but also more students left without completing the course – at Cambridge perhaps as many as one in three, pensioners as well as sizars in the period from 1760 to 1780. Growing expense may have contributed to both these developments, especially in the case of poorer boys, but in times of war, academic and clerical careers perhaps had fewer attractions for younger sons of the gentry than commissions in the army or navy, or the prospects of fortune-making in India.

About 1780 things began to change for the better. Admissions started slowly to rise. Some colleges set their houses in order and began to take their educational responsibilities more seriously. Demands for reform were heard from within – for the abolition of religious tests, for the right of fellows to marry, for competitive elections for fellowships, for more searching examinations for degrees. But effective reforms to modernize the universities were long delayed by vested interests and the dead hand of tradition. 'We may scarcely hope', wrote Gibbon, 'that any reformation will be a voluntary act; and so deeply are they rooted in law and prejudice, that even the omnipotence of parliament would shrink from an inquiry into the state and abuses of the two universities.'[106]

Throughout the eighteenth century, in the education of the nobleman and the gentleman the university continued to be supplemented by the grand tour almost as a matter of course, though its value was now sometimes questioned.[107] Italy with its relics of the classical past was the chief attraction. Bred in the language and literature of Greece and Rome at Eton or Westminster and then at Oxford or Cambridge, and impressed by the visible remains of the ancient world seen on their travels, young milords shipped home cargoes of antique and Renaissance statuary, bronzes, marbles and mosaics to adorn their splendid neo-Palladian mansions, classically correct in every detail, which cultivated taste and growing rent rolls had prompted them to raise in their landscaped English parks. Educated men of this class easily saw themselves through the eyes of the Romans; their attitudes to politics and government, conduct, manners and style mirrored those of the world of Horace and Virgil and testify to the influence of the classical discipline in which they had been trained.[108]

Science education

If the universities and the classical curriculum helped to form the aristocratic outlook that adorned the age, they contributed nothing to the economic developments that were gradually trans- forming it. The industrial revolution was effected by men educated along more utilitarian lines in private schools and academies, men like the ironmasters John Wilkinson and Matthew Boulton, or by working mechanics with little or no formal schooling, like Newcomen, pioneer of the steam engine and an ex-blacksmith; Brindley, the canal engineer, an ex-wheel-wright; and James Hargreaves, inventor of the jenny, a weaver and carpenter. Among the technical innovators Edmund Cartwright, father of the power loom, stands out as an exception because he was Oxford-educated and a parson.

For men excluded from the universities by religious conscience or lack of means there were other opportunities for higher education. Apart from the Scottish universities and the dissenting academies, growing numbers of private schools and teachers gave instruction in scientific, technical and commercial subjects unknown at Oxford and Cambridge. More informally, in London and the larger towns, educated men associated for intellectual improvement through conversation and argument in literary, artistic and scientific clubs meeting in coffee houses. One of the best known of the literary clubs was that formed in 1763 at the Turk's Head in Soho over which Dr Johnson presided. Even in small county towns societies of this kind sprang up to provide a forum for the local intelligentsia. Undoubtedly, these activities were stimulated by a steadily increasing output of books, newspapers and periodicals, and by the growth of circulating libraries organized by booksellers, and private subscription libraries which might themselves be literary clubs.[109]

Without some diffusion of scientific and mathematical knowledge among the commercial and manufacturing middle class, the industrial revolution could hardly have taken place. True, some technical improvement was brought about by unlettered workmen, but the chief organizers and entrepreneurs tended to be men interested in scientific knowledge and experiment. Scientific advance came mainly from the activities of groups and societies meeting at first in the London coffee houses, and from public lecture courses given by scientists who were often of some note in their day; J. T. Desaguliers, FRS, one of the most celebrated, lectured regularly in London for thirty years until his death in 1744. Although these clubs were patronized largely by medical men, dissenting ministers and manufacturers, some were organized by and for skilled craftsmen, like the Spitalfields Mathematical Society founded in 1717, of which the future optical instrument maker, John Dollond, was a member. Much of this activity sprang directly from an interest in improving methods of production, and a national stimulus to this was provided after 1754 by the Society for the Encouragement of Arts, Manufactures and Commerce, which offered premiums for new inventions and processes and itself grew out of a scientific club which met at Rawthmell's Coffee House in Covent Garden.[110]

Later in the century, science clubs and itinerant science lecturers became common in the provinces. Many of these were self-educated men – private schoolmasters, teachers of navigation, surveyors, scientific-instrument makers – who made tours of the larger towns to give public or private subscription lectures with demonstrations and experiments in subjects such as mechanics, optics, pneumatics, hydrostatics and astronomy.[111] From about 1769 the Lunar Society of Birmingham was active. This was a small informal group of midland manufacturers and other scientifically minded men which included at different times the steam-engine partners Matthew Boulton and James Watt;

Josiah Wedgwood, the pottery magnate; Joseph Priestley, chemist and unitarian divine; and Erasmus Darwin, physician and botanist.[112] More institutional and permanent were the literary and philosophical societies soon to be established in other important provincial towns; the Manchester society, started in 1781, was the most influential. Active promoters of these societies included men who owed nothing to the universities, but who had been raised in the nonconformist educational tradition which had begun with the Restoration. The connection between this tradition and the scientific invention, industrialization and concern for social improvement of the late eighteenth century was a close one.

About 1780 changes were taking place which in the space of two or three generations were to transform the ancient, seemingly immutable, pre-industrial social and economic order based on the village and the land. It is these changes that make this period the turning point in the evolution of education in England.

Notes

1 For the form of subscription see E. H. CARTER, *The Norwich Subscription Books 1637–1800* (London, 1937), pp. 7–13.

2 H. MCLACHLAN, *English Education under the Test Acts* (Manchester, 1931), pp. 16 ff.

3 Ibid., pp. 49, 62, 76.

4 E. CARDWELL, *Synodalia, a collection of . . . Proceedings of Convocations of Canterbury*, II (Oxford, 1842), pp. 712–13, 718.

5 LEACH, *Charters*, pp. 542–4.

6 J. E. G. DE MONTMORENCY, *State Intervention in English Education* (Cambridge, 1902), pp. 176–8.

7 WOOD, *Life and Times*, I, p. 423.

8 KEARNEY, *Scholars and Gentlemen*, pp. 146–52. For Locke as a college tutor see J. L. AXTELL, *The Educational Writings of John Locke* (Cambridge, 1968), pp. 36–44.

9 The Royal Society's motto *Nullius in Verba* implied that knowledge is not to be derived from words (i.e. from ancient authorities) but from observation and experiment.

10 AXTELL, *Educational Writings of John Locke*, pp. 69–87, discusses Locke and scientific education.

11 See below, p. 211.

12 *English Scholars* (London, 1939), pp. 15, 26 ff.

13 CARTER, *Norwich Subscription Books*, pp. 81–130, for schools in Norfolk and Suffolk. For schools in Leicestershire, JOAN SIMON, 'Post-Restoration developments . . . 1660–1700', in B. SIMON (ed.), *Education in Leicestershire 1540–1940* (Leicester, 1968), pp. 27–54.

14 See below, pp. 182–4.

15 M. G. MASON, 'John Locke's proposals on workhouse schools', *Durham Research Review*, XIII (1962), pp. 8–16.

16 W. A. L. VINCENT, *The Grammar Schools 1660–1714* (London, 1969), pp. 23–39, for the Wase inquiry.

17 Quoted AXTELL, *Educational Writings of John Locke*, p. 254, note 3.

18 C. B. FREEMAN, 'The Children's Petition of 1669 and its sequel', *British Journal of Educational Studies*, XIV (1966), pp. 216–22.

19 STONE, *Crisis of the Aristocracy*, p. 687.

20 A. BANISTER, *A Model for a School for the Better Education of Youth* (London, c. 1675), pp. 1–8.

21 G. C. BRAUER, *The Education of a Gentleman: theories of gentlemanly education in England 1660–1775* (New York, 1959), discusses some of the contemporary literature.

22 'A Dialogue . . . of the Want of Respect due to Age' and 'A Dialogue concerning Education' in *Several Tracts of . . . Edward Earl of Clarendon* (London, 1727), pp. 285–348.

23 Boevey's treatise (BM. Add.MS.28531) has been edited by S. H. ATKINS, *The Art of Building a Man* (London, 1966).

24 J. E. STEPHENS, *Aubrey on Education* (London, 1972) is the only published version.

25 York, Borthwick Institute, R.IV.B.c.3, fo. 54^{v}.

26 His book *Of Education, especially of Young Gentlemen* (Oxford, 1673) ran through six editions by 1699.

27 *The Complete Gentleman: or Directions for the Education of Youth as to their Breeding at Home and Travelling Abroad* (London, 1678).

28 Axtell's edition (1968) is the most fully annotated.

29 Ibid., p. 114.

30 Ibid., p. 289. For Locke's views on public and private education, pp. 165–71.

31 Ibid., pp. 321–4.

32 Ibid., p. 52.

33 J. LAWSON, 'An early disciple of John Locke: John Clarke (1686–1734)', *Durham Research Review*, XIII (1962), pp. 30–8.

34 STONE, 'Educational revolution', p. 51.

35 *Of Education, especially of Young Gentlemen*, pp. 117–18.

36 N. SYKES, *Church and State in England in the Eighteenth Century* (Cambridge, 1934), p. 212.

37 H. J. HABAKKUK, 'The English land market in the eighteenth century', in J. S. BROMLEY and E. H. KOSSMAN (eds.), *Britain and the Netherlands* (1960), pp. 154–73.

38 Professor Stone's note in *Past and Present*, XXIV (1963), pp. 101–2.
39 *Considerations concerning Free Schools*, pp. 1–2.
40 *A Step towards an English Education* (2nd ed., 1740), pp. 1–8.
41 For particular educational charities see *Reports of . . . Commissioners . . . concerning charities . . . for the education of the poor* (32 volumes, London, 1819–37).
42 J. E. JACKSON, *Shinfield C.E. School 1707–1957* (Shinfield, 1957), pp. 4–6.
43 M. G. JONES, *The Charity School Movement* (Cambridge, 1938), pp. 36–84. The SPCK's role is reassessed in the light of the Leicestershire evidence by Joan Simon, 'Was there a charity school movement?', *Education in Leicestershire*, pp. 55–100.
44 So observed Matthew Arnold in 1886, epitomizing Bishop Butler's charity-school sermon of 1745.
45 *Victoria County History City of York.*, p. 91.
46 JONES, *Charity School Movement*, pp. 297–314; G. WILLIAMS, 'Welsh circulating schools', *Church Quarterly Review*, CLXII (1961), pp. 455–66.
47 R. S. FERGUSON (ed.), *Miscellany Accounts of the Diocese of Carlisle . . . by William Nicolson, late Bishop* . . . (Cumberland and Westmorland Antiquarian Society, 1877), pp. 4, 5, 13, 30, 77, 106.
48 *An Account of Several Workhouses . . . as also of several charity schools for promoting work and labour* (London, 1732), p. ix.
49 *Miscellany Accounts*, pp. 106, 23, 75, 14, 51.
50 A. FRIEDMAN (ed.), *Collected Works of Oliver Goldsmith*, IV (Oxford, 1966), p. 295, lines 193–216.
51 [V. N. WRIGHT], *John Day, a village poet* (Sigglesthorne, Yorks., 1968).
52 J. BERESFORD (ed.), *The Diary of a Country Parson*, I (Oxford, 1924), pp. 20–1.
53 DE MONTMORENCY, *State Intervention*, p. 179.
54 J. S. PURVIS, *Educational Records* (York, 1959), pp. 95, 97.
55 S. L. OLLARD and P. C. WALKER (eds.), *Archbishop Herring's Visitation Returns* (5 volumes, Yorkshire Archaeological Society, 1928–31).
56 H. A. LLOYD JUKES (ed.), *Articles of Enquiry . . . of Dr Thomas Secker 1738* (Oxfordshire Record Society, 1957).
57 W. P. BAKER, *Parish Registers and Illiteracy in East Yorkshire* (East Yorkshire Local History Society, 1961).
58 F. J. HARVEY DARTON, *Children's Books in England* (Cambridge, 1932), pp. 122–40. V. E. NEUBURG, *Popular Education in Eighteenth-century England* (London, 1972), pp. 115–38, discusses the role of chapbooks and other cheap popular literature.
59 The infant mortality rate is uncertain. In London (where it was exceptionally high) some 75 per cent of all baptized children may have died before the age of five about the mid-century.
60 W. L. SARGANT, 'On the progress of elementary education', *Journal of the Statistical Society of London* (March 1867), p. 50.

61 For the grammar schools' dilemma in reconciling the traditional curriculum with changing educational needs see R. S. TOMPSON, *Classics or Charity?* (Manchester, 1971).

62 The school suffered at this time from disagreements between the town corporation and New College, Oxford, which had the patronage. *Victoria County History Beds.*, II, pp. 168 ff.

63 *Victoria County History Yorks.*, I, p. 423.

64 C. WORDSWORTH, *Scholae Academicae: university studies in the eighteenth century* (Cambridge, 1910), p. 76.

65 T. W. HUTTON, *King Edward's School Birmingham* (Oxford, 1952), pp. 37–8; L. R. CONISBEE, *Bedford Modern School* (Bedford, 1964), pp. 12–13.

66 CARLISLE, *Endowed Grammar Schools*, II, pp. 47–54.

67 J. SARGEAUNT, *Annals of Westminster School* (London, 1898), pp. 158 ff.

68 J. CARLETON, *Westminster School* (London, 1965), pp. 21, 32.

69 For the social origins and later careers of Etonians see R. A. AUSTEN-LEIGH, *The Eton College Register 1698–1752* (Eton, 1927), *1753–1790* (Eton, 1921).

70 MAXWELL LYTE, *Eton College*, pp. 292–3, 313, 319.

71 Ibid., pp. 317–34.

72 LEACH, *Winchester College*, pp. 367–84.

73 MAXWELL LYTE, *Eton College*, pp. 345–9; LEACH, *Winchester College*, pp. 396–407.

74 CARLISLE, *Endowed Grammar Schools*, II, pp. 125–61.

75 Ibid., II, pp. 374–96, 662–86.

76 Ibid., II, pp. 2–37.

77 Articles on Jones and Priestley in *Dictionary of National Biography*.

78 N. HANS, *New Trends in Education in the Eighteenth Century* (London, 1951), Table III, pp. 26–7. These figures are based on entries in the *Dictionary of National Biography* and therefore probably unrepresentative.

79 Hans' is still the only study, but unreliable in detail.

80 JOSEPH RANDALL, 'An account of the Academy at Heath', in *An Introduction to History Ancient and Modern* (1749), pp. 181–211. See also F. WATSON, 'A private-school master in 1750', *The Educational Times*, 1 November 1911 (p. 455), 1 April 1912 (p. 159).

81 W. A. C. STEWART and W. P. MCCANN, *The Educational Innovators 1750–1880* (London, 1967), pp. 3–13, 35–52.

82 'The Bee', 10 November 1759, in *Collected Works*, I, p. 456.

83 H. MCLACHLAN, *Warrington Academy* (Chetham Society, 1943).

84 D. F. BOND (ed.), *The Spectator*, III (Oxford, 1965), pp. 132–5. See also BRAUER, *The Education of a Gentleman*, pp. 195–228.

85 WILLIAM COKE (master of Thame grammar school), *A Poetical Essay on the Early Part of Education* . . . (Oxford, 1785), pp. lvi–lviii.

86 *Miscellaneous Observations relating to Education*, p. 50. TOMPSON,

Classics or Charity?, pp. 36–48, quotes contemporary anti-grammar-school arguments.

87 'The Vicar of Wakefield' (1766) in *Collected Works*, IV, pp. 63–4.

88 C. MORRIS (ed.), *The Journeys of Celia Fiennes* (London, 1949), pp. 220, 224, 227.

89 R. W. CHAPMAN (ed.), 'Emma', *The Novels of Jane Austen*, IV (Oxford, 1923), pp. 21–2.

90 GARDINER, *English Girlhood at School*, pp. 408–13, 426–38, 461–9.

91 EDWARD HUGHES, 'The professions in the eighteenth century', *Durham University Journal*, XIII (1952), pp. 46–55.

92 See above, pp. 129–30.

93 WORDSWORTH, *Scholae Academicae*, for university studies.

94 Ibid., p. 46.

95 V. KNOX, 'Of some parts of the discipline in our English universities', *Essays Moral and Religious* (1795 ed.), pp. 328–34.

96 D. WINSTANLEY, *Unreformed Cambridge* (Cambridge, 1935), p. 168.

97 NICHOLAS AMHURST, *Terrae Filius, or the secret history of . . . Oxford*, I (Oxford, 1726), p. 52.

98 For the eighteenth-century Cambridge colleges see WINSTANLEY, *Unreformed Cambridge*, chapter 4, and for Oxford, MALLET, *Oxford*, III, *passim*.

99 JOHN PEILE, *Christ's College* (London, 1909), p. 217, quoted *Victoria County History Camb.*, III, p. 434.

100 *Autobiography* (Oxford World's Classics edition, 1907), p. 40.

101 W. N. HARGREAVES-MAWDSLEY (ed.), *Woodforde at Oxford 1759–1776* (Oxford Historical Society, 1969), *passim*.

102 Ibid.

103 Estimates based on Hans' figures from the *Dictionary of National Biography* (*New Trends*, pp. 26–7).

104 *Victoria County History Oxon.*, III, pp. 111, 223, 236, 281.

105 WINSTANLEY, *Unreformed Cambridge*, p. 186.

106 *Autobiography*, p. 37.

107 BRAUER, *Education of a Gentleman*, pp. 156–94.

108 R. M. OGILVIE, *Latin and Greek: a history of the influence of the classics on English life from 1600 to 1918* (London, 1964), pp. 46 ff.

109 T. KELLY, *History of Adult Education* (Liverpool, 1962), chapter 6.

110 W. H. G. ARMYTAGE, 'Augustan academic honeycombs', *The Changing Curriculum*, History of Education Society (London, 1971), pp. 46–7.

111 A. E. MUSSON and E. ROBINSON, *Science and Technology in the Industrial Revolution* (Manchester, 1969), and, for developments in one county, DIANA HARDING, 'Mathematics and science education in eighteenth-century Northamptonshire', *History of Education*, I (1972), pp. 139–59.

112 R. E. SCHOFIELD, *The Lunar Society of Birmingham* (Oxford, 1963).

Further Reading

J. L. AXTELL, *The Educational Writings of John Locke* (Cambridge, 1968).

G. C. BRAUER, *The Education of a Gentleman: theories of gentlemanly education in England 1660–1775* (New York, 1959).

E. H. CARTER, *The Norwich Subscription Books . . . 1637–1800* (London, 1937).

A. D. GODLEY, *Oxford in the Eighteenth Century* (London, 1908).

N. HANS, *New Trends in Education in the Eighteenth Century* (London, 1951).

M. G. JONES, *The Charity School Movement* (Cambridge, 1938).

H. MCLACHLAN, *English Education under the Test Acts* (Manchester, 1931).

V. E. NEUBURG, *Popular Education in Eighteenth-century England* (London, 1972).

D. OWEN, *English Philanthropy 1660–1960* (London, 1965).

D. ROBSON, *Some Aspects of Education in Cheshire in the Eighteenth Century* (Chetham Society, 1968).

R. S. TOMPSON, *Classics or Charity? The dilemma of the eighteenth-century grammar schools* (Manchester, 1971).

W. A. L. VINCENT, *The Grammar Schools . . . 1660–1714* (London, 1969).

D. A. WINSTANLEY, *Unreformed Cambridge* (Cambridge, 1935).

C. WORDSWORTH, *Scholae Academicae: university studies in the eighteenth century* (Cambridge, 1910).

C. WORDSWORTH, *Social Life at the English Universities in the Eighteenth Century* (Cambridge, 1874), abridged in R. B. JOHNSON, *The Undergraduate* (London, 1928).

See also pp. 266, 471–3.

CHAPTER VII

Education in a changing society

1780–1830

The momentum of change

In the half-century beginning in the 1780s education became one of the main areas of conflict in a profoundly changing society. The provision of mass education, and to a much lesser extent the reform of the endowed schools and ancient universities, became persistent public issues. Sustained social change sharpens questions about the adequacy of existing social institutions, and from the late eighteenth century, in fact, sustained change became, to an extent unparalleled in previous centuries, the major characteristic of English society. This was not the first time, as we have seen, that schools, ideas about education, and systems of education, responded to larger changes in society, or were seen as instruments of such change. From the late eighteenth century, however, social change was continuous and pervasive. Although Britain was still predominantly rural, social relationships and assumptions about the organization of society were no longer what they had been. A growing population, agricultural change, the growth of towns and the dissemination of new ideas had given rise to deeper uncertainties and a sense of precariousness in the social structure.

The population had risen steadily in the second half of the eighteenth century, although it is still not certain whether the main impetus was given by a rise in the birth rate (perhaps as a result of earlier marriage) or a fall in the death rate (as a result of environmental and other improvements). The population of England and Wales, probably approaching 6 million in the middle of the eighteenth century, had reached nearly 9 million by the end of the century. From the 1780s towns began to grow, most rapidly and dramatically round the factories of Lancashire, but also in the Midlands, Scotland and the West Riding. Ports and centres of commerce like Liverpool and London also expanded. Even a town like Nottingham, not at the centre of the main processes of industrialization, grew quickly in the later decades of the century, from 12,000 in 1750 to 18,000 in 1780 and to over 28,000 by the end of the century.

It was the concentration of population that produced the main and unprecedented educational problem. It was also a profoundly cultural problem, since the canals, the cotton mills, iron foundries and – later – the railways, brought into being communities working to new forms of industrial discipline, dislocating old patterns of life and the traditional culture and pursuits of the countryside. Child labour and child crime became major social phenomena. Familiar landmarks of behaviour and relationships were destroyed. The new urban communities were cut off from the familiar attentions of squire, vicar, poor-law overseer and school-master. The new towns spread without planning, without local government, franchise, churches or schools.

In many parts of the countryside itself, in the final decades of the century, the impact of new methods, enclosures, increased population and nearby urban development was being felt. Poverty and illiteracy were no less acute in rural areas during this period than they were in towns. One of the first inspectors of elementary schools, reporting on Norfolk in 1840, described how the consolidation of farms and enclosure of commons had altered the position of the farm labourer and social relationships in the countryside since the second half of the eighteenth century. Social change had 'placed vast intervals between classes which were formerly in easy juxtaposition, it has interrupted to a great extent the social sympathies'.[1] The disturbance of a way of life was accompanied by no signposts or compensations. The rural poor and rural rebellion were as much a reality of the early nineteenth century as were urban squalor and urban protest.

In a society of strong traditions and relatively unchanging status and standards of life, schooling for the poor had in general appeared irrelevant. A young man in that situation who attempted to 'improve his condition' was seen as 'a disaffected person, who was not satisfied with the station in which God had placed him, but, forgetting the humility that belonged to his condition, was contriving how to raise himself out of his proper place'.[2] The breakdown of settled ways of life, however, opened – at least for some – new horizons. The stirrings of new political and social ideals, new ideas about justice, rights and education, helped to formulate new aspirations. By the end of the eighteenth century there were more young men attempting to 'improve their condition' – if only in the sense of colouring their existence with some hardwon contact with the world of education and ideas.

The new educators

From the 1780s thinking about popular education was conditioned both by the evolution of new social ideals and by responses to the problems of social change. In this situation new educational ideas and efforts to establish schools emerged from a variety of sources – the political radicalism of the 1790s, traditions of philanthropy, the utilitarianism associated with Jeremy Bentham and the *laissez-faire* economists, the evangelical movement in the Church of England, and the educational radicalism connected with the ideas of Rousseau.

There had been movements for constitutional reform earlier in the eighteenth century, but the radicalism of the 1790s was something new in English political and social life. The combination of social changes and the impact of the early French revolutionary period made the last decade of the eighteenth century a decisive historical turning point. The English radicals made education as central to their thinking as the philosophers who influenced the French revolution had done. Locke's views on education had been explicitly accepted into the thinking of the French eighteenth-century Enlightenment, and through the political radicals of the 1790s such ideas were again made common currency in England, as part of radical programmes of social reform. The Corresponding Societies were symbolic of the new audience for ideas of human educability and progress. The London Corresponding Society, formed largely by working men in 1792, established branches in many parts of London, and corresponded with similar societies elsewhere, particularly in the Midlands and the north. These were England's first working-class political organizations, and were illustrative of one type of response to the social changes.

The eighteenth-century French *philosophes*, who had far-reaching influence in England, placed great emphasis on conceptions of human perfectibility. Education, they considered, could do a great deal, or even 'everything'. Helvétius, who greatly interested the new generation of English radicals, went furthest in ascribing to education total influence over human conduct – 'l'éducation peut *tout*'. For Helvétius, as for Locke, man was at birth nothing, and became what education (by which he meant circumstances in general) made him. The English radicals of the 1790s saw education as one of the objectives in their search for a just and sensible social order. Embedded in Tom Paine's *The Rights of Man* or Mary Wollstonecraft's *A Vindication of the Rights of Woman* are assumptions about education in the context of the pursuit of human rights. These assumptions are more thoroughly explored in William Godwin's *Political Justice* (all three of these works were published within four years of the start of the French revolution).

For Godwin, 'if education cannot do everything, it can do much'.[3] He built a social philosophy on the twin pillars of justice and a rational approach to education. James Mill, the utilitarian, in 1819 outlined Helvétius' view of mankind as being all 'equally susceptible of mental excellence'. If this is true, says Mill, 'the power of education embraces every thing between the lowest stage of intellectual and moral rudeness, and the highest state, not only of actual, but of possible perfection. And if the power of education be so immense, the motive for perfecting it is great beyond expression.'[4]

Through cheap editions of radical pamphlets and books (outstandingly those of Tom Paine), through the public meeting, the radical organization and rudimentary libraries, a confidence in the power of education was disseminated at many different levels of society.

Not the least important medium for the dissemination and discussion of ideas was the early literary and philosophical society. Such societies, in places like Birmingham, Manchester and Newcastle, very often had as active members men who were familiar with the continental philosophers and had perhaps received their education at dissenting academies and Scottish or continental universities. Some of the societies, most notably the

Manchester one, published papers and had international reputations. The Birmingham Lunar Society was at its peak in the 1780s, declined in the next decade and disappeared by 1800. The Manchester Literary and Philosophical Society ('philosophical', it should be remembered, in its sense of 'scientific') was founded in 1781. Erasmus Darwin, after leaving Birmingham, founded philosophical societies in Lichfield and Derby. The Newcastle society was created, on the Manchester model, in 1793. Their libraries were one of their most important concerns. The Derby and Birmingham societies both established libraries in 1784. The

Indigent Blind Female School, Southwark, 1799

Newcastle society's library contained, in the 1790s, works by Bentham, Helvétius, Godwin, Priestley and Mary Wollstonecraft and by 1829 had over 9,000 volumes. The organization of lectures, meetings, libraries and even (as later at Leeds) museums continued to be a feature of the societies in the nineteenth century. The later societies, however, did not have the same important role to play in the dissemination of formative ideas as had the earlier ones, which appeared at a crucial moment in the history of ideas. It was to be a matter of importance that the membership of the Manchester society in the 1790s included a cotton spinner called Robert Owen, who was to play no small part in crystallizing this movement of ideas into educational action.

At the level of both corresponding society and philosophical society, therefore, social realities were being discussed and social ideals being formulated – to be handed on as a tradition to the new movements of the early decades of the nineteenth century.

The *laissez-faire* economics of Adam Smith and the utilitarian philosophy of Jeremy Bentham gave nineteenth-century England its most influential body of ideas. For the Benthamite the objective of social action was happiness, 'the greatest happiness of the greatest number'. *Laissez-faire* economics and utilitarian social philosophy both declared that society was best regulated by the interplay of free forces, with minimal legislative interference (although they considered such interference justified in the case of education). The doctrine of utility included a preoccupation with useful knowledge, and hence with education. The utilitarians formulated views which led to widespread action in the field of education – monitorial schools for the poor, the reform of secondary education, a middle-class university for London, and the mechanics' institute and useful knowledge movements. The utilitarians were anxious to educate the different social classes for their different social roles – the poor to work intelligently and the middle classes to govern intelligently. In spite of its limitations, the utilitarian view accepted that the people were educable, and that they should be educated. Of ordinary people James Mill believed that 'a very high degree is attainable by them . . . a firm foundation may be laid for a life of mental action, a life of wisdom, and reflection, and ingenuity, even in those by whom the most ordinary labour will fall to be performed'.[5] This was a secular theory. It was restricted but it was new.

The evangelical movement which grew up in the Church of England in the late eighteenth century was in some respects the religious counterpart to utilitarianism in its awareness of the changes taking place in society. Its objective, however, was different – to reserve the population for traditional, Christian roles. It aimed, not to adapt people to new conditions, but consciously to warn against social and moral dangers, in order to reinforce traditional religious codes of behaviour. It was a movement at once to redeem an apathetic church, to educate an illiterate populace and to protect the social order.

The early evangelical movement – Wesleyan Methodism – had made a direct appeal to the poor, and it was, as its critics contemptuously called it, 'enthusiastic'. The new evangelicals in the church were equally anxious to save souls, the church and society from spiritual torpor, but were also anxious to win the support of the influential and the great. William Wilberforce, who became their most influential spokesman, wished to 'do within the church, and near the throne, what Wesley had accomplished in the meeting, and amongst the multitude'.[6] With support from the great they hoped to begin the process of rescue from merely nominal Christianity, moral corruption and revolutionary danger. They formed societies (such as the Society for the Suppression of Vice) which prosecuted purveyors of licentious and obscene books (by which they meant primarily anti-religious works like those of Tom Paine). Hannah More, leader of the evangelical educators, warned the lax divines not to acquiesce in 'modish curtailments of the Christian faith'. She was aware, as the evangelicals were constantly forced to be aware, that seriousness in religion was unpopular and suspect in the church, because of its association with Methodism. If coarse and vulgar preachers, she responded, had 'given offence by their uncouth manner of managing an awful doctrine, that indeed furnishes a caution to treat the subject more discreetly, but it is no just reason for avoiding the doctrine'.[7] The evangelicals were as anxious as the eighteenth-century church in general to preach to the poor acceptance of their subordinate status, but they believed it necessary to take active measures. Their main weapons became the printing press and the Sunday school.

The evangelical tracts, of which Hannah More was the most famous author, were simple moral tales illustrating basic Christian virtues and the rightness of the social order. Two million of Hannah More's tracts were reputed to have been sold in 1795. Legh Richmond's *The Dairyman's Daughter* is also said to have sold 2 million copies. But it is difficult to estimate the real size of the readership, since a tract sold or distributed was far from meaning a tract read. The printed word had certainly come to be seen, however, as an important weapon in the armoury of education. Evangelical publications, like their campaigns for Sunday observance and against immorality and vice, became important influences on the character of Victorian life. One of the influences explicitly attacked by the evangelicals

was that of Rousseau. Although Rousseauism as a political
doctrine was woven into the revolutionary and radical movements
of Europe in the late eighteenth century, his educational doctrine
had immediate influence in England largely in terms of middle-
class experiments. Rousseau and the English Rousseauites were
not specifically concerned with the problems of mass education
in an industrialized society. They were not concerned, like
Helvétius and Godwin for example, with education as a factor
in social reform. The major contribution of Rousseau and his
English followers was to focus attention on the development of
the individual child. For Rousseau the natural growth of the
individual was of paramount importance. In a later phase of
radical educational thought, in fact, John Dewey was to criticize
Rousseau for believing that the native faculties could be
developed 'irrespective of the use to which they are put. And it is
to this separate development that education coming from social
contact is to be subordinated.'[8] *Émile* was a major influence in
educational theory, however, precisely because it focused
attention on natural development. Rousseau took ideas which had
been alive in educational thought since the Renaissance,
Comenius and Locke, and placed them in a new theoretical
framework of the 'natural man'. For Rousseau the child was
good, and corrupt society corrupted him. The right education,
therefore, was that which most fully protected him from the
constraints and corruptions of society, that which gave him fullest
freedom to develop.

The English Rousseauites, notably Thomas Day and Richard
Lovell Edgeworth, conducted experiments: the first brought up
two orphan girls in the hope that one might make him a perfect
wife, and the latter brought up a son, to demonstrate Rousseau's
principles. Both failed: Day considered both products imperfect
and found them husbands elsewhere, and Edgeworth's son grew
up wild and was packed off to boarding school. Edgeworth and
Day had both been active members of the Birmingham Lunar
Society, and both made important contributions to the literature
of education, the former with his daughter Maria, whose own
books, including her *Moral Tales*, were heralds of a renewed
interest in literature about and for children at the end of the
eighteenth century. The Rousseauite educational experiments
themselves had little influence. Criticism was made even by
progressive educators of the danger inherent in Rousseau's

concentration on the individual. Critics could agree with him 'that the severest evil which children suffer is the bondage which they endure', but pointed out that 'to be the object of constant attention, as the Emilius of Rousseau must have been, would, without any vanity on his part, lead him into the error of supposing that himself and his education were the great business of the world'.[9] Wordsworth was also suspicious of an education as total as that of the Rousseauite educator. The child protected was, in Wordsworth's view in 1805, the reverse of free, and hence his contempt for would-be

> keepers of our time,
> The guides and wardens of our faculties,
> Sages who in their prescience would control
> All accidents . . .[10]

Just as, mainly in the seventeenth century, Europe arrived at a new conception of childhood, so in the late eighteenth century Rousseau and the Romantics in their different ways helped to establish the child as a major theme in literature, and as a proper subject of study and concern. In the mid-eighteenth century Thomas Gray had idealized the innocence of Eton schoolboys in contrast to the adult world that awaited them:

> Yet see how all around 'em wait,
> The Ministers of human fate,
> And black Misfortune's baleful train![11]

Blake, in the *Songs of Innocence*, had in 1789 made a major contribution to the tradition. Coleridge emphasized the innocence of childhood, Wordsworth both its innocence and wisdom. For Wordsworth, in a famous phrase, the child was 'father of the man'. What, he asked, looking at a 6-year-old child, 'hast thou to do with sorrow, or the injuries of tomorrow?' His own career, he explained at the turn of the century, was dedicated to exploring 'this infant sensibility, great birthright of our being'.[12] The Romantic view was far removed from that of the natural depravity of children.

Late eighteenth-century society had discovered, then, the educational problems of a mass society, and those of the individual child. The answers to the problems were not easy. There were profoundly different views, for example, about the role of the state in achieving a 'national' education. Joseph Priestley and

William Godwin were opposed to state involvement in education, since government would tend to use education to buttress its own position. The evangelical educationalists were concerned with a philanthropic enterprise for the spiritual good of the nation, and in such a work the state had no part. Paine, on the other hand, was willing to let government lay the groundwork of a national system. Adam Smith and Malthus were both in favour of publicly provided education, as it was too important to be left to philanthropy. These diverse positions were to be a feature of educational controversy far into the nineteenth century.

All of these educational policies and programmes, it is important to note, met with resistance, based on fear of an educated populace and suspicion of the motives of educators. The nature of the opposition to extreme radical views such as those of Paine and Godwin is not difficult to picture, and the more orthodox educators joined in the opposition. Just as evangelicalism was tainted by its identification with Methodism, so were even the orthodox educators tainted by identification with revolution. The bishop of Rochester was proclaiming in 1800 that 'schools of Jacobinical rebellion . . . schools of atheism and disloyalty abound in this country; schools in the shape and disguise of Charity Schools and Sunday Schools'.[13] Hannah More and her sister met persistent and virulent opposition to their Sunday schools in Cheddar, from the farmers and dignitaries of the church. Hannah More was as little anxious as her opponents to upset the social order, but she believed that the ability to read was essential for a Christian society. Her opponents saw her work as undermining the natural and necessary ignorance of the poor, and therefore the social order. *The Anti-Jacobin* was in the late nineties waging a violent campaign against the Sunday schools, describing them as 'nurseries of fanaticism'.[14] Attempts to found schools in rural areas met with apathy or opposition from farmers afraid that their labourers would become disaffected. Sunday schools were described in Hull in 1788 as 'a preposterous institution, replete with folly, indolence, fanaticism and mischief'. Ignorance was necessary for the poor: 'what ploughman who could read the renowned history of *Tom Hickathrift, Jack the Giant-killer*, or the *Seven Wise Men*, would be content to whistle up one furrow and down another, from the dawn in the morning, to the setting of the sun?'[15] Early Sunday-school teachers in Glasgow were suspected of conspiracy and required by the sheriff to take the oath of allegiance.[16] As Joseph Priestley pointed out in Birmingham, libraries were looked on with suspicion by the Anglican clergy, and when they could not prevent them being organized, 'they have endeavoured to get the control of them, for the sake of keeping out such books as they wish the common people not to read'.[17] None of this resistance was to disappear quickly or easily.

The extent of the problem

In the early 1820s an attempt to establish a nonconformist 'British' school in Lambeth was explained on the grounds that even a limited inquiry in part of the parish had shown

> that out of forty-one families, comprising one hundred and twenty-four children between the ages of six and fourteen, there were only twenty-six who received daily instruction; thirty had occasionally attended Sunday Schools; whilst the remaining seventy were wholly without education. In another part, comprising three hundred and forty-one children between the ages of six and fourteen, two hundred and two were found to be uneducated.[18]

In ensuing decades this kind of inquiry was to be carried out more widely and systematically, and in dense urban areas always with the same result — that there existed a high percentage of children without schooling. Paradoxically, the literacy rate in towns was often higher than in country districts, but the concentration of population in the towns made the problem of education in the areas of greatest density and poverty a more intractable one. In some cases the amount and proportion of illiteracy rose in the early industrial towns.

There is no doubt that overall literacy as measured by the signatures of brides and bridegrooms increased in the late eighteenth century. The East Riding figures, as we have seen, show a rise in the literacy rate between 1754 and 1800, in the case of bridegrooms from 64 to 67 per cent, and brides from 39 to 48 per cent. A national sample of the evidence for roughly the same period showed an average rise from about 42 to 54 per cent in country parishes and a drop from 56 to 53 per cent in towns.[19] The figures hide, of course, considerable regional differences, and although the overall national improvement was clear, it was not spectacular. Early industrial England probably had a literacy rate of under two-thirds for men and nearly a half for women. Although such figures remain an important comparative guide, it is difficult even for this period to assess their meaning in qualitative terms. The numerical problem was more straightforward. The first parliamentary committee to consider education, in 1816, estimated that 120,000 London children were entirely without educational facilities. This was only the first official recognition of the magnitude of the problem.

From the late eighteenth century changes in available reading matter were quite substantial, and became an increasingly important factor in questions of education and literacy. In the first instance many of the changes were of most direct concern to middle-class readers. The price of new books was high throughout the eighteenth century, but after a copyright decision in 1774 cheap reprints of various kinds of literature became available. Although high stamp duty made newspapers prohibitive to the common reader throughout this period, the radical press was beginning to reach out to a wider audience (in 1794, for example, the *Sheffield Register* was claiming a circulation of 2,000 copies a week).[20] Libraries were beginning to assume importance. In the 1790s working-class subscription libraries are known to have been created at two places in Scotland and at Kendal and Birmingham in England (the latter in conjunction with a works Sunday school). Workers' mutual improvement societies set up their own informal libraries. In parts of the north of England in particular libraries began to be run as clubs or businesses even in the smaller towns. Others were run in conjunction with a Sunday school, a chapel or a public house. Circulating libraries and those attached to literary and philosophical societies served various categories of middle-class taste.[21]

From the 1780s an increasing number of working men, either self-educated or with a flimsy basis of schooling, were able to gain access to books in all kinds of ways, including loans from wealthier acquaintances in the neighbourhood in religious or political movements. Books can never have been far away from radical organizations. Francis Place, a tailor who was later to become prominent in reform movements, joined the London Corresponding Society in 1794. At his division in Covent Garden the members subscribed for books which 'were read by all the members in rotation who chose to read them before they were finally consigned to the subscriber'. At Sunday evening meetings they had

> readings, conversations, and discussions. . . . The Chairman (each man was chairman in rotation) read from some book a chapter or part of a chapter, which as many as could read the chapter at their homes, the book passing from one to the other, had done, and at the next meeting a portion of the chapter was again read and the persons present were invited to make remarks thereon.[22]

Similar activities were often part of other traditions, including the Methodist and Owenite ones.

Older contributions to literacy also continued to appear. Spelling books, primers and readers, grammars, catechisms, pocket histories and geographies, introductions to arithmetic and natural history, were produced in large quantities in the late decades of the eighteenth century. Chapbooks continued to be popular fare. All of these types of reading matter, and not least the great quantity of evangelical tracts, must be seen as contributory evidence of the picture of literacy at the beginning of the nineteenth century.

Schooling for the poor

Existing schools which provided for the children of the poor were not always, as came to be increasingly the case, demarcated along strict class lines. Many of the endowed schools had, as we have seen, become wholly or in part English and petty schools, taking children from a wide variety of backgrounds – although some of them were by now beginning to acquire a higher status and becoming middle-class or even upper-class preserves. In Lancashire, the attendance of middle-class children at a charity school such as the one in Lancaster, and of poorer children at a grammar school such as the one in Bury, made the two kinds of school barely distinguishable.[23] Generally speaking, however, charity schools at the end of the eighteenth century were training poor children for a specific status in society and for specific occupations, while the endowed schools were struggling to reconcile their roles as providers both of basic literacy and of a higher education in the classical tradition. Some schools maintained the uneasy balance, most gravitated in one direction or the other.

The choice was a social one, as was illustrated in the 1820s by the corporation of Bristol. Under pressure to widen the grammar-school gates to 'the children of persons of a very inferior condition' they preferred to have no school at all, and with dwindling numbers the school in fact closed from 1829 for nineteen years.[24] The real nineteenth-century status of these schools began to be defined more strictly as the education of the poor was itself provided in schools designed explicitly for them, and as, at the other end of the scale, the children of the wealthier classes left the grammar schools for the widening network of residential public schools.

The charity schools were themselves able to make only a limited contribution to education in the changed situation. Some counties, such as Lincolnshire and Derbyshire, had a fair scatter of charity schools (in 1800 Derbyshire had seventy-four charity schools well distributed over the county).[25] New ones were still being founded, as, for example, a day school of industry founded at St Marylebone, in London, in 1791, where the boys were employed in shoe-closing, shoemaking, and pin-heading, and the girls in wool-spinning and reeling, knitting and needlework. Subscribers were invited to give orders for their shirts, shifts and table linen. The 200 children in the school were trained 'to the habits of virtue and industry'.[26] Charity schools were continuing, therefore, to contribute to the provision of education for the poor, often in the form of schools of industry, but they were soon to be superseded by the monitorial schools, which were seen to be able to handle more children, more cheaply.

A new dimension in schooling for the poor was achieved with the Sunday-school movement of the 1780s. Though these were not the first such schools, it was Robert Raikes, evengelical churchman and editor of the *Gloucester Journal*, who launched the movement. In 1783 he published his experience of Sunday work with street urchins, and the movement was quickly taken up by Methodists, evangelicals and the church more widely. The purpose of the schools was simple – to teach children to read the Bible, and, in Hannah More's words, 'to train up the lower classes in habits of industry and piety'.[27] In 1791 the children of Lincoln were 'taught to read, to say the Church Catechism, and short Morning and Evening Prayers. . . . They are instructed in such plain religious truths as they can understand; such as will direct and fix their faith, improve their hearts, and regulate

'The Schoolmistress' by J. Coles after F. Wheatley

their manners.'[28] Hannah More considered writing an unnecessary accomplishment for the poor, and this view was widely held. The Wesleyans particularly opposed the teaching of writing in their Sunday schools.

In Wales the social implications of the Sunday-school movement were wider. After the collapse of the circulating schools at the end of the 1770s a charity-school movement, begun by Thomas Charles in north Wales in the 1780s, also gave rise to Sunday schools, but with a difference characteristic of Welsh education. They brought in adults and children alike, and were self-governing, democratic organizations, in the words of an official report of the 1840s — 'a mixture of worship, discussion, and elementary education, which the congregation performs for itself'.[29]

In England the movement rapidly became nationwide. Some factory owners opened Sunday schools at their works. It is remarkable that, in the period of reaction against revolution in France and radicalism at home, the Sunday schools should have been singled out for attack as subversive. Hannah More's schools, where the teaching was based on 'the Catechism, broken into short questions, Spelling Books, Psalter, Common Prayer, Testament, Bible', and where the children repeated Watts's hymns every Sunday, learned the collect, the sermon on the mount, and 'many other chapters and psalms',[30] came under special attack, mainly because of her known evangelical sympathies. In the famous 'Blagdon Controversy' between 1800 and 1804 one of her schools became the focus of her struggle with a virulently conservative faction in the church. Eventually the school had to close.

The success of the Sunday schools, some of which extended their activities to weekday evenings, helped to prepare for the next phase of development – the weekday schools on the monitorial system. The monitorial schools, it should be noted, frequently met with the same apathy (including from clergymen) as Sunday schools had done, but not with the same hostility – although the separate Church of England and nonconformist monitorial movements were hostile enough towards each other.

A writer in 1819 expressed his belief that Dr Andrew Bell and Joseph Lancaster, the two founders of the monitorial system, would be honoured 'with sentiments more elevated and spiritual than those due to the talents of a Watt and an Arkwright'.[31] They were hailed, indeed, as inventors of a piece of social machinery that was both simple and economical, an instrument suited to the needs and outlook of the times. No one took up the system more enthusiastically than Bentham and the utilitarians. To its supporters it appeared faultless, and teachers who were trained for National Society schools were forbidden to depart from 'the beautiful and efficient simplicity of the system'.[32]

Joseph Lancaster, a Quaker, opened a school for poor children in 1798. It attracted widespread interest since, as an active supporter put it, Lancaster provided the possibility of making 'arrangements for the education of every poor child in the kingdom at a very trifling expense to the public'.[33] The Royal Lancasterian Society was formed in 1808 to expand the work and rescue it from Lancaster's ruinous finances; six years later, without Lancaster, it became the British and Foreign School Society. Dr Andrew Bell, a clergyman of the Church of England, conducted a monitorial experiment in Madras, which he described in

An Experiment in Education in 1797. On this basis, and in opposition to the undenominational Lancasterian Society, the Church of England in 1811 set up its National Society for promoting the Education of the Poor in the Principles of the Established Church. Disputes about the claims of the two men to be considered the founder of the system were long and impassioned, as were those about the relative merits of their only slightly differing systems. The monitorial (or 'mutual') system was to dominate popular education for half a century. British and National schools appeared in competition all over the country – with the National Society by far the larger of the two.

National and British schools were conducted in single large schoolrooms, in which the master could keep the whole school under scrutiny. Under the Lancasterian arrangement the central area was filled with rows of benches for writing drill, and the surrounding space, where the bulk of the time was spent, was occupied by 'drafts' of children standing for instruction by their monitor, usually with the aid of cards hung on the wall. Under Bell's arrangement the desks for writing occupied the outer space, facing the wall, and the central area was used by classes of children standing in squares for instruction by their monitors (called 'teachers' and 'assistants' under the National system). The number of children under a monitor was normally about ten, though under the National system it could be as many as twenty. The work consisted of reading, writing and arithmetic in the boys' schools, plus needlework in the girls' schools. Reading was from the Bible or other religious texts. The monitor drilled his group in work in which he had been previously drilled by the master. General monitors supervised the overall work in the different subjects as well as the general discipline. The role of the monitors was to teach the units of work, to recommend pupils for promotion and to keep order. In a well-organized school a monitor might be given tuition out of hours by the master. He was likely to be about 10 or 11 years old. In other schools he might receive perfunctory instruction, and be more or less the same age as his class. The whole process was regulated by a system of rewards and punishments, and was seen as in itself a course of moral training. It could operate in large and small schools alike. At a school for 150 boys at Usk, in Monmouthshire, for example, the best boy of the week in a class earned $\frac{1}{2}$d., the best catechism boy of the day could earn a medal with riband

and in some cases $\frac{1}{2}$d. Promotion earned $\frac{1}{4}$d., and monitors could earn, in various circumstances, $\frac{1}{2}$d., 1d. or 2d. a week, merit tickets or books. All tickets and rewards were forfeited 'by neglect to attend at the Hour appointed for procession to respective places of Worship on Sunday'. Punishments for swearing, lying, quarrelling, talking, coming to school dirty or late, playing truant, telling tales, being disobedient or absent from church included confinement in a closet, suspension in a basket, the pillory, being handcuffed behind, being washed in public, wearing a fool's cap and expulsion.[34] While the upper-class boy in the public school had to be content with flogging as a punishment, the boy from a poor family had a wide range of punishments – though in these schools in this period rarely corporal punishment. Even otherwise enlightened schools followed the monitorial pattern, and children at the Hills' progressive school at Hazelwood, for example, were confined in dark closets for punishment.

The British Society and the National Society both trained teachers, though the training amounted to nothing more than mastering the intricacies of the system. The schools, like their predecessors, aimed to discipline 'the infant poor to good and orderly habits, to train them to early piety'. A typical expression of the purpose of a National school was 'to confer upon the Children of the Poor the Inestimable Benefit of Religious Instruction, combined with such other Acquirements as may be suitable to their Stations in Life, and calculated to render them useful and respectable Members of Society'.[35] In the circumstances of early industrial England this seemed an ideal machine – it was not only simple and inexpensive, it was sufficient. As a form of school organization it was adopted outside the British and National systems. Endowed schools doing elementary work adopted it widely, and some were converted into National schools. Others adopted it for their lower schools. Even Charterhouse introduced the system in 1813. As late as the 1830s and 1840s grammar schools went over to the monitorial system (for example, Stockport in the early 1830s and the lower school at Brigg grammar school from 1841 to 1847).[36]

The central criticism of the system was, of course, that pupils 'who were little more than infants, without training, without special instruction, with no qualifying test, were set to waste their own time and that of their still younger companions under the nominal supervision of the teacher'.[37] A 7-year-old boy

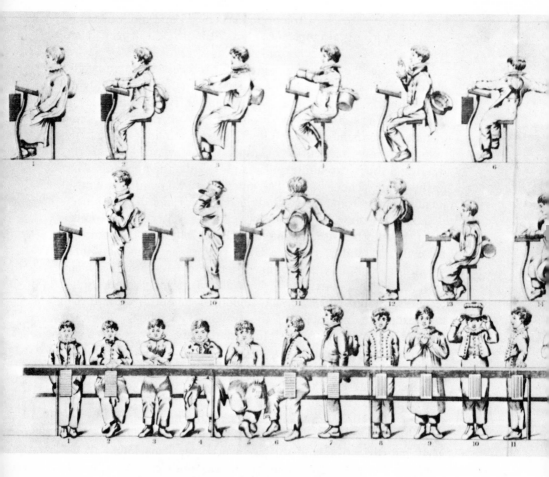

Vocabulary of Commands and Order of Occupation

The following are the usual commands, which may be communicated either visibly or audibly.

Nine o'clock

The school commences. The children, on entering, proceed to their desks, and the master reads a chapter from the Bible, the boys remaining perfectly quiet.

Fifteen minutes past nine

The training of the monitors: the mass of the school writing on slates. Preparatory to writing, the general monitor of order would say 'Recover'; the boys bring their hands to the string of the slates (Fig. 2) – 'Slates' shown up (Fig. 4), 'Lay down slates', as expressed – 'Clean' (Fig. 5) 'Slates'; the writing is rubbed out – 'Hands'; they cease rubbing the slate – 'Down'; they sit pre-

pared for writing – 'Eighth class monitor begin'; a word is dictated for his class to write.

Forty-five minutes past nine

The boys would be exercised out to their reading drafts. The following commands would be given by the master or general monitor. 'Hands'; the boys clap on the desks (Fig. 2), 'Down' (Fig. 1), 'Clean' (Fig. 5), 'Slates'. The writing is then rubbed out. 'Hands', 'Down', 'Look'; the boys then observe the hand of the general monitor, and turn in the direction he moves it in (Fig. 6). 'Out'; the boys jump out. 'Front'; they then face the platform (Fig. 8). 'Look'; the general monitor turns in the direction of their reading draft stations. 'Go'; they are then led to their drafts by the class monitors, either quite quietly, or repeating their tables.

Eleven o'clock

The general monitor says aloud, 'Stop reading' – 'Turn' – 'Go'; they are then led by the monitors back to their desks. . . . The general monitor of arithmetic then says 'Cipherers – front'; (the boys face the platform), 'Recover' (they clap on the desks), 'Slates', they unstring the slates, and lodge them against the screw on the desk. 'Show slates', they then hold them before them (Fig. 12). 'Look'; they turn in the direction of his hand. 'Go' and they are then led to their ciphering drafts.

Twelve o'clock

The school is dismissed. The commands for this are 'Sling'; each boy touches the slate sling with his left hand, and the lower end of his slate with his right hand. 'Slates'; each is lifted over the upper end of the desk and suspended. 'Hands down' – 'Look' – 'Turn' – 'Out'; they jump out of the seats and stand as shown in Fig. 7. 'Front'; they face the monitor (Fig. 8), 'Unsling'; bring up the fingers of both hands to the strings which fasten their hats to the backs (Fig. 10). 'Hats'; untie the strings and place the hats on the desks. 'Put on hats', 'Hands behind', 'Look' – they are then turned in the direction of the doors. 'Go'; led out quietly, or repeating tables. A class of elder boys, of from twenty to thirty, would remain behind to receive additional and personal instruction from the teacher.

From *Manual of the system of Primary Instruction, pursued in the model schools of the British and Foreign Schools Society* (British and Foreign Schools Society, London, 1831).

arriving at Newport Pagnell, Buckinghamshire, was sent to the National school, he later recalled,

> to learn but very little. The boys who could read moderately well were appointed to teach the young or lower classes. I was one of these and I had very little time allowed me for either writing or arithmetic, and none for grammar or geography. Our schoolmaster, Mr Johnson, was the parish clerk, and he had to see to the bells being chimed for prayers on Wednesdays and Fridays; he sent the biggest boys to perform the chiming business, I being amongst them.[38]

The main defence of the schools was that they provided at least a modicum of education, in a way that no other system could have done at the time, and where otherwise none might have existed. Some of the schools were, in fact, efficient and humane, and as time went on were able to improve their methods. One of the outstanding problems was the lack of or the inadequate training for teachers, a high proportion of whom became teachers only after having tried other occupations. Schools which were efficiently managed and remunerated teachers tolerably well did succeed in obtaining a supply of suitable candidates. In general, however, progress in the quality of schooling was not to be made until the monitorial system declined and a new approach to the training of teachers was inaugurated at the end of the 1830s.

One critical supporter of the monitorial schools was Robert Owen, whose infant schools at New Lanark were one of the outstanding educational phenomena of the nineteenth century. Owen's views and his very language derived from the eighteenth-century Enlightenment, which he encountered as a member of the Manchester Literary and Philosophical Society. He had received a Welsh village education, by the 1790s had become a leading Manchester cotton spinner, and in 1800 became director of the New Lanark cotton mills, which he made one of the showplaces of Europe. He gave Bell and Lancaster financial support, treated the monitorial system as an important step forward, but at New Lanark proved that something better was possible. The lack of a proper number of teachers in monitorial schools was, in his view, its main defect: 'it is impossible, in my opinion, for one master to do justice to children, when they attempt to educate a great number without proper assistance.'[39]

The schools at New Lanark took children mainly from the

ages of three to ten (when parents normally wanted the children to start work in the mills). In 1816 there were 300 children attending school during the day and another 400 taking part in evening studies and activities. Ten or eleven teachers were employed in the day schools, and another two or three in the evenings. The children were governed 'not by severity, but by kindness'. There were no rewards or punishments. What the children had to learn was 'conveyed to them in as pleasant and agreeable a manner as can be devised'. The curriculum consisted of reading, writing and arithmetic, sewing, natural history, geography, history, religious knowledge, singing and dancing. The infants spent half the time in small groups doing simple lessons, and half the time, under supervision, 'they are allowed to amuse themselves at perfect freedom, in a large paved area in front of the Institution'.[40] It was the infant school in particular that established Owen's reputation. In *A New View of Society* he set out his belief that 'any general character, from the best to the worst, from the most ignorant to the most enlightened, may be given to any community, even to the world at large'.[41] Owen considered his work at New Lanark to have been incomplete and imperfect, and he spent the rest of his life trying to establish conditions in which less imperfect experiments could be conducted, and propagating his principles of a rational and humane approach to education and to society.

Owen's work at New Lanark helped to create a confidence in the possibility of overcoming the problems of industrialization and change. His ideas gained their most enduring hearing at the popular level. A working-class Owenite movement was born in the 1820s, with the objective of establishing co-operative communities, and placing great emphasis on education. New social ideals, imbued with the Owenite commitment to education, were handed on to the Chartist and other radical movements of the thirties and after. The memory of New Lanark and its infant school was strong in popular movements right through the century.

Owen's work gave rise to an infant-school movement. He gave his teacher for the first infant school to be founded on the New Lanark model in London. The infant school idea, taken up by Samuel Wilderspin, was turned into a nationwide movement. An Infant School Society was founded in 1824, with Wilderspin as its energetic organizer of schools. David Stow created the

Glasgow Infant School Society in 1827. Dr Charles Mayo and his daughter took up the cause in the late 1820s and in 1836 set up the Home and Colonial Infant School Society. The schools which emerged from this movement had a more emphatic moral and intellectual character. They had their music, their toys, their equipment and their kindness. The influence of the late eighteenth-century continental educators, especially Pestalozzi, began to be felt, including the 'object lesson' which became a major feature of nineteenth-century English schooling. Pestalozzi intended that teaching should be done more by things than by words, but in the event this came to be accepted in the formal sense that there should be separate lessons in which objects, or pictures of objects, were the basis of demonstration and the learning of information. At its best the object lesson was promoted as a means of teaching simple natural history, physiology, geography or domestic economy, or a combination of these. The Pestalozzian model could however, a contemporary pointed out, easily be corrupted: 'I never yet saw this book [Dr Mayo's book on object lessons] in the hands of a teacher without finding that the little pupils during the greater part of their lesson were not really learning the properties of Glass, or Chalk, or Copper Wire, but were in fact learning the meaning of sundry hard words, such as "*transparent, opake, friable, malleable, ductile, insipid, sapid*"....'[42] The temptation in the infant school was to emphasize its role as a moral training centre and preparatory department for the monitorial school. For Mayo an object such as a leaf or a flower would

> form an interesting groundwork for a lesson. Alive to impressions made through their senses, the little ones will by such means be roused to attention, and when the intelligence is awake and stirring, the teacher should gradually lead them to the moral lesson or the holy doctrine, connected in Scripture with the object he has shewn them.[43]

The kindergarten movement in the second half of the century was to see itself as supplying 'what the early infant schools, always excepting Owen's original attempt, with their various key-notes – Biblical instruction, catechism, or the three R's – ignored. The key-note of the Kindergarten was always the child himself, his natural development, and his natural activity.'[44]

By the end of the 1820s different forms of popular education had been developed on a mass scale in response to the new features of the changing society. The range of private-venture schools that we have seen in the earlier period also continued to flourish. Although new forms of schooling developed most dramatically as part of the new pattern of urban growth, it must be remembered that at this and later periods the village school was of great importance in the overall pattern of education. Some were supported by the parish or subscriptions, some were established as charity schools, others were decayed endowed schools or indistinguishable from dame schools. The majority of them were Church of England schools and became National schools, often adopting the monitorial system in spite of their small size. It was not uncommon throughout the century for village schools to have average attendances of twenty or thirty, though many were very much larger. Those village schools which were sponsored in this way, and found an adequate financial basis, continued in many cases with only small changes through to the mid-twentieth century.[45]

Two early Factory Acts, in 1802 and 1819, sought to regulate the cotton mills and the treatment of pauper apprentices, but had little effect; their educational clauses were largely inoperative, since the means of implementing such legislation did not begin to exist until the 1830s. Owen's schools, though the most outstanding, were not the only attempt to provide schools for factory children in this period. Before the main developments in factory education, mills like those of the Strutts in Derbyshire and the Gregs in Manchester were providing education in one form or another.

A bill introduced in Parliament by Samuel Whitbread in 1807, attempting to link education with problems of the poor law and factory children, failed to overcome fears about an educated populace. From this time onward the problems of finance and control which this bill sought to solve were to be central to disputes about the wider provision of education. The Church of England was anxious to preserve what it saw as its guardianship of spiritual, including educational, matters. The nonconformists were anxious to prevent education from coming under the control of the established church. Suspicions became increasingly acute on both sides as attempts were made to promote educational expansion through the state. This is evident in the case of the work of Henry, later Lord, Brougham, a leading Whig reformer with a major interest in education of all kinds. In 1816 his efforts in Parliament resulted in a select committee to inquire into the education of 'the lower orders' in London, and later of the whole country. This was Parliament's first real incursion into education. Brougham also introduced a bill in 1820 'for better promoting the means of education for His Majesty's subjects in England and Wales'. His proposal was that schools should be aided by local rates, and that teachers should be members of and appointed by the Church of England. In seeking to placate the hostility of the Church of England, however, Brougham now provoked the opposition of the dissenters. The bill failed. The history of the main period of dispute about the roles of Parliament, rates, voluntary effort, the church and nonconformity had begun.

The endowed schools and universities

The 'industrial revolution' coincided with the period when the endowed schools, great and small, contributed least to the education of English children. The schools made little response in this period to the changes taking place in the society about them, although adaptation was difficult, even when sought, for schools governed by statutes. The schools were faced with fluctuating or declining numbers. A symbol of the inefficiency, or disappearance, of many of the schools was their persistent failure to reply to questions addressed to them by Nicholas Carlisle, when conducting the survey on which his description of *The Endowed Grammar Schools* was based in 1818.

The reasons for the drop in numbers included parental reaction to the inefficiency of the schools and their inappropriate curriculum, successful competition from the private academies, and the practice of private education in wealthier homes. The decay of Manchester grammar school at the end of the eighteenth century was probably due to commercial depression (reducing the number of wealthy boarders), a decline in the value attached to classical education, and inefficient teachers. Factors such as these were at work in other towns, and inefficiency due to teachers' age, incompetence or even illiteracy is widely commented upon. At Manchester the result was that between 1770 and 1810, when the population of the city more than doubled, admissions for each of the four decades were 548, 490, 285 and 288. The number of students who went from the school to Oxford and Cambridge in the four decades was 67, 71, 58 and 29. At Bristol grammar school numbers declined from 100 in 1764 to a handful at the end of the century and none at all in the first decade of the nineteenth century. After a brief recovery, numbers dwindled again in the 1820s, and the school was empty, as we have seen, from 1829 for nineteen years. Cheltenham grammar school was described in the 1850s as having 'fallen in reputation and usefulness' over the previous half-century, so that only a few boys were ever on the foundation. At Pocklington in the early nineteenth century the master was permanently absent and the usher, deaf and infirm, incapable of teaching. The schoolroom was let to a carpenter for a sawpit.[46] Many schools were discontinued altogether in this period. Carlisle's reports on Cornwall are particularly depressing, with many sixteenth- and seventeenth-century grammar schools in places like St Ives, Penryn and Saltash being described by such phrases as 'not kept up for many years past'. In many places the masters held sinecures and the endowments were misappropriated. Some masters drew their salaries, admitted no children on the foundation and conducted a private school on the premises. At the grammar school at Monk's Kirby, in Warwickshire, a dissenting minister was appointed to the mastership in 1771. After a fight with the usher both withdrew from the school and neither attended for the next sixteen years. When the master retired a successor was appointed who was 'most illiterate and unfit for the office. He attends occasionally at the School, "where he has nothing to do"!'[47]

In a large proportion of the schools the level of work was still elementary. Many had of necessity introduced commercial subjects, or were conducted in 'sides' (classical and commercial) or departments, teaching English to the children on the foundation and Latin to the scholars and boarders. The schools still admitted children as young as six or seven (at Darlington 'as soon as they are able to read').[48] Schools also organized themselves where possible in lower and upper divisions, and in the case of some of the major schools, set up 'feeder' schools for younger pupils.

Some schools did, of course, go through periods of success, often related to the popularity of the headmaster. In the 1780s and 1790s Hull grammar school, under the evangelical Reverend Joseph Milner, enjoyed considerable popularity among the wealthy middle class of the East Riding of Yorkshire, and prospered under his successors until the beginning of the 1820s.

A new master at Manchester grammar school in 1807 restored its fortunes by aiming to 're-establish it as a high-class boarding school'.[49] Such reforms, coming alongside the development of monitorial education, tended to make the grammar schools more completely middle-class preserves, especially as reform normally meant the restoration of the classical curriculum. This emerges most clearly from the Leeds grammar school case of 1805. Application had been made to use part of the endowment for teaching modern subjects, including French and German. It was submitted that 'the Town of Leeds and its neighbourhood had of late years increased very much in trade and population . . . and, therefore, the learning of *French* and other modern living languages was become a matter of great utility to the Merchants of Leeds'. The lord chancellor, Lord Eldon, took Dr Johnson's definition of a grammar school as one 'for teaching grammatically the learned languages' and declared the purpose of the original charity to be the 'free teaching thereof'.[50] The school continued with its classical curriculum.

Under an Act of 1812 some schools were later enabled to apply to revise their curricula, and an Act of 1840 gave them freedom to do so. The principal effect of the Eldon judgement and the subsequent legislation was to confirm the classical curriculum as the central work of the grammar schools. Modern work was seen as extra and subject to separate fees. Governors and headmasters found themselves in many cases at loggerheads over the desirability and nature of reform. The headmaster of Bradford grammar school, for example, clashed with the governors over 'the depressed condition of the foundation of which they were the guardians'. The headmaster favoured 'restoring to it a purely classical discipline, in order to raise and elevate its character'. Having failed to win their support he published a pamphlet imploring them to 'restore their school to its original constitution'. He asked

> whether sound and liberal learning is to flourish in the school, or those subordinate branches of tuition must predominate. . . . It is a struggle whether the youth of Bradford are to be trained up in the study and imitation of the ancients, and thus become great and good, or they are to enter on their future parts in life, uninspired by a laudable ambition, uninfluenced by the thirst of excellence.[51]

Reform invariably meant a drop in the number of 'free' or poor scholars. In 1819, for example, reversion to a classical curriculum at Colfe's grammar school, Lewisham, resulted in the immediate drop in the number of free scholars from thirty-one to two or three.[52] In broadening their curriculum, but tending to introduce fees for subjects other than the classical languages, the schools were consolidating their status, achieving a certain stability and competing more favourably with the private academies. At the same time they were becoming more remote from the children of the poor. From 1818 Brougham's Commission of Inquiry into Charities was engaged for two decades in the investigation of abuses. Some legal action was taken as a result of these investigations, and some financial abuses were corrected. The overall effect on educational standards, however, was limited. The nature of the reforms did not fail to arouse controversy, since in choosing to be *grammar* schools, it was widely argued, the schools were failing to be *free*; the charging of fees excluded the children for whom the schools were intended. The whole process, argued one critic, distorted the intentions of the founders 'by letting the sons of the rich go free, and charging for the education of the sons of those parents ill able to pay'.[53] The earlier broad social basis of the schools was rapidly being eroded.

Among the endowed schools seeking to consolidate their status there were some in this period which reached out for that of the great schools. Harrow, as we have seen, moved into the top rank of schools earlier in the eighteenth century. From the beginning of the 1770s Rugby did the same. Under a new head, Thomas James, the school established a strong national reputation, and under another head, John Wooll, Thomas Arnold's predecessor, it consolidated its eminence, even though numbers declined in Wooll's later years. When Samuel Butler became headmaster of Shrewsbury in 1798 it had eighteen boys. From its earlier pre-eminence it had suffered a decline over a century and a half. Butler won back for the school not only its local but wider regional support. In 1817 there were 130 boys, about a third of them free scholars on the foundation. Status and numbers, even at this level, were nevertheless precarious. The alternatives of domestic education and the private academy were tempting to parents in a period of increasing doubts about the effectiveness and morality of the public school. Under a James or a Butler numbers could sharply rise. Under another head, or the same head in his later years, numbers could just as easily fall. In the late eighteenth century, numbers at the established great schools generally rose, but there was no security in their increase. The total number of boys at Charterhouse, for example, averaged about 80 before the 1780s, rose to 480 in the period 1816–26, dropped to 90 in 1833 and was back up to 173 in 1844. Numbers at Westminster had fallen to about 100 in the late eighteenth century and continued to fall until the middle of the nineteenth century, standing at 67 in 1841.[54]

The demarcation line between public and grammar school in this period is uncertain. The great schools like Eton and Winchester remained an identifiable group, patronized by the aristocracy and the gentry, with Rugby and Shrewsbury acquiring something of their eminence by the early 1800s. Between these schools and the classical grammar schools the differences were ones of status and social composition. Differences of curriculum or teaching methods were insignificant. The Eton grammars continued to provide the main thoroughfare of knowledge for St Paul's or Hull, Stockport or Harrow. Flogging continued to be the ritualized inducement to sound learning, and was seen as the corrective for all misdemeanours, including apparently, genius. At the grammar school at Norwich, Dr Parr, formerly of Harrow, responded to signs of genius in a pupil by advising the master – 'then begin to flog tomorrow morning'. His lictor was a man who had been sentenced to be hanged, but had been cut down and resuscitated. From his hand Parr 'used to receive the birches with a complacent expression of countenance'.[55] At Merchant Taylors' school, one boy with a long memory returned from college to take his revenge by horsewhipping a master 'before the admiring and approving scholars until he roared for mercy'.[56]

Flogging and cruelty were sometimes the cause of disorder in the schools, but other causes were often mentioned, including the influence of revolutionary France. Most of the troubles related in some way, however, to the autocratic structures of the schools. Eton's famous rebellion in 1768 was followed by five serious rebellions at Winchester between 1770 and 1818. In 1770 some of the boys had pistols, and in 1793 they unpaved a court, and carried the stones to the top of a tower to defend their stronghold, in a dispute over the disciplining of a prefect and other

Sewing class

'petty miseries'.[57] At Harrow in 1771, when Dr Parr was unsuccessful in his application for the vacant headmastership, the
boys, who had supported him, attacked the house where the
governors were meeting, and destroyed the carriage of one of
them. Order was not restored for three weeks.[58] Eton and
Harrow had other rebellions, as did Charterhouse, Merchant
Taylors' and Shrewsbury. Rugby had its rebellions from the
1780s, and even under Thomas Arnold a near-rebellion in 1833.

The criticisms of the public schools that were beginning to be
strongly made were not only of *abuses* (such as the diversion of
endowments away from poor scholars), but of the very *practice*
of the schools. At worst, believed the critics, the schools were
degrading, at best they were inefficient and irrelevant. Criticism
focused on the classical curriculum, and the immorality and
brutalizing effect of the schools. Salient among the early attacks
was that by Sydney Smith in 1810 on the narrow curriculum
to which a boy was subjected: 'the great system of facts with

which he is the most perfectly acquainted, are the intrigues of the Heathen Gods: with whom Pan slept? – with whom Jupiter? – whom Apollo ravished?' Linguistically, there was a search for 'a needless perfection'.[59] Sydney Smith was arguing from experience, and even in his old age 'used to shudder at his recollections of Winchester'.[60]

Boarding schools for girls continued in this period to provide an austere regime and, increasingly, amounted to a coaching for success in the game of matrimony. The range of quality was wide, and criticism of these schools was also beginning to mount. For middle- and upper-class girls, more than for boys, domestic education and the governess remained a powerful rival to the boarding school.

In the early nineteenth century, therefore, middle- and upper-class education remained in general committed to ancient rituals and established forms. Only after 1830 were serious new developments to occur.

The eighteenth-century decline in university numbers, at its worst in 1760, had been checked by 1780, and by the end of the century numbers were back to what they had been a century before. Eighteenth-century Oxford and Cambridge, as we have seen, had seemed to critics like Wesley places of 'pride and peevishness, sloth and indolence, gluttony, sensuality, and a proverbial uselessness'.[61] Newman described the universities' eighteenth-century history as a 'century of inactivity'.[62] Adam Smith and Edward Gibbon had attacked their curriculum and practices. At the end of the eighteenth century, in the words of a modern historian, 'Oxford may have not entirely deserved Gibbon's contemptuous phrases, but it was for the most part sunk in a learned torpor, though there were groups here and there eager to preserve learning if not to propagate new ideas.' This did not prevent the life of the small Oxford college in the early nineteenth century remaining one of 'much triviality, some scholarship, a modicum of gossip and more than a modicum of dispute'. Life for the fellows was punctuated by the routine of chapel and dinners, and 'the long leisurely evening, patterned with cards, conversation and port'.[63]

The picture of decadence has doubtless been exaggerated in the past. In the last two decades of the century some colleges did make moves to improve their teaching. Holders of some chairs which had earlier been sinecures now took their research and lecturing seriously, including in science. These exceptions are important, but Oxford and Cambridge at the end of the eighteenth century remained much the same – socially exclusive, concerned (like the public schools) with the formalities of learning, and resistant to reform. The Scottish universities had their own deficiencies, but remained real centres of learning in such fields as medicine and moral and natural philosophy.

At the turn of the century reform of the two ancient universities became an important public issue. Oxford in 1800 began to reform its degree examinations, and in the next decade continued the process, creating a school of mathematics and physics and introducing the division of degrees into classes. From 1809 public criticism of the universities grew sharper, and although further attempts at reform, especially at Oxford in the 1820s, were unsuccessful, changes were beginning to be made. Facilities for chemical research at Oxford and the teaching of geology at Cambridge were improved. In the early decades of the nineteenth century, however, the universities were torn – like educational opinion more generally – between the conservative fear of institutional change, and the wish of a minority of reformers to see the universities actively participate in the processes of change. A substantial percentage of students at the two universities continued to be the sons of the gentry, clergy, professional and merchant groups. These four groups accounted for some 90 per cent of early nineteenth-century Cambridge, for example, and the proportion and status of the 'poor' scholar at both universities remained little changed. Of a sample of 281 Cambridge graduates (whose social composition will not exactly match that of all *students*, many of whom did not graduate) in 1781–1802, the fathers of 88 were 'gentry', of 71 were 'clergy', of 31 were 'other professions', and of 42 were 'merchants' – some 82 per cent altogether (the only other large group being 32 sons of 'farmers'). Such calculations are difficult to make with accuracy, but give a broadly reliable picture of the social composition of the universities in this period.[64]

The University of London, the basis of which was laid in the 1820s, was intended, in the words of one of its founders, to provide an education in the arts and sciences for 'the youth of our middling rich people, between the age of 15 or 16 and 20'.[65] This institution, which was opened in 1828, was designed to be a university, but in the end became University College. Supported by many dissenters and reformers who had been involved in other educational movements, the new institution was undenominational. Like all educational innovations it met with hostility and suspicion, in this case largely because of its association with the forces of utilitarianism and dissent. The curriculum at University College was designed at the beginning to be broad and to last four years. Students took a range of courses which included Latin, Greek and mathematics, logic, philosophy and chemistry, with English, modern languages, political economy, law and other subjects as options. Anglican and other opposition prevented the college's incorporation as a university, and founded a rival in King's College, which opened in 1831. Thomas Arnold's famous description of University College as the 'Godless institution on Gower Street' highlighted the issue at stake. 'The Gower Street College', he considered, was 'Anti-christian, inasmuch as it meddles with moral subjects – having lectures in History – and yet does not require its Professors to be Christians.'[66] King's College did, in general, make this a requirement of its principal and professors, as well as of its students. The University of London was incorporated in 1836 purely as an examining body for the students of the two colleges (and subsequently others).

Social distinctions had been sharpening between the great public schools and the grammar schools, and from the 1830s this was to be the case between the older public schools and the new generation of proprietary public schools. The traditions of Oxford and Cambridge, on the one hand, and the new middle-class colleges of London, on the other, reflected a similar process of social differentiation.

Adults and literacy

By the beginning of the 1830s there were forty-three towns with populations of over 20,000 (there had been fifteen in 1801); they now contained over 25 per cent of the population by comparison with 17 per cent in 1801. The total population of England and Wales in 1831 was nearly 14 million (it had been nearly 9 million in 1801). In the first thirty years of the nineteenth century Manchester doubled its population and Greater London almost doubled (to nearly 2 million). In the same thirty years the amount of raw cotton imported increased fivefold and the amount of coal produced more than doubled. The railway age began in earnest in

1830 with the opening of the Liverpool–Manchester railway. At the beginning of the 1830s England had great industrial and urban communities with high mortality rates, inadequate and unhealthy water supplies, large areas of insanitary and overcrowded housing and little or no local or national machinery to implement basic reforms. In this context words like 'society', 'town' and 'education' had by 1830 come to have quite different implications from those of half a century before.

The percentage of literacy, as measured by ability to sign the marriage register, rose in these early decades of the nineteenth century. The East Riding figures show an increase between 1801–10 and 1831–40 from 64 to 70 per cent for bridegrooms and from 43 to 54 per cent for brides, increases which are paralleled elsewhere, with the greatest gain among women. Literacy in the country as a whole was about two-thirds for men and about a half for women in 1840.[67] It is difficult to convert the details of schools and literacy rates into a picture of the quality of literacy among the adult working population in the social situation of these early decades of the nineteenth century. The nature of the reading public was changing. Cheaper books became available in the 1820s with the advent of cheaper paper and new machinery. The daily and Sunday press remained too expensive for working men. Libraries played a small but increasing part, especially after the mechanics' institutes had begun to build up their libraries from the mid-1820s.

One of the most important and revealing developments in this period was William Cobbett's production, in 1816, of a cheap edition of his *Weekly Political Register*. Cobbett, defender of some of the older values of the pre-industrial age and at the same time a champion of the rights of the poor and a hero of the popular reform movement, opened the way to the cheap radical press, which was to play a central part in the social and political developments of coming decades. His *Register*, selling originally at over 1s. because of the tax, had been read before 1816 'in meetings of people in many towns and one copy was thus made to convey information to scores of persons'. The landlords of public houses were objecting to such meetings, however, for fear of losing their licences. He saw that his readers, or 'hearers', must either

be driven out into the high-roads and waste lands, or that they must be supplied with reading at a *cheap rate*. Two or three

journeymen or labourers cannot spare a shilling and a halfpenny a week; but they can spare a halfpenny or three-
farthings each . . . Then there is time for reflection, and the
opportunity of reading over again . . . The *children* will also
have an opportunity of reading . . . The wife can sometimes
read if the husband cannot.[68]

In just over a year he sold 200,000 copies of the famous issue
No 18 of the *Register*. Ideas and information, not only about
politics, but about history and literature, for example, were to
come for the first time within the reach of large numbers of
working men through the periodical press, especially from the
1830s. In 1831, in defiance of stamp duty, Henry Hetherington
brought out his weekly *Poor Man's Guardian* (a newspaper, not a
pamphlet like the *Register*), appealing to his readers to 'circulate
our papers – circulate the truths which we write, and you *shall*
be free'.[69] Hetherington and those who sold his paper were
prosecuted and gaoled.

Popular movements for political and social reform which had
continued in various forms from the 1790s were given a new
vigour by the appearance of a cheap popular press, created above
all by Cobbett and later the working-class radicals of the 1830s.
'Knowledge', said the motto at the head of the *Poor Man's
Guardian*, 'is power.' Popular movements had also begun, in some
of their forms, to be actively concerned with education, including
adult education. The co-operative community movements of the
1820s elaborated educational objectives, organized schools, issued
publications, and held discussion groups and classes for adults.
One of the most famous of the many co-operative journals, *The
Co-operator*, produced in Brighton, advised supporters in 1828 not
only to meet to discuss co-operative principles but to 'form themselves into classes for mutual instruction . . . labour must be
directed by *knowledge*, and therefore they will acquire all the
useful knowledge they possibly can'.[70] Such advice was widely
acted on.

Those attempting in the early nineteenth century to organize
education for adults found that the deficiencies in the elementary
education of their students were an obstacle to the spread of
knowledge. The mechanics' institutes found that one reason for
their failure to attract working men was the inadequate basic
education of the artisans for whom they were designed. The

Quaker school under John Bunyan's Meeting House, Southwark, early nineteenth century

mechanics' institute movement began to take shape from the opening of the London mechanics' institution in 1824, after which the movement spread rapidly, for the most part sponsored and organized by middle-class subscribers. The institutes and the Society for the Diffusion of Useful Knowledge, which was set up under similar auspices in 1827, aimed primarily at teaching artisans the scientific principles underlying their trades, and at imparting useful information. The institutes and the publications of the SDUK deliberately avoided politics and religion, and in doing so alienated the working man interested in ideas. Suspicion of the motives of the institutes and their middle-class sponsors was widespread, and in the late thirties Owenite halls of science and Chartist halls became more acceptable alternatives for many working men. Nevertheless, although the institutes proved more attractive to men in whitecollar and commercial occupations, they provided an opportunity for large numbers of working men to encounter systematic courses of learning. They provided another means of access to books and periodicals (although censorship often limited the range): many had only tiny collections, but by mid-century some of them had very extensive libraries.

Basic to all these educational phenomena was the fact of self-education or mutual education on the part of working men. In the 1850s a lecturer reminded his mechanics' institute audience of the time earlier in the century, when 'men in your own class, who formerly pursued knowledge under difficulties, were forced to study in the hours filched from the scanty time allowed for sleep'.[71] A spell at Sunday school, however inadequate, might be the basis on which a man would build, and the *Life* of Thomas Cooper, Chartist, lecturer and poet, is only the best-known record of the acquisition of languages, the learning of plays, the feverish search for a wide range of knowledge, in hours 'filched from sleep' at morning and night. Timothy Claxton, son of an illiterate labourer, recalled in his *Hints to Mechanics* in 1844 that he had had two unsuccessful years of schooling and then, as an apprentice, with his first money bought himself a Bible and cyphering book, and taught himself arithmetic, when he might have excused himself 'from extra labour, after working ten or eleven hours for my employer'. He had the good fortune, like so many of the self-taught artisans, to find someone with books, in this case a journeyman carpenter with 'several books full of examples in mensuration of superficies and solids'.[72] Such men gave one another invaluable help and encouragement, and the history of adult education is not only that of the mechanics' institutes, but also that of small, informal, mutual improvement societies, reading societies, and men filching time to study their scanty supply of books and periodicals. The radical political movement and the pursuit of knowledge under difficulties are essential counterparts to the story of monitorial, private-venture and Sunday schools at the beginning of the nineteenth century.

Notes

1 *Minutes of the Committee of Council on Education 1840–41* (London, 1841), pp. 446–7.

2 JAMES BOOTH, *On the Self-improvement of the Working Classes* (Leeds, 1858), p. 7.

3 WILLIAM GODWIN, *The Enquirer* (London, 1797), p. 3.

4 JAMES MILL, 'Education', *Supplement to the Encyclopaedia Britannica*, (London, 1819), pp. 18–19.

5 Ibid., p. 29.

6 Quoted from WILBERFORCE in FORD K. BROWN, *Fathers of the Victorians* (Cambridge, 1961), p. 76.

7 HANNAH MORE, *Strictures on the Modern System of Female Education*, II (London, 1799), pp. 299–300.

8 JOHN DEWEY, *Democracy and Education* (New York, 1916; 1966 edition), p. 113.

9 MATTHEW DAVENPORT HILL, *Plans for the Government and Liberal Instruction of Boys* (London, 1822), pp. 195, 201.

10 WILLIAM WORDSWORTH, 'The Prelude', Book V, lines 353–6.

11 THOMAS GRAY, 'On a Distant Prospect of Eton College', lines 40–2.

12 WORDSWORTH, 'My heart leaps up' (1807), line 7; 'To H.C.' (1807), lines 25–6; 'The Prelude', Book II, lines 270–1. See also WILLIAM WALSH, *The Use of Imagination* (London, 1959), chapter 1, 'Coleridge and the age of childhood'.

13 Quoted in GUY KENDALL, *Robert Raikes* (London, 1939), p. 122.

14 BROWN, *Fathers of the Victorians*, pp. 168–9.

15 Quoted in J. LAWSON, *Primary Education in East Yorkshire 1560–1902* (York, 1959), p. 13.

16 WILLIAM FRASER, *Memoir of the Life of David Stow* (London, 1868), pp. 21–2.

17 Quoted in THOMAS KELLY, *Early Public Libraries* (London, 1966), p. 130.

18 *An Address to the Inhabitants of Lambeth, on the Propriety of Establishing Schools . . . on the British and Foreign System* (probably 1817).

19 BAKER, *Parish Registers and Illiteracy in East Yorkshire*, p. 12; SARGANT, 'On the Progress of Elementary Education', pp. 49–50.

20 DONALD READ, *Press and People 1790–1850* (London, 1961), p. 70.

21 See KELLY, *Early Public Libraries*, pp. 126–49, 209–18, 220–5.

22 Quoted in R. K. WEBB, *The British Working Class Reader* (London, 1955), pp. 36–7.

23 See J. MICHAEL SANDERSON, 'The grammar school and the education of the poor, 1786–1840', *British Journal of Educational Studies*, II (1962), pp. 28–43.

24 C. P. HILL, *The History of Bristol Grammar School* (London, 1951), p. 69.

25 See MARION JOHNSON, *Derbyshire Village Schools in the Nineteenth Century* (Newton Abbot, 1970), p. 15.

26 *A Brief Statement of the Saint Mary-le-Bone Day-school of Industry* (1794).

27 R. BRINLEY JOHNSON (ed.), *The Letters of Hannah More* (London, 1925), p. 183.

28 REX C. RUSSELL, *A History of Schools and Education in Lindsey, Lincolnshire 1800–1902*, II (Lindsey, 1965), pp. 11–12; see p. 61 for rules and regulations of the Wesleyan Methodist Sunday School, Grimsby, 1820.

29 Quoted from an 1847 report in 'The Welsh Intermediate Education

Act, its origin and working', *Special Reports on Educational Subjects*, II (London, 1898), p. 4. For more detailed references see DAVID EVANS, *The Sunday Schools of Wales* (London, 1883), chapter 10.

30 *Letters of Hannah More*, p. 184.

31 HENRY GRAY MACNAB, *The New Views of Mr. Owen . . . of the Rev. Dr. Bell, and that of the New British and Foreign System of Mutual Instruction* (London, 1819), p. 212.

32 Quoted in R. W. RICH, *The Training of Teachers in England and Wales during the Nineteenth Century* (Cambridge, 1933), p. 2.

33 Quoted in DAVID SALMON, *William Allen* (London, 1905), p. 7.

34 E. T. DAVIES, *Monmouthshire Schools and Education to 1870* (Newport, 1957), pp. 68–70.

35 *Statement . . . to the Inhabitants of Kennington, South Lambeth . . . Disposed to Assist in the Instruction of the Infant Poor* (1823); rules and orders of Kennington District school (1824).

36 EDWARD C. MACK, *Public Schools and British Opinion 1780 to 1860* (London, 1938), pp. 224–7; BENJAMIN VARLEY, *The History of Stockport Grammar School* (Manchester, 1957), p. 127; F. HENTHORN, *The History of Brigg Grammar School* (Brigg, 1959), p. 110.

37 HENRY CRAIK, *The State in its Relation to Education* (London, 1896), p. 33.

38 W. H. CHALONER (ed.), 'The reminiscences of Thomas Dunning (1813–1894)', *Transactions of the Lancashire and Cheshire Antiquarian Society*, LIX (1948), pp. 89–90.

39 *Select Committee on the Education of the Lower Orders of the Metropolis* (London, 1816; 1968 edition), p. 241.

40 Ibid., p. 240; ROBERT DALE OWEN, *An Outline of the System of Education at New Lanark* (Glasgow, 1824), pp. 32–3.

41 'A new view of society', in HAROLD SILVER (ed.), *Robert Owen on Education* (Cambridge, 1969), p. 71.

42 HENRY MALDEN, *On the Introduction of the Natural Sciences into General Education* (London, 1838), pp. 19–20.

43 CHARLES and MISS MAYO, *Practical Remarks on Infant Education* (London, 1837; 1849 edition), pp. 3–6.

44 E. R. MURRAY, *A Story of Infant Schools and Kindergartens* (London, undated [1912]), p. 93.

45 See for example R. R. SELLMAN, *Devon Village Schools in the Nineteenth Century* (Newton Abbot, 1967), chapter 1.

46 ALFRED A. MUMFORD, *The Manchester Grammar School 1515–1915* (London, 1919), p. 232; HILL, *History of Bristol Grammar School*, pp. 52–69; ALFRED HARPER (ed.), *History of the Cheltenham Grammar School* (Cheltenham, 1856), p. 4; P. C. SANDS and C. M. HAWORTH, *A History of Pocklington School* (London, undated), pp. 70–1.

47 CARLISLE, *Endowed Grammar Schools*, I, pp. 138, 142–3; II, pp. 459–61.

48 Ibid., I, p. 400.

49 LAWSON, *Town Grammar School,* pp. 171–5, 191–2; REGINALD W. CORLASS, *The Hull Grammar School* (Hull, 1878), pp. 10–12; MUMFORD, *Manchester Grammar School,* p. 258.

50 See CARLISLE, *Endowed Grammar Schools,* pp. 842–7; for further details (though a confusing argument), see R. S. TOMPSON, 'The Leeds grammar school case of 1805', *Journal of Educational Administration and History,* III (1970), pp. 1–6.

51 SAMUEL SLACK, *Considerations on the Nature and Tendency of Classical Literature* (London, 1822), pp. v, 114–15.

52 LELAND L. DUNCAN, *The History of Colfe's Grammar School 1652–1952* (London, 1910; 1952 edition), pp. 95–7.

53 GEORGE GRIFFITH, *The Endowed Schools of England and Ireland* (London, 1864), p. 9.

54 [WILLIAM LUCAS COLLINS], *The Public Schools* (Edinburgh, 1867), pp. 356, 382; CARLISLE, *Endowed Grammar Schools,* p. 388; *Charter-House, its Foundation and History* (London, 1849), pp. 80–1.

55 COLLINS, *Public Schools,* p. 281 (quoting a pupil of Parr's).

56 F. W. M. DRAPER, *Four Centuries of Merchant Taylors' School 1561–1961* (London, 1962), p. 113.

57 T. F. KIRBY, *Annals of Winchester College* (London, 1892), pp. 404–24.

58 COLLINS, *Public Schools,* pp. 278–80.

59 W. H. AUDEN (ed.), *Selected Writings of Sydney Smith* (London, 1957), pp. 263–5.

60 KIRBY, *Annals of Winchester College,* p. 418.

61 Quoted in G. R. BALLEINE, *A History of the Evangelical Party in the Church of England* (London, 1908; 1933 edition), p. 2.

62 JOHN HENRY NEWMAN, *On the Scope and Nature of University Education* (1852; Everyman edition, 1943), p. 1.

63 V. H. H. GREEN, *Oxford Common Room* (London, 1957), pp. 11, 36–7.

64 HANS, *New Trends,* p. 43; SHELDON ROTHBLATT, *The Revolution of the Dons* (London, 1968), p. 87.

65 THOMAS CAMPBELL, quoted in H. HALE BELLOT, *University College London 1826–1926* (London, 1929), p. 52.

66 T. W. BAMFORD (ed.), *Thomas Arnold on Education* (Cambridge, 1970), p. 162.

67 BAKER, *Parish Registers and Illiteracy in East Yorkshire,* p. 12; SARGANT, 'On the progress of elementary education', p. 51.

68 Quoted in WILLIAM H. WICKWAR, *The Struggle for the Freedom of the Press 1819–1832* (London, 1928), p. 54.

69 *The Poor Man's Guardian,* 24 June 1831, p. 2 (the first two issues, of which this was the first, were not numbered, in an attempt to evade description as a 'serial' publication, and thus to escape tax).

70 *The Co-operator,* No. 6 (1828), p. 4.

71 BOOTH, *Self-improvement of the Working Classes,* p. 7.

72 TIMOTHY CLAXTON, *Hints to Mechanics on Self-education and Mutual Instruction* (London, 1844), pp. 5–9.

Further Reading

W. H. BURSTON (ed.), *James Mill on Education* (Cambridge, 1969).

A. E. DOBBS, *Education and Social Movements 1700–1850* (London, 1919).

THOMAS KELLY, *Early Public Libraries: a history of public libraries before 1850* (London, 1966).

EDWARD C. MACK, *Public Schools and British Opinion 1780–1860* (London, 1938).

J. MICHAEL SANDERSON, 'The grammar school and the education of the poor, 1786–1840', *British Journal of Educational Studies*, XI (1962), pp. 28–43.

HAROLD SILVER, *The Concept of Popular Education; a study of ideas and social movements in the early nineteenth century* (London, 1965).

HAROLD SILVER (ed.), *Robert Owen on Education* (Cambridge, 1969).

BRIAN SIMON, *Studies in the History of Education 1780–1870* (London, 1960), chapters 1–4.

W. A. C. STEWART and W. P. MCCANN, *The Educational Innovators 1750–1880* (London, 1967), part 1.

MABEL TYLECOTE, *The Mechanics' Institutes of Lancashire and Yorkshire before 1851* (Manchester, 1957).

R. K. WEBB, *The British Working Class Reader 1790–1848: literacy and social tension* (London, 1955).

See also pp. 473–5.

CHAPTER VIII

The state and voluntary effort

1830–1869

Committee of Council

In 1840 one of Her Majesty's inspectors of schools described the handloom weavers of Norwich, either unemployed or earning 7s. a week, working fourteen to sixteen hours a day, and most of them unable to send their children to school. They and their families were almost without furniture and possessions, their clothing and food scanty, and their faces emaciated. Every Monday morning about 400 men, women and children attended the children's market hoping to hire out the children's labour.[1] The handloom weavers were only one illustration of the poverty which acted as an obstacle to education. Sir James Kay-Shuttleworth, who played an outstanding part in the educational developments in this period, described the great changes that had taken place in the previous half-century: formerly the workers

> considered their poverty and sufferings as inevitable . . . now, rightly or wrongly, they attribute their sufferings to political causes. . . . The great Chartist petition . . . affords ample evidence of the prevalence of the restless desire for organic changes, and for violent political measures, which pervades the manufacturing districts.

These districts, which he knew from personal experience as a doctor in Manchester, had brought together illiterate and often semi-barbarous populations from the Lancashire and Yorkshire valleys, the Derbyshire highlands, the Welsh border areas and

Ireland. They had accumulated in districts without adequate water supply, sanitation or policing, without church or school.[2] The social tensions generated in such conditions were damaging to the confidence of growing commercial England. By the end of the 1840s, after the decline of Chartism and with the beginning of the economic growth that marked the Victorian 'golden age', confidence was restored. The Great Exhibition of 1851 was Britain's demonstration of her manufacturing supremacy, challenges to which only began to cause anxiety from the late sixties.

The first measure of parliamentary reform took place in 1832, and its failure to enfranchise working men intensified popular radical movements. The reformed Parliament, strongly influenced by utilitarian ideas, implemented the first workable Factory Act in 1833 by including in it the principle of inspection. Brougham was now in the Lords and no longer in favour of legislative action in education. John Arthur Roebuck, on behalf of the parliamentary radicals, pressed for an education bill. Failure had its small compensation in the shape of the first parliamentary grant for education — £20,000 in 1833 to be distributed through the National and British societies. Grants were from now on made annually, and until the Committee of the Privy Council on Education was created in 1839 the state 'merely stood in the position of a subscriber to the two great voluntary societies'.[3] From the 1840s the authority of the state increased, through the inspection associated with the grants, through inquiries and commissions. By the end of the 1860s Parliament had investigated the main public schools, the endowed schools and popular education, had introduced major reforms at the ancient universities and passed legislation to reform the endowed schools. All these developments and compromises, in the face of reluctance, resistance and controversy, amounted to what has been described as 'the beginning of the tinkering system in education'.[4]

The Committee of the Privy Council on Education was created in 1839, with Dr James Kay (later Sir James Kay-Shuttleworth) as its first and most famous secretary. The new body was the outcome of pressures for a body to supervise the proper use of parliamentary grants, and was placed under the Privy Council partly in an attempt to keep education out of parliamentary controversy. Its status under the council gave it a degree of autonomy and authority which was bitterly resented by the Church of England in particular.

The committee dealt not so much with the societies as with their schools, and grants were conditional on inspection. The Church of England forced two important concessions. A proposal that the committee should supervise the opening of an establishment to train teachers was dropped, and it was agreed that inspectors of National schools should be appointed only with the approval of the archbishops of Canterbury and York. It was similarly agreed with the British Society in 1843 that inspectors of their schools would not be appointed without its agreement. Church suspicions that the committee represented an undermining of church authority were intensified in 1846, when the committee began to lay down conditions for the management of National schools. The National Society was much the larger of the two societies and its schools attracted the larger share of grant, which was distributed in proportion to the amount of voluntary contributions raised. In the 1840s some £500,000 was distributed by the Committee of Council, and four-fifths of it went to National Society schools. This fact, and government attempts to conciliate church opinion, caused disquiet in nonconformist circles. John Bright, spokesman for Liberal nonconformity, told the House of Commons in 1847 that many of the dissenters had regarded the creation of the Committee of Council 'as a step leading away from that power which the Church of England wished to usurp, of educating the whole people . . . But from 1839 to this year we have found no step taken by the Government which has not had a tendency to aggrandize the Established Church.'[5]

The committee did succeed, however, in extending its work. From 1843 grants became available for furniture and apparatus as well as for school-building. Support for the building of denominational training colleges was given, and in 1846 Kay-Shuttleworth brought about a new era in teacher training with Minutes which inaugurated the pupil teacher scheme – the replacement of monitors by apprentices. Financial rewards for trained and efficient teachers were designed to improve the quality of teaching. Financial incentives to appoint pupil teachers, and the introduction of Queen's scholarships to be competed for by pupil teachers and tenable at training colleges, were designed to provide a flow of trained recruits into the elementary schools. Pupil teachers had to be at least thirteen years of age, and had to pass an annual examination conducted by the inspectors. In 1853 the state was induced to make a further limited step by offering maintenance grants to schools in rural districts and small towns, on the basis of attendance and the employment of certificated teachers.

The state and the voluntary agencies were beginning to collaborate, circumspectly, in a system designed explicitly for the children of the poor. What had begun as a rescue exercise for the children of the 'lower orders' or 'labouring classes' had become consolidated into a separate system with a separate ideology. The inspectors appointed under the Committee of Council in 1839 were instructed to 'ascertain the number and character of the schools for the children of the poorer classes'. The code of 1860 defined the object of grants as 'to promote the education of children belonging to the class who support themselves by manual labour'.[6] The fact that some of the schools, such as the Wesleyan schools, existed 'for the sake of the children of trades-men, of farmers, and of mechanics of the higher class, rather than for the sake of the children of the poor',[7] only highlights the general picture. Working-class and middle-class education in the nineteenth century had clear identities. They were separated by different curricula, length of school life, attendance rates and cultural and social objectives.

The continued existence of 'two nations' in education reflected a basic social reality. Commentators at mid-century were point-ing not only to England's unprecedented industrial advance, but also to its disparate social effects. In the previous quarter of a century, said one writer in 1845, Britain in its industrialization had 'exhibited the most extraordinary spectacle that the world has perhaps ever witnessed'. Equally unparalleled, however, was the

> co-existence of so much suffering in one portion of the people, with so much prosperity in another; of unbounded private wealth, with unceasing public penury . . . of the utmost freedom consistent with order, ever yet existing upon earth, with a degree of discontent which keeps the nation constantly on the verge of insurrection.

The nation had come to accept 'this extraordinary combination . . . as unavoidable'.[8] If such vastly different conditions of living were accepted as 'unavoidable', so also were the different types of education. Men like Kay-Shuttleworth, hostile to Chartism as 'an armed political monster', saw it as an expression of the separate nation whose children they were involved in educating. William Cobbett, from the other side of the fence, had in the 1820s watched with indignation the poverty which he saw and which the rulers ignored: 'the king is advised to tell the parliament, and the world, that we are in a state of *unexampled prosperity*, and that this prosperity must be *permanent*, because *all the great interests are prospering! The working people are not, then, "a great interest"! They will be found to be one, by and by*.'[9] Clearcut conceptions of the two classes or 'nations' or 'interests' were familiar features of Victorian educational, social and political discussion. The concept of a 'ladder' from one educational system to another was only hinted at in the late 1860s, was not defined until the 1870s, and was not substantially acted upon until the twentieth century.

An important assumption about the elementary schools was that religious instruction was the main element in their work. One of the inspectors summarized the reasons: 'The "classics" of the poor in a Protestant country must ever, indeed, be the Scriptures: they contain the most useful of all knowledge.'[10] Another frequent assumption was that the elementary schools protected society against the dangers of radicalism, including Chartism and Owenite socialism. In 1840, for example, after the first peak of Chartist agitation, two reports published by the Committee of Council underlined the theme. An Anglican clergyman commented that 'before the working classes . . . can be proof against the delusive seductions of Socialism . . . far more extended and energetic efforts must be made to improve them. They must not merely be schooled but educated.'[11] Another report pointed out that mechanical schooling was not enough: 'if the legitimate educator does no more than this, there are those who will do more; the Chartist and Socialist educator – the publisher of exciting, obscene, and irreligious works – he who can boldly assert and readily declaim upon false and pernicious dogmas and principles'.[12] The Committee of Council sent this same HMI to investigate education in Monmouthshire in 1839, as a result of Chartist riots, and the National Society increased efforts in the mining areas at the same time for the same reason. The 'legitimate educator' was responding to relentless economic and social change, of which active social movements had become a prominent feature.

Resistance to the idea of mass education, though weaker, had not disappeared. There was opposition to the 'over-education' of the poor. Mechanics' institutes were still considered by many to be subversive. In the 1860s it was being said that suspicions of education as 'an engine of destruction', though not as strong as earlier, were 'by no means extinct even yet'.[13] In 1862 the principal of St Mark's College, Chelsea, warned that education was 'in many quarters secretly slighted, if not openly decried'.[14] Against such a background, the importance of the Committee of Council, Kay-Shuttleworth, the inspectors and their published reports can be more adequately measured. Matthew Arnold reflected in 1862 that the existence of such a department was 'opposed to so great a body of English habits and English prejudices, that one wonders how it ever found means to establish itself'.[15]

The influence of the inspectors, even though undermined by the payment by results they had to administer from 1862, was among the main strengths of the Committee of Council. The early inspectors were all 'men of respectable origins and of university training',[16] many of them clergymen. They were among the first to benefit from the expansion of the railway system in the 1830s and 1840s. The Reverend John Allen's first assignment, for example, was to report on education in the mining districts of Durham and Northumberland. On the advice of the bishop of Durham he fixed his headquarters at Newcastle-upon-Tyne, 'from which town the railroads and other means of communication afforded an easy access to those coal-fields lying along the Tyne and the Weare'.[17]

The system of grants administered by the Committee of Council suffered from the weakness that it failed to provide assistance where it was most needed. In a discussion of this period the secretary of the Education Department (into which the Committee of Council had been merged in 1856) was later asked about the rule that a grant was not to exceed the level of voluntary subscription raised. Had this not meant that wealthier districts got more and poorer districts less? Of course, he replied, 'the poorer the districts were, the less they got.' The whole system, he agreed, 'acted as a penalty on poverty'.[18]

Factories and voluntaryists

The state was becoming involved in education in a variety of ways. With the creation of a government school of design in 1837, for example, it became concerned with education in the practical arts and sciences. The Great Exhibition of 1851 was a signal for further efforts and the Department of Science and Art was born in 1853 (and brought together with the Committee of Council office in 1856 to form an Education Department, still under the Privy Council). The state was also involved in regulating factory conditions, including the education of factory children.

The Factory Act of 1833 was a limited response to pressure for a ten-hour Act. It forbade the employment of children under nine in the main branches of textiles, and for children under thirteen it restricted working hours to nine a day and made schooling obligatory for two hours a day, six days a week. It provided for the appointment of factory inspectors. The Act was widely evaded, and 'education' was often given in factory corners by illiterate factory employees. One factory inspector reported that it was 'not at all an unusual thing to have certificates presented to us subscribed by the teacher with his or her *mark*'.[19] Some children were sent to local schools, but attendance was often erratic. Children had to produce a certificate of attendance signed (hence the *mark*) by the teacher. Medical certificates which testified to children's 'physical age' were highly unreliable, and the compulsory registration of births was introduced in Britain in 1837 as a result of this and other pressures.

There were, before and after 1833, factory schools which did more than the law required of them and had good educational and social facilities. A large firm like McConnel's of Manchester, in 1833 the largest employer of labour in the English cotton industry, did not, however, directly concern itself with education before the 1833 Act. In this 'they were sufficiently "normal" to need the spur of legislation before taking active steps of their own'.[20] Once the 'spur' had been felt, however, the factory inspector could report that McConnel's had an exemplary school, where the facilities were liberal and the curriculum enlightened, and where six adult operatives acted as a 'visiting committee'.[21] Two years earlier the same inspector had reported that in nineteen factories in the district over half of the 2,000 children were unable to read.[22] The legislation, the activities of the inspectors, albeit restricted, and other pressures were pointing the way to more serious factory improvements.

In 1843 Lord Shaftesbury made an influential speech in Parliament, deploring the state of the manufacturing districts and the lack of adequate educational facilities, and pressing for new measures to regulate the conditions and education of factory children. Sir James Graham introduced a bill 'for regulating the employment of children and young persons in factories, and for the better education of children in factory districts, in England and Wales'. A Factory Act of 1833 had laid down the principle of compulsory part-time education, and Graham saw his bill as an attempt to extend the principle. Its aim was the compulsory education of factory, but also of pauper, children. It proposed to reduce working hours and increase the hours of schooling. Schools were to serve manufacturing *districts* as a whole, and were to be built with funds raised through the poor rate. They were to be under the control of the Church of England, which would appoint the teachers, but separate classrooms were to be provided where children whose parents so desired could receive their own form of religious instruction. Lord John Russell's hope that the plan would 'reconcile the consciences of all denominations'[23] proved in vain. The nonconformists were profoundly antagonized, petitions against the measure were signed by 2 million people, and it was withdrawn. The dissenters believed it 'better that popular instruction should still be left to voluntary machinery for some time longer, than that new authority and new fields of ecclesiastical control should be opened to the privileged church'. Many nonconformists, however, irate at what had been attempted, went further. Under the leadership of Edward Baines, editor of the *Leeds Mercury*, the 'voluntaryist' position entered educational politics, as a movement totally opposed to any form of state intervention, and advocating the ending of government grants and regulations. At the end of the decade Cobden was bemoaning the 'split in the Liberal party, caused by Baines', and regretting that Baines and his followers, 'the very salt of liberalism, have managed to snatch away from us more than half of our old cry of "National Education"'.[24]

The Congregational Board of Education and the Voluntary School Society broke away from the British Society, and refused government grants. By 1853 the Congregational Board had 431 schools. Baines was the backbone of the movement. In 1843 he published an influential booklet on *The Social, Educational, and Religious State of the Manufacturing Districts*, designed to show that Shaftesbury's picture of the manufacturing districts had been 'excessively erroneous and unjust', and that Graham's bill had been 'the greatest outrage on Civil and Religious Liberty attempted in modern times'. His statistics were aimed to show 'the power of *voluntary Christian zeal*, to provide the means of Education and Religious Instruction, even for rapidly increasing population'.[25] In 1846 he published *Letters to the Right Hon. Lord Russell*, with the aim of forestalling another attempt at legislation, arguing that the deficiencies of the voluntary system were being exaggerated. In 1848, agreeing that there were wretched voluntary schools, he argued that 'we have as much right to have wretched schools as to have wretched newspapers, wretched preachers, wretched books, wretched institutions, wretched political economists, wretched Members of Parliament, and wretched Ministers. You cannot proscribe all these things without proscribing Liberty.'[26] In 1861 a voluntaryist minority on the Newcastle Commission was still expressing its belief that 'the annual grants now made should be gradually withdrawn'.[27]

The movement was losing ground, however. It was the inability of the voluntary principle to achieve more or better schooling beyond a certain point that led finally to the collapse of the outright voluntaryist position. Baines confessed a change of heart in 1867, and Edward Miall, leading voluntaryist on the Newcastle Commission, gave his support in 1869 to the programme of the National Education League, including compulsory attendance and rate support for schools. 'We have lived', said one of the speakers at the league's first general meeting in 1869, 'to hear the recantations of a Miall and a Baines – to hear them declare that their mistakes about voluntaryism were what we all knew them to be – well intentioned; and that voluntaryism is quite an inadequate basis for a national system.'[28] The proposals and responses of 1843, however, were a crucial moment in the history of educational opinion in the nineteenth century, and made a national system of elementary education impossible for over a quarter of a century. The half-time proposals were rescued from the collapse of 1843 and came into effect under a Factory Act of the following year, raising to three hours a day (five hours a day on alternate days in some cases) the obligatory school attendance of children in textile mills. The factory half-timer was not to disappear finally until 1918.

Statistics

The growth of traditions of local and national investigation is closely related to the education question. The new statistical societies (Manchester having the first in 1833) were sensitive to education and its relation to poverty. Manchester was quickly followed by London, Liverpool, Birmingham and others. Lord Kerry's parliamentary return of 1833 made the first attempt to calculate the proportion of eligible children actually receiving education. The Central Society of Education made further efforts, mainly in London and Manchester, to collect reliable figures. The controversies of the 1840s were an incentive to collect and marshal data, notably about numbers of places, the length of school life, and the proportion of children in attendance. The education census compiled between 1851 and 1854 by Horace Mann acknowledged a debt to the work of Baines in particular. Two rival education bills for Manchester and Salford were put forward in 1852, and the voluntaryist opposition to both involved a complex controversy about figures. One section of the

Clapham School, built 1810, and 'conducted on the system . . . invented by Andrew Bell' (see p. 241)

National Association for the Promotion of Social Science, created in 1857, was devoted to education. The reports of the Committee of Council continued to provide a close analysis of the financing and operation of schools, an analysis on which the Newcastle Commission tried not too successfully to improve at the end of the 1850s.

The central issue in the investigations tended to be the proportion of children who could be, and were, receiving schooling. The ratio of children attending day schools to the total population was estimated by Brougham in 1818 to be 1:17, by Kerry in 1833 to be 1:11 and by Mann's Census to be 1:8. None of the figures are reliable, but the trend is clear. Brougham thought a ratio of 1:8 or 1:9 was desirable. Baines accepted the latter figure, and when his returns showed the number of day scholars in Yorkshire, Lancashire and Cheshire in 1843 to be one in ten of the population he confessed to a 'great and agreeable surprise'.[29] The figures could be interpreted optimistically. There were, however, serious weaknesses in the picture given by the figures. Baines and Horace Mann made their assumptions about the number of children able to benefit from education after they had excluded certain categories. Mann accepted 'as a sufficient reason for school absence the simple fact of a child's employment, however premature the age at which his occupation commenced'. This, as one of the Newcastle assistant commissioners pointed out, simply ignored the problem of the proper education of a million children, a fifth of the whole. Baines explicitly left out of his calculations the adequacy of means of education for the most destitute and criminal classes. The educational problem would be immensely simplified, commented the assistant commissioner, 'if, by a mere *tour de chiffres*, we could eliminate its most puzzling data'.[30]

The overall statistics also concealed two of the most important problems. They failed to demonstrate the magnitude of the educational problem in the most populous areas of the manufacturing north and London in particular. Investigations in some districts of Manchester in the early sixties, for example, found that under half the children considered of school age by the census of 1861 (three to twelve or five to fourteen) were not attending school.[31] They also failed to bring out the disparity between the number of children on the books and the number in attendance, the latter figure being consistently inflated in all returns (as the Newcastle Commission discovered). The statistics therefore failed to show the extent of erratic attendance and the real length of school life. In the agricultural districts numbers fluctuated widely with the season of the year. In towns they fluctuated with trade, the weather and a thousand other factors. At Hornsea, in the East Riding, in 1847–8 there were 400 children on the roll, with an average attendance of 58.[32] At a boys' school in Hull in 1846 the average stay of the boys was rather more than eleven months, and at a girls' school, of 137 children admitted in the previous year, 89 had left in the course of it. In Salford in the same year a master had been in the school twenty months, during which time 581 children had been admitted and 378 had left. The average stay had been five months.[33] The statistics collected regionally or nationally were liable to give an over-optimistic view of the processes taking place.

Only limited and impressionistic data were collected at the time about literacy. Some evidence was produced in the reports of the HMIs. The report on Norfolk, in 1840, for example, considered that when people were able to read and write in a parish it was 'exceptional' – that 'very few of the adults of either sex, from 20 to 50, could read or write, seemed to be generally acknowledged'. In one parish a woman had acted as clerk for the previous two years, as no adult male could read. At a sewing school set up in Manchester in the early 1860s for unemployed girls between the ages of sixteen and twenty-three, most of whom had been to factory schools, only 199 out of 963 could read and write.[34] The 1851 census, while optimistic in tone, contains some far from optimistic evidence. Marriages in 1851 showed what Mann called the 'extraordinary fact' that of some 32,000 minors who married (about three-quarters of them girls) no less than 52·6 per cent were unable to sign their names. Of the 13,879 dame schools which completed his census returns 708 masters and mistresses signed with their *mark*, as did 35 in public elementary schools.[35] One of the inspectors quoted from the registrar general's figures, showing that in 1844 only 67 in 100 men and 51 in 100 women wrote their names in the marriage register. This showed an increase of only 1·2 per cent for the men and 1·1 per cent for the women in the previous four and a half years. Improvement was 'very slow, and the unapproached mass of ignorance very great'.[36]

Progress was slow in the growth of libraries, though more

factories, Sunday schools and day schools were organizing them (the first instructions to inspectors in 1840 required them to report whether there was a library associated with any school they visited). The mechanics' institutes in the 1840s tried to improve their service, particularly in the technical field — in which they were unique until the public libraries took over their function. The Public Libraries Act of 1850 first made it generally possible for authorities to use a ½d. rate to subsidize the provision of libraries. This was permissive and limited legislation, passed — as all educational measures were — in the face of keen resistance, and easy to obstruct or delay locally. A second Act, in 1855, raised the permitted rate to 1d., but even by 1869 only thirty-five places had adopted the Act and opened public libraries.[37] The ones that were opened, however, were patronized by working men, especially where, as in the pioneering case of Warrington as early as 1848, they opened in the evenings. One of the leaders of the National Education League believed that the new free libraries had 'created and strengthened an interest in thousands and tens of thousands of the working and poorer classes'.[38]

The range of journals available at the popular level included both the radical press and religious journals, such as the *Penny Magazine*. Some, like the *Saturday Magazine*, were purely collections of 'useful information'. A typical issue might contain an account of some famous building, a piece on Mexico, extracts from Dr Johnson and something about elephants. The line drawings were not the least feature of the popularity of many of these journals.

A reduction in the newspaper tax enabled the *News of the World* to appear (in 1843) as a Sunday paper at 1d. The abolition of the newspaper taxes led to a 1d. *Daily Telegraph* in 1855. The range of children's reading widened, especially in the 1860s, which saw the appearance not only of *Alice in Wonderland* but also of a growing number of magazines for boys and girls. All of these developments are parts of the story of schooling and literacy summarized in the statistics.

The population of England and Wales rose from under 14 million in 1831 to nearly 18 million in 1851. By mid-century half the population lived in urban areas. The close association between poverty, dirt and disease was being realized by reformers, but action to achieve improvements was delayed by hostility and apathy. Cholera, not yet known to be a waterborne disease, struck

Britain in the early 1830s and late 1840s, and was one of the factors which persuaded the government to pass the important 1848 Public Health Act. Sanitary engineering, a growing awareness of the environmental hazards to life, and the appointment of local medical officers of health, were important steps towards the improvement of urban conditions, but the areas least touched by education continued to be those least touched by other aspects of social reform. The Church of England and nonconformist churches were willing to make educational gestures through the National and British societies, but were basically unable to adjust to the conditions of the growing towns. Individual clergymen might make valiant efforts, but large urban parishes were given little support by the Church of England as a whole. In 1846 an HMI found only one National school covering the whole of a great manufacturing town. No parochial clergyman saw it 'among the prescribed duties or the responsibilities of his office, and it has *received the supervision of none*'.[39] Poverty, overcrowding, disease, crime and illiteracy continued to be part of one and the same phenomenon, and where it was worst it tended to receive the least attention.

Schools, teachers and children

Dame and private-venture schools declined in numbers in the 1830s and 1840s, but continued to provide a large quantity of poor-quality education. The Manchester Statistical Society found them in 1834–5 'in the most deplorable condition. The greater part of them are kept by females, but some by old men, whose only qualification for this employment seems to be their unfitness for every other.' A not untypical Yorkshire teacher, hunchbacked, 'very deaf and ignorant' had been placed in his post by the parochial authorities 'that he may not be burdensome to them for his support'.[40] Investigations of education invariably found teaching of this quality in this kind of school.

The Sunday school, wrote David Stow's biographer in 1868, 'has been by far the most efficient instrument for excavating a portion of the heathen population from the general mass of ignorance and depravity'.[41] In 1841 the Sunday schools in Norfolk were described by one inspector of schools as 'until recently the chief instrument of instruction, and in many parishes still such'. In the same year another inspector thought that the

Sunday schools, and especially one at Bolton, were the most efficient form of education in Lancashire.[42] There was disagreement about the effectiveness of the Sunday school as an instrument of basic education. In St Marylebone the children at Sunday schools could not 'be said to receive intellectual instruction' and they were not included by the Central Society in the total of children receiving education. This was a widely echoed opinion. So was the opinion that, especially in the agricultural districts, the Sunday schools accomplished a great deal. The problem by mid-century was that the Sunday schools were still 'doing the work of the day-school on the Sabbath'.[43] Only with increased

Playground of the Home and Colonial
Infant School Society, 1843

literacy did the Sunday schools concentrate on their religious purpose, and from the 1870s their role changed. On the Sunday in 1851 when attendance was counted throughout the country, of the 2·4 million children on the books of the Sunday schools there were over 1·8 million present. Not least of the effects of the schools, Horace Mann pointed out, was the influence on the Sunday-school teachers themselves. They were obliged, 'in order to discharge their voluntary functions, to acquire, by careful study, an intelligent acquaintance with the Scriptures'. This was what Stow's biographer described as 'the reflex influences of their labour of love on the teachers themselves'.[44]

The religious and moral purposes of the infant school were also being intensified in the 1840s. The Home and Colonial Infant School Society defined the 'primary object of early education' as being 'to cultivate religious principles and moral sentiments; to awaken the tender mind to a sense of its evil dispositions and habitual failings, before it is become callous by its daily intercourse with vice'.[45] An inspector, reporting on the British Society's infant schools in 1845, described their purpose as being 'wholly drawn from, based in, or illumined by the words of Holy Writ'. The children were led, by object lessons, 'line upon line and precept upon precept . . . to a perception of God's bounties'.[46]

The infant schools were torn between giving a self-sufficient education and preparing children for the next phase of education. It was widely believed that infant schools for children from the age of three would become a universal feature of the educational system. The Newcastle Commission was impressed by this view at the end of the 1850s, and deduced from its evidence that 'infant schools form a most important part of the machinery required for a national system of education'.[47] Many infant schools acquired during this period a variety of apparatus and books, and used music, recreation and physical education. Generally speaking, however, the whole was subservient to 'the most important branch of all — religious instruction'.[48] By the age of seven an infant was expected to have a range of intellectual accomplishments, and 'be able to regulate his own conduct by the precepts of morality and religion'.[49] In practice most infant schools combined formalized scripture lessons with reading, writing and arithmetic (often taught by monitors), and varying degrees of physical exercise and play.

The object lesson, in infant and other schools, lent itself to the danger of teachers producing infants who knew 'of pachydermatous animals, and monocotyledonous plants, absurdities which,' said an inspector, 'are often witnessed'.[50] Overintellectual infant teaching was encouraged under the system of payment by results, introduced — as we shall see — by the revised code of 1862, with its division of schooling into 'standards'.

This affected infant schools and departments since standard I children were often together with infants, and infants had to be prepared to pass into standard I. Although some of the more informal features of infant education were preserved, the overall situation under the code had its influence. Froebel's ideas were brought to England in the mid-1850s and were immediately the source of experiments, but they were only taken up by the Home and Colonial Society and the British Society in the 1860s and 1870s; from then on they formed the basis for the reinterpretation of infant and junior teaching that was central to the new education movement at the end of the century.

The attempt to educate the most depressed class of children devolved on three kinds of schools – workhouse schools, ragged schools and industrial and reformatory schools. The Poor Law Amendment Act of 1834 was designed to be a harsh deterrent. It proposed, not entirely successfully, that all relief should be given in workhouses, and it tried to ensure the daily education of pauper children. Efforts to establish district schools away from the workhouse premises and bringing together children from workhouses in different parishes had the backing of legislation in 1845 but produced only six such schools by 1859. Poor-law guardians were frequently hostile to the idea of educating pauper children. A government grant of £30,000 a year for teachers' salaries in workhouse schools was introduced in 1846 in an attempt to improve the wretched conditions of the teachers. Out of Kay-Shuttleworth's interest in improving the teaching in these schools arose the pupil-teacher system. In 1847, an inspection of forty-one workhouses in the northern counties found that the teachers in twenty-five of them were themselves paupers, most of them 'grossly incompetent, cannot write, or spell, or ask a question in a proper manner'.[51] The situation was scarcely better for the children of people receiving outdoor relief, and some counties took no action to educate the children of outdoor paupers, as permitted in the 1850s. The campaigners for workhouse improvements knew that education was almost impossible for children living in the workhouse environment: 'the utter helplessness and incapacity of workhouse children has become almost proverbial . . . Their acquaintance with life is bounded by the four blank walls of their school and dormitory, and their dreary yard called a playground.'[52] In 1840 the workhouse master at Boston described the teachers in workhouse schools as being often incompetent and the teaching as 'barren and unsatisfactory'. In most cases teachers were 'utterly ignorant of any system of collective teaching'. The solution, he believed, was the union of schools in separate establishments, causing 'a diminution in the required number of schoolmasters and school-mistresses for workhouses', making it possible to increase salaries and attract better qualified candidates. It would take children away from the atmosphere of the workhouse, which was 'very dangerous for children to breathe in', separate them 'from contagion and vice, and the degradation of dependence'.[53] Not until the end of the century did the practice of keeping children in workhouses with adults begin to break up.

The 'ragged school' movement began in the early 1840s. The seed was sown by John Pounds, a Portsmouth cobbler, who collected ragged children together and tried to give them some care and a training 'in virtue and knowledge'.[54] The idea was taken up elsewhere, prominently by Lord Shaftesbury in the evangelical tradition, who in 1844 helped to form the Ragged

Brook Street Ragged and Industrial School, London, 1853

School Union. Voluntary funds were raised, and the aid of voluntary teachers was enlisted. Horace Mann described their purpose as 'to convert incipient criminals to Christianity'.[55] The motive was, in fact, a blend of Christian mission and the need to provide a simple level of care for the most deprived children, if education was to be possible at all. Some of the schools lodged the children, most fed them. They sought out vagrant children and used whatever makeshift accommodation they could find. They helped the children to work as shoeblacks and some of them to emigrate. Even when the board schools began to function in the 1870s there was still a 'residuum', as the chairman of the union described them in 1887, for whom the ragged schools catered: 'even board school teachers do not like to take shoeless, shirtless, and capless children into their schools.'[56] In 1870 the union was running 132 schools, containing nearly 25,000 children, although there were other such schools outside the union. Some of the ragged schools asked to be taken over by the school boards after 1870, and the union concentrated on ragged Sunday schools up to the 1890s.

Industrial schools developed in this period as schools to which children under fourteen could be committed as vagrants, and in 1861 they were placed under Home Office inspection. They generally provided, apart from a basic education, a training in some craft in the case of boys, and domestic skills in the case of girls. In 1854, under the Youthful Offenders Act, official recognition was also given to reformatory schools, and offenders under sixteen, who had served a minimum of fourteen days in prison, could be committed to them. Not until the 1890s was the reformatory school made a complete substitute for a prison sentence.

In spite of optimism about the spread of National and British schools, criticism was also growing from the 1830s. Joseph Kay, in 1838, talked of the teachers 'actually *demoralizing* the children'. Twenty years later one of the Newcastle assistant commissioners reported an HMI as saying that 'he knew schools in which he could estimate a pupil's length of stay by the stupidity impressed upon his countenance'.[57] The brevity of school life, fluctuating numbers, the poverty of the monitorial method and the low standard of teachers continued for most of this period to be the major problems. There were, of course, schools of high quality, like many of the Wesleyan schools, but in general higher standards were dependent on a new approach to teacher training. This was the intention of the introduction of the pupil teacher system by the Minutes of 1846, as we have already seen. The social purposes of these plans were defined explicitly by Kay-Shuttleworth:

> to raise the character and position of the schoolmaster . . . the establishment and support of a larger number of Normal schools; to feed those Normal schools with candidates having much higher attainments and greater skill and energy than those which have hitherto entered them; to render the school popular among the poor, as a means of introducing their children to more honourable and profitable employments, and by its increased efficiency to create in the minds of the working class a juster estimate of the value of education for their children.[58]

The pursuit of such objectives was to gain momentum, but the monitorial system continued to dominate popular education in the 1840s. The inspectors' reports for the period are usually a compendium of complaints about the poverty of the system, about 'the general rout of many a British School', about monitors who, after two or three years in a school, 'are almost as ignorant as the classes whom they instruct'. Even village schools were found slavishly following the monitorial system – dividing, for example, forty-four boys in one case and twenty-six in another, into little classes, taught in the first instance by six monitors and in the second by five.[59] Schools (including infant schools) are reported as being without apparatus or not knowing what to do with the apparatus they possess. Maps might exist, but not be used – 'objects apparently still of respectful and distant wonder alike to master and pupils'. If geography was taught the children might be able to 'tell the names of every known tribe of barbarians in Africa' or 'every petty island in the Pacific, without knowing the name or course of "the river" which ran through their respective towns'.[60]

Schooling for girls, as the literacy figures show, broadened in these decades, but with the same defects. Needlework was ubiquitous (and a condition of grants after 1862), and very often replaced arithmetic. At the National schools in Kennington the girls spent four afternoons a week doing needlework provided by 'several respectable families in the neighbourhood'. Profits were spent in 1831 'in providing Forty of the deserving Girls with Cloaks, Frocks, Bonnets, and Tippets, in which they appear at Church on Sundays'.[61] Some of the endowed schools made provision for girls, but it was probably the Sunday schools that made the greatest contribution to improving literacy among girls in the early and middle nineteenth century. It was a virtue of some of the mechanics' institutes and social movements, especially the Owenites, that they provided a form of adult education for women.

The main point of the inspectors' reports in the late 1840s, therefore, was either that the monitorial schools were narrow and inefficient, or that, at their best, the achievement was not commensurate with the effort. The substitution of pupil teachers for monitors, and the foundation of training colleges in the 1840s began to effect change in the 1850s.

David Stow had opened a training college in Glasgow in 1824. Kay-Shuttleworth, after the defeat in 1839 of the plans for a 'normal' or training college to be supervised by the Committee of Council, opened a college privately in Battersea and handed it over to the National Society in 1843. The denominational school societies began to extend the number of colleges, and the 1846 regulations provided a national framework within which elementary-school children could become trained, being paid as pupil teachers between the ages of thirteen and eighteen, and then eligible to compete for 'Queen's scholarships', tenable at the colleges. This was to be the basis of the training of elementary-school teachers until the twentieth century.

Since the schools were so firmly encompassed by religious definitions, it was natural that the religious bodies should see teacher training as an exclusively religious preserve. By the early 1850s there were some forty colleges in England and Wales, thirty-four of them belonging to the Church of England, with a total of some 2,000 students. The Newcastle Commission found that over 87 per cent of pupil teachers successfully completed their apprenticeship, and 76 per cent competed for Queen's scholarships – which most of them obtained.[62] The students in training at the colleges were most commonly from working-class homes, usually having served some years in clerical or manual occupations. Most of them had been educated at National or

British schools, and had done Sunday-school teaching. The average age of students at Battersea in 1845 was twenty-two, and their average stay was one year and nine months. The programme for students in that year was as shown opposite.[63] Wide though this curriculum was it was also, and remained, a very heavy programme, although the colleges were criticized, by the Newcastle Commission among others, for their excessive working hours and memory work.

The increasing supply of trained teachers meant the beginnings of a sense of professional status. The ex-working-class teacher was now in a professional role, but his background and duties separated him from the professional middle class. His relationships with his managers – especially the clergy, the inspectorate and parents – were full of ambiguities. The principal of St Mark's College, Chelsea, described in 1862 how the term 'social status' in connection with parish schoolmasters had come into use some twenty years earlier. The master of the parish school was admitted, 'if more than usually respectable, to the hospitality of the clergyman's kitchen', but was 'looked down upon with sovereign contempt by the domestics'. He was pitied and despised by the farmer and shopkeeper. It was only beginning to be seen that 'the "status" as is was called, – of the men through whose instrumentality the social regeneration of the largest class of the community was to be effected, was the one thing needful'.[64] The search for this new status, deliberately fostered by Kay-Shuttleworth, was the basis of attempts at professional organization, most effective after 1870.

The revised code

In elementary education the last decade of this period was dominated by the effects of the Newcastle Commission and the revised code, summarized in the phrase 'payment by results'. The Newcastle Commission was appointed in 1858 and reported three years later on 'what measures, if any, are required for the extension of sound and cheap elementary instruction to all classes of the people'. Its main proposal was for the payment of grants to schools in two forms, the first on the basis of certain general criteria, and the second on the basis of the individual examination of each child. The commission's report was widely criticized for its oversimplification of the problems. Teachers and

ROUTINE

5 a.m. Rise, Wash, Dress, and Make Beds.
6 a.m. Prayers.
8 a.m. Breakfast.
9 a.m. First Division of Teachers go to the Village School.   ditto   ditto   return from Village School.
12 Noon Ditto

1¼ p.m. Dinner.
2 p.m. Second Division of Teachers go to the Village School.   ditto   Ditto School.
4 or 5 p.m.   return from Village   return from Village School.

6¼ p.m. Supper.
9 p.m. Prayers.
10 p.m. Retire to rest.

		Monday	Tuesday	Wednesday	Thursday	Friday	Saturday
6	1	Garden	Garden	Garden	Garden	Garden	Garden
	2	Do.	Do.	Do.	Do.	Do.	Do.
7	1	First principles of Arithmetic	Principal	Private Study of Ecclesiastical History	Principal	Principal (Liturgy)	Leisure
	2	English Composition	Do.	Do.	Do.	English Composition	Do.
9	1	Descriptive Mechanics	Drill	Garden	English History	Drill	9 to 10¾ Examination Papers
	2	Do.	Do.	Do.	Do.	Do.	Examination Papers
10	1	Mr. M'Leod	Mr. M'Leod	Mensuration	Mr. M'Leod Elementary Music	Mechanics Elementary Music	10¾ to 11½ Garden
	2	Scripture	Do.	Scripture			
11	1	Garden	Garden	Natural Philosophy	Grammar	Algebra	11½ to 1 Examination Papers
	2	Do.	Do.	Derivation	Mental Arithmetic	Principal	Examination Papers
12	1	Chemistry	Mathematical Geography	Scripture	Mensuration and Geometry	English History	Examination Papers
	2	Do.	Descriptive Do.	Do.	Grammar	Do.	Do.
2	1	Leisure	Derivation	Principal	Garden	Garden	Historical Geography
	2	Do.	Miscell. Calculations	Do.	Do.	Do.	Do.
3	1	Grammar	Mechanics	Practice of Chanting	Grammar & Derivation	Globes	Household Work
	2	Arithmetic	Music	Problems on Work	Do.	Music	Do.
4	1	Algebra	Music	Arithmetic	Scripture	Music	
	2	Derivation	Arithmetic	Do.	Do.	Arithmetic	
5	1	Mr. M'Leod	Scripture	Leisure	Geography	Chemistry	
	2	Grammar	Do.	Do.	Do.	Do. Dictation Class	
7	1	Penmanship	Leisure	Drawing	Penmanship	Drawing	
	2	Do.	Do.	Do.	Do.	Do.	

managers attacked the report, and Kay-Shuttleworth pamphle-
teered from retirement on their behalf, against proposals that
would reduce the income of the schools. Payment by results had
been the basis of Science and Art Department grants, was given
prominence by the commission and was raised to the status of a
dogma in the revised code of 1862.

Robert Lowe, vice-president of the Committee of Council,
made his famous statement to the House of Commons that he
could not promise 'that this system will be an economical one,
and I cannot promise that it will be an efficient one, but I can
promise that . . . if it is not cheap it shall be efficient; if it is not
efficient it shall be cheap'.[65] Annual expenditure on education
had, indeed, risen from £125,000 in 1848 to over £800,000
in 1861. The effect of the new code was to reduce the figure to
something over £600,000 in the mid-sixties, although it rose
again in the late sixties and after the 1870 Act, among other
reasons because of improved attendance.

The revised code ended grants in augmentation of teachers'
salaries (introduced in 1846 and paid direct to the teacher), grants
to pupil teachers and for school maintenance. Overall grants were
now to be paid direct to managers, who would negotiate salaries
individually with teachers. Grants were to be conditional
primarily on the proficiency of the children as tested individually
by the inspectors. The machinery introduced by the code was
narrower than that proposed by the Newcastle Commission. Each
child over the age of six was to earn the school a grant of 4s.
on the basis of attendance, and 8s. 'subject to examination'. Of
the latter 2s. 8d. was forfeited for failure to satisfy the inspector
in reading, 2s. 8d. in writing and 2s. 8d. in arithmetic. Children
were to be presented in six 'standards', and not a second time in
the same or a lower standard. Children under six were exempted
from examination only under last-minute pressure (and these
earned a grant of 6s. 6d. subject to a general report by the
inspector as to the suitability of their education). A decline in the
numbers attending evening classes followed the application of
payment by results to these classes also (pupils attending, for
example, cookery classes had also to be presented for examinations in the standard elementary subjects).

The effects were not solely financial. As T. H. Huxley later put
it: 'the Revised Code did not compel any schoolmaster to leave off
teaching anything; but, by the very simple process of refusing to

Final teaching assessment, St Mark's, Chelsea, 1849

pay for many kinds of teaching, it has practically put an end to them.'[66] Matthew Arnold, poet and HMI, was the inspector most responsive to the effects of the code. Under the old system a good inspector heard selected children read and questioned whole classes on all their subjects: 'the whole life and power of a class, the fitness of its composition, its handling by the teacher, were well tested.' Under the new system, however, he was unable to test any of these: 'he hears every child in the group before him read, and so far his examination is more complete than the old inspection. But he does not question them; he does not . . . go beyond the three matters, reading, writing, and arithmetic.'[67] The result was generally an increase in rote learning, and even inspectors not opposed to the principle of the revised code reported its deadening and disheartening effects. The need to drill the children to meet the inspection requirements was reflected in the schools' activities throughout the year. Frequent testing became common. Some of the improvements of the 1850s in curriculum and method in many schools were cut short. Even religious instruction was sometimes dropped as the inspection approached. The logbooks which the code required teachers to keep record obsessively attendance fluctuations due to weather, the races and a host of other factors over which the teacher had no control but on which standards and income depended. The possibility of new thinking about educational methods and about the curriculum became paralysed by the operation of the code. When it was modified in 1867 to provide, among other things, for the teaching of 'specific subjects' (such as history or geography), for which individual children could earn a grant, Arnold responded with contempt. This palliative merely drew attention to the neglect of subjects other than the three Rs, and gave them the same 'character of an intricate and mechanical routine'.[68]

The training colleges were among the first to be hit by the new code, since it reduced their grant, their numbers (by decreasing the number of Queen's scholars) and their standards. Schools dealing with the lowest class of children were hit hard, as were pupil teachers, the number of whom had been 14,000 in 1861 and dropped to 9,000 in 1866. Doubts about the future supply of teachers were strongly expressed. Payment by results was a view of the nature of elementary education from which it took the system generations to recover. Edward Thring looked back at the experience of payment by results and the inspection of minds like 'specimens on a board with a pin stuck through them like beetles', and appealed to teachers to get rid of the vestiges of the system: 'strive for liberty to teach, have mercy on the slow, the ignorant, the weak'.[69] A former inspector looked back in 1911 at the thirty or more years of 'Code despotism' in which he had been involved, and thought the effects were still being felt of 'that deadly system . . . which seems to have been devised for the express purpose of arresting growth and strangling life, which bound us all, myself included, with links of iron'.[70] There had been those who, like Matthew Arnold, had forecast from the very outset how it would be. By the triumph of the revised code, he wrote in 1862, 'there would be only one sufferer: — *the education of the people*'.[71]

Social movements

The variety of educational efforts among working-class and radical movements, especially in the 1830s and 1840s, was considerable. Their main concern was with the education of the adult, but they also opened schools and discussed plans for education on the widest basis. The main impetus had come from Owenism, which passed through its most important phase in the early and mid-1830s. The Owenite co-operative movement and its publications constantly appealed to their members to open schools for the children and to hold adult classes. The Salford co-operators, for example, opened a Sunday school with over 100 males and females, adults and children. It taught 'really useful knowledge' on Sunday mornings and afternoons, and mathematics, drawing, political economy and other subjects to senior scholars three evenings a week.[72] The activities of Owen and the various types of Owenite organization in the first half of the 1830s constituted the most deeply rooted popular education movement of the century. In the late 1830s the Owenite halls of science became centres of political and secularist discussion, education and recreation. The Rochdale co-operators, who inaugurated a practical form of co-operative retailing in 1844, retained the earlier interest in education, meeting in the evenings for discussion and 'mutual and other instruction'. They had a 'bounteously filled' newsroom open from 9 a.m. to 9 p.m. and a free library, the lending section of which had over 5,000 books in 1862. From 1850 to 1855 they ran a school at a charge of 2d. a month.[73]

From the late 1830s to the early 1850s the Chartist movement acted as the main focus of popular discontent. The demand for parliamentary reform was associated in the minds of Chartists with other demands and ideals. The Chartist press, meetings, lectures, programmes and protests constituted for many people what has been called 'a defiant self-culture',[74] and Chartist energies spread into many local activities. The working men, said one Chartist publication in 1841, 'have passed the Rubicon – they have their own movement – their own circulating libraries – a newspaper press they claim as their own. The present age beholds them combining for the education of their own off-spring.'[75] *Chartism; a New Organization of the People*, published by William Lovett and John Collins in 1841, was an enlightened programme for schools and halls of every kind, to be built with government support, but controlled and maintained locally.

After 1850 the dynamic of this kind of social movement declined. The new radical politics and movements of the 1860s and after were less concerned with education from below than with pressures for free, compulsory, state-provided education. The second Parliamentary Reform Act of 1867 enfranchised a large proportion of working men in the towns, and the first Elementary Education Act followed three years later. The 'new model' trade unions of skilled workers after 1850 produced trade union leaders like Robert Applegarth, general secretary of the Amalgamated Society of Carpenters and Joiners, who were active in educational pressure groups, principally the National Education League from 1868. They campaigned for an Education Act, for free and compulsory education. There is little wonder, said Applegarth, 'that the working class should desire to give compulsion a trial when they know how utterly the voluntary system has failed to provide themselves with the advantages of education'. Applegarth's union also started technical education classes, 'probably the first instance', he wrote, 'in the industrial history of the country, of a Trade Union undertaking to provide a plan for the education of its members'.[76] The Owenite trade unions had forestalled him in the 1830s, but their ideals had been very different. The TUC, founded in 1868, had a wide interest in education, including teaching methods, Sunday opening of museums and half-timers. A TUC delegation even persuaded the archbishop of Canterbury to withdraw a National School textbook which described the trade unions as wicked institutions.[77]

Other movements of ideas played a part in educational developments. A combination of phrenology and utilitarianism, for example, produced a group of reformers who founded secular schools. George Combe, Britain's most famous phrenologist and one of the most interesting educationists of the nineteenth century, had a view of education based on social or economic science that was shared by William Ellis, founder of the Birkbeck schools, and W. B. Hodgson, well-known educationist and Newcastle assistant commissioner. Combe and James Simpson were active in founding secular schools in Scotland, and contributed to the important campaign for secular schools in Lancashire. The first such school was founded in Edinburgh in 1848 by Combe, with financial help from William Ellis. Ellis's own first such school, the first Birkbeck school, was opened in the hall of the London mechanics' institute also in 1848, and in the same year he helped the former Chartist leader, William Lovett, to open a school in Holborn, both for working-class children. By

School for mill operatives, Manchester, 1862

1852, 2,000 boys and 250 girls in London, Manchester, Edinburgh and Glasgow were attending schools founded by Ellis or associated with his efforts.[78] The main focus of the schools was a form of social science or economics, to prepare the children for the realities of society (and incidentally to discourage strikes).

The mechanics' institutes had in many places lost their initial impetus. Some conducted haphazard courses of lectures and provided recreational facilities, but others continued to serve a more consistent educational function. There were in 1851, according to Mann's census, over 1,000 'literary, scientific and mechanics' institutes' and of these the largest concentrations were in the West Riding (155) and Lancashire (97). A large percentage of their members, certainly outside the manufacturing districts, consisted of tradesmen and clerks, but the classes run in towns like Huddersfield and Leeds continued to attract manual workers, and provided important forms of training, including in subjects like mechanical drawing and chemistry. The difficulties of the institutes were only partly overcome in the 1850s by attempts to co-ordinate their efforts, the Yorkshire Union of Mechanics' Institutes being the most successful. Their functions came sooner or later to be carried out by specialist public bodies, notably the public libraries and the technical colleges (many of which were created later in the century out of the mechanics' institutes themselves).

Other forms of adult, usually evening, education were being attempted. Courses of lectures were organized under many auspices. At Bilston, in Staffordshire, for example, a course of miscellaneous lectures in 1847, for which a season ticket cost 1s., had audiences of 300–700, of whom it was estimated that more than two-thirds were artisans and colliers.[79] Evening schools for young adults were run by many schools. The Newcastle Commission heard evidence from Somerset of the failure of many evening classes for lack of teachers, funds or support. Sometimes, however, 'a journeyman carpenter or shoemaker, having acquired a moderate education by his own perseverance, desires to help his fellows; he sets up a night school in his house or workshop; retired ink-jars hold the candles, and fingers act as snuffers . . . such a man is not to be despised.'[80] The evening class has a continuous history from this period, featured in the work of the school boards after 1870, the resolutions of the TUC in the 1880s, and embodied in the university extension movement and workers' education programmes in the final decades of the century. There is also a tradition from the 1840s of more substantial courses of education for working men. The Sheffield People's College, with early morning and evening courses, was born in 1842, to be followed by the more permanent Working Men's College in London, providing teaching rather than lecturing, and with a less vocational range of courses than the institutes.

Self-education remained a common road to knowledge in the middle of the nineteenth century. The starting points, however, were becoming more diverse in an increasingly articulated educational system, and access to books and ideas less difficult. The inadequacy of the basic education provided by the elementary schools and the harsh realities of industrial, agricultural and urban conditions remained the main obstacles.

Reforms and foundations

For landed and aristocratic England the process of change in education was above all one which committed them more firmly to the public school, and defined more explicitly the education of gentlemen. For middle-class England educational change had to be related to changes in political and social status. The changes lay more in the provision of new schools than in the transformation of the old – which did not come about until after the Taunton Commission (sometimes referred to as the commission on middle-class education) had investigated the endowed schools in the 1860s.

In the three decades up to 1870 there were the beginnings of important reforms at the ancient universities, the great schools and the grammar schools – all as a result of parliamentary intervention. Reform at Oxford and Cambridge was the earliest to take shape. The internal reforms of the beginning of the century had not heralded major changes. In many respects, in fact, the two universities continued little changed into the later decades of the century. John Stuart Mill expressed the view in 1867 that 'youths come to the Scottish Universities ignorant, and are there taught. The majority of those who come to the English Universities come still more ignorant, and ignorant they go away.'[81]

Even before the royal commission on the universities was appointed in 1850, however, changes had begun to take place at least in some of the colleges of Oxford and Cambridge, although the curriculum continued relatively unchanging (with moral philosophy given emphasis at Oxford and mathematics at Cambridge, both taught and examined with great formality). Classical studies retained their pre-eminence. Modern subjects, including science, continued to be largely extracurricular accomplishments. The most important focus of change before 1850 was the role of the tutor, through whom the reformers hoped moral and intellectual improvements would come. Mark Pattison at Oxford in the 1840s was the model of the new tutor and the new don. The academic reputation of Lincoln College was 'mainly the fruit of Pattison's work as tutor, but . . . the College was itself changing; elections to fellowships had at last brought a nucleus of real learning and conscientious teaching capacity to the common room'.[82] For some students, in some colleges, the mood was one of greater concentration on scholarship, together with a more earnest interpretation of religion, learning and the nature of an educated gentleman. Training for the professions, principally in service to church and state, was synonymous with training to be a gentleman. The percentage of students coming to Oxford and Cambridge from the major schools increased in the first half of the nineteenth century. In 1864–7, of all students entering the two universities 23 per cent came from Eton, Harrow, Winchester and Rugby.[83]

The liberals, anxious to improve both administration and the range and quality of studies, campaigned inside and outside the universities for a greater measure of reform. They eventually won the appointment in 1850 of the royal commission, with whom the authorities in the two universities, especially at Oxford, refused to co-operate. The commissioners accepted as the main criticism of both universities the inefficiency of the teaching; they made recommendations for adequate professorial and lecturing arrangements, proposing in particular the creation of new chairs in the scientific disciplines. They made proposals for the improvement of the administration of the universities, and of their examination systems. They put forward no clear conclusions on the question of the religious tests still in force at the two universities.

Two parliamentary Acts followed, one for Oxford in 1854 and one for Cambridge two years later. Both Acts were important advances, but neither went as far as the universities' critics had hoped. A half-way measure of religious toleration was introduced, enabling students (except those of divinity) who were not members of the Church of England to take bachelors', though not masters', degrees. The bar on masters' degrees meant that university government was retained firmly in the hands of members of the established church. Colleges could continue to refuse to admit dissenters to fellowships. When nonconformists began to win some of the most prized distinctions, but were barred from fellowships, it was not surprising, as one historian comments, 'that sensible men in both Universities came to the opinion that the colleges were losing far more by the tests than the Church of England gained'.[84] The Acts had shown the trend of opinion. The organs of university government had been made more representative, although a proper balance of relationships between college and university (involving questions of finance and power) was the subject of controversy for the next quarter of a century. The way to curriculum reform had been opened. The principle of competition had been introduced into the scholarship system, and closed scholarships were now to be reformed. Fellowships were open to competition. The half measure of religious reform could not fail to provoke demands for more.

The effects of the Acts and reforms were felt in the public and grammar schools: the opening of scholarships to competition meant, as did competition for places in the civil service, a move towards higher standards and a tendency for the schools to retain pupils longer. The campaign to remove the last religious restrictions within the two universities continued through the 1860s and in 1871 the battle to abolish the religious tests was won.

London University was in this period undergoing steady expansion. Colleges of various kinds in different parts of the country and the empire were affiliated to it (there were over eighty by mid-century), and their students were prepared for the centrally set examinations. From 1858 individual external students could also take the university's examinations. Durham University, founded in the 1830s out of the wealth of Durham Cathedral, was from the outset an independent, Anglican institution, receiving its charter in 1837. Owens College, Manchester, established in the 1850s, came as did similar foundations later in the century under the tutelage of London University. Owens College was founded from a private benefaction, had no religious tests, and was intended to be a college appropriate to the needs of its surrounding community. It established itself quickly in scientific fields, but also organized faculties in traditional university disciplines. As the future Manchester University it was an important departure. It had strong local connections, including with the schools (the grammar school established exhibitions to the college), and was open to continental scientific and technological influence. It showed that the ambitions held by many cities to have their own university institutions could be fulfilled. Owens College and London external degrees, both coming in the same decade, were outstanding developments in higher education in the nineteenth century.

Some of the university developments coincided with or gave rise to others in education for the professions. In the early nineteenth century most medical teaching had been arranged privately by physicians or surgeons at the hospitals, and the medical schools at Oxford and Cambridge existed virtually in name only. Modern medical teaching began in England with new university medical schools (and the provincial ones which were affiliated to London University). The medical school at University College, London, was its first department to open in 1828. Interest in the reform of legal education was directed primarily towards various abortive plans in the second half of the century for the creation of a legal university. A parliamentary select committee of 1846 looked at legal education and a royal commission on the Inns of Court and chancery in 1854 resulted eventually in the dissolution of the latter, and improvements in lecturing arrangements and examinations for solicitors. At University College, lectures in law, as in surgery, were given in the evenings. The conception of professional education as primarily one of apprenticeship was being broadened, but not without difficulty, particularly in those cases in which professional organization and status were still uncertain. The education and qualification of architects, for example, were matter for controversy throughout the century, to the detriment of the schools of architecture which had first appeared in the eighteenth century. Chairs in architecture were created at King's College, London, in 1840 and at University College in the following year. Chairs in civil engineering were established at the two colleges in 1838 and 1841. Cambridge acquired its first chair of 'mechanical and applied science' in 1875. The general story of professional education in the middle and late nineteenth century is one of attempts by the professions to establish or reform their own institutions and codes of apprenticeship and conduct, and of slow movements in the universities to provide related academic courses.

The grammar and public schools continued, to a greater extent than Oxford and Cambridge, along traditional paths. Even the new schools showed some of the old symptoms. Marlborough, founded in 1843, had its rebellion eight years later, and it was not the last to do so. Rote learning of the classics continued to be the staple fare, and the practice of boys 'standing up' or being 'called up' to recite and construe passages remained the main pedagogical method. Private education for boys at home declined throughout the period; even near the end of the century at Cambridge, however, 18 per cent of students were recorded as having had their previous education by 'private tuition or home'.[85] The great schools had defined themselves more strictly in social terms by separating off the sons of tradesmen and the lower orders. New public schools were founded in the 1840s, when increased demand coincided with the fillip given to boarding education by the railways. Marlborough opened with 200 boys, and five years later stood second only to Eton in numbers. Wellington, built as a memorial to the duke, who died in 1852, was intended primarily for the orphans of army officers. The Prince Consort hoped it would be the prototype of a modern school with an emphasis on science; the school soon turned, however, into a traditional public school. Some of the new schools (such as Cheltenham and later Malvern) explicitly defined their function as places of education for the sons of gentlemen. Many of the newer schools quickly established academic reputations equal with if not superior to those of the older schools. 'I believe it to be the case', the Clarendon Commissioners were told by Christ Church, Oxford, 'that the great prizes are not won now by Eton, but by such schools as Rugby and Marlborough.'[86]

The changes that took place in the established public schools from the 1830s are normally associated with Thomas Arnold and Rugby: the acceptance of the public school by the middle and upper classes was in part the result of his reputation. Although what he accomplished at Rugby became something of a myth, the myth was a powerful influence. Arnold became headmaster of Rugby in 1828. 'My object will be,' he said in advance, 'if possible, to form Christian men, for Christian boys I can scarcely hope to make.'[87] It is this view that accounts for his stress on the sixth-form prefects, through whom he promoted the ideal of the Christian gentleman, and for the severity with which he treated offences such as lying. Without sound religious principles and a sense of gentlemanly conduct he considered intellectual attainment valueless. His influence began to be felt at Oxford, where, the headmaster of Winchester later recalled, 'his pupils brought quite a different character with them . . . than that which we knew elsewhere . . . his pupils were thoughtful, manly-minded, conscious of duty and obligation'.[88] The history of the public school in the nineteenth century has been written in terms of the transition from this combination of religion and education ('godliness and good learning') exemplified by Arnold, to the cult of 'manliness' and games in the second half of the century.[89]

Arnold and Rugby were not the only models. Edward Thring, transforming Uppingham after 1853 from a small grammar school into a public school of some eminence, made a contribution of a different order, in relation to the curriculum and a sympathetic understanding of children. The pupil learning Latin and Greek was for him often 'the unintelligent dealing with the unintelligible'. He was dedicated to the study of English, opened the first public-school gymnasium and made music commonplace at the school. He believed every child could do *something* well. 'If a stupid lad excelled in the carpenter's shop,' said a former pupil, 'or a fool in form made good hits to leg, or took his hurdles easily, or a duffer at Greek prose bowed his violin well, we had the feeling that the Headmaster looked on him as a *good fellow*.'[90]

Curriculum change came slowly in the public schools, although science, for example, began to appear seriously in some of the major schools in the 1850s and 1860s. The newly established schools were often resistant to curriculum change, for example the Woodard schools which were designed to provide a nation-wide system of secondary boarding schools for middle-class children. (Canon Woodard, organizer of this unofficial Church of England movement, created schools of different grades to suit different social divisions. Lancing, founded in 1848, catered for two separate class divisions, paying different fees and using separate halls. Ardingly was designed ten years later as a school for the lower middle class.) Although some of the schools introduced modern subjects, Woodard was no innovator. 'My view', he said, 'is not to introduce new elements either into our religious or educational departments, but rather to try our strength on the present system, which has stood the test for many generations.'[91]

New local proprietary schools were part of the same pattern of response to middle-class educational needs. The proprietary schools competed successfully with the grammar schools through-out the century. They were founded as joint-stock enterprises, and unlike the private-venture schools they had properly con-stituted managements, generally with a clear view of the purpose of their schools. Some, for example, were denominational, others – later – provided for the education of middle-class girls. Whether philanthropic or profitmaking institutions they were able to com-pete with the grammar schools for staff, and their success – and the grammar schools' weakness – lay generally in the appeal of their denominational basis to particular communities and of their modern curriculum to the commercial middle class. The private schools still flourished, and in the 1860s there were, in fact, more boys attending these than the endowed grammar schools.[92]

Some of the grammar schools were provoked, by competition from the proprietary schools particularly, into making improvements but in general they waited for the 'spur' of the Taunton Commission and the Act that followed in 1869. Some schools encouraged science, though it was unusual for a school to have as serious a scientific programme as Cheltenham grammar school, for example, which was visited by Lyon Playfair in 1853 and had a letter of encouragement from another of the outstanding campaigners for science, Prince Albert. Mathematics had a wide but uncertain place in the schools. At Manchester grammar school, in 1849, the mathematics post had fallen into abeyance.[93] The momentum of interest in science was increased by, among other things, the publication of Darwin's *Origin of Species* in 1859, the campaign for science education waged by such men as T. H. Huxley in the 1850s and 1860s, and the publication of Herbert Spencer's *Education* in 1861 – the nineteenth century's most uncompromising plea for realism and science in education. In 1867 the Taunton Commission on the grammar schools that was then at work received a letter from Lyon Playfair 'stating that the Industrial Exhibition at Paris in 1867 furnished evidence of a decline in the superiority of certain branches of English manufacture over those of other nations, and that, in his opinion, this decline was partly due to a want of technical education in England'. The commission approached 'competent observers' and found that 'the opinion was general'.[94] The main effects of the 'general opinion', however, were to be felt in a later period.

Criticism of the public and grammar schools led to the appointment of two commissions. The Clarendon Commission was appointed in 1861 to inquire into the nine great schools – Eton, Winchester, Westminster, Charterhouse, Harrow, Rugby, Shrewsbury, St Paul's and Merchant Taylors'. Its report was published in 1864, and a Public Schools Act followed in 1868. The commission's report was the signal for pressure for a commission to inquire into those schools which had not been covered by the Newcastle or Clarendon Commission. The Taunton Commission (the official title of which was the Schools Inquiry Commission) was appointed in 1864, and reported in 1868. The distinction that the two separate commissions seemed to imply between the nine schools and the rest caused resentment among many headmasters, including Thring – and the result was the establishment of the Headmasters' Conference, which became the voice of the public schools.

Private school for girls at Campden House, London

The Clarendon Commission criticized the studies, methods and administration of the nine schools. Following its proposals and the Act of 1868 the definition of the schools as upper-class preserves was, in fact, strengthened, by the opening of foundation scholarships to competitive examination (inevitably favouring boys from preparatory schools). The governing bodies of the schools were reformed, and it was left to them to implement the suggested reforms of both curriculum and teaching methods. The commission responded to the body of scientific opinion with which it was presented by agreeing that 'the introduction of the elements of natural science into the regular course of study is desirable, and see no sufficient reason to doubt that it is practicable'.[95]

The Taunton Commission selected eight districts, covering a third of the area and three-fifths of the population of England and Wales, in which assistant commissioners inspected endowed, proprietary and private schools for boys and girls, and studied parental demand for education and the extent to which it was met. The reports constitute a massive indictment of the schools. The initial need, and the main concern of the 1869 Endowed Schools Act, was the reform of the charities on which the schools were based. Newly constituted endowed schools commissioners (absorbed into the Charity Commission in 1874) were empowered to prepare schemes for the reorganization of governing bodies and the revision of charities, including their extension to the education of girls. The Taunton Commission's wider proposals for a national system of secondary schools, graded according to the age to which parents were willing to keep their children at school (fourteen, sixteen and eighteen or nineteen), was not adopted. The commission considered that English lan-

guage and literature could be an elevating part of education, but
realized the difficulty of finding teachers able to teach it in such
a manner. It agreed that Latin should retain its place, though
Greek could be dropped in all except the first-grade schools. It
advocated the extension of political economy and mathematics in
the curriculum, and on science expressed the view that 'we
cannot consider any scheme of education complete which omits
a subject of such high importance'.[96] The commission did not
consider one grade of education preparatory to another, but did
look forward to the possibility 'that real ability shall find its
proper opening'. In the reorganization of endowments after 1869
lies one source of the concept of the 'ladder' to secondary education that was beginning to take shape from the 1870s.

The Taunton Commission came at an important point in the
history of education for middle-class girls. Girls in the early

Victorian family were trained to be dependent, 'distrusting their own conclusions, and shrinking from responsibility, till they sink into mere puppets, useless to themselves and to others'.[97] Educational improvements were only achieved when the pattern of Victorian family life began to change, and when girls began to seek economic independence. The focus of change was found in the governess system in the 1850s, was turned into a major campaign in the 1860s, and produced real fruits in the 1870s.

The unenviable position of governess in the large Victorian middle-class family (often as much part of the Victorian middle-class taste for 'conspicuous affluence' as the crinoline, the large house and the large number of well-groomed children) provided almost the only career open to the unmarried middle-class girl. The private boarding school gave parents 'the satisfaction of saying that they have spared no expense in the education of their children', but was merely a prelude to the 'traffic and arrangement' of matrimony.[98] None of this, said the critics, was as good as the education supplied by a governess under the supervision of the mother. A Governesses' Benevolent Institution was founded in 1843 for their protection, and five years later it opened Queen's College, in London, for girls over twelve years of age. One of its major achievements was its curriculum, one of the most extraordinary in nineteenth-century England. Lectures or classes from which the girls could choose included modern languages, mechanics, geography with geology, English grammar with Latin, and English literature. Botany, chemistry, philosophy, political economy and other subjects were later added, a range of interests reflected in the evening classes which were also introduced.[99] The second of its achievements was the quality of the support (including lecturing) it obtained, notably from F. D. Maurice and the staff at King's College. Maurice played an important part in the campaign of the 1860s, considering girls to be 'the most pitiable of all the victims of ignorance'.[100]

Students at Queen's College included Frances Mary Buss and Dorothea Beale, the former of whom became headmistress of North London Collegiate School in 1850 and the latter principal of Cheltenham College for Young Ladies in 1858. The campaign of the 1860s was one by women for education, as a gateway to other rights and opportunities. Queen's College and Bedford College (founded in 1849) and the schools of Miss Buss and Miss

Beale had shown the possibilities. The movement found a forum in the recently created National Association for the Promotion of Social Science. Under pressure (including from this association) the Taunton Commission agreed to include girls' schools in their investigations. A college for girls was founded at Hitchin in 1869 and, as Girton College, moved to Cambridge five years later; by the end of the decade classes were being arranged for women at University College, London.

By the 1860s, therefore, important changes in middle-class education were being indicated, if not yet accomplished. The changes accompanied increased middle-class prosperity and self-consciousness. Education reflected at the same time a growing mid-Victorian belief in raising standards by competition. Payment by results was one example; the spread of examinations generally was another. Competition in education reflected commercial and Darwinian influences. The Oxford and Cambridge 'locals' were established in 1858, as the beginning of the secondary-school examination system. The Royal Society of Arts and other organizations were conducting examinations. The 1850s saw the beginning of the reform of the civil service by the introduction of competitive examinations. Entrance to Sandhurst and Woolwich was made dependent on examinations in the 1850s. The effect of public examinations of this kind on the grammar schools in particular was immediate. Preparation for the examination requirements (including arithmetic, spelling and writing – responsible for the failure of 250 out of the 309 rejected for the civil service in 1856)[101] became an important function of the grammar schools. Many of them set up 'civil service' classes. Competition had been introduced for scholarships to the major public schools, and the Endowed Schools Act was about to increase the number of grammar-school scholarships open to competition.

Even before this process began Thomas Arnold saw that it was inevitable: 'every profession, every institution in the country, will be strung up to a higher tone: examinations will be more common and more searching . . . All this *will* be certainly . . . and I think also, that it ought to be.'[102] Edmond Holmes, looking back on the process in 1911, however, saw it as a symptom of the concern of Western civilization with the superficial: 'In every Western country that is progressive and "up to date", and in every Western country in exact proportion as it is progressive and "up to date", the examination system controls education, and in doing so arrests the self-development of the child, and therefore strangles his inward growth.'[103] In the second half of the nineteenth century the different needs of educational systems and of children were growing more apparent.

School, 1849

Notes

1 *Minutes of the Committee in Council 1840–1*, pp. 425–30, 438, 441.
2 JAMES KAY-SHUTTLEWORTH, *Four Periods of Public Education* (London, 1862), pp. 100–1, 229.
3 FRANCIS ADAMS, *History of the Elementary School Contest in England* (London, 1882), p. 92.
4 Ibid., p. 108.
5 JAMES E. THOROLD ROGERS (ed.), *Speeches on Questions of Public Policy by . . . John Bright* (London, 1868; 1869 edition), p. 530.
6 *Minutes 1840–1*, p. 124; M. E. SADLER and J. W. EDWARDS, 'Summary of statistics, regulations, &c., of elementary education in England and Wales, 1833–1870', in *Special Reports on Educational Subjects*, II (1898), p. 80.
7 FRANCIS SANDFORD (ed.), *Reports on Elementary Schools 1852–1882 by Matthew Arnold* (London, 1889), pp. 4–5.
8 ARCHIBALD ALISON, *England in 1815 and 1845* (Edinburgh, 1845), pp. 5, 15.
9 KAY-SHUTTLEWORTH, *Four Periods*, p. 230; WILLIAM COBBETT, *Rural Rides*, I (London, 1830; Everyman edition, 1948), p. 296.
10 *Minutes 1846*, II, p. 75.
11 *Minutes 1840–41*, pp. 176–7.
12 Ibid., p. 437.
13 ARTHUR JOHN BOOTH, *Robert Owen* (London, 1869), p. 56.
14 DERWENT COLERIDGE, *The Teachers of the People* (London, 1862), p. 5.
15 R. H. SUPER (ed.), *The Complete Prose Works of Matthew Arnold, II: Democratic Education* (Ann Arbor, 1962), p. 233.
16 DAVID ROBERTS, *Victorian Origins of the British Welfare State* (New Haven, 1960; 1961 edition), pp. 185–202.
17 *Minutes 1840–41*, p. 125.
18 Royal Commission appointed to Inquire into the Working of the Elementary Education Acts (CROSS COMMISSION), *First Report* (London, 1886), p. 5.
19 *Reports by the Four Factory Inspectors on the Effects of the Educational Provisions of the Factories Act* (London, 1839), p. 6.
20 W. C. R. HICKS, 'The education of the half-timer', *Economic History* (February 1939), pp. 225–6.
21 *Reports by the Four Factory Inspectors*, pp. 5–6.
22 CARLO M. CIPOLLA, *Literacy and Development in the West* (Harmondsworth, 1969), p. 67.
23 Quoted in EDWARD BAINES, *Letters to . . . Lord John Russell . . . on State Education* (London, 1846; 1847 edition), p. 16.
24 JOHN MORLEY, *The Life of Richard Cobden* (London, 1879; 1903 edition), pp. 300, 505, 610.

25 EDWARD BAINES, *The Social, Educational, and Religious State of the Manufacturing Districts* (London, 1843), pp. iii, 3, 11.

26 CONGREGATIONAL BOARD OF EDUCATION, *Crosby-Hall Lectures on Education* (London, 1848), p. 39.

27 SADLER and EDWARDS, 'Summary of statistics', p. 57.

28 *Report of the First General Meeting of . . . the National Education League* (Birmingham, 1869), pp. 13–14, 33–4.

29 *Education in Great Britain, Being the Official Report of Horace Mann* (London, 1854), p. xxi; BAINES, *Manufacturing Districts*, p. 26.

30 Commission appointed to Inquire into the State of Popular Education in England (NEWCASTLE COMMISSION), III, *Reports of the Assistant Commissioners* (London, 1861), pp. 507–8.

31 T. S. ASHTON, *Economic and Social Investigations in Manchester 1833–1933* (London, 1934), pp. 63–4.

32 LAWSON, *Primary Education in East Yorkshire*, p. 21.

33 *Minutes 1846*, I, pp. 436–7.

34 *Minutes 1840–41*, p. 452; *Education of the Manual-labour Class* (Education Aid Society of Manchester, 1866), p. 5.

35 *Education in Great Britain*, pp. xxxiii, xxxvi.

36 *Minutes 1846*, II, p. 21.

37 See W. A. MUNFORD, *Penny Rate* (London, 1951; 1967 edition), pp. 26–9.

38 JESSE COLLINGS, *Free Education* (Birmingham, 1871), p. 10.

39 *Minutes 1846*, I, p. 166.

40 KAY-SHUTTLEWORTH, *Four Periods*, p. 102; *Minutes 1846*, II, p. 113.

41 FRASER, *David Stow*, pp. 56–7.

42 *Minutes 1840–41*, pp. 319, 451.

43 CENTRAL SOCIETY OF EDUCATION, *Second Publication* (London, 1838), pp. 267–8; *Minutes 1846*, II, p. 29.

44 *Education in Great Britain*, p. lxxiii; FRASER, *David Stow*, p. 55.

45 *Minutes 1846*, II, p. 550.

46 *Minutes 1845*, II, pp. 221, 224.

47 NEWCASTLE COMMISSION, I, pp. 31–2.

48 *Minutes 1846*, II, p. 546.

49 JAMES CURRIE, *The Principles and Practice of Common-school Education* (London, 1862; undated new edition), pp. 174–5.

50 *Minutes 1846*, II, p. 545.

51 *Minutes 1847–8–9. Schools of Parochial Unions*, pp. vi–ix, 159–60.

52 LOUISA TWINING, 'Workhouse education', *Transactions of the National Association for the Promotion of Social Science 1861* (London, 1862), p. 335.

53 *Sixth Annual Report of the Poor Law Commissioners* (London, 1840), pp. 178–9.

54 C. J. MONTAGUE, *Sixty Years in Waifdom or, the Ragged School Movement in English History* (London, 1904; 1969 edition), p. 37.

55 *Education in Great Britain*, p. lxv.
56 CROSS COMMISSION, *Third Report* (1887), p. 439.
57 JOSEPH KAY, *The Education of the Poor in England and Europe* (London, 1846), p. 145; NEWCASTLE COMMISSION, III, p. 509.
58 [JAMES KAY-SHUTTLEWORTH], *The School in its Relations to the State, the Church, and the Congregation* (London, 1848), pp. 42–3.
59 *Minutes 1845*, II, p. 235; *Minutes 1840–41*, p. 175; *Minutes 1846*, I, pp. 172–3.
60 *Minutes 1840–41*, p. 437; *Minutes 1846*, II, p. 100.
61 *Annual Report on the State of the Charity Schools of the Kennington District* (London, 1832).
62 NEWCASTLE COMMISSION, I, p. 107.
63 For details of students' social and educational backgrounds see *Minutes 1845*, I, p. 241; II, pp. 36–49; *Minutes 1846*, I, pp. 503–14 (the last two, reports on Battersea, give details, among other things, of the 'previous condition' and 'acquirements at the time of admission' of students. Timetable from *Minutes 1845*, II, p. 51.
64 COLERIDGE, *Teachers of the People*, pp. 24–5.
65 Quoted in B. J. JOHNSON, 'The development of English education, 1856–1882, with special reference to the work of Robert Lowe' (MEd thesis, University of Durham, 1956), p. 116; this thesis is a sympathetic view of Lowe's work.
66 THOMAS H. HUXLEY, *Science and Education* (London, 1893; 1899 edition), p. 379.
67 SANDFORD (ed.), *Reports by Matthew Arnold*, pp. 98–9.
68 Ibid., pp. 123–4.
69 Quoted in H. D. RAWNSLEY, *Edward Thring* (London, 1889), p. 19.
70 EDMOND HOLMES, *What Is and What Might Be* (London, 1911), pp. vi–vii.
71 SUPER (ed.), *Matthew Arnold: Democratic Education*, p. 243. For a different view of the revised code, as a necessary instrument for simplifying and improving the administration of education, and as a victory for the state over the churches, see JOHN HURT, *Education in Evolution* (London, 1971), chapter 7.
72 HAROLD SILVER, *The Concept of Popular Education* (London, 1965), p. 177.
73 G. J. HOLYOAKE, *Self-help by the People: the history of the Rochdale pioneers 1844–1892* (London, 1893), pp. 12, 23, 50, 134–6.
74 MONTAGUE, *Sixty Years in Waifdom*, p. 184.
75 Quoted from *Chartist Circular* in A. TYRRELL, 'Political economy, Whiggism and the education of working-class adults in Scotland 1817–40', *Scottish Historical Review*, XLVIII (1969), p. 164.
76 R. APPLEGARTH, *Compulsory Attendance at School. The Working Men's View* (Birmingham, 1870), p. 1; A. W. HUMPHREY, *Robert Applegarth* (Manchester, 1913), p. 195. For details of classes run by the carpenters and joiners see P. W. MCCANN, 'Trade unionist, co-operative and

socialist organisations in relation to popular education 1870–1902'
(PhD thesis, University of Manchester, 1960), pp. 106–11.

77 W. J. DAVIS, *The British Trades Union Congress*, I (London, 1910), p. 78.
78 FREDERIC W. ROBINSON, 'William Ellis and his work for education' (MA thesis, University of London, 1919), p. 83.
79 *Minutes 1846*, I, pp. 189–91.
80 NEWCASTLE COMMISSION, I, p. 45.
81 JOHN STUART MILL, *Inaugural Address delivered to the University of St Andrews* (London, 1867), p. 6.
82 GREEN, *Oxford Common Room*, p. 127.
83 T. J. H. BISHOP and RUPERT WILKINSON, *Winchester and the Public School Élite* (London, 1967), p. 128.
84 D. A. WINSTANLEY, *Later Victorian Cambridge* (Cambridge, 1947), p. 39.
85 Bryce Commission, quoted in ROTHBLATT, *Revolution of the Dons*, p. 60.
86 E. G. W. BILL and J. F. A. MASON, *Christ Church and Reform 1850–1867* (Oxford, 1970), p. 28.
87 ARTHUR PENRHYN STANLEY, *The Life of Thomas Arnold* (London, 1844; abridged edition, 1903), p. 60.
88 Dr G. Moberly, quoted in ibid., p. 146.
89 See DAVID NEWSOME, *Godliness and Good Learning* (London, 1961), especially chapter 4, 'Godliness and manliness'.
90 RAWNSLEY, *Edward Thring*, pp. 17, 50.
91 K. E. KIRK, *The Story of the Woodard Schools* (London, 1937), p. 75; B. W. T. HANDFORD, *Lancing* (Oxford, 1933), *passim*.
92 For a discussion of the private and proprietary schools in the 1860s see FRANK MUSGROVE and PHILIP H. TAYLOR, *Society and the Teacher's Role* (London, 1969), chapter I and Appendix.
93 HARPER, *Cheltenham Grammar School*, pp. 46–8, 69–75; MUMFORD, *The Manchester Grammar School*, p. 309.
94 Schools Inquiry Commission (TAUNTON COMMISSION), I, *Report of the Commissioners* (London, 1868), p. 11.
95 Quoted in EDWARD C. MACK, *Public Schools and British Opinion since 1860* (New York, 1941), p. 36.
96 TAUNTON COMMISSION, I, pp. 25–6, 34.
97 MARIA G. GREY and EMILY SHIRREFF, *Thoughts on Self-culture, Addressed to Women*, II (London, 1850), p. 30.
98 'Female education, and modern match-making', *Fraser's Magazine*, XII (1835), pp. 312–13.
99 SHIRLEY C. GORDON, 'Studies at Queen's College, Harley Street, 1848–1868', *British Journal of Educational Studies*, III (1954–5), pp. 144–7.
100 CHARLES KINGSLEY, *Address on Education* (London, 1869), p. 12.
101 HARPER, *Cheltenham Grammar School*, p. 198.

102 BAMFORD (ed.), *Thomas Arnold on Education*, pp. 117–18.
103 HOLMES, *What Is and What Might Be*, p. 8.

Further Reading

MATTHEW ARNOLD, 'The twice-revised code' and 'A French Eton', in R. H. SUPER (ed.), *The Complete Prose Works of Matthew Arnold, II, Democratic Education* (Ann Arbor, 1962).

T. W. BAMFORD (ed.), *Thomas Arnold on Education* (Cambridge, 1970).

GEORGE C. T. BARTLEY, *The Schools for the People: containing the history, development, and present working of each description of English school for the industrial and poorer classes* (London, 1871).

W. F. CONNELL, *The Educational Thought and Influence of Matthew Arnold* (London, 1950).

V. H. H. GREEN, *Oxford Common Room: a study of Lincoln College and Mark Pattison* (London, 1957).

BRIAN HENRY, *Mission to the Middle Classes: the Woodard Schools 1848–1891* (London, 1969).

LOUIS JAMES, *Fiction for the Working Man 1830–1850: a study of the literature produced for the working classes in early Victorian urban England* (London, 1963).

JAMES KAY-SHUTTLEWORTH, *Four Periods of Public Education* (London, 1862).

S. E. MALTBY, *Manchester and the Movement for National Elementary Education 1800–1870* (London, 1918).

JAMES MURPHY, *The Religious Problem in English Education: the crucial experiment* (Liverpool, 1959).

DAVID NEWSOME, *Godliness and Good Learning: four studies on a Victorian ideal* (London, 1961).

JOHN ROACH, *Public Examinations in England 1850–1900* (Cambridge, 1970).

ADAM HENRY ROBSON, *The Education of Children Engaged in Industry in England 1833–1876* (London, 1931).

SHELDON ROTHBLATT, *The Revolution of the Dons: Cambridge and society in Victorian England* (London, 1968).

BRIAN SIMON, *Studies in the History of Education 1780–1870* (London, 1960), chapters 5–7.

W. A. C. STEWART and W. P. MCCANN, *The Educational Innovators 1750–1880* (London, 1967), part 2.

See also pp. 473–5.

CHAPTER IX

Education and social policy
1869–1900

An Act to provide for public elementary education

The Elementary Education Act of 1870 was the most workable piece of compromise legislation in English nineteenth-century history. It did not introduce free or compulsory education, but it made both possible. It did not supersede the voluntary schools, it supplemented them. It brought the state into action in education as never before. It created, in the school boards, the most demo-cratic organs of local administration of the century, but left the board's opponents in positions of strength.

A sequence of parliamentary debates and unsuccessful bills in the 1850s and 1860s had created a sense that an elementary Act was sooner or later inevitable. The most vociferous voluntaryist opinion had abated in the late 1860s. A more powerful form of educational pressure group had appeared. The 1867 Reform Act convinced many waverers of the need to educate the newly enfranchised working men in the towns. Edward Baines indicated the shift in public opinion in 1871, twenty-eight years after he had launched hardline voluntaryism, and four years after abandoning his position. Voluntary action, he explained, had been successful, but the 1870 Act represented necessary new 'giant steps'. He was enthusiastic about the Act, the Education Com-mittee of the Privy Council and the new boards – particularly the London school board. The Act, Baines believed, would have 'the most important consequences to the social and political condition of England'.[1] The Church of England and its sup-porters in many districts, on the other hand, were less enthusiastic, and often openly hostile to the boards, since it was with the church schools that these were seen to be most directly in competition.

Although the 1870 Act did not embody the programme of the National Education League, the latter's seven years of activity from 1869 were of considerable importance. The league was centred on Birmingham, but it had significant predecessors in Manchester, which in the thirties and forties had been the home of societies advocating either non-sectarian or secular education (including the Lancashire, subsequently the National, Public School Association in 1847). Unsuccessful education bills for Manchester and Salford were promoted in 1852. To Manchester, said one contemporary after 1870, 'we owe the line of ideas and influence, educational and political, which has brought the nation into the possession of the present Education Act'.[2] The Education Aid Society of Manchester had, from 1864, shown a possible way forward in joint efforts by religious and secular educators to bring children into schools, paying the fees where necessary. The society employed qualified visitors 'to go from house to house to inquire into the circumstances of applicants for aid'; in two years it succeeded in getting several thousand children to school.[3] This Manchester model was repeated in Birmingham in 1867, and out of it grew the National Education League. It considered voluntary action to be inadequate: 'that it is a failure in country parishes', Charles Kingsley told the league, 'I know from 27 years' experience as a parson.'[4] The voluntary system, an MP told them, 'is like the multiplication table; if you multiply 10 by 10 you get 100, but if you multiply nothing by 10 you still get nothing at all': this was the condition of 'that large section of the community, which the voluntary system has failed to serve'.[5]

The league wanted local boards to be set up in all districts, education to be compulsory, and free and unsectarian schools to be founded and maintained out of rates – and aided and inspected by the government.[6] The core of the league's support was non-conformist and Liberal, and there was a good deal of support from national trade unions and local trades councils. The league's parliamentary spokesmen delayed introducing a bill in 1870 when it learned that W. E. Forster, on behalf of Gladstone's government, was to introduce one.

Forster had shared many of the views of the league, but finally considered it necessary to carry church opinion and leave the voluntary schools intact. Robert Applegarth, trade union leader and one of the founders of the league, records a conversation with Forster before the bill was introduced; he told Forster that he was conceding too much to the church party, and 'when I told him that the members of the League would surely fight him on the religious difficulty he was creating, he tartly replied, "Then they will have to fight."'[7] Forster chose the course that would, in his own words, 'supplement the present voluntary system – that is . . . fill up its gaps at least cost of public money, with least loss of voluntary co-operation, and with most aid from the parents'. Forster was not alone in choosing this course: his approach was also that of the prime minister, Gladstone. As a churchman Gladstone was making substantial concessions even in supporting the education bill as it was finally framed. He sought to preserve 'along with full freedom of conscience the integrity of religious instruction', and was behind Forster when he placed himself in the position 'of appearing to care more for his enemies than for his friends'.[8] Forster's policy brought him, in fact, support from former Conservative enemies and attacks from former friends; it made him 'more than any other politician of his time . . . the subject of a controversy which dealt not merely with his methods and results, but with his motives'.[9] His Act 'to provide for public elementary education in England and Wales' was described by the secretary of the league as a 'a compromise upon a compromise',[10] between the practical compromise already effected by the Manchester educationists and the programme of the National Education Union, a church body set up to oppose the league and protect the voluntary system.

The aim of the Act was to provide school accommodation 'for all the children resident in such district for whose elementary education efficient and suitable provision is not otherwise made'.[11] Where such provision was inadequate 'a school board

shall be formed for such district and shall supply such deficiency'. The voluntary agencies were given six months in which to claim their last building grants for new schools. A clause added to the bill in its final stages (the Cowper-Temple clause) laid down that for board schools 'no religious catechism or religious formulary which is distinctive of any particular denomination shall be taught in the school'. Boards could take over voluntary schools transferred to them by their managers. It was laid down that 'every child attending a school provided by any school board shall pay such weekly fee as may be prescribed by the school board' (not more than 9d. a week) but boards had the power to remit fees, and — a cause of much later controversy — could pay the fees of poor children attending schools other than board schools (seen by the league in particular as a subsidy to schools not publicly accountable).

The 'public elementary schools' to be provided by the boards, it should be emphasized, were intended to and did rest on the same central assumption as the voluntary schools which they were called on to supplement – they were for the children of the poor, providing an independent system for the lower class. Although lower-middle-class children came to some extent to benefit from their existence, the elementary schools were viewed as catering for the class of children ranging from the 'street Arabs' to those of the 'respectable' working class. They were self-contained and not preparatory to a grammar school or any other education. Although the voluntary and public elementary schools were rival systems in one respect, they formed a socially coherent system in another respect: the identification of this system with the working class did not alter in the remainder of the nineteenth century and was only slowly eroded in the twentieth century. A pamphlet on the public elementary schools published by the National Union of Teachers early in the twentieth century begins with the typical statement: 'Six million children are in the Public Elementary Schools of England and Wales. They are the children of the workers, to be themselves England's workers a few years hence.'[12]

School boards were to have between five and fifteen members and were to be elected on the basis of a cumulative voting system, by which a voter could give all his votes to one candidate or distribute them among the candidates. All ratepayers could vote and stand for election, including women. Boards were enabled to enact by-laws making attendance compulsory between five and thirteen, with total or partial exemption between ten and thirteen for children certified by one of Her Majesty's inspectors to have 'reached a standard of education specified in such bye-law'.

The election and composition of the boards proved to be of great social importance. As single-purpose authorities they were able, in large towns like London and Birmingham, to attract candidates of high quality. The chairman of Birmingham school board in 1902 reflected that the boards' successes had been mainly due to 'the calibre of those whom they attracted as members, especially in their earlier years. School Boards enlisted the activity and zeal of many eminent men and women of strong philanthropic instincts who, for various reasons, had not hitherto enjoyed any similar opportunity of public service. . . . A seat on the School Board was a highly-coveted honour.'[13] It must be remembered that this was true only of the large urban school boards. In a number of towns women were elected in the 1870s. The working men enfranchised in 1867 were able to vote, and trades councils put up candidates. Although few were successful in the early elections, such educational activity was to be an important extension of trade union functions in the 1870s and 1880s.[14] The boards became a focus of new social pressures and of a new interest in democratic processes. One of the leading supporters of the boards declared in 1873 that by leaving the clergy to administer part of the educational system

> we threw away one of the rarest and most convenient opportunities, first of inculcating and diffusing a new sense of the value of instruction, and . . . secondly, of deepening those habits of local self-government which . . . are at the very root of our superior political advancement. And we threw away this opportunity especially in the rural districts, where it was most desirable to seize it.

Objections to the establishment of school boards were 'simply objections to self-government'. Voluntary school managers were a 'private and irresponsible body'; a school board was a 'responsible body of representatives' through which 'we gradually diffuse the notion of the school being an object of public care'.[15]

The boards' lessons in democracy, however, were not always salutary. Elections were often sectarian battles between Church of England and nonconformity, between candidates pledged to educational development and those pledged to save the ratepayers' money, or between political parties. The cumulative vote not only protected minorities, it sometimes gave them disproportionate power. In the first board election Birmingham's locally dominant Liberals ran fifteen candidates, but the Tories won control of the board by putting up only eight candidates and concentrating their votes. Political faction-mongering often overshadowed educational issues. Some of the smaller boards in rural areas were controlled by people who had opposed their creation, and were pledged to restrict their activities. One school inspector even recorded two cases of school boards set up by accident: in Wales for a parish in one county instead of for one of the same name in another county, and in England for a parish whose deficit of 13 school places was mistakenly copied out as 130.[16] The fact that almost half the country's school boards were forced upon reluctant localities helps to explain the view that 'there never was any real School Board system, no cohesion among Boards, no systematical advance of their work and interests'.[17]

Many of the boards developed, nevertheless, their internal loyalties and a new sense of educational purpose. They contributed to the movement of opinion which, from the 1880s, saw the state and public authorities as more active agents of social policy. T. H. Green and an influential school of idealist philosophers were at the same time giving prominence to the state in discussions of education, equality and social justice. From the early 1880s the Social Democratic Federation, the Fabian Society and other bodies gave new currency to socialist concepts of social responsibility. In 1885 Joseph Chamberlain, at the time still a Liberal, could agree with his opponents who called his programme socialism. 'Of course it is Socialism,' he retorted, 'The Poor Law is Socialism; the Education Act is Socialism; the greater part of municipal work is Socialism; and every kindly act of legislation by which the community has sought to discharge its responsibilities and obligations to the poor is Socialism.'[18] Discounting the rhetoric, it is clear to what extent thinking about social policy had changed. The existence of the school boards had contributed to the change.

Between 1870 and 1896 nearly 2,500 school boards were created in England and Wales, almost a half serving communities with a population of under 1,000; of the 116 village school boards in Devon 89 had one school and 25 had two. Average national attendance at board schools in 1895 was nearly 1,900,000. At voluntary schools average attendance rose from just over 1,200,000 in 1871 to double that figure in 1895. When the 1870 Act was passed there were some 8,800 inspected voluntary schools in England and Wales (6,000 of them connected with the Church of England); in 1900 there were nearly 14,500, by which date the number of board schools was almost 5,700. The initial impetus given to voluntary-school building by the passing of the Act could not be maintained. In the 1890s the number of voluntary schools in fact fell by over 350, and the number of board schools rose by nearly 1,000.[19]

The test of the efficacy of the 1870 Act lay in the areas of greatest need, of which London and Birmingham were two. It took the London school board only twelve years to catch up with the 250,000 or so children in voluntary schools, and by the time the board came to an end it had twice as many, with over 500,000 school places.[20] The church made widespread efforts to prevent the election of school boards. The arguments were, as in the past, less concerned with education than with religion, politics, power and finance. In Derbyshire people 'were little concerned with children and their education, but very much concerned with future workers, congregations, godliness and godlessness, the forestalling of revolution, rates, and the like. It was these questions which delayed the election of School Boards, and hindered their work once they were established.'[21] The rapid increase in church school-building, encouraged by the period of grace allowed in the Act, had been a serious blow to the league, which had hoped that the boards would gradually spread and take over most of the existing schools. The new church schools, in Chamberlain's words, were created 'to prevent the election of School Boards in hundreds of districts, and thereby to render impossible the compulsory attendance of children'. Since the board schools collected a large number of hitherto neglected children, it was said in Birmingham that 'many of the more decent and more respectable poor preferred the denominational schools'.[22] The number of British and other nonconformist schools also rose, but some schools were handed over to the school boards, and from a peak at the end of the 1870s the number dropped in succeeding decades. The number of Roman Catholic schools, however, rose from 400 in 1871 to 1,000 or so at the end of the 1890s.

The 1870 Act made further legislation, especially with regard to attendance, inevitable. After 1870 the NEL was one of a variety of organizations (the TUC was another) campaigning for free education. In the early 1870s the league was an educational force of a new kind; it had 26 branches in 1869 and 315 two years later. It influenced opinion most successfully on the question of compulsory education, taking its cue from the compulsory provisions in the Factory Acts. An Act of 1876 made obligatory the election of school attendance committees in districts not covered by school boards (a provision which the league attacked as giving 'a new lease of life to the denominational system').[23] By 1880 only 450 of the 2,000 or so school boards and 20 of the 190 school attendance committees had adopted by-laws enforcing school attendance, and an Act passed in that year made such by-laws obligatory. Education was made compulsory up to the age of thirteen, with exemptions from the age of ten (raised to eleven in 1893 and twelve in 1899). An Act of 1891 enabled board and voluntary schools to admit children free and claim a fee grant in compensation.

After 1870, therefore, the legislative basis of elementary education was extended, as was the authority of the Education Department, whose scope was continually widened in the next thirty years, and 'its importance in the hierarchy of Government Departments emphasised'.[24] T. H. Huxley believed the powers of the department to be excessive and sought to strengthen the London school board, of which he was a member, as a counter-balance to the influence of the state. For Scotland, following the Argyll Commission, which reported in 1865–8, an Education Act was also passed in 1872, creating school boards which had powers in secondary as well as elementary education, and made attendance compulsory. The Scottish boards were able immediately to take over a high percentage of existing schools.

Inevitably the largest boards had the greatest influence, and London more than any other. The architecture and layout of the London board's schools were widely followed. Its leading figures, like T. H. Huxley, commanded national respect. The decisions of the London board from the end of 1870 affected 'not only the vast population under its immediate administrative control, but also, indirectly, all those areas in which School Boards were about to be established'.[25]

Within the national and local organization of education after 1870 the inspectorate played an increasingly important part. The early inspectors had been prodigiously hardworking and sensitive to the social realities surrounding education. Since 1862, however, the examination process under the system of payment by results had absorbed so much of their time that they had been deprived, in Matthew Arnold's words, 'of the needful freshness and spirit . . . for joining with it, on the same occasion, the old inspection'.[26] After 1870 the inspectorate was reorganized in districts, covering both board and voluntary schools, and Her Majesty's inspectors continued to wield great power over the income of schools and the very jobs of the teachers. At the same time the school boards began to appoint their own inspectors, London and many other cities making their first appointments within a year or two of the Act. Local inspectors, unlike HMIs, were recruited mainly from experienced elementary-school head teachers.

The boards were a representative social phenomenon. The organs of social administration were in general becoming larger and more complex. The organization of public services and the balance between central and local government control were becoming themes of increasing public interest. So was the recruitment of civil servants, and related attempts, primarily through examinations, to make the process more efficient. In 1870 an Order in Council made senior grades in the civil service open to competitive examinations. Although patronage declined in public administration, education was exempted from the working of the 1870 Order and patronage continued. G. W. Kekewich, later secretary of the Education Department, was appointed as an 'examiner' there in 1868 in a manner which prevailed until the end of the century. His father, an MP, asked the chancellor of the exchequer to find young Kekewich, straight from Oxford, a civil-service appointment. He was interviewed for a post as examiner (never having previously heard of such a thing, or of the Education Department). He was appointed because someone mistakenly credited him with a first in classics. The interviews were 'of exceedingly short duration, and included no inquiry whatever into my knowledge of education or of the system then in operation, of which I was of course absolutely ignorant'.[27]

In general the professions which were related to expanding public services were growing in numbers and status. Under a Public Health Act of 1872 new urban sanitary districts acquired an increasing range of local government responsibilities. After the third of the Parliamentary Reform Acts of the century, in 1884, county and county borough councils were created in 1888. The scale of the average industrial and commercial enterprise was also growing. Between 1881 and 1901 the number of males employed in 'general and local government' increased from 97,000 to 172,000, and the number of females from 7,000 to 26,000. The number of female commercial and business clerks increased in the same period from 6,000 to 56,000. New professional institutions, the trade unionism of the unskilled, and greater job opportunities for girls were other features of the changes in social structure and organization.

From the beginning of the 1870s, then, education became a vital element in the development of social policy. For many Liberals and nonconformists the compromises in the 1870 Act had seemed, in fact, a defeat in the field of social policy. A pamphlet published by 'A Nonconformist M.P.' in 1873, and addressed to his Liberal leader, Gladstone, made two emphatic points. Education, firstly, was now 'of more importance than the army or navy, affecting, as it does, the physical, intellectual, and moral progress of the people'. Yet education was administered by only part of a state department, and expenditure on education was one-seventeenth of that on the armed services. Forster's bill, secondly, had put 'every sect in battle array'; the Act was 'an ecclesiastical, nearly as much as an educational measure'. It was felt widely that Forster 'ought to have proposed his bill from the Conservative benches'.[28] The National Education League issued a leaflet to show that the Liberal leaders had passed the bill only with Conservative support. Social policy, it is clear, was not formed from an easy consensus of opinion. The school boards demonstrated the new emphasis in public opinion, but also the difficulties and ambiguities in approaches to social policy.

Literacy and attendance

The figures for the final decades of the century show the almost complete elimination of illiteracy as measured from parish registers. The gains were greatest for women. For the years 1871, 1881 and 1891 the registrar general gave a national literacy rate for males of approximately 80, 87 and 94 per cent respectively, and for females 73, 82 and 93 per cent. By the end of the century it was approximately 97 per cent in both cases. Literacy among brides in the East Riding parishes was 74 per cent in the decade up to 1870, 88 per cent in the following decade and 92 and 98 per cent in the last two decades.[29]

Had it not been for the 1870 Act progress in literacy would have slowed down, 'simply because illiteracy was by that time concentrated in those classes and regions that were hardest to provide for under the voluntary system'. The 1870 Act was responsible for a 'mopping-up operation'.[30] The main advances in literacy in the final decades of the century related, therefore, to the increased number of school places, but equally to improvements in attendance and length of school life. In the countryside, schools were opened where none had previously existed. In towns it was among the most depressed classes that the effects of the 1870 and subsequent Acts were most felt. Questioned about the ragged Sunday schools in 1887, the chairman of the Ragged School Union said that 'the Education Act had been enormously beneficial. The number of children who came to our ragged schools unable to read previous to the Education Act, was very large. Now almost every child is able to read the Bible or the Testament.' Children, he thought, could 'read intelligently, for the most part'.[31]

Although the statistics reflected a qualitative as well as a numerical improvement, there was small ground for complacency. In the mid-1890s Sir John Gorst, Conservative vice-president of the Council, told Parliament that a quarter of a century after the 1870 Act there were 'nearly three-quarters of a million of children whose names ought to be on the books of some elementary school, and who do not appear at all . . . Of those who are on the books of the elementary schools, nearly one-fifth are continually absent.' In 1897 average attendance was 81·5 per cent. In 1898 Gorst described the main problems of education as being 'to get more children into the existing schools, to get them there in a condition fit to receive instruction, and to keep them to an older age'.[32] Manchester and Salford in 1869 had some 100,000 children between the ages of three and twelve; 55,000 were on school books and 38,000 in average attendance. At schools in receipt of parliamentary grant the percentage in attendance rose from 68 in 1870 to 82 in 1900. When the Birmingham school board was created children were absent on average nearly four half-days a week; thirty years later the figure had been cut by half.[33]

Legislation was not the only contributory factor: a machinery of enforcement had been necessary. The most persistent absentees could in some areas, including London, be sent to 'truant schools', which had an atmosphere of deterrence intended to make regular schooling more palatable. The main pressure brought to bear, however, was that of the attendance officer (familiarly known as the 'board man') and ultimately a summons. Authorities were often unwilling to prosecute or convict parents, either because the procedure was expensive and not always successful, or because – in country areas especially – magistrates were sympathetic to farmworkers who kept their children away from schools, and with farmers who wanted the children's labour. An Agricultural Children Act in 1873 was intended to improve attendance, but fines imposed were often derisory, when imposed at all. In 1887 an attendance officer in Lincolnshire declared 'that it was useless his taking out summonses because the Magistrates *would not convict*' at the village of Bardney; a fine imposed in 1894, reported the teacher, was the first case of conviction in ten years.[34]

By the beginning of the twentieth century the number of children at school in the main centres of population had grown enormously (although it must be remembered that the population of England and Wales also rose from over 22 to over 32 million between 1870 and the end of the century). Improvements in the schools, and a changing climate of opinion about the value of education, were additional factors inducing some parents to send their children to school. An official report in the late 1890s commented on the change since 1870: 'the value of a good school has become more widely appreciated, and parents evince an increasing desire to secure the benefits of efficient teaching for their children'.[35]

The extent and nature of literacy in this period were also reflected in the dramatic increase in cheap commercial publications and the arrival of the mass-circulation newspaper. The 1880s saw, for example, the proliferation of 'penny journals', to be found 'in back streets, in small dark shops, in the company of cheap tobacco . . . put forth from Heaven knows what printing-houses in courts and alleys, to lie for a few days only on the counter in huge piles'. This was a periodical, romance literature, written to a formula and 'in a forest of verbiage'. Like earlier improving magazines it included snippets of information, to the effect that, for example, 'needles were first made in England in Cheapside, in the reign of Queen Mary, by a negro from Spain', or 'the family name of the Duke of Norfolk is Howard, although the younger members of it call themselves Talbot'.[36] This kind of literature was based on past traditions, and was to prepare the way, in the 1890s, for Northcliffe, *Tit-bits* and the *Daily Mail*, and the growing empire of serialized and paperback fiction. Alfred Harmsworth, later Lord Northcliffe, produced the *Daily Mail* against a background of the inertia of the existing press. He installed his new rotary presses, attracted advertising revenue, made unprecedented use of the cable as a source of news, and produced a ½d. paper with short leading articles, and vivid news presentation.[37] From the end of the century newspaper circulations were counted in millions. The widening range of cheap reading matter assumed a degree of literacy that could not cope with sustained effort.

At one level, therefore, there was an attempt to cater for simple reading tastes on a mass scale. At another level there was also increasing library provision. In 1902 Sidney Webb could point to the 750,000 volumes in London's lending libraries, and nearly 150,000 in their reference departments. In 1880, when proper records began, just over 2,000 schools had their own libraries. In 1895 the number was nearly 6,400.[38] The commercial libraries continued to circulate fiction to a mainly middle-

*Warrington Mechanics'
Institute travelling
library, 1860*

class audience, and the end of the century saw the foundation of Boots' library through their chain of chemists' shops.

In both manufacturing and agricultural areas, of course, the quality of literacy was governed by factors other than directly educational ones. The factory legislation of the late 1860s and 1870s, in particular, encompassed children in industries not before covered, such as the metal industries. From the 1870s the future pattern of leisure and holidays began to take rudimentary shape. Bank holidays were enacted in 1871. Brunner-Mond was the first large firm to give some of its workers an annual week's holiday with pay, from 1884. The practice of half-day working on Saturdays had become widespread after 1850 and was almost universal in industry by the end of the century. New skilled and semi-skilled occupations were being created. Whitecollar occupations were expanding, and the status of large numbers of clerical and supervisory workers was becoming more difficult to define.

The mass of urban and rural poverty, however, remained. Charles Booth, the father of the English social survey, launched his great work on *The Life and Labour of the People of London* in 1887, convinced that socialist claims about the extent of poverty were exaggerated. To his astonishment he discovered that between a quarter and a third of the population fell within his definition of 'living in poverty'. Seebohm Rowntree, refining Booth's definitions and methods, came to similar conclusions at the end of the century in York. Poverty was reflected not only in housing and health, but in education. It is an essential background to the discussion of attitudes to schooling and the concept of literacy.

Schools, codes and subjects

'When we small school-boys noted the disappearance of some of the interesting features in our classwork and were lined-up at the inspector's visit for a rigid examination in the three R's, we were conscious that a change had come.' This was one memory of the introduction of the revised code; to the more liberal school managers and inspectors payment by results 'proved repugnant'. A 'starvation period' set in. In the seventies and eighties school work remained 'undeniably hard, . . . preparation for these examinations, chiefly mechanical, practically monopolized the labours both of teachers and children'.[39] Not the least of the pressures against the code was that of the elementary-school teachers and their union, known at first as the National Union of Elementary Teachers, founded in 1870.

After 1870 some relaxations of the rigidities of the 1862 code began to be introduced. Schools could earn extra grant even from 1868 for 'specific subjects' taught in addition to the three Rs; in 1871 a grant of 3s. was introduced for each child successful in an examination in not more than two such subjects, including geography, history, algebra, geometry, the natural sciences, political economy, languages, 'or *any* definite subject of instruc-

tion . . . taught according to a graduated scheme'.[40] Only about
2–3 per cent of children on the registers were presented in
specific subjects in the 1870s. Under the code of 1875 'class subjects' were also introduced; grants for these were made to schools
on the basis of the proficiency of classes, not the examination of
individual children. Three further dates mark the remaining
history of payment by results.

The code of 1882, the work of A. J. Mundella, Liberal vice-
president of the Council, added a standard VII for grant-
earning examination purposes; it introduced a classification of
schools as 'fair', 'good' or 'excellent', with three corresponding
levels of merit grant; it related attendance grants to total attendance in the school; it extended the specific and class subjects, and
encouraged school libraries and savings banks.[41] New attitudes
were being formulated, but the constriction of payment by results
remained. The National Union of Elementary Teachers (which
became the NUT in 1889) had been conducting a prolonged and
vigorous campaign against the system, wider concepts of educational processes were gaining currency – including among some
key educational administrators – as was the view that educational
finance needed to be more firmly related to the needs of schools.
The result was that in 1890 payment by results was fundament-
ally undermined, to the delight of the teachers. General inspection without notice was substituted for one on an appointed day.
'Absurd and mischievous deductions from the grant' were ended,
and the system abandoned by which 'the worse a school was, the
more the means of improving it should be taken away'.[42] A
small element in the grant per child, however, was still dependent
on the inspector's examination. The examination of individual
children in efficient schools was disappearing in the mid-1890s,
and in 1898 inspectors were finally instructed that they 'should
not include any of the processes heretofore employed in formal
examination'.[43] The consequences must not be exaggerated.
A long process of conditioning had been taking place. Men who
grow accustomed to semi-darkness, explained Edmond Holmes,
formerly chief inspector for elementary schools, were blinded on
being brought out into the daylight; for thirty-three years the
teachers were 'treated as machines, and they were suddenly asked
to act as intelligent beings'.[44]

The philosophy of 1862, therefore, whatever its intentions, had
a constricting effect on the schools. It was to be a long time after

that date before the elementary-school system began to respond to wider concepts of culture, to a more generous view of educational objectives. Lyon Playfair, one of the great names in science education, said of the schooling provided for working-class children in 1870: 'What an equipment for the battle for life!' The low quality of education was 'impoverishing the land. It is disgracefully behind the age in which we live, and of the civilization of which we boast.' John Ruskin, one of the great names in the arts, proclaimed six years later: 'Commiserate the hapless Board School child, shut out from dreamland and poetry, and prematurely hardened and vulgarised by the pressure of codes and formularies. He spends his years as a tale that is *not* told.'[45] By the twentieth century some of the boards, especially the larger ones, had accomplished important changes, and new ideas were beginning to be acted upon. The board schools had for the most part implemented the principle of separate classrooms. Long benches were gradually replaced by desks. In 1903 Sidney Webb wrote a panegyric to the London school board era, which had effected

> the change from frowsy, dark, and insanitary rooms, practically destitute of apparatus or playgrounds, in which teachers, themselves mostly untrained, mechanically ground a minimum of the three R's required by the wooden old code into the heads of their scanty pupils, to the well-lighted and admirably decorated school buildings of the present day, with ample educational equipment . . . served by a staff of trained professional teachers, encouraged to develop the growing intelligence of their scholars in whatever subjects and by whatever educational methods they find best.

Yet, he added, 'great as was the stride taken by the establishment of the London School Board, the dominant idea was still merely the education of the poor'.[46]

In 1871 the prescribed subjects of instruction were reading, writing, arithmetic and, for girls, needlework and cutting out; in addition there were the optional specific subjects from standard IV (as well as drill for boys). In 1896 the obligatory subjects were the three Rs, needlework for girls, drawing (for older boys), object lessons or one class subject. In addition schools could provide (with certain restrictions) such class subjects as singing, recitation, drawing, English, geography, science, history and domestic economy. Welsh was an optional class subject in

Wales. Specific subjects (again within limits) included mechanics, chemistry, physics, animal physiology, agriculture, navigation, languages and shorthand. Girls could also be taught cookery, laundry and dairy work, and boys could be taught gardening. Explicit provision was also made for manual instruction, physical exercise (including swimming and gymnastics), and visits to institutions of educational value.

Some curriculum developments were the subject of extensive discussion. The object lesson, for example, was emphasized not only in timetables, but in the writings about the principles of education which were an important feature of these decades. The phrase was used sometimes to mean simple demonstrations in science, sometimes to mean using concrete examples to convey abstractions (especially in number work), and sometimes as a process of discrimination among colours, forms and so on. Such lessons ranged, in general, 'over all the utilities of life, and all the processes of nature. It begins upon things familiar to the pupils, and enlarges the conceptions of these.'[47] Science became more widely taught, often by peripatetic teachers, following the example of Birmingham, which in 1900 had a 'central science staff' of one chief science demonstrator, seven assistant demonstrators and seven porters to trundle the apparatus about.[48] Only after the 1870s were important advances made in physical education and manual training. As late as 1875, William Jolly, HMI, was complaining that 'systematic physical education has been altogether ignored, until quite recently, in our common schools'.[49] By the end of the century, however, various forms of drill and physical exercise had become an established part of school life. The manual education movement also made great progress in elementary schools in the last two decades of the century. Elementary education retained, however, in a new age and in new forms, its role as 'apprenticeship to a calling',[50] preparation for a defined status of life.

'I am well aware', wrote a headmaster in 1889, 'that even yet there are great differences of opinion regarding the amount of education to be expected from an elementary teacher. Some persons seem ever afraid lest the poor be instructed beyond their station.'[51] The social definition of the elementary teacher remained, in fact, at this late point in the century, as sharp as that of the separate system of which he formed a part. Early attempts to create some form of Registration Association to make teaching

Board school, 1876

one of the 'liberal professions' were for teachers other than those in elementary schools. This was true of bills debated in Parliament in 1869, 1879 and 1881. The first attempt to design a bill which included all teachers was in 1890, one of the promotors being the National Union of Teachers. All were unsuccessful.[52]

When the 1870 Act was passed there were somewhat over 12,000 certificated teachers, about half of them women. Ten years later there were over 31,000, and in 1895 there were almost 53,000, the proportion of women steadily increasing to about three-fifths at the latter date. In the same period the number of pupil teachers rose from over 14,000 to 34,000: from just over 1,000 the number of adult assistant teachers rose to 28,000 by 1895.[53] The creation of the school boards had, of course,

provoked an unprecedented demand for teachers, and had
improved the security if not the status of a large number of them.
Teacher training remained until the 1890s the monopoly of the
voluntary religious agencies and the main criticism levelled
against them, including by inspectors, was the weakness of their
work in secular subjects. The pupil-teacher system was coming
under increasing attack for putting immature and inefficient
apprentices in the classroom, and giving them extremely poor
instruction. An attempt was made by a group of head teachers in
London to bring pupil teachers together in centralized evening
classes in 1876. The venture collapsed, but was taken up again in
1882, when evening and Saturday morning classes were successfully begun. In 1885 the London school board opened its first

day centres for pupil-teacher classes, and such classes – day or evening – were taken up in many towns. Classes were most difficult to arrange in science, a chief inspector reported in 1900, because of the need for equipment and practical work. In West Suffolk a teacher and apparatus were supplied 'sufficient for such experimental work as can be carried out with improvised arrangements in an elementary schoolroom'. Porth, in South Wales, possessed 'a model of what the premises of a pupil-teacher school should not be'.[54]

Until the end of the century pupil teachers were recruited at thirteen or fourteen (the age was raised to fifteen in 1900, though with the possibility of a probationary period from thirteen to fifteen). They did some twenty hours of teaching a week. Demands for secondary education for pupil teachers were one of the main pressures towards the expansion of the scholarship ladder and the system of secondary schools.[55]

In the 1890s day training colleges came into existence in association with the newly emerging university colleges: students took combined university and college courses. Birmingham, Cardiff, Manchester, Newcastle, Nottingham and King's College, London, were the first to be created, all in 1890. Reading admitted eighty or so students to its first intake in 1899, and such numbers helped to strengthen the small new university institutions themselves.[56] The day training colleges were the first important step away from the denominational basis of training, and although in elementary education it was to be the local authority training colleges of the twentieth century that proved important, some of the foundations in the 1890s were intended to train both elementary and secondary teachers. Schemes for joint training coincided, for a moment of time, with the interest among some educationists in raising the professional status of teachers. J. J. Findlay, later professor of education at Manchester, was anxious, for example, to base the distinction between secondary and elementary teacher training not 'upon social or caste distinctions, but *upon the standard of attainment*'.[57] The schemes of the 1890s did not result in a unitary system of training or registration. The universities eventually developed postgraduate courses for secondary education, and local authority colleges, alongside the denominational ones, were to be engaged mainly in training elementary teachers.

The grammar schools

A quarter of a century after the Taunton Commission and the Endowed Schools Act of 1869 the Bryce Commission was appointed to look at secondary education. Four main developments had taken place. First, the endowments and management of the grammar schools had been widely reformed (of the total of 1,448 in England which came within the terms of the Act, the Bryce Commission found that only 546 had 'not felt the reforming hand of the Commissioners').[58] Secondly, and consequent upon such reforms, the curricula of the grammar schools had become subject to greater scrutiny and change. Thirdly, the middle-class character of the schools had been further strengthened, although a narrow ladder had begun to be erected for the recruitment of a small number of working-class children to the secondary system. Fourthly, secondary education for middle-class girls had made considerable strides.

In spite of the reforms, however, many schools remained insecure. The Bryce Commission found that in the nineties many of them, mainly the smaller ones, were prone to fluctuating numbers and decline. 'The most general cause of their decay', said the commission, 'is poverty', but geographical position and the inefficiency of headmasters also contributed. Many of the schools were conducting a 'hard fight for existence, often doing creditable work, yet doomed, apparently, to dwindle'.[59] They continued to suffer in competition with private and proprietary schools. The higher-grade schools of the boards, as we shall see, provided further competition. In Hull there was even talk in the 1880s of handing over the grammar school to the school board.[60] Recruitment of children at an early age was still common. A report to the London County Council in 1892 estimated that 24 per cent of the boys and 28 per cent of the girls attending seventy-one secondary schools in London were under twelve years of age. Even in 1927 it could be pointed out that attendance by very young children in preparatory departments of grammar schools was 'an anomaly which can only be defended on the ground that "it works" '.[61] The Bryce Commission found in general 'two excellent things, an enlarged education and a wider and more intelligent interest in it'.[62] The 'enlarged education' reflected the fact that the Taunton Commission, the Endowed Schools Act, and the pressure of middle-class opinion had by the end of the century begun to remould the grammar-school curriculum, preserving the status of Latin and adding modern subjects. The new range of studies was not uniform or fixed, but the trend was clear. In 1887 Hull grammar school, at a low ebb in its fortunes, with only forty or so boys, provided a standard course consisting of Latin, French, English, scripture, history, geography, writing and mathematics, with drill twice a week and singing for the first two forms. Greek and German were optional in the top two forms, and classes in book-keeping and shorthand were available. At the tiny Read's grammar school at Corby the timetable included divinity, Latin, reading, writing, mathematics, English grammar and literature, French, mechanics, geography, vocal music and drawing.[63]

In 1887 a Charity Commission return on the Welsh endowments subject to the Endowed Schools Act listed thirty-one schools for which schemes had been approved. On the question of 'any special provisions made in them for technical or scientific instruction' over half were shown as having 'none', seven had land surveying, mensuration, navigation or a combination of two or all three, two had 'cookery for girls' and only two were shown as providing science in the real sense of the term.[64] Science was becoming established, but still with difficulty. A Royal Commission on Scientific Instruction and the Advancement of Science (the Devonshire Commission) reported in 1875 on the teaching of science in public and endowed schools. The better-endowed schools had been circulated and of the 128 which replied, science was stated to be taught in 63. Only 13 had a laboratory and 18 any apparatus. Thirty allotted 'no regular time whatever to scientific study; 7 only one hour a week; 16 only two hours; while out of the whole number only 18 devote as much as four hours to it'. Science, concluded the commission, 'is as yet very far from receiving the attention to which, in our opinion, it is entitled'. Some grammar and public schools, such as Dulwich College, University College school and Manchester grammar school (all of whose laboratories were illustrated in the report) had serious science programmes, although within each school science was not taught uniformly to all. At Manchester grammar school the 'classics forms' were taught mathematics but not physics or chemistry. At Harrow science was taught to all boys on the 'modern side' and to upper forms on the 'classical side'.[65]

Even grammar schools willing to turn to science found difficulties. Not all were as fortunate as William Ellis school in north London which, when it was refounded as a secondary school in 1889, had chemistry and physics laboratories (a new and better chemistry laboratory being built five years later). At Stockport a headmaster appointed in 1888 said that 'if someone would come forward and equip the school with a laboratory, he would engage the best science master he could get, but with his limited means it was impossible to undertake the teaching of science'.[66] By the time the Bryce Commission reported, the Science and Art Department was dispensing £143,000 a year. This sum, reported the commission, 'virtually goes in aid of secondary instruction, and a large part of it is spent on day schools'.[67] 'Secondary' instruction, of course, was not confined to 'grammar' schools. Pressures towards an expansion of secondary education, in order to meet a variety of social needs, were endorsed by proposals of the Bryce Commission and produced the 1902 Education Act. The question of access to secondary schools was on the point of becoming a major social issue.

Ladders

The 1870 Act itself made access to higher-than-elementary education inevitably a more prominent issue. Apart from evening and adult education such access became available mainly in two ways – the evolution of a higher stage within the elementary system, and the scholarship ladder from the elementary to the grammar school.

Under some school boards elementary schools kept children in extra-grade classes or 'higher tops'. Others provided central facilities for children in the upper grades to be grouped in schools which were seen initially as elementary and later, especially by the Bryce Commission, as secondary. Some church opinion protested that such higher education supported out of public funds, even in voluntary schools, was 'an education the curriculum of which cannot possibly be defined as "elementary" '.[68] In London, church and other opposition in the school board prevented the creation of higher-grade schools until the 1890s.[69] A feeling that the higher-grade schools competed unfairly with the grammar schools was widely expressed, especially where grammar schools with entrance scholarships for boys from elementary schools found the supply of good candidates diminishing when a good higher-grade school was established locally.

The higher-grade schools resulted from an awareness of the reservoir of ability produced by the working of the 1870 Act. Many of the schools organized their higher work to conform to the grant arrangements of the Science and Art Department and were known as organized science schools: by 1900 there were approaching 200 such schools in receipt of its grants. In 1894 there were 60 higher-grade schools outside London, 35 of them in Durham, Lancashire and Yorkshire. Courses varied to some extent according to the employment possibilities of the district. London's higher-grade work at the end of the century was described as 'scientific, literary, and commercial. Each of these three branches has some recognition in every case, though the stress of work may, and does, vary considerably. In the literary direction some language besides English is taught in every Higher Grade school.'[70] A systematic course of study in the upper grades of schools, including such subjects as physics, chemistry, mechanics, machine drawing and mathematics, encouraged their introduction in the lower standards, and in the higher-grade schools the curriculum, however broad, generally placed strong emphasis on scientific and practical subjects.

The higher-grade schools acted in some cases as stepping-stones to the grammar school and university but were seen generally as routes to skilled and clerical occupations. The chairman of the Manchester school board expressed the view in 1887 that neither the higher-grade schools nor the scholarship ladder to the Manchester grammar school was really catering for the children of the poor, but for a slightly higher class which was now benefiting from the elementary system, including the children of the 'labour aristocracy', the better-paid 'upper strata' of the working class whose social position was very often identical with that of the lower middle class.[71] The grammar-school scholarships were going to children of clerks, warehousemen and shopkeepers. Asked whether the thirty or so scholarships to the grammar school were going to 'what you call the poor', he replied: 'No; I am afraid that Manchester is an example of what the ladder is not.' The higher-grade schools, also, charged a 9d. fee, 'which is prohibitory so far as the labouring classes are concerned. The higher grade schools are not open to the labouring classes as they ought to be.'[72] The higher-grade schools remained socially identified, however, with the working-class elementary system.

The concept of a ladder to higher education was associated in these decades partly with the greater emphasis being placed on social justice, and partly with the indignation among men like T. H. Huxley at the social waste of failing to recruit all available talent. The ladder itself evolved as a direct result of three main developments – the establishment of entrance scholarships as part of the reform of the endowed schools after 1869, an awareness of the increasing number of able working-class children being revealed in the board schools, and developments in technical education, notably at the end of the 1880s. The most important development took place in Wales. The Aberdare Committee 'to inquire into the present condition of Intermediate and Higher Education in Wales' reported in 1881, and its central proposal was for more local 'intermediate' or secondary schools, to which scholarships would be available. The Intermediate Education Act of 1889 provided Wales with a system of secondary education administered by the counties, which was to influence the views of the Bryce Commission and the 1902 Education Act. The question of scholarships was fundamental to the new departure in Wales.[73]

Attempts to organize a systematic scholarship ladder began in the 1870s. Provision for the admission of poor scholars to the endowed schools had, as we have seen, been severely curtailed, and the social composition of the classical grammar schools narrowed in the nineteenth century. The reforms of the Charity Commissioners and those under the 1869 Act began to increase the number of scholarships available. A variety of local schemes began to emerge, though the number of poor children who attained grammar-school education remained very small. In London in the 1890s the scholarships to St Olave's grammar school, Southwark, were worth £11. 11s. 0d. a year for two years (but renewable on the headmaster's recommendation), plus school fees and £5. 5s. 0d. for books and travelling expenses. Scholarships to Dame Alice Owen's school, Finsbury, were worth £10 a year for three years.[74] A boy's success, at board or voluntary school, was a matter for pride and celebration.

After the Technical Instruction Act of 1889 county and county borough councils were enabled both to make grants to secondary schools and provide scholarships, as part of their efforts to

encourage technical education. In 1893–4 the West Riding of
Yorkshire spent nearly £10,000 on scholarships, and about a
third of that amount in grants to secondary schools; Hertfordshire spent £239 on scholarships and nearly four times as much
on schools. To cater for boys coming to Manchester grammar
school with such scholarships the school received a grant from the
corporation to extend its workshops and its art, chemistry and
physics facilities.[75]

The Bryce Commission looked in detail at the question of
scholarships and reported on the 'deficiency of means for trans-
ferring pupils from one grade of education to another'. The
demand, it concluded, 'has not yet been satisfied'. The last chairman's address to the Birmingham school board, in 1902, stressed
that if 'the oft-mentioned educational ladder' was 'not to remain a
dream and is to be in any sense a reality, then classes must grow
smaller, and the number of teachers qualified to give special
instruction in languages, and probably in mathematics, must be
greatly increased'.[76] At the end of the century, therefore, there
was keen awareness of the deficiencies in the scholarship system.
There were also, in other circles, worries and hesitations about
the social effects of extending it. Sir John Gorst in 1901 believed
that 'every boy and girl showing capacities above the average
should be caught and given the best opportunities for developing
these capacities', but he did not believe it right to 'scatter broad-
cast a huge system of higher instruction for any one who chooses
to take advantage of it, however unfit to receive it'.[77] Whereas
'over-education' had been discussed earlier in the century as likely
to disturb the social order, it was now being talked of in more
personal terms: secondary and university education were for the
'fit'. The Cross Commission, in 1886, was questioning one of the
chief inspectors: 'Do you think that in the long run we do any
real good to a clever boy belonging to the working classes if we
give him an exhibition to the University, and lift him out of his
own social station, and put him in one which is not congenial to
him? – If it is not congenial to him you clearly have done him
mischief.'[78] In this question and answer, and in Gorst's comment about the 'unfit', there is an acceptance of a narrow ladder
from the gutter to the university, but a difficulty in reconciling
its widening with old assumptions about education and social
status.

The education of girls

The education of working-class girls, as we have seen, went side by side with that of boys. Working-class girls were not, however, promoted up the educational ladder in the same way as boys. The secondary education of working-class girls had to await a more generous view of their social position, greater job mobility, and the construction of a wider system of secondary schools to which girls could have access.

The movement for the social emancipation of women was making significant progress by the 1870s, during which decade the first of the Married Women's Property Acts and Matrimonial Causes Acts reflected the beginnings of changes in the status of women in the family. Some unmarried daughters were looking for occupations outside the family. The philosophy governing the education of girls was, however, only slowly beginning to change. In the 1850s and 1860s, recalled one writer of her early life in a 'well-to-do but not wealthy' family, there was 'a desire on the part of our parents to give us some intellectual interests . . . but the chief stress lay on the accomplishments of music, drawing, and sewing'. Whenever 'any need of economy arose it was always the dismissal of our instructors in intellectual subjects that took place before any other curtailment was suggested'.[79] In the last quarter of the century the 'need of economy' was, in fact, felt sharply among the middle class, anxious to maintain or improve its standard of living in a period of falling prices and profits. Middle-class families were induced 'to explore some way of escaping from the trammels of a large family'.[80] The smaller family, and the changes in the role of wife, mother and daughter in such a family, as well as other pressures for change, affected the view of the kind of education most appropriate to the middle-class girl.

The obsession with feminine 'accomplishments', it was being suggested, was socially wasteful: women needed to take an intelligent interest in the welfare of their families. Samuel Smiles, always a sensitive spokesman for Victorian middle-class society, wrote in 1878 that 'to instruct woman is to instruct man . . . to enlarge her mental freedom is to extend and secure that of the whole community. For Nations are but the outcomes of Homes, and Peoples of Mothers.'[81] By the end of the century the smaller family, higher servants' wages, smaller houses in growing

Girton College, Cambridge, girls' fire brigade, 1897

suburbs and other domestic changes were transforming the position of middle-class women. In 1898 a well-known Scottish schoolmaster-writer expressed the opinion that

> of all the social improvements that have adorned this wonderful Victorian epoch, I think that the amelioration of woman's position in the vital matters of education and training, intellectual and physical, may rightly claim the place of honour. I purposely add 'physical' to 'intellectual', for are we not living under the dispensation of the health-giving and space-destroying bicycle?[82]

The bicycle and its effect on women's clothing became, in fact, one of the symbols of the changing social role of middle-class girls.

Some of the charities reviewed under the 1869 Act were used to provide schools for girls. The Taunton Commissioners found only twelve endowed schools for girls in England; in the 1890s the Bryce Commission found eighty, and affirmed that since

1868 'there has probably been more change in the condition of the Secondary Education of girls than in any other department of education'.[83] A new pattern of proprietary schools for girls had also taken shape. The Women's Education Union was founded in 1871, and in the following year it created the Girls' Public Day School Company (or Trust, as it became), with the aim of establishing 'good and cheap Day Schools for Girls of all classes above those attending the Public Elementary Schools'.[84] By 1894 the Trust had thirty-six schools. Although they provided some subjects appropriate to the domestic duties and possible careers open to women, they did so within an academic framework modelled on the boys' secondary schools. The girls' secondary schools in general were less anxious to pioneer new curricula than to establish girls' education on the same footing as that of boys.

The developments in the late 1860s which, as we have seen, produced Girton College and classes for women at University College, London, were followed in the 1870s by Newnham, Cambridge, Somerville and Lady Margaret Hall, Oxford, and in the 1880s by Royal Holloway College for Women and Westfield College, London. Although London admitted women to degrees from 1878, it was to be over forty years before Oxford and Cambridge did likewise (and seventy years before women were admitted as full members of Cambridge University and to its degrees on a completely equal footing with men). From the late 1880s other departures in the education of women were also taking place. Lectures for women were being organized; a North of England Council for the Higher Education of Women was formed in 1867, laying a foundation on which Cambridge University built its 'university extension' work from 1873.[85] Out of the work of the Women's Education Union came a concern for the training of women teachers. Government-supported training colleges, it pointed out, trained elementary teachers only. Many men secondary-school teachers had university degrees. The response to public lectures instituted by the union on teaching methods was so encouraging that in 1878 it opened Maria Grey College, as a 'training college for teachers in higher grade girls' schools'.[86]

The secondary and higher education of girls was inevitably shaped as a separatist movement. Coeducation was common in Scotland, some of the higher-grade schools and what the Bryce

Commission described as a good many 'private second grade schools . . . scattered about the towns of Lancashire'. Few endowed or proprietary schools in England, however, took both boys and girls. Yet there was an important measure of support for the idea, influencing the Bryce Commission into a viewpoint which, for 1895, was surprisingly categorical: 'this system has been tried with so much success in other countries, and to some extent in Great Britain itself, that we feel sure its use may be extended without fear of any undesirable consequences, and probably with some special advantages for the formation of character and general stimulus to intellectual activity.'[87]

The public schools

The elementary and endowed and private school systems remained broadly defined by the criteria of social class. The Taunton and Bryce Commissions, some quarter of a century apart, identified 'grades' of schools which corresponded with strata of the middle class. The three grades earlier described by Canon Woodard and the Taunton Commission were re-echoed in evidence to the Bryce Commission by Cecil Reddie, headmaster of Abbotsholme, the first of a new kind of 'progressive' school. There should be, said Reddie, 'the school for the Briton who will be one of the *muscle-workers* . . . the school for the Briton whose work requires knowledge of the modern world . . . the school for the Briton who is to be a *leader*'; the leaving ages would be fourteen, sixteen and eighteen respectively.[88] Against the background of such prevalent models, which were merely idealized social realities, it is not surprising that the public schools managed to maintain their social identity.

Criticism continued to be levelled against the schools, against their traditions and preoccupation with games and athleticism. Reddie and the progressive public-school educators criticized their curriculum, but wished to combine their tradition of giving 'English boys the manly bearing and independent habits which fit them peculiarly for life' with 'those influences which modern culture and the present needs of society have shown to be desirable'.[89] The public schools perpetuated an aristocratic element in English education, and the proprietary and endowed schools continued to uphold it as the educational ideal. The sons of the expanding commercial and industrial middle class were being trained in the older traditions and codes of gentlemen. Economically the price paid was the education of a middle class ill prepared for its role in an increasingly competitive world; politically and socially, however, the schools achieved what their patrons most required.

In the last three decades of the century the public schools made minor adaptations, acquired in some cases new buildings but in few cases new ideas. The accent moved from godliness to manliness. Between 1860 and 1880 'games became compulsory, organised and eulogised at all the leading public schools'.[90] At Eton in the 1880s and 1890s its headmaster had 'an infallible prescription for achieving his purposes: games . . . only through games could "fortitude, self-rule, public spirit – measure in victory, firmness in defeat" be secured . . . He thus made games frankly the center of Eton life.' The rise of imperialism, says Edward Mack, was also to put 'a new premium on discipline, authority, and team spirit . . . a discipline which would create responsible, honorable boys, willing to give their lives unquestionably to the preservation and expansion of empire'.[91] Adaptation to new social ideals took other forms, including tentative changes in the curriculum itself. Modern subjects were often left optional. At Uppingham the curriculum devised by Edward Thring showed that it was possible to innovate within the established tradition. In 1880 all boys learned classics and mathematics; all learned a modern language or drawing or science; all learned some history or geography, and all 'learn singing who can'. Of 320 boys, about 25 were learning science. The 'languages or drawing or science' of Uppingham (and 'verses or science' at Marlborough at the same time) indicate the adaptability of the tradition. The establishment of the Headmasters' Conference, in Thring's words, broke up 'the exclusiveness of the old schools' and cemented a sense of common purpose among the public schools; it helped them to face up to the hazards of change.[92]

Technical and university education

We have seen at a number of points how science was becoming accepted at school level in the late nineteenth century. In the 1880s the science education movement gained a recruit of great importance in Professor Henry E. Armstrong, who campaigned for a more enlightened approach to the teaching of science. In most cases, he explained, science was being taught because it had become fashionable, 'and is a subject in which public examinations are held; more or less under compulsion; without real belief in its worth or efficacy as an educational instrument'. He attacked existing teaching methods and advocated 'heuristic' or discovery methods: 'In future, boys and girls generally must not be confined to desk studies: they must not only learn a good deal *about* things, they must also be taught how to *do* things . . . so that children from the outset may learn to acquire knowledge by their own efforts.'[93] Through Armstrong the science education movement was linked both to new philosophies of education and to the technical education movement.

Technical and scientific education was slowly responding in the closing years of the nineteenth century to concern about Britain's economic position. Other countries were taking greater advantage of new industrial and scientific processes and better education. A Royal Commission on Technical Instruction (under Sir Bernhard Samuelson) issued its final report in 1884, and gave a typical warning of danger from foreign competition: 'our industrial empire is vigorously attacked all over the world. We find that our most formidable assailants are the best educated peoples.' How is it, asked one of the members of the commission, that 'we are talking to-day about "holding our own" and "still keeping the lead", when a few years ago we were not conscious of competitors?'[94] Responses to such an awareness were both public and private. The members of the Samuelson Commission toured the country addressing audiences, and some of them were involved in setting up a National Association for the Promotion of Technical and Secondary Education in 1886. Under pressures of this kind the first Technical Instruction Act was passed in 1889, enabling the new county and county borough councils to support technical education out of rates. The Act, in the words of Philip Magnus, one of the major figures in these developments, gave technical education 'that encouragement and momentum which was afforded to elementary education by Mr Forster's celebrated Act of 1870'.[95] In the following year, surplus govern- ment funds ('whisky money') resulting from the abandonment of some provisions of a Local Taxation (Customs and Excise) Act were made available to local authorities for technical educa- tion. Evening classes were given a great stimulus in the mid-1890s by the recognition of students over twenty-one for grant purposes.

Private responses to the situation had begun earlier. The ancient gilds of the City of London were induced, in 1876, to consider supporting technical education from their unused resources, 'with the view of educating young artisans and others in the scientific and artistic branches of their trades'.[96] In 1880 the City and Guilds of London Institute was created, with Philip Magnus as its first secretary and organizing director, to encourage the teaching of practical subjects by conducting examinations. In 1883 the institute also opened Finsbury technical college, which became a model for future technical education, and from whose laboratories Armstrong propounded his new view of science teaching. Three years after the City and Guilds Institute was founded an Act of Parliament also required that the substantial resources of the City of London parochial charities should be devoted to 'objects within the Metropolis', of which technical education might be one. In Regent Street special commissioners found Quintin Hogg providing, at the Polytechnic, classes and leisure facilities of all kinds for the poorer sections of the community. It was on this model that the City Parochial Foundation created the London polytechnics, including, by the end of the 1890s, the People's Palace and East London Technical College (now Queen Mary College), Northern, Borough, Battersea and Chelsea polytechnics. The polytechnics were designed to 'promote the industrial skill, general knowledge, health, and well-being of young men and women belonging to the poorer classes' of London.[97] Some of them developed higher-level technical and scientific work which also attracted wider support, and brought them into association with the University of London.

The motives which underlay developments in technical education were to some extent also responsible for university expansion. The new colleges in towns like Liverpool and Sheffield were similarly conditioned by the heightened public awareness of increased competition from foreign countries. The principal of the new college at Sheffield emphasized that 'out of London the only places where a more or less thorough and scientific training in technical subjects suited to the needs of a Captain of Industry can be obtained are in connection with Local Colleges'[98] – for example the engineering school at Owens College, Manchester, the department of textile industry and dyeing at Yorkshire College, Leeds, and the school of metallurgy at Firth College, Sheffield.

Between 1870 and the end of the century university colleges were founded at Newcastle (1871), Leeds (1874), Bristol (1876), Sheffield (1879), Birmingham (1880), Nottingham and Liverpool (1881) and Reading (1892), all teaching for external London degrees until they achieved independence or (in the case of Leeds and Liverpool) joined Victoria University. Some were designed as science colleges (Newcastle was at first the University of Durham College of Physical Science, and Leeds was the Yorkshire College of Science). Some of them (such as Bristol and Reading) arose directly out of the university extension movement, through which, in the 1870s, Cambridge, Oxford and London became involved in adult education. The new colleges aroused strong local patriotism, and some sprang from major local benefactions (such as Mason College, Birminghan:, and Firth College, Sheffield). Nottingham was unique in that, with almost no benefactions, its foundation was undertaken by the town council. The largest of them hoped, unsuccessfully at first, to achieve the status of independent universities. Victoria University was created in 1880 as an examining university on the model of London; as a federal university it encompassed Owens College, Manchester, followed in 1884 by Liverpool and in 1887 by Leeds. The federation broke up and all three became independent universities in 1903–4. Mason College had already become the University of Birmingham in 1900. From a shaky beginning in 1872 University College, Aberystwyth, revived in the 1880s, at the same time as new colleges were founded at Cardiff (1883) and Bangor (1884) – all of which formed a federated University of Wales in 1893.

The new university colleges had a variety of emphases, problems and standards. The minimum age of entrance at Leeds and Liverpool was at first fourteen and fifteen respectively. Most of the colleges, where scientific and modern studies were stressed, were in constant financial difficulty, being, said Sir Bernhard Samuelson, 'inadequately provided with funds and not very numerously frequented'.[99] The state entered into a new kind of commitment in 1889 with the appointment of a committee to advise the government on the distribution of grants to the new colleges (the forerunner of the University Grants Committee). An Act of 1900 made London a teaching university, and the recently created London School of Economics was admitted as one of the newly named 'schools of the University'. The status of 'institutions with recognized teachers' was given to some of the polytechnics and similar colleges doing a proportion of higher-level work.

Oxford and Cambridge were in 1891, according to Henry Armstrong, 'not improperly described as, in the main, classical trade unions'.[100] Both universities had in the 1860s and 1870s begun to make scholarships available in the natural sciences, and to improve courses and examinations in science, but the results were slow to come and the initiatives to encourage science and technology weak. Influences which had been at work in the public schools were affecting late Victorian Oxford and Cambridge, including the cult of games and manliness. Leslie Stephen, 'regarded as sickly and weakly by his father, felt that he had triumphed over his nature – made himself a better man – when he excelled at athletics and sports in Trinity Hall'.[101]

By the 1870s the ancient universities had made their structural reforms, and the following decades were concerned more with the definition of moral attitudes and the improvement of standards than with the curriculum content. Pure science was the most important area of development: at Cambridge in particular the natural sciences were placed on a new footing with a considerable improvement in laboratory accommodation. The establishment of the Cavendish laboratory at Cambridge, with Clerk-Maxwell as its first professor of experimental physics, signalled an important departure in university science. The role of the universities was further extended from 1869 when Cambridge was persuaded to extend its system of local examinations to include a more advanced examination for girls over eighteen. This development of the influence of the universities beyond their traditional one was carried further by their involvement with extension work. The lectures, begun in 1873 by Cambridge, were followed by similar lectures organized by London from 1876 and by Oxford from 1878. The work dovetailed with a growing interest by the labour movement in adult education, a particular demand for such lectures from groups of women in many towns, and eagerness in many communities to establish university-type educational facilities.

New departures

Some of the late-century developments that we have discussed, themselves the products of slowly changing attitudes, set the scene for larger, later changes. The final decades of the nineteenth century produced, as we have seen, marked changes in population trends, but also in the general economic climate, as we have also suggested in relation to technical education. The changes and the problems were also reflected in other fields of social and educational policy. The main industrial changes were those connected with mechanization, a process which was accelerated and completed in many industries in these decades. It was a process which produced new skilled trades, and increased the demand for semi-skilled workmen — both trends inevitably influencing approaches to education. The fact that the economy still flourished did not prevent people noticing the slowing down of growth; the fact that real incomes were rising on average did not prevent a growing awareness that the submerged poor were not benefiting. In general, Britain now faced the problems of an established economy, with traditional, staple industries and a society which had survived the crises of industrial and urban change, but in a world which presented new challenges. The difficulties of international commercial competition and falling world prices did not persuade British industry to reorganize or reinvest, but they gave substance to the demand for educational and social changes; they intensified the demand for state and public action to remedy deficiencies in the workings of British society.

The 1880s and 1890s saw a growing realization of the extent of social problems which, in a society seeking to evade too large a measure of state and public involvement, had remained unsolved. The largest problem was poverty, and the outstanding analysis of it, as we have previously mentioned, was Charles Booth's highly influential survey of the *Life and Labour of the People of London*, which coincided with growing support for the idea of social responsibility and state intervention.

The welfare of the child was a focus of new attention. Philanthropic effort, sometimes in association with school boards, found new outlets. In Birmingham, for example, a Schools' Cheap Dinner Society supplied lunches for school children in the poorer districts from 1884. Birmingham board-school teachers contributed, among other charities, to a Poor Children's Boot Fund, and a Country Holiday Society (the first efforts to provide country holidays for poor London children date from the 1870s). An anonymous donor provided the

Penny dinner for board-school children, 1885

children at a board school in the poorest part of Birmingham with free breakfasts.[102] From 1867 the Factory Acts had been extended to cover trades which had not previously been affected and in which illiteracy was most acute. The first Act which both forbade work by boy chimneysweeps and provided a workable enforcement machinery was passed in 1875. A Summary Jurisdiction Act of 1879 resulted in most child offenders appearing before the magistrates and not the assizes or quarter-sessions. Objections were being raised in the 1880s to reformatory and industrial schools being treated under the law 'as something growing out of the prison system'.[103] The London school board appointed a medical officer in 1890. The history of special education begins seriously in the 1890s, with Acts providing for the education of blind and deaf, physically and mentally defective, and epileptic children.

Opposition, even among Liberals, to legislation of this kind was far from having been overcome, but the appearance of new social and political movements pledged to public forms of action was of considerable importance. In the 1880s a new socialist movement was created, and the working man, after the Reform Act of 1884, was a voter to be won. The school boards provided one focus for organized radical action, around programmes which included, generally, free and secular education. Seats were won by socialists and radicals on school boards. 'The first thing we need', said Robert Blatchford in his famous *Merrie England* in 1894, 'is education, and the second thing we need is a Socialist Party.'[104] In the 1880s and 1890s the TUC was constantly pressing for free education and more evening classes. Fabian socialism was profoundly involved, from its inception in 1882, with educational as with other social policies. Robert Applegarth, as a member of the deputation from the National Education League to Gladstone and Forster in 1870, speaking as a trade unionist, described 'the great determination there is on the part of the working classes to speak for themselves on these great questions'. A conference of miners' delegates had declared 'not that they wanted more wages, not that they wanted shorter working hours, or any special remedy of that sort; but the first and most important thing they have declared is, that they must have compulsory education for their children'.[105] Working-class movements were becoming a factor to be balanced in the formulation of political and social policy.

To many sections of the labour movement the school boards represented the most advanced model of democratic control available in British society. To others, notably Sidney Webb and some of the Fabians, the principle of *ad hoc* authorities appeared outmoded; for them the future lay with the new, multipurpose authorities created under the Local Government Act of 1888. The responsibility given to the latter for technical education disappointed the school-board supporters. The existence of the new local authorities, of people like Webb who were prepared to use them againat the boards, of Tory and church opposition to the boards, and of the financial difficulties of the voluntary schools – all these provided the context for the Education Act of 1902.

In education changing approaches to social policy were signalled by the new interest in studying the child, and the concern with education as a science, the latter motivated partly by developments in psychology and partly by the desire of educationists, teachers and teachers' organizations to improve the status, not only of the teacher, but also of education.

The concept of education as a science dates back, in England, to the rationalist psychology domesticated from the French Enlightenment in the early nineteenth century, largely by the utilitarians. James Mill explained in 1819 that 'the whole science of human nature is . . . but a branch of the science of education'. Education could not 'assume its most perfect form, till the science of the human mind has reached its highest point of improvement'. To Matthew Davenport Hill in 1822 public education was 'of the nature of a science'. Phrenologists, psychologists and philosophers were increasingly concerned with the serious study of education, which, in Herbert Spencer's view in the 1850s, 'should culminate . . . [in] the Theory and Practice of Education'. Alexander Bain, biographer of James Mill, was in the 1870s influentially defining education as a science, in terms of 'the teaching art . . . from a scientific point of view' – mainly the formulation of general psychological and physiological rules.[106]

Between the 1870s and the first decade of the twentieth century educational thought became as never before open to international influences. One of the main contributors to the new concern with psychological methodology was the German J. F. Herbart, who died in 1841 but whose *Science of Education* had an important impact in England at the end of the century. The most influential, though mechanically applied, feature of Herbart's psychology was his formulation of 'steps' in educational method (from preparation to presentation, comparison, generalization and application). Handbooks of educational method at the end of the century, many of them American, discuss and interpret Herbartian principles of character formation, in order 'to lay scientific foundations for the art of teaching'. The Montessori method of teaching young children was introduced into Britain as 'scientific pedagogy'.[107]

This search for a scientific approach to teaching and for a more profound understanding of the teaching process was accompanied by the beginnings of the 'progressive school' and 'new education' movements. The most important development in this connection in the final decades of the century was in infant education. That 'the English infant-school system is one of our chief educational advantages' was agreed in the 1870s and after.[108] In no branch of elementary education, it was also agreed at the end of the century, 'have greater strides been made in the last 30 years than in the methods of teaching infants from 4 to 7 years of age'.[109]

'It is difficult to believe', said one education handbook in the last year of the century, 'that there ever existed a prejudice against play as a waste of time.'[110] Froebel and the kindergarten introduced into infant education in England from the 1850s a new element of activity. Froebel placed a new emphasis on the idea of growth. He devised a series of toys or 'gifts' and 'occupations', all intended to promote 'the harmonious growth of the intellectual, moral, and physical powers of the child'.[111] This concept of the relationship between play and growth contributed something quite different from the Herbartian notion of 'steps', as contemporary commentators were aware: 'Herbart studied the child to find the best that could be done for it; Froebel studied it to learn how it could be aided in working out its own best development. Herbart magnified the work of the teacher; Froebel magnified the work of the child.'[112] In the early days of the Birmingham school board the work of the infant schools 'was almost confined to the mechanical teaching of the three R's with only a very little in the way of singing, needlework and physical exercises beyond'. The early 1880s saw a 'great advance in the use of more rational and scientific methods, and the true principles of Kindergarten began to permeate all the teaching'.[113]

These methods often degenerated, however, into formalities. Stern warnings against over-rigid application of the Froebel 'system' were being expressed in the 1890s. Froebel, said one, 'was a teacher, not an official'.[114] The new school of infant educators which appeared in the early twentieth century, focusing on the ideas of the American John Dewey and the Italian Maria Montessori, was to be concerned with rescuing infant education from the mechanical application of Froebel's ideas. Froebel's contribution to the study of children, Dewey emphasized, was 'perhaps the most effective single force in modern educational theory in effecting widespread acknowledgment of the idea of growth' yet such mechanical applications were inevitable, because of a basic flaw. In postulating a goal – growth towards a 'completed product' – Froebel had, in Dewey's view, prevented growth from being seen as an end in itself.[115] The new educationists were to place greater emphasis on activity for its own sake. Although the impact of the new ideas in England

was not to be felt until the twentieth century, the criticisms on
which they rested were beginning to be expressed earlier.

The new interest, in Europe and the United States, in the
individual child, was symbolized by the creation in London in
1894 of a Child Study Society. It also found direct embodiment
in the early progressive schools, although the progressive school
movement was not to be an important phenomenon until the
early twentieth century. Experimental schools had been conducted before. From the 1820s the Hills' schools at Bruce Castle
and Hazelwood, for example, tried to encourage independent
thought and behaviour by placing 'as much as possible, all power
in the hands of the boys themselves. . . . Impositions, public dis-
grace, and corporal pain, have been for some years discarded
among us.'[116] Thring had made curriculum innovations at
Uppingham. Abbotsholme, created by Cecil Reddie in 1889,
provided a new impetus in a period more responsive to change.
The school, while accepting the traditional role of the public
school, aimed also 'to develop harmoniously all the powers of the
boy – to train him in fact how to *live*'. Reddie defined his
purposes in straight moral terms: he told the Bryce Commission
that it was necessary 'that education become once more saturated
with religion, and that the moral training of the nation be made
the first and final aim'. All boys at Abbotsholme were obliged to
take part every day in outdoor activities, including drill, football
and cricket, carpentry and gardening. The main features of the
timetable read:

>   6.55   Rise (in Summer – Rise, 6.10 . . .).
>   7.15   Military Drill, Dumb Bells, or Run (according to the
>   weather).
>   7.30   Chapel.
>   7.40   Breakfast – after which Dormitory Parade (bed-making
>   and teeth-cleaning), and Violin Practice.
>   8.30–10.45   School . . .
>   10.45–11.15   Lunch, and if fine, Lung drill in the open air,
>   stripped to the waist (to teach breathing).
>   11.15   School.
>   (In Summer, if fine and warm enough, 12, Singing; 12.20,
>   Bathing in the River.)
>   1.0   Dinner.
>   1.30–1.45   Music Recital . . .

    2–6   Drawing, Workshop, Gardening, Games, or Excursions on Foot or Bicycle . . .

    6.0   Tea – after which Violin Practice.

    6.45–7.30   Singing . . .

    7.30   Shakespeare Reading, Lecture, Rehearsal of Play, Concert . . .

    8.30   Supper.

    8.40   Chapel.[117]

Stern though this was, its philosophy was new. Reddie's innovation was to take the public-school tradition and reshape it, with the intention of producing an élite better able, physically and mentally, to cope with the problems of ruling in the new conditions of the late nineteenth century.

Abbotsholme was the starting point for that part of the progressive school movement which produced Gordonstoun and Outward Bound. Bedales (founded four years after Abbotsholme) broke down many of the rigid features of the earlier school and influenced the movement towards a more open kind of progressive school. Bedales made history in particular as a coeducational school. It tried, like Abbotsholme, to involve pupils in academic, creative, outdoor and social activities, but it tried to give more options across the whole range of activities. J. H. Badley, the creator of the school, was particularly anxious to get away from the identification of 'school work' with 'headwork', and placed greater stress than Reddie on creative activities. The school parliament did not have the far-reaching powers of its predecessor at Hazelwood, but it was an important feature of the school. Work was organized in assignments, with some class lessons and some of the time allocated for individual work. Badley and his staff were to become enthusiastic supporters of the Montessori approach to children and education. In many respects Bedales, rather than Abbotsholme, was 'the parent of the progressive school movement in England'.[118]

A range of new departures was becoming evident in English education in the 1890s. There were new schools and new interests in child study and child development. Music, literature, modern languages and other subjects were finding a new place in schools. Craft subjects and physical exercise, games and drill, were becoming features of education at all levels. The constraints imposed by payment by results were being removed from the

elementary schools, and new approaches in the infant school
were beginning to have an influence on the higher classes.
Technical subjects and science were not only finding a place in
schools, but were also the focus of new thinking about methods
and objectives in teaching. For most of the nineteenth century
the major changes in education had been in terms of supply and
structure. Under new pressures, changes in the final decades also
began to focus on content and method, and on children. The
search for a new understanding of children and of educational
processes was closely related to the wider changes of emphasis in
discussions of the individual, society and social policy.

By the end of this period the context of educational developments had altered radically. By the end of the century all of
these aspects of educational change were related to new inter-
pretations of the processes of society and the state, and of the
individual within them. Looking back on the difference between
the Working Men's College in London when it was founded in
1854 and as it was in 1904, its principal reflected that 'the spread
of education . . . and its supply at the expense of the State, is an
outward and visible sign of a revolution in public opinion. In
1854 reformers laid unlimited stress upon the virtue of self-help
. . . In 1904 the tendency of opinion is to lay immense, some may
think excessive, emphasis upon the duty of society to help its
individual members.'[119] This emphasis was to become even
stronger after the end of the century.

Notes

1 *Transactions of the National Association for the Promotion of Social Science 1871*, pp. 76–7.
2 JAMES H. RIGG, *National Education in its Social Conditions and Aspects* (London, 1873), p. 379.
3 EDUCATION-AID SOCIETY, *Education of the Manual-labour Class*, p. 7; ADAMS, *Elementary School Contest*, p. 193.
4 *Report of the First General Meeting*, p. 17.
5 *Report of the National Education League's Meeting* (Liverpool, 1870), p. 6.
6 See, for example, *Report of the First General Meeting*, p. 25.
7 HUMPHREY, *Robert Applegarth*, pp. 221–2.
8 JOHN MORLEY, *The Life of William Ewart Gladstone*, I (London, 1903; 1908 edition), pp. 699–700.

9 T. WEMYSS REID, *Life of . . . William Edward Forster*, I (London, 1888), pp. 464, 483.

10 ADAMS, *Elementary School Contest*, p. 193.

11 Details of the Act are from National Education Union, *A Verbatim Report . . . of the Debate in Parliament . . . together with a Reprint of the Act* (Manchester, 1870).

12 W. B STEER, *Our Public Elementary Schools, and How they are Staffed* (London, undated).

13 E. A. KNOX, *Chairman's Annual Address to the School Board* (Birmingham, 1902), pp. 4–5.

14 See MCCANN, 'Trade unionist, co-operative and socialist organizations', chapters 2 and 6.

15 JOHN MORLEY, *The Struggle for National Education* (London, 1873), pp. 43–5, 131.

16 E. M. SNEYD-KYNNERSLEY, *HMI* (London, 1910), pp. 16–17, 138.

17 KNOX, *Chairman's Annual Address*, p. 8.

18 Quoted in J. L. GARVIN, *The Life of Joseph Chamberlain*, II (London, 1933), p. 78.

19 M. E. SADLER and J. W. EDWARDS, 'Public elementary education in England and Wales, 1870–1895', *Special Reports on Educational Subjects 1896–7* (London, 1897), pp. 6, 16, 22; *Report of the Board of Education 1900–01*, II, pp. 456–7; SELLMAN, *Devon Village Schools*, p. 55.

20 STUART MACLURE, *One Hundred Years of London Education 1870–1970* (London, 1970), p. 27.

21 JOHNSON, *Derbyshire Village Schools*, p. 125.

22 J. CHAMBERLAIN, *The Educational Policy of the Government* (Birmingham, 1872), p. 11; KNOX, *Chairman's Annual Address*, p. 9.

23 NATIONAL EDUCATION LEAGUE, *Report . . . presented at the Eighth Annual Meeting* (Birmingham, 1876), pp. 14–15.

24 LEWIS AMHERST SELBY-BIGGE, *The Board of Education* (London, 1927; 1934 edition), p. 9.

25 T. A. SPALDING, *The Work of the London School Board* (London, 1900), p. 31.

26 SANDFORD (ed.), *Reports by Matthew Arnold*, p. 103.

27 G. W. KEKEWICH, *The Education Department and After* (London, 1920), pp. 4–7.

28 A NONCONFORMIST MP, *A Letter to . . . W. E. Gladstone . . . on Educational Legislation* (London, 1873), pp. 7–10.

29 RICHARD D. ALTICK, *The English Common Reader* (Chicago, 1957), p. 171; BAKER, *Parish Registers and Illiteracy in East Yorkshire*, p. 12.

30 ALTICK, *English Common Reader*, pp. 171–2.

31 CROSS COMMISSION, III, p. 439.

32 Quoted in JAMES C. GREENOUGH, *The Evolution of the Elementary Schools of Great Britain* (New York, 1903), p. 24.

33 *Report of the First General Meeting of . . . the National Education League*,

p. 22; *Report of the Board of Education 1900–01*, II, pp. 456–7; E. F. M. MACCARTHY, *Thirty Years of Educational Work in Birmingham* (Birmingham, 1900), pp. 6–7.

34 RUSSELL, *Schools and Education in Lindsey*, IV, p. 51.

35 SADLER and EDWARDS, 'Public elementary education 1870–1895', p. 8.

36 JAMES PAYN, 'Penny fiction', *The Nineteenth Century*, IX (1881), pp. 145–54.

37 See MAX PEMBERTON, *Lord Northcliffe* (London, undated), pp. 59–83.

38 SIDNEY WEBB, *London Education* (London, 1904), pp. 183–5; SADLER and EDWARDS, 'Public elementary education 1870–1895', p. 7.

39 G. A. CHRISTIAN, *English Education from Within* (London, 1922), pp. 9, 18, 33.

40 SADLER and EDWARDS, 'Public elementary education 1870–1895', p. 60.

41 W. H. G. ARMYTAGE, *A. J. Mundella 1825–1897* (London, 1951), pp. 210–13; SADLER and EDWARDS, 'Public elementary education 1870–1895', pp. 40–1.

42 KEKEWICH, *The Education Department and After*, pp. 56–7.

43 Quoted in JOHN LEESE, *Personalities and Power in English Education* (London, 1950), p. 151.

44 HOLMES, *What Is and What Might Be*, p. 111.

45 LYON PLAYFAIR, 'Address . . . on education', *Transactions of the National Association for the Promotion of Social Science 1870*, pp. 46–7; JOHN RUSKIN quoted in T. RAYMONT, *A History of the Education of Young Children* (London, 1937), pp. 247–8.

46 WEBB, *London Education*, pp. 6–7.

47 ALEXANDER BAIN, *Education as a Science* (London, 1878; 1886 edition), pp. 132–3, 247; see also pp. 247–72, 439–44.

48 MACCARTHY, *Thirty Years of Educational Work*, pp. 23–5.

49 WILLIAM JOLLY, *Physical Education for Common Schools* (London, 1875), p. 3.

50 DEWEY, *Democracy and Education*, p. 312.

51 A. PARK, *The Higher Education of the Elementary Teachers* (Ashton-under-Lyne, 1889), p. 6.

52 See FRANCIS STORR, 'Registration and training of secondary teachers', in LAURIE MAGNUS (ed.), *National Education* (London, 1901), pp. 57–62.

53 SADLER and EDWARDS, 'Public elementary education 1870–1895', p. 46.

54 CHRISTIAN, *English Education from Within*, pp. 22–3; *Report of the Board of Education 1900–01*, II, pp. 252, 274–5.

55 See, for example, Fabian Tract LV, *The Workers' School Board Program* (London, 1894), pp. 14–15.

56 PETER SANDIFORD, *The Training of Teachers in England and Wales* (New York, 1910), pp. 53–4; W. B. CROUCH, 'From day training college to school of education', *University of Reading Staff Journal*, VII (1969), p. 9.

57 J. J. FINDLAY, 'On the study of education', *Special Reports on Educational Subjects*, II, pp. 24–5.

58 Commission on Secondary Education (BRYCE COMMISSION), I, *Report* (London, 1895), pp. 8–9.

59 Ibid., I, pp. 45–7.

60 LAWSON, *Town Grammar School*, p. 247.

61 FLANN CAMPBELL, *Eleven-Plus and All That* (London, 1956), p. 9; SELBY-BIGGE, *The Board of Education*, p. 39.

62 BRYCE COMMISSION, I, p. 16.

63 Lawson, *A Town Grammar School*, p. 250; ALAN ROGERS, 'A grammar school curriculum 1887', *History of Education Society Bulletin*, II (1968), p. 47.

64 CHARITY COMMISSIONERS (WALES AND MONMOUTHSHIRE), *Return* (London, 1887), pp. 2–3.

65 Royal Commission on Scientific Instruction and the Advancement of Science (DEVONSHIRE COMMISSION), *Sixth Report* (London, 1875), pp. 1, 179–82, 184.

66 T. D. WICKENDEN, *William Ellis School 1862–1962* (London, undated), pp. 39, 49; BENJAMIN VARLEY, *The History of Stockport Grammar School* (Manchester, 1957), pp. 133–4.

67 BRYCE COMMISSION, I, p. 28.

68 THOMAS MOORE, *The Education Brief on behalf of the Voluntary Schools* (London, 1890), pp. 18–19.

69 DAVID RUBINSTEIN, *School Attendance in London 1870–1904* (Hull, 1969), pp. 32–3.

70 *Report of the Board of Education 1900–01*, II, pp. 632–7, for list of schools of science; SPALDING, *London School Board*, p. 197.

71 See E. J. HOBSBAWM, 'The labour aristocracy in nineteenth century Britain', in *Labouring Men* (London, 1964).

72 CROSS COMMISSION, I, p. 796.

73 'The Welsh Intermediate Act, 1889', *Special Reports on Educational Subjects*, II; BRYCE COMMISSION, I, pp. 13–14.

74 St Mark's boys' school, Kennington, logbook 1880–95.

75 BRYCE COMMISSION, I, p. 34; MUMFORD, *Manchester Grammar School*, p. 411.

76 BRYCE COMMISSION, I, pp. 63–4, 167–8; KNOX, *Chairman's Annual Address*, p. 19.

77 Quoted in OLIVE BANKS, *Parity and Prestige in English Secondary Education* (London, 1955; 1963 edition), p. 51.

78 CROSS COMMISSION, I, p. 138.

79 ALICE WOODS, *Eduational Experiments in England* (London, 1920), p. 12.

80 GRACE G. LEYBOURNE and KENNETH WHITE, *Education and the Birth-Rate* (London, 1940), p. 57; this theme is expanded in J. A. BANKS, *Prosperity and Parenthood* (London, 1954).
81 SAMUEL SMILES, *Character* (London, 1878; 1905 edition), p. 64.
82 D'ARCY W. THOMPSON, *Day-dreams of a Schoolmaster* (London, 1912), p. 131.
83 BRYCE COMMISSION, I, p. 75.
84 WOMEN'S EDUCATION UNION, circular (undated).
85 See 'The origins of university extension' (report of lecture by SHEILA LEMOINE), *History of Education Society Bulletin*, VI (1970), pp. 13–16.
86 TEACHERS' TRAINING AND REGISTRATION SOCIETY, *Training for Teachers in Higher Grade Girls' Schools* (undated leaflet).
87 BRYCE COMMISSION, I, pp. 159–60, 285.
88 CECIL REDDIE, *Abbotsholme* (London, 1900), p. 164.
89 Ibid., p. 22.
90 NEWSOME, *Godliness and Good Learning*, p. 222.
91 MACK, *Public Schools since 1860*, pp. 107–8, 130.
92 GEORGE R. PARKIN, *Edward Thring* (London, 1898), II, p. 201; I, p. 208; for Marlborough see DEVONSHIRE COMMISSION, VI, pp. 131–4.
93 HENRY E. ARMSTRONG, *The Teaching of Scientific Method* (London, 1903; 1925 edition), pp. 3–10.
94 F. C. MONTAGUE, *Technical Education* (London, 1887), p. 12; W. MATHER, *The Relation of Technical Instruction to the Progress of the Engineering and Kindred Trades* (Manchester, 1885), p. 7.
95 PHILIP MAGNUS, *Educational Aims and Efforts 1880–1910* (London, 1910), p. 110.
96 Quoted in A. M. HOLBEIN, *The Work of the City and Guilds of London Institute* (London, 1949), p. 2.
97 General Regulations, quoted in CITY PAROCHIAL FOUNDATION, *Report of Sub-Committee* (London, 1935), p. 20.
98 W. M. HICKS, *Local Colleges and Higher Education for the People* (Sheffield, 1886), pp. 8–9.
99 Preface to MONTAGUE, *Technical Education*, p. vii.
100 ARMSTRONG, *Teaching of Scientific Method*, p. 3.
101 Quoted in ROTHBLATT, *Revolution of the Dons*, p. 246.
102 MACCARTHY, *Thirty Years of Educational Work*, pp. 46–8; ELIZABETH ROSSITER, 'Child life for children', *The Nineteenth Century*, X (1881), pp. 567–72.
103 E. LYULPH STANLEY, 'Industrial schools and the Home Office', *The Nineteenth Century*, X (1881), p. 916.
104 ROBERT BLATCHFORD, *Merrie England* (London, 1894; undated edition), p. 130.
105 NATIONAL EDUCATION LEAGUE, *Verbatim Report of the Proceedings of a Deputation* (Birmingham, 1870), pp. 18–19.
106 MILL, *Supplement to Encyclopaedia Britannica*, p. 12; HILL, *Plans for*

the *Government of Boys*, p. 193; HERBERT SPENCER, *Education* (London, 1861; 1905 edition), p. 70; BAIN, *Education as a Science*, p. v.

107 HERMAN HARRELL HORNE, *The Psychological Principles of Education: a study in the science of education* (New York, 1915), p. vii; MARIA MONTESSORI, *The Montessori Method: scientific pedagogy as applied to child education* (London, 1912).

108 RIGG, *National Education*, p. 336.

109 MACCARTHY, *Thirty Years of Educational Work*, p. 26.

110 P. A. BARNETT, *Common Sense in Education and Teaching* (London, 1899), p. 75.

111 NEWCASTLE COMMISSION, III, p. 463.

112 JAMES L. HUGHES, *Froebel's Educational Laws* (New York, 1897; 1906 edition), p. 40.

113 MACCARTHY, *Thirty Years of Educational Work*, p. 26.

114 BARNETT, *Common Sense in Education*, p. 77.

115 DEWEY, *Democracy and Education*, pp. 58–9.

116 HILL, *Plans for the Government of Boys*, pp. 1–2.

117 REDDIE, *Abbotsholme*, pp. 21, 63, 155–6.

118 MACK, *Public Schools . . . since 1860*, p. 255; see also J. H. BADLEY, *Bedales* (London, 1923), especially chapter 9.

119 A. V. DICEY in J. LLEWELYN DAVIES, *The Working Men's College 1854–1904* (London, 1904), p. 245.

Further Reading

FRANCIS ADAMS, *History of the Elementary School Contest in England* (London, 1882).

ERIC ASHBY, *Technology and the Academics: an essay on universities and the scientific revolution* (London, 1963).

CHARLES ALPHEUS BENNETT, *History of Manual and Industrial Education 1870 to 1917* (Peioria, 1937).

ERIC EAGLESHAM, *From School Board to Local Authority* (London, 1956).

FRANK FODEN, *Philip Magnus: Victorian educational pioneer* (London, 1970).

ANGELA GILL, 'The Leicester school board 1871–1903', in BRIAN SIMON (ed.), *Education in Leicestershire 1540–1940* (Leicester, 1968).

PETER GOSDEN, 'Technical instruction committees', in *Studies in the Government and Control of Education since 1860* (History of Education Society, London, 1970).

EDWARD C. MACK, *Public Schools and British Opinion since 1860* (New York, 1941).

DAVID RUBINSTEIN, *School Attendance in London 1870–1904: a social history* (Hull, 1969).

MALCOLM SEABORNE, 'Education in the nineties: the work of the technical education committees', in BRIAN SIMON (ed.), *Education in Leicestershire 1540–1940* (Leicester, 1968).

R. J. W. SELLECK, *The New Education 1870–1914* (London, 1968).

BRIAN SIMON, *Education and the Labour Movement 1870–1920* (London, 1965).

T. A. SPALDING, *The Work of the London School Board* (London, 1900).

D. A. WINSTANLEY, *Later Victorian Cambridge* (Cambridge, 1947).

See also pp. 473–5.

CHAPTER X

Towards a unified system
1900–1938

The new century

This period began with the Boer War, contained the First World War and ended on the brink of the Second; it was a period dominated by economic difficulties and social conflict. It experienced a slump and a general strike; it saw major departures in social legislation, and great changes in mass communications, leisure and entertainment. The nineteenth century had been marked by sustained change; the acceleration of this process in the period up to the Second World War was accompanied by two related processes. First, the sense of collective responsibility for serious social problems (some of which became more prominent in this period of economic crisis) was quickened by, among other things, the very magnitude of the problems themselves and the voices of organized protest. Second, educational decision-making was becoming increasingly part of the struggle to determine financial priorities as the range of social services increased. The national economy itself was becoming subject to new international vicissitudes. Education became more and more a public service governed by public policy. It became a part of local and national government election manifestos, an issue in the conflict between the political parties (including, from its formal creation in 1906, the Labour Party). It became an element in a new pattern of social policy at a time when Britain's world economic dominance had begun to decline, in an age both of increasing international competition, not only between nations but between empires, and of world war.

Education began from the end of the nineteenth century to reflect new social and political ideals. In 1959 the Crowther Report *(15 to 18)* was to describe a double task for education in the technical age – on the one hand 'to set young people on the road to acquiring the bewildering variety of qualifications they will need to earn their living. On the other hand . . . the development of human personality and . . . teaching the individual to see himself in due proportion to the world in which he has been set.'[1] Changes in education in the twentieth century can be analysed generally in terms of this axis of economic (and occupational) pressures and an explicit attempt to relate education to widely acceptable ideals of the individual and society.

Near the turn of the century Alfred Russel Wallace, co-founder with Darwin of evolutionary theory, looked back with bitterness at a century in which, 'with the increase of wealth there has been a positive and very large *increase* of want'. During the second half of

> this most marvellous of all the centuries, while science has been enlarging man's power over nature . . . resulting in possibilities of wealth-production a hundred-fold that of any preceding century, the direst want of the bare necessaries of life has seized upon, not only a greater absolute number, but a larger proportion of our population.[2]

Whether or not Wallace was entirely right there were certainly at the end of the century an increasing number of people who shared the view that nineteenth-century England had failed to solve its basic problem of the just distribution of wealth. There was at the beginning of the twentieth century no less an awareness than before of the existence of 'two nations', of the barriers of social class. Elementary education continued to be seen as something specifically provided for the working class. Increased school and university provision had not altered the definitions that surrounded the different strata of education. Socialists in the 1920s were to describe the distinction between 'elementary' and 'secondary' education as 'educationally unsound and socially obnoxious', and to campaign for the abandonment of the nineteenth-century concept of elementary education as 'the discipline of a class'.[3] Few of the features of nineteenth-century society had markedly altered by the First World War. Social unrest –

in the form of mass strikes, the suffragette movement and near-civil war in the north of Ireland – was as acute in the period 1910–14 as at any point in the nineteenth century.

Not until the end of the First World War was a 48-hour working week introduced and not until the eve of the Second World War were holidays with pay becoming an important feature of British life. By the turn of the century average family size had begun to drop substantially (from an average of 6·1 children in the 1860s it had fallen to 4·1 in the 1890s and to 2·6 in the 1910s). Infant mortality, which stood at about 150 per 1,000 live births for most of the second half of the nineteenth century, fell from 154 to 105 per 1,000 between 1900 and 1910. The death rate fell dramatically from 1900. The population of England and Wales, which had been almost 18 million in 1851 and 26 million in 1881, reached 32·5 million in 1901 and 36 million ten years later. Urban development was particularly striking. Between 1871 and 1901 Greater London grew from under 4 million to over 6·5 million. The twenty years from 1871 often saw spectacular growth, as with Cardiff, which grew from 40,000 to 129,000, and Nottingham, from 87,000 to 214,000. The twenty years from 1891 also saw major increases. Seaside towns like Bournemouth and Blackpool more than doubled (and Southend went from 12,000 to 63,000). Manchester and Liverpool each grew from approximately 500,000 to 750,000.

The increase in scale is in fact a distinguishing characteristic of early twentieth-century English society and applied equally to education. By 1900 the trade unions, for example, had 2 million and by 1915 over 4 million members. The scale of industrial and commercial units was increasing through mergers and the creation of monopolies. By the First World War Woolworth's and the chain grocery firms were well established. The Federation of British Industries was created during the war and the TUC general council after it. By the First World War there were nearly 400,000 licensed road vehicles, a large network of trams in many towns and an electric underground railway in London. The early twentieth-century reorganization of education was profoundly affected by considerations of the scale and complexity of social institutions and problems. Changes in social attitudes and the clash of political ideals were to be highlighted most clearly in relation to questions of welfare.

The 1902 Education Act

At the end of the nineteenth century important factors were altering attitudes towards the pattern of education as it had evolved since 1870. The elementary system had produced what seemed to some people anomalous pseudo-secondary features in its higher-grade schools and evening classes. The still insecure financial basis of very many grammar schools was in many cases being further eroded by these developments. The voluntary schools were being outpaced by the school boards; many of them, in a period of general decline in church attendance, were in serious financial difficulties, bearing what A. J. Balfour (shortly, as prime minister, to carry through the 1902 Act) called an 'intolerable strain'. The voluntary agencies, though divided as to the desirability of further state aid and intervention, were increasingly pressing for greater assistance, as 'a due recognition of the magnificent work they have done, not for a quarter of a century, but for many centuries, in training up the people in godliness and honesty'.[4] State intervention was in society generally being more actively advocated and tolerated. The Bryce Commission had recommended in 1895 the creation of a central authority for education, although, it hastened to add, 'not in order to control, but rather to supervise the Secondary Education of the country, not to override or supersede local action, but to endeavour to bring about among the various agencies which provide that education a harmony and co-operation which are now wanting'.[5] A Board of Education was created in 1899. Local councils had also entered the education field (mainly under the Technical Instruction Acts) as competitors of the school boards. The boards' supporters viewed the creation of technical instruction committees under the councils as an 'outflanking policy' to undermine the boards.[6] The work of the councils, through these committees, was extensive enough for them to be seen by one historian as 'far more than shadowy forerunners of the 1902 LEAs. The more closely one examines the structure, organization and scope of the work of the counties under the Technical Instruction Acts, the less significant a watershed does 1902 appear to be.'[7]

Such changes threatened the uneasy 1870 settlement; school boards came under fire before the end of the century, particularly for their higher-grade schools, and what the church party especially considered excessive expenditure of ratepayers' money. Leading Conservatives were severely attacking the boards in the nineties, and promoting bills in Parliament to reduce their powers or transfer them to the county and county borough councils. The boards themselves, nonconformist and labour bodies expressed hostility to such moves, and defended the record and role of the boards. Although the labour movement was, generally speaking, in favour of the boards, some of the Fabians, and Sidney Webb in particular, played a crucial part in formulating the philosophy which underlay the 1902 Act and thus destroyed them. Sir John Gorst led the attack on the boards; Sidney Webb defined an alternative policy; Robert Morant masterminded the Act; Balfour steered it through Parliament.

Webb's main target, from his vantage point as chairman of the LCC's technical education board, was the improvement of education through a more streamlined administrative machinery, and his chosen instrument was the all-purpose council. His 'tactic of reform', it has been explained, 'was neither to attack the School Board nor assail, directly, the system of separation. It was, rather, so skilfully to extend, aggrandise, and make efficient the . . . Technical Education Board . . . that the case for handing control over education as a whole to the Council became irresistible.' His policy could only be achieved by the destruction of the school boards. Webb's policy was deeply resented by other Fabians and socialists who were committed to the boards as agents of educational democracy.[8] Robert Morant, recently returned from tutoring the crown prince of Siam, and shortly to become one of the key figures in English education, met and was influenced by Webb and his policy for educational reorganization. Fabian Tract No 106, *The Education Muddle and the Way Out*, mainly Webb's work, proved influential enough to be distributed in the Conservative cabinet.[9] From a relatively junior position in the Education Department Morant was able to engineer a test case in which London school board expenditure on higher elementary classes was disallowed by a district auditor, Cockerton, in 1899. Through the Cockerton judgement Morant and Gorst achieved a dual objective – the prevention of further post-elementary developments in board schools, and the possibility of using the councils as all-embracing educational authorities. The higher work of the boards was legalized for one year and Morant, who became Gorst's private secretary in 1899 (and permanent secretary of the Board of Education in 1903), drafted the new education bill, with the aim of bringing elementary and secondary education under one authority, and at the same time bringing relief to the voluntary schools.

Support for the boards was at this point strongly expressed. The TUC called a conference which protested at the proposal to abolish them. Nonconformists proposed 'such a resistance as will defeat a policy which threatens to kill democratic control of education, decrease educational efficiency, add to the State endowments of sectarianism, and fix more securely than ever the tyranny of the State Church over the life of the land'.[10] Large meetings and rallies of nonconformists made angry protests. The most telling of the criticisms seized on the issue of democracy. A. J. Mundella, for example, the former Liberal vice-president of Council, published an address entitled *Democracy and Education*, which emphasized that the school boards were 'the most democratic education authorities we possess. Their work is done with a thoroughness, an efficiency, and a progressive development which have carried it further than the most hopeful educationists of the last generation thought possible . . . The reason is that the Boards have had behind them the driving force of a compelling and

Arithmetic lesson, 1907

approving democracy.' The aim of the new bill, he believed, was 'to eliminate, as far as possible, the democratic element'. The Act of 1902, he later added, 'eliminated the effective democratic element by destroying the directly elected School Boards and substituting nominated committees'.[11] The National Education Association, a successor of the league, described the Cockerton case as one of 'many manœuvres, obscure in themselves, but all parts of a consistent policy' by which 'the principle of popular control has been removed from a large field in which it had become established'. The government's policy was 'a reactionary policy . . . a very Tory clerical theory of local self-government'.[12]

There were, of course, legitimate criticisms of the boards. Many of the smaller ones were inefficient. The separate administration of board schools, grammar schools, Science and Art Department grants, technical instruction committees (and the independent management of voluntary elementary schools) was chaotic. The new council education authorities, what is more, would have advantages. Some trade unionists saw the possibilities of co-option onto education committees. The Conservative chairman of the Birmingham school board contrasted the lack of cohesion in the work of the school boards with the greater continuity of membership open to the councils and the chief advantage to be gained 'in those places, where, as in Birmingham, both secondary and University education as well as technical will be brought into close contact with primary'.[13] For all the criticism that greeted the Act, it was afterwards rapidly accepted (except for the religious controversy over rate-aid for voluntary schools). Bradford's Independent Labour Party was able to look back in the 1920s on 'Balfour's admirable Act of 1902'.[14]

The Act itself designated as local education authorities the councils of counties and county boroughs.[15] Under part II of the Act they were to 'take such steps as seem to them desirable . . . to supply or aid the supply of education other than elementary, and to promote the general co-ordination of all forms of education'. Non-county boroughs with a population of more than 10,000 and urban districts with more than 20,000 were, however, to be reponsible for elementary education in their areas, and since elementary education was dealt with in part III of the Act these councils became known as part III authorities. Instead of dealing with 2,500 school boards and the managers of over 14,000 voluntary schools, the Board of Education would now deal with

318 local education authorities. The Act converted, said one supporter, 'our long-endured educational chaos into something approaching a regulated system'.[16]

The Act did not make it mandatory for part II authorities to provide secondary schools; it did require them, however, to perform the functions previously performed by the school boards and technical instruction committees. Local authorities were to be responsible for maintaining voluntary schools (including the payment of teachers), subject to certain provisions, the central one of which was that the managers of such schools 'shall provide the schoolhouse free of any charge . . . to the local authority for use as a public elementary school, and shall, out of the funds provided by them, keep the schoolhouse in good repair'. The authority would make good any 'fair wear and tear'.

It was this solution to the problem of the voluntary schools that provoked the most fierce and lasting resistance, inside and outside Parliament. Labour opposition was intense. The nonconformists and Liberals, especially in Wales, bitterly fought the measure. Kekewich, whom Morant supplanted at the Board of Education, had warned in advance: 'I pointed out that Nonconformists would naturally object to be compelled to pay for the teaching of the Anglican creed. The answer that was given to me at the time was that it would not matter to the Government, as all Nonconformists were already opposed to them in politics.'[17] It was the fight against the settlement with the voluntary schools, not the fight to keep the boards, that loomed largest and lasted longest, and influenced the landslide return to power of the reforming Liberal government at the end of 1905.

The most far-reaching effect of the 1902 Act was its influence on the structure of elementary and secondary education. The Act, says Professor Eaglesham, 'helped to contain, to repel, and in some respects to destroy the upward striving of the elementary schools'.[18] Morant has been defended against the charge of hostility to the scientific and technical work that was central to the experience of the higher-grade schools,[19] but it is clear that his view of the nature of secondary education was in the public-school mould. On the question of advanced work under the school boards, he wrote in a memorandum '. . . it cannot be doubted that this policy of letting School Boards supply a sort of Pretence-Secondary School has headed off the natural local pressure in the big towns for the development of true Secondary Schools'.[20]

His view of elementary education was based on a strong sense of social hierarchy. He and Balfour had 'similar middle-class educational values, similar doubts about the abilities of the masses'.[21] By defining the board schools as strictly elementary, and then bringing them into a relationship with the newly strengthened grammar schools, Morant (and with him Gorst, Balfour and Webb) defined also a strictly class relationship to be tempered only by the introduction of a formal system of transition from one system to the other.

Secondary education to 1918

The Act gave the grammar schools a new financial security and a clear structure within which to work. The role of the schools provided or aided by the local authorities was defined more explicitly in the *Regulations for Secondary Schools* issued in 1904, in which Morant echoed some of the doubts about the higher-grade type of curriculum. The regulations, according to a well-known description, 'failed to take note of the comparatively rich experience of secondary curricula of a practical and quasi-vocational type which had been evolved in the Higher Grade Schools'.[22] The regulations did require science to be taught, and in this sense were an advance for those schools where it had been absent. The curriculum had to contain a minimum of $4\frac{1}{2}$ hours a week for English, history and geography, $3\frac{1}{2}$ for one language and 6 for two languages, and $7\frac{1}{2}$ for science and mathematics. Where two languages other than English were taken and Latin was not to be one of them, 'the Board will require to be satisfied that the omission of Latin is for the advantage of the school'.[23] The intention was to preserve as much as possible of the traditional grammar- and public-school emphasis and spirit, and the assumption was that secondary education should be designed with university requirements in mind. Although Morant, the 1902 Act and the 1904 regulations have been defended against the charge of such a traditional bias, the balance of evidence is with the author of the passage in the Spens Report of 1938 which asserted: 'The new Regulations were based wholly on the tradition of the Grammar Schools and the Public Schools . . . the Board did little or nothing after the passing of the Education Act of 1902 to foster the development of secondary schools of quasi-vocational type designed to meet the needs of boys and girls who desired to enter industry and commerce at the age of 16.'[24] The 1902 Act created a more impersonal educational administration, as part of an expanding, multipurpose local government machinery. It made education less amenable to direct public influence. It resulted in the confirmation of the traditional role of the grammar school. On the other hand, the Act made secondary education a more stable element in a coherent pattern of education. It established a new relationship between central and local government in the education field. It transformed the financial position of the grammar schools.

Secondary schools run by voluntary bodies were able, following the 1902 Act, to receive grant from both the local authority and the Board of Education. After 1919 these schools had to choose between receiving grant from the LEA or direct from the Board; those in special relationship with the Board (there were nearly 250 by the Second World War) acquired 'direct grant' status. In terms of social composition they were or tended to become closer to the independent public schools than to the provided or aided grammar schools.

The new local authorities immediately began to survey the secondary education needs of their areas. The story of secondary education from 1903 to the First World War is a combination of two main themes – the building up of the system of schools and, as we shall see, the introduction of the free-place system. The number of grant-aided secondary schools increased from nearly 500 in 1904–5 to over 1,000 in 1913–14 (and the number of pupils from nearly 64,000 to nearly 188,000).[25] The number of schools continued to increase into the 1920s, but the main feature of wartime and post-war expansion was the size of schools, as the demand for grammar-school places grew. The average number of pupils in grant-aided secondary schools was 182 in 1913 and 290 in 1921. In the first decade of the century London was educating some 5 per cent of its children aged ten to fifteen in public secondary schools.[26] In 1904 Morant created a secondary branch of the inspectorate. The free-place system was introduced in 1907; it made recognition for a grant dependent on the school taking upwards of a quarter of its children from elementary schools. The new system both brought relief to the grammar schools and introduced a greater element of social-class diversification into their structure.

Although the regulations covering grammar-school curriculum

were altered in 1907 to allow greater freedom, it remained
largely determined by the established principles. About English
education in general before 1914 it has been said that 'teachers,
with a few adventurous exceptions, seemed content to tread the
paths they already knew'.[27] The Bryce Commission, as we have
seen, had pointed with enthusiasm in 1895 to the 'enlarged
education' in the grammar schools. Morant had made the pattern
of grammar-school subjects into a prescription, and developments
up to the First World War were more in terms of ideas than new
practices. Armstrong's heuristic method in science had been
argued about and turned into limited practical routines. The
position of biology was being particularly criticized as having
'the humiliating status of the shabby sister in "the family of
knowledges" '.[28] When, in wartime, a committee was appointed
under the physicist J. J. Thomson to report on 'natural science
in education', it found that science had a far from stable or
satisfactory position. The committee reported in 1918 that
although in many schools pupils spent a fair proportion of time
on science, especially in upper forms, 'in a considerable number of
schools the time for Science might be as little as four three-
quarter-hour periods a week, or even less. In some schools, owing
to the pressure of other subjects, the time allotted to Science has

been reduced in recent years.' The fact that science courses were designed as a preliminary to university entrance meant that most boys completed only part of an overspecialized course. Appeals by the Thomson Committee and others for an approach to science in terms of 'opening the mind', 'training the judgement' and 'stirring the imagination' were not really to be acted upon for several decades.[29] The commitment to science teaching had become more widespread since the 1904 regulations, but its position in schools was subordinate. A writer in 1919 talked about the policy of the Board after 1902 as having 'put a stop to the triumphant progress of science and destroyed its privileged position as a grant-earning subject'. The ending of the special grant arrangements for 'schools of science' meant that – in the elementary schools particularly – 'the attention given to science has very sensibly diminished'. Science had been levelled up in the grammar and public schools which had previously stuck to the classical curriculum, and levelled down in those which had previously accepted the grants of the Education Department for science subjects.[30] The social status of science remained low in the community at large, its position in the secondary-school curriculum was frequently one of tolerance, and the prestige of university education continued to be highest in the traditional literary subjects. Only in the second half of the century were there to be substantial changes in Britain in the social position of science, resulting from the intensity of argument about the place of science in human culture, and the intensity of social and economic pressures for improvements in the educational position of science.

Sixth-form work was uncertain or nonexistent in many of the grammar schools until their numbers rose during and after the First World War, by which time progress towards wider studies and more consistent standards was beginning to be made. In this as in other fields the mechanism to regulate and encourage change was the examination system. The tangle of competing examinations available to secondary schools was cut through in 1917 by the introduction of the school certificate and higher school certificate, the former of which required candidates to pass in five or more subjects, including at least one from each of three groups – 'English' subjects, languages, and science and mathematics; a fourth group including music and manual subjects was available but not obligatory. The new examinations, increasing numbers and special grants gradually strengthened sixth-form work.

Cookery class, 1910

The position and role of the grammar schools were shaped in 1900–4, and by 1918 their numbers, processes and objectives had been readjusted and redefined. The blurring of the secondary–elementary definition by the higher-grade schools had not been entirely overcome at the turn of the century. Some of them were absorbed into the secondary system; others became 'higher elementary schools', offering a largely scientific and vocational course, but deliberately designed to be lower in standard than secondary schools. The Board of Education was less than enthusiastic about them, and the new local authorities were not eager to adopt such a concept until, in 1911, in the shape of the Central School, it appeared as 'another example of the general tendency of the national system of elementary education since 1870 to throw up experiments in post-primary education'.[31] The pace was set by London, which had fifty such schools by 1914. Other towns followed suit. From 1913, similarly, 'junior technical schools' (or 'technical high schools') were given official blessing, and recruited children from elementary schools at thirteen or fourteen; their courses were strictly defined as training skilled employees for the needs of local industry (some were known as 'trade schools'), and not to be seen as competing with the grammar schools. The 1926 Hadow Report on *The Education of the Adolescent*, which discussed all these developments, described them as 'the half-conscious striving of a highly industrialised society to evolve a type of school analogous to and yet distinct from the secondary school, and providing an education designed to fit boys and girls to enter the various branches of industry, commerce, and agriculture at the the age of 15'.[32]

The public schools in this period and between the wars remained relatively unchanged, though their popularity led to a small number of new foundations: Stowe and Canford, for example, were both created in 1923 and the former in particular rapidly emulated the prestige of the old public schools. The complacency of the public schools in this period has been described as being partly responsible for 'two great failures of British national leadership' – the military mistakes of the First World War, and the overconfidence in the face of the growth of fascism in the 1930s. The former were possible, it is argued, because of unquestioning loyalty to leaders (even when known to be wrong) and lack of imagination – both fostered by the public-school tradition: among officers 'the education system failed to offset the intellectual shortcomings that military habits tend to breed'. In the thirties 'the public school set of values failed to perform countervailing functions that might have produced a quicker national response to the German threat'.[33] What is certainly true is that the adaptations we have seen taking place in the schools at the end of the nineteenth century had not profoundly altered their generally fixed and complacent outlook. The values of the public schools were being constantly criticized in these decades by radical and leftwing critics, and in a spate of critical novels.[34] Morant had tried to influence the public schools into accepting inspection by the Board, and when inspection was offered from 1908 most of them invited it (inspection of private schools was made possible in 1914, but not until after the Second World War was the problem of the 10,000 or so private schools in England and Wales confronted seriously).

Elementary education to 1918

In the new pattern of thinking and administration the influence of welfare policies on elementary education increased. Some relationship between elementary education and other aspects of

OTC at Westminster between the wars

social policy had been seen from the beginnings of mass education. Education had been considered by some to be a service
under the poor law or a charity. Specialized educational services
had, as we have seen, begun to be created under the impact of
new social and psychological interests. The provision of special
schools had begun in the 1890s; between 1914 and 1918 it
became mandatory to make provision for mentally and physically
'defective' children. In 1913 a Mental Deficiency Act was
passed, a Central Association for Mental Welfare was founded,
and a psychologist (Cyril Burt) was appointed by the LCC, among
other things 'to investigate cases of individual children who
present problems of special difficulty . . . and to carry out, or
make recommendations for, suitable treatment or training of such
children'.[35] But the health and welfare of children became more
widely interpreted. Educational services were being pioneered.
School meals in particular, and a preoccupation with child welfare more generally, were promoted by the Independent Labour
Party, for example, in the 1890s, outstandingly in Bradford under
the influence of Margaret McMillan. The Fabian Society was in
the 1890s pressing for swimming, games, physical training and
free meals in elementary schools.[36]

The Boer War revealed the extent of what became known as

'physical deterioration', when a government committee investigated the causes of the poor physical condition of would-be recruits. Against such a background of charitable effort, radical pressures and evidence of the real physical condition of the poor, legislation of a new kind was enacted. In 1906 an Education (Provision of Meals) Act enabled, but did not compel, local authorities to provide school meals out of rates. In the following year another Act required local authorities to institute school medical examinations. In all of these developments in child health a leading role was played by Margaret McMillan, and also by Robert Morant – in securing the legislation of 1906 and 1907 and in setting up a medical department of the Board of Education. Local campaigns sometimes had to be conducted to ensure that this legislation was acted upon.

The reform programme of the Liberal government from 1906 extended the framework of social policy. A Probation of Offenders Act was passed in 1907, and old age pensions were introduced for the first time in 1908 – the first major break in poor-law attitudes. The 1911 Act which provided for health and unemployment insurance laid bare, said Lloyd George in Parliament, 'a good many . . . social evils, and forces the State, as a State, to pay attention to them'.[37] A Maternity and Child Welfare Act was passed in 1918. It is this acceptance of state responsibility for wide areas of welfare that makes the social and educational legislation of 1900–18 as decisive a break in educational history as that of 1833–9.

Although the new administrative structure of education in England and Wales established itself rapidly after 1902, there remained a widespread feeling that something had been lost in the transition. In preparation for the 1913 meeting of the British Association, directors of education for local authorities in England and Wales were asked: 'Would you prefer the Educational Authority to be one elected *ad hoc*, as in the days of School Boards, rather than the system as at present established?' Roughly half of the 121 replies received said yes, but in the boroughs and urban districts the figure was 72 per cent. There was a strong feeling, also mainly in the towns, that the inclusion of education under multipurpose authorities had led to a 'decay in local interest' in education.[38] The commitment to separate *ad hoc* authorities for education remained firm in Scotland, where the trade unions, for example, supported the school

London schoolboys on strike for the abolition of the cane and an extra half-day's holiday, 12 September 1911

boards in 1918 in their campaign to retain the *ad hoc* principle. Although in 1918 the number of authorities was reduced from nearly 1,000 to 38 county authorities, the latter were directly elected and the intention to reorganize Scottish education on the English post-1902 model was defeated. The *ad hoc* authorities remained in Scotland until 1930.

The content of elementary education in this period changed only slowly. 'A cynic', says Professor Eaglesham, 'might argue that . . . *Morant aimed at and achieved a standstill in elementary education.* There is evidence to support such a conclusion.' Elementary education under the 1904 code was to be 'training in followership rather than leadership training, suited to the working classes'.[39] The ending of payment by results and the ideas of the new educationists were having only slow results in the elementary field, and those mainly in the education of younger children. Curriculum developments were sometimes of a confused or conservative kind. The interest in speech training, for instance, was one such new emphasis, accompanied by a resistance to new reading methods. A widening interest in geography matched a growing awareness of empire, and strengthened a tradition of interest in the exotic rather than the more immediate. Boys at St Mark's, Kennington, for example, were being taken in 1900 to an exhibition 'where many addresses were given explaining the manners and customs of the people of India: Burmah: Madagascar: Australia: South Africa &c'.[40] The object lesson was in decline. H. G. Wells describes Mr Polly near the beginning of the novel (published in 1910) as having attended a National School, where he was 'given object-lessons upon sealing-wax and silkworms and potato-bugs and ginger and iron and such-like things'. Nature study and elementary science were beginning to offer more systematic alternatives, though in the latter case apparatus was limited or nonexistent. Swimming and games were beginning to benefit from the growth of municipal amenities. School outings became more common (with even village schoolmasters raising money to take children to the seaside). Visits by school parties to 'institutions of educational value' were counted as attendance at school from 1896 under the code of that year. Girls at St Mark's, Kennington, for example, in 1899 visited various museums, the Tower, the Tate Gallery, Westminster Abbey and Kensington Palace.[41]

The training of elementary teachers was also undergoing a slow transition. The number of pupil teachers fell as the minimum age of acceptance was raised; pupil-teacher centres were closed or absorbed into the secondary system. Local authorities were urged to give secondary-school scholarships to intending teachers, and a new system introduced in 1907 enabled them to stay at school to the age of seventeen or eighteen. From over 11,000 new pupil teachers in 1906–7 the number fell to under 1,500 in 1912–13; only in rural areas did the system really continue beyond that date. Training facilities sharply increased as local authorities opened training colleges (in 1922 there were twenty-two local authority and fifty voluntary training colleges).[42]

The need to provide more secondary-school places for intending elementary teachers was an important factor in attempts to improve the ladder from the elementary schools. In 1906 approximately half of the scholarships in secondary schools were held by pupils pledged to teaching. As a result of the 1902 Act

there was to be, in one description, 'a ladder, not a stairway —
to the universities for the poor boy and girl of parts; there was to
be a reservoir from which would come the ten thousand teachers
required each year by the state elementary schools'.[43] In
1907 the free-place system was introduced, by which grants to
secondary schools were made dependent on their keeping at least
a quarter of their places, without fee, for pupils from elementary
schools. Entrance was conditional on passing an 'attainment
test' at approximately the age of eleven, which had grown
in popularity as the best age of transfer since the end of the
nineteenth century. Of almost 200,000 pupils in recognized
secondary schools in 1916–17 nearly 62,000 held free places.
Of the holders of scholarships in London in 1905, 24 per cent
were described as having parents of 'lower middle' class status,
49 per cent 'skilled working' and 25 per cent 'unskilled working'
(a few were 'unclassified'). In 1920–1 the proportions of successful candidates were 42 per cent 'lower middle', 41 per cent 'skilled
working' and 17 per cent 'unskilled working'. The areas in which
fewest children attended grammar schools tended also to be those
with greatest poverty, overcrowding and infant mortality.[44]
Demands were to increase in the years that followed for the
ladder to be made into a stairway, and for fees to be reduced or
abolished. Not all educationists favoured the ladder concept.
J. J. Findlay, for example, was in 1911 advocating a system on
the American model, under which public authorities would spend
all their educational budget on schools, not on pupils. The latter
would have to finance themselves above the primary stage entirely
from 'unofficial sources', including through employment. Payment and personal sacrifice made education more appreciated:
'And while, no doubt, advancement to the highest standards of
learning is hindered or delayed by serving as waiter or office
clerk, these . . . afford the student an insight into some practical
conditions of the work-a-day world . . . Natural selection might
be left to operate more freely.'[45] English education remained,
however, devoted to the principle of the careful selection of the
'fit'. One effect of the free-place arrangements was to increase
the pressures in the elementary schools to prepare children for the
examinations. There was also a greater temptation for lower-
middle-class parents to send their children to elementary schools
up to the age of eleven, though middle-class parents generally
continued to have the choice of private and preparatory schools,

and the junior classes or departments of many of the grammar schools themselves.

All these trends of opinion and organization were confirmed by the 1914–18 war, which, wrote Kekewich in 1920, 'has made no difference in kind to the needs of education. But it has made their satisfaction more urgent.'[46] It showed clearly the deficiencies in British scientific and technical education, but also crystallized the view of elementary education as part of a continuing social policy. State intervention in the form of wartime controls and planning went further than ever before, in agriculture and the railways, for example. The need to respond to social difficulties during the war, and to plan for post-war solutions, made social policy more directly a public concern.

In 1913 the Chief Medical Officer of the Board of Education had estimated that of the 6 million children in public elementary schools in England and Wales

10% suffer from a serious defect in vision.
 5% suffer from defective hearing.
 3% suffer from suppurating ears.
 3% have adenoids, or enlarged tonsils.
50% suffer from injurious decay of their teeth.
10% have uncleanliness of the body.

Medical examination, 1911

2% have tuberculosis.
1% have heart disease.
1% have ringworm.[47]

Health and housing become prominent wartime issues, and in 1918 the Ministry of Health was created. Wartime shortages both of teachers and of school buildings (with many commandeered for other purposes, and building at a standstill) drew attention to the state of elementary education, and with more stable jobs and incomes in many regions and industries the demand for longer and better education for working-class children increased. The Education Act of 1918 was the outcome.

In the war, said H. A. L. Fisher, in promoting his Act of 1918, we had

> overdrawn our account with Posterity . . . I conceive that it is part of the duty of our generation to provide some means for compensating the tragic loss which our nation is enduring, and that one means by which some compensation may be provided is by the creation of a system of education throughout the country which will increase the value of every human unit in the whole of society.[48]

The aim was grandiose, some believed unrealistic: the Act 'set out to conquer a kingdom without the means of even taking a province'.[49] It gave the Board of Education powers to compel local authorities to provide 'for the progressive development and comprehensive organization of education in respect of their area'. In return the state committed itself to the provision of aid in proportion to local expenditure. The Act provided for the establishment of nursery schools, continuation and more central or 'senior' schools.

The Act ended the half-time system and established fourteen as the uniform compulsory leaving age (in 1914 some 40 per cent of children were leaving before that age). Instead of raising the leaving age to fifteen, as had been considered, the continuation schools were to provide a post-school, part-time education. These and the nursery schools were the first victims of post-war economic stringency. They were the kingdom that was not conquered either then or in the half-century that followed. The expansion of the system of senior elementary schools continued, and extended the tradition of experiments with post-primary education; it was to prove important in the re-examination of the pattern of education in the 1920s.

The war ended with an ambitious Education Act, a report on the insufficiency of science teaching, and the creation of the Burnham Committee, in which teachers and the local authorities were to negotiate teachers' salaries. All three reflected trends in social organization and social and educational philosophies apparent since the late nineteenth century. The 1918 Act was intended to provide a new national momentum in implementing established ideas; like many other hopes for the post-war implementation of radical social policies it ended in a struggle to cope even with existing provisions, given the demands for economy in public spending from the beginning of the 1920s.

The 1920s and 1930s

The 1920s and 1930s saw the growth of a movement to end the parallel systems of elementary and secondary education, and to replace them by an end-on system of primary and secondary education. 'Secondary education for all' was the slogan; the Hadow Report of 1926 was its most representative document. By the beginning of the 1920s the NUT and the labour movement were pressing for a remodelling of the system. In 1922 a major policy document of the Labour Party entitled *Secondary Education for All*, edited by R. H. Tawney, considered that the only proper definition of 'secondary' education was in fact 'the education of the adolescent' – the phrase that came to be used for the title of the Hadow Report; R. H. Tawney was also a member of the committee which produced the latter. Although there were calls for experiments with 'multiple-bias' schools, the general aim of the movement was to establish a two-stage educational process, with the grammar schools as one type of secondary school, and with maximum opportunity for entry.

This movement to revise the relationship between elementary (the word was not officially interred until 1944, two decades after the Hadow Committee proposed that it should be) and secondary schools had its roots not only in the increased demand for secondary education, but also in the economic and political conditions of the inter-war years, including juvenile unemployment. The poverty and unemployment of the twenties and thirties were overwhelmingly regional in character, in the mining and ship-building areas most dramatically. Elsewhere, increased output in such industries as electrical and light engineering and motor-car production contributed to new economic growth. Although average real wages rose between the wars, the calamitous level of unemployment (nearly 17 per cent in 1921 and 22 per cent in 1932) and the social distress in large areas of the country widely affected attitudes to educational and social policy.

Important social and cultural changes of other kinds were taking place. Talking films from 1928 and the mushroom growth of radio (about a million people owned radio sets in 1925, and nearly 9 million in 1939)[50] were two such salient changes, as was the circulation warfare of the mass newspapers (the circulation of the morning daily newspapers was some 12 million by the Second World War). The motor car, the seaside holiday and the continued increase in the use of birth control were other features of the period (average family size was almost down to two children by 1939). The position of women had been profoundly altered by the war, and relationships between parents and children were changing. When the Board of Education in 1937 produced a revised edition of its *Handbook of Suggestions* for elementary-school teachers it felt impelled to describe the changes of the previous decade:

> The general standard of life has improved, and life itself is being lived at a faster rate. The universality of motor-transport, of broadcasting, and of the sound-film in the cinemas presents new features in the common life, while better housing, the increasing use of electrical and other mechanical devices, the probability of increased leisure and wider social contacts for all, with their opportunities for the enrichment of experience, make it necessary for those engaged in education to review their task afresh.[51]

The review was to take place mainly in wartime.

The important feature of education in the 1920s and 1930s was, then, the attempt to bring elementary and secondary education into an organic relationship. It is necessary at this point to consider the condition of schooling in the two systems, and then to examine the attempt to relate the two.

The content and approach of elementary education were undergoing little change. In its second report (*The Primary*

Lesson with radio, 1936

School, 1931) the Hadow Committee stressed, under the influence of the ideas of John Dewey, that the curriculum should be thought of 'in terms of activity and experience rather than of knowledge to be acquired and facts to be stored'. The aims of schooling in earlier industrial society, the committee believed, were no longer adequate: 'the schools whose first intention was to teach children how to read have thus been compelled to broaden their aims until it might now be said that they have to teach children how to live'.[52] The committee was, however, expressing a desire rather than describing a widespread reality. Attempts were certainly being made to reinterpret the elementary curriculum.[53] English, for example, was continuing to be reassessed in terms of oral work as much as written routines – a trend represented most clearly by the report of the Newbolt Committee in 1921 on *The Teaching of English in England*.[54] The teaching of mathematics was beginning to be re-examined. The Hadow Committee itself pressed for younger children to be taught less through subjects than through manual and aesthetic experience, integrated schemes and project work.[55] There were, however, serious obstacles to such efforts.

The economic constraint was of paramount importance. New apparatus and equipment were difficult to obtain. Attempts to modernize school buildings were frustrated, especially after the major financial crisis of 1931, when school-building was (as is generally the case) one of the worst-hit victims. New ideas about school-building, incorporated in the Board's *Suggestions for the Planning of Buildings for Public Elementary Schools* in 1936, were only beginning to be acted upon when war came.[56] The quality of the teachers, also, was conditioned by the resources available for training and salaries. The search for professional status was profoundly undermined by cuts in teachers' salaries during the economic crises of 1922–3 and 1931.

The elementary-school teaching force was now quite different from what it had been in the late nineteenth century. The number of adults teachers in public elementary schools in England and Wales rose from approximately 114,000 at the turn of the century to nearly 170,000 in 1920–1. Of the latter number less than half were trained. When the board schools began there were roughly equal numbers of men and women teachers. Ten years later the gap had widened (16,000 men to 25,000 women) and by 1904 three elementary teachers out of four were women. The disparity was even greater by 1920 (37,000 men to 132,000 women).[57] By the 1920s the pattern of recruitment had been redrawn by the virtual disappearance of the pupil-teacher system. The most common route for elementary teachers by the 1920s was from elementary school to secondary school (on a scholar-ship) and then either straight to college for a two-year course, or to an elementary school as a 'student teacher' and then to college. Although there are obvious differences of content between the timetable (on pp. 390–1) of a municipal training college for girls in 1921 and that which we have seen at Battersea in 1845,[58] the student of 1921 was still subject to a strenuous timetable, and in most colleges (especially for girls) to a rigorous, highly supervised social situation.

The number of grant-aided secondary schools remained almost stationary in the thirties (increasing by only fifty-nine between 1928 and 1937), but the number of pupils increased by nearly 100,000 and the average size of school rose to nearly 350. In 1924 nearly 68 per cent of children in secondary schools had come from public elementary schools, and in 1937 the percentage had risen to 77, as a result of the increased numbers of special places, and greater pressures from the parents of elementary-school children. The grammar-school curriculum remained essentially 'academic' and was now moulded by the requirements of the school certificate and higher school certificate. In two decades, in the eyes of the Spens Committee, whose report on *Secondary Education* was published in 1938, the school certificate had helped to raise secondary-school standards in general. The examination had been based, however, on the principle that it would 'follow the curriculum and not determine it', and the committee saw indications that 'in practice this principle has been reversed'. The number of candidates in the school certificate offering craft, technical, domestic and commercial subjects, art and music increased in the thirties. Although botany declined, the newly introduced biology prospered. Only English, French and mathematics were offered by more than 90 per cent of entrants in 1937; chemistry was offered by 35 per cent, physics by 27 per cent, physics-with-chemistry by 10·3 per cent and geography by 69 per cent.[59] In school science laboratories, experiments were generally given great prominence in spite of the warning by the Thomson Committee that 'in many schools more time is spent in laboratory work than the results obtained can justify'.[60] English teaching, in secondary as in elementary schools, was influenced by the report on *The Teaching of English in England*. The Spens Report described the first aim of English teaching as 'to enable a child to express clearly, in speech or writing, his own thoughts, and to understand the clearly expressed thoughts of others'; the second aim was 'the development of the power thus acquired to benefit the child as a social being'. Political, social and educational changes had already, said the Spens Committee, produced the result that 'a typical school of the present day is to be regarded as not merely "a place of learning" but as a social unit or society'. It was clear to the committee, as to the schools, however, that 'formal learning, the curriculum, in the narrower sense of the word, must always retain its central place'.[61]

The aim of the 1902 Act had been to weld together a system of secondary education under local authority control, and by the 1920s and 1930s this objective had been accomplished. The new secondary schools had developed a pattern of curriculum, staffing and attainment similar to that of the old-established schools. They had developed sixth forms and won the same kind of parental and

Morning

		8.50	9.30	10.10	10.50	11.45	12.25
Monday	2nd yr		a. Education	a. Advanced English		a.⎫ Ordinary b.⎭ Music	Adv. Music
		b. Education	Phys. Trng				
		c. Adv. Eng. (Shakespeare)		c.⎫ d.⎭ Phys. Trng	c.⎫ d.⎭ Education	c.⎫ d.⎭ Education	Ord. Maths Biology (2)
	1st yr	a.⎫ b.⎭	English		Drawing History		
		c.	Biology	Education	Phys. Trng	c.⎫ d.⎭ Education	Ord. Maths
		d.	History		Biology		Biology (2)
Tuesday	2nd yr	a.⎫ b.⎭ Education	a.⎫ b.⎭	Advanced Maths	History	Advanced Geography	Advanced Botany
			c. Phys. Trng				
	1st yr	a.⎫ English b.⎭ Method		1. Practical Housecraft *or* 2. Biology		Education	Music
		c.	Geography	English			
		d.	Demonstration Lessons				
Wednesday	2nd yr	Advanced Mathematics	Practical Housecraft (1)	Ordinary Drawing	Advanced Drawing	b.	Advanced English
		Ordinary Drawing	Biology (1)			d.	(Romantic Revival)
						b.	Ordinary English
						d.	c. Education Handwork (1)
	1st yr	a.⎫ b.⎭ Education	⎫Geography ⎭Method	English Maths		Gardening	
		c.	Handwork	Music *or*		Needlework	
		d. Phys. Trng Education		⎭ Maths		Gardening	
Thursday	2nd yr		Practical Housecraft (2)		Adv. Maths	Handwork (3)	
			Advanced Botany		Ord. Drawing (2)	Ordinary Drawing	Advanced Geography
					History		
	1st yr	a.⎫ Arithmetic b.⎭ Method	History	Phys. Trng Handwork	Ord. Music	Geography	
		c.	Drawing		Geography	Phys. Trng	Drawing
		d.	English		Drawing		Phys. Trng
							Biology
Friday	2nd yr		History	a. Adv. Eng.	a. Phys. Trng	Handwork (4)	
			Advanced Geography	b. Phys. Trng	b. Ord. Eng.	Ordinary Maths	
			Rural Science	c. Adv. Eng. (Shakespeare)	d. Ord. Eng.	Adv. Music	Adv. Music
	1st yr	a. Drawing	a. English		Geography	Phys. Trng	Education
		b. Phys. Trng			Drawing	Education	Relig. Instr.
		c.	English		Biology	Education	Drawing
		d.	Handwork		Drawing	Drawing	Education

The letters *a, b, c, d,* indicate different groups of students. Brackets show the occasions when two or more groups are combined for purposes of instruction. Unappropriated periods are at the students' disposal for private study and recreation.

Afternoon

	4.45	5.25	6.5	6.45	8.15

a. Phys. Trng   Ordinary   b. ⎱ Adv. Eng.   Theory of
          Geography   d. ⎰ (Romantic Movement
                         Revival)
c. ⎱ Ord. Music   b. Ordinary
d. ⎰   d. · English

1. Housecraft Demonstration
or 2. Biology   Theory of
Geography   Adv. Maths ⎱   Movement
           English   ⎰ Biology   b. ⎱
           Phys. Trng ⎰ Method   c. ⎰ Music
                               d. ⎰

2. Housecraft Demonstration
Biology (1)
b. ⎱ Advanced English
d. ⎰ (Romantic Revival)
                            c. ⎱ Ord. Music
                            d. ⎰

...emonstra-   Discussions   Country
...ion Lessons   Dancing
                      c. ⎱ Education c. History
                      d. ⎰   d. Relig. Instr.

...ardening   a.   Adv. Eng. (Shakespeare)
                   Handwork (2)   Musical
...dvanced   c.   Advanced English   Biology (2)   Society
Drawing   d. Education

a. ⎱ History
b. ⎰   Maths   Adv. Maths   Musical
                    Homecraft   Society
c. ⎱ History
d. ⎰   Maths   English

              Biology (2)
Choral   Country
          a. ⎱ Ordinary   Ordinary   Dancing
          b. ⎰ Music   Geography

          a. Relig. Instr.   Rural Science
Choral   b. Maths   Adv. Maths   Maths Method
          c. History   Relig. Instr.
          d. Maths   Rural Science

Educational Handwork

...⎱ Needlework
...⎰

c. Needlework
c. ⎱ Educa-
    ⎱ tional
d. ⎰ Drawing

public confidence; the distinctions between the old and new
secondary schools, inevitable when the latter were created, had
been eradicated in a very short space of time.

When the Labour Party issued its policy statement *Secondary
Education for All* in 1922 it used data obtained in Bradford to
show that secondary education had become 'the aspiration of
families who, twenty years ago, would have withdrawn . . .
[children] from school at the earliest age which the law allowed';
throughout the country, however, large numbers of children were
still debarred by their parents' poverty or the shortage of free
places. The existing scholarships and places were described in the
document (varying the 'ladder' image) as 'bridges' or 'slender
hand-rails' between the elementary and secondary systems. For
more than 90 per cent of the children concerned 'the primary
school is like the rope which the Indian juggler throws into the
air to end in vacancy'. Its proposal was 'the creation of a system of
universal secondary education extending from the age of eleven
to that of sixteen'.[62] The Hadow Committee's main conclusion
was that education should be conceived as two stages, primary
and secondary, with a break at about eleven. In addition to
existing grammar schools, schools on the pattern of selective and
non-selective central schools – to be known as 'modern schools' –
should be made available for all children. Existing elementary
schools could at least be divided into junior and senior departments. The movement for secondary education for all accepted
the Hadow Report 'as ground on which we think the battle for
improvement can hopefully be fought . . . It aims at secondary
education, not for a selected few, but for all children. To this
principle we admit no exception.'[63]

Secondary Education for All and the Hadow Report marked the
climax of movements of opinion which aimed to raise the elementary education of older children to 'secondary' status. The ideal
of labour organizations, for example, had become to provide
diverse forms of secondary education for all children; the idea of
introducing a break at about the age of eleven for every child had
been canvassed throughout the century in such organizations.
At the beginning of the century, for example, the Fabian Society
had heard a lecture on 'The irreducible minimum in education',
the main point of which was that in addition to grammar schools
and higher elementary schools there should also be schools for
children 'unprepared for education according to either of these

types. . . . To such a new kind of school, the term secondary
should . . . be applied, as well as to the schools now known as
Higher Elementary.' This was not merely a question of name;
it was that of

> the right of every child to education, not merely in a vague
> sense, but to the education fitted to his age and capabilities –
> (1) to primary, *i.e.*, undifferentiated, education up to the age of
> about eleven or twelve; (2) to secondary education of the type
> which, having due regard to the time which he is to remain at
> school, makes the best possible use of that time for the
> development of his powers.[64]

Such arguments for different types of secondary school were,
generally speaking, to predominate in the labour movement until
after the middle of the century.

The Hadow Report won swift and widespread support. The
Board of Education in 1928 published a pamphlet applauding its
recommendations and urging local authorities to adopt the
principles laid down in it, and to prepare public opinion for the
changes.[65] Many authorities tried to implement the scheme in
full; others began to open new senior schools and to create
senior departments. In 1928 Bradford, for example, entirely
reorganized its elementary schools along Hadow lines, with a new
system of 'modern' schools for children from the age of eleven,
and involving an extensive redistribution of staff and children.
By March 1930 there were 1,186 departments 'affected by reorganization schemes'. At this stage it was the reorganization of
schools into departments that was under way; by 1937–8 of all
pupils over eleven 63.5 per cent were in senior departments or
senior schools.[66] An important obstacle to reorganization was
the existence of the voluntary schools, which might be unable
or unwilling to participate in local reorganization schemes. The
Hadow Report itself could do no more than acknowledge the
problem and appeal to the voluntary bodies to make suitable
arrangements, perhaps closing some of their junior schools and
concentrating their resources on modern schools. In 1936 it
became possible for 'non-provided' senior schools to be built by
the religious bodies with a building grant of up to 75 per cent,
in return for some loss of autonomy.

Such expansion or reorganization did not go without opposition. Fisher's Act, and especially its proposal for continued

education beyond the school leaving age, provoked the wrath
of the Federation of British Industries, whose education committee declared that industry would be unable to bear the burden
of releasing its juvenile labour over the age of fourteen for eight
hours a week, and that only a small minority of children were
'mentally capable of benefiting by secondary education'. It
warned against creating, as in India, 'a large class of persons
whose education is unsuitable for the employment which they
eventually enter'.[67] In 1928 a former school medical officer
insisted similarly that most elementary-school children could not
benefit from secondary education because of 'the shallowness of
their mental impress . . . and of the generally exaggerated
appraisement of school education for the masses as a whole'.
The vast majority would be manual workers and therefore 'even
that extra year in the Public Elementary Schools . . . would
prove superfluous to the majority of them'. He found the Hadow
proposals unacceptable because of '(1) The too low educability of
many of the children. (2) The compulsory nature of the after-
lives of the scholars . . . No theoretical schemes for equal education of all the children can get away from these basic and fixed
conditions.'[68]

In spite of the 'fixed conditions' some children were climbing
the rope which ended in vacancy. The historian of Manchester
grammar school described, in 1919, the typical 'free placer' at the
school: he was highly selected, since only 10–20 were chosen out
of 200–250 candidates. He was 'of quick apprehension . . . of
good physical, as well as of mental, stability. He generally comes
from a home which possesses a moral thoughtfulness.'[69] The
number of pupils with free places in grammar schools doubled
between 1920 and 1932, when the 209,000 free-place children
amounted to over 48 per cent of the total. By the latter date the
free-place system had been converted, following the economic
disasters of 1931, into the 'special place' system, which required
that parents who could afford to should pay all or part of the
fees. A large proportion of scholarship winners continued, however, to have their places free (in London in 1934 only 85 special-
place holders paid full fees, 299 partial fees, and 2,940 no
fees).[70]

For the individual grammar school the free and special places
meant a broadening of its social basis. For the nation as a whole
at the outbreak of the Second World War education was still,

in Tawney's words, based on a combination of 'a not unkindly attitude to individuals with a strong sentiment of class and a deep reverence for wealth'.[71] The benefits of the ladder were unevenly distributed geographically and among the different social strata eligible to benefit from it. A study of the free-place system by Kenneth Lindsay in 1926, entitled *Social Progress and Educational Waste*, not only showed the limitations of the ladder but also heralded the sociological concern with education and social class. 'Success in winning scholarships', Lindsay summarized, 'varies with almost monotonous regularity according to the quality of the social and economic environment.' The poorer the district the lower the success rate. Not less than 40 per cent of the nation's children of 'proved ability', he concluded, were 'being denied expression'. The solution was that 'selection by differentiation must replace selection by elimination'.[72]

In this highly selective system a preoccupation with the age and methods of selection naturally increased. Even the Cross Commission had been told in 1886 by a chief inspector of schools of the difficulty of securing 'encouragement for those who are slow at learning at first, but who are not necessarily slow afterwards'. Transfer at eleven plus came to be justified in the twenties and thirties in terms of physical and psychological growth. The Hadow Committee described 'a tide which begins to rise in the veins of youth at the age of eleven or twelve'. The Spens Committee declared that 'general intelligence' was best measured up to the age of eleven, 'when certain qualitative changes in the child's personality . . . become noticeable'.[73] The early free-place examinations consisted of papers in English and arithmetic, sometimes a general paper, and, increasingly from the 1920s, intelligence tests. The claims for such tests were at first tentative. In 1928, for example, the Board of Education reported that twenty-one out of seventy-five local authorities investigated were using intelligence tests (four or five using 'standardized' or 'recognized' tests, and about half of the others using tests constructed by expert examiners). The board indicated that opinion was 'deeply divided upon the question of the value and suitability of the tests themselves, and upon the relevance of the usual arguments for and against them'. Its conclusion was that 'a general use of these tests in making awards would be premature'. In the 1930s claims for the tests became more insistent; the Board of Education followed the research cautiously,

Open-air lesson, 1933

but by 1936 could say: 'Evidence has accumulated which suggests that the value of what are known as intelligence tests is higher than had been supposed provided that such tests are constructed, and their results used, under expert guidance. It is therefore recommended that such a test be included in every examination for the award of special places.' [74] The Spens Committee, two years later, was impressed by evidence that 'with few exceptions, it is possible at a very early age to predict with some degree of accuracy the ultimate level of a child's intellectual powers'. This confidence in the possibility of identifying different levels of ability seemed also to justify the emerging pattern of secondary education, with grammar, modern and technical schools. 'Different children from the age of 11,' said the Spens Report, 'if justice is to be done to their varying capacities, require types of education varying in certain important respects.' Although the committee saw the need for experiments with 'multilateral' schools, it 'could not advocate the adoption of multilateralism as a general policy'.[75]

The committee also recommended the eventual raising of the school leaving age to sixteen. An Education Act had determined that the leaving age would be raised to fifteen in September 1939, but war intervened.

The new education

New departures, on a limited scale, can be traced in this period in every type of education. They were often sporadic, sometimes conflicting, but were aimed primarily at educating a more creative, less inhibited individual, or alternatively a true democrat, a man capable of a high level of service. The progressive educators were disillusioned with what Edmond Holmes in 1911 described as the path of 'mechanical obedience', and chose one form or another of the path of 'self-realization'.[76] The movement had truly international parentage, including American, German and Russian philosophers; it looked to Rousseau and Pestalozzi, Froebel and Tolstoy, Montessori and Dewey and Freud. King Alfred school in Hampstead listed its ancestors as 'Pestalozzi, Froebel, Herbart, Herbert Spencer, and others working on similar lines'.[77] Foreign educators came to Britain, and British progressive educators were conscious of their membership of an international fraternity. The Dalton plan came to England from Massachusetts

Break for milk, 1936

and the New Education Fellowship was part of an international movement.

The views of John Dewey underlay a great deal of the new English thinking. Dewey's aim was to promote individuality, to base education on the concept of children as children, not as future adults, on the idea of growth in children as an end in itself, not as a preparation. The experience of the child must be real; learning, in the most famous of Deweyite slogans, must be by doing.[78] Much of the experimentation with the 'play way' in education, influential books such as Percy Nunn's *Education: its Data and First Principles* (1920) and the very language of the Hadow and Spens reports, in their concern with education as 'activity', derived from Dewey. The other paramount influence was Maria Montessori, whose demonstration of what she called the 'exercises of practical life'[79] and freedom for children in a prepared environment reinvigorated kindergarten and infant education. The Montessori method involved a greater measure of control than Dewey's philosophy, but the cumulative effect of the two on the education of the younger child particularly was profound from the 1920s. The New Education Fellowship, founded in 1920, was intended to bring together all those dedicated to a radical renewal of education, and therefore of society.

New schools associated with this movement took different

paths. Bedales was followed by, for example, King Alfred (1897) and Bryanston (1928), both with the objective of 'wholeness' and a large measure of self-disciplined activity and learning. King Alfred was coeducational. Both, like Bedales, were influenced in the 1920s by the Dalton plan, which was intended to enable children to programme their own studies (and was itself indebted to Dewey's conception of democracy and the individual).[80] Dartington Hall, founded in 1925, was also coeducational, and was planned on this Devon estate by its founders as part of a wider social experiment to revive rural life and the arts. A. S. Neill opened Summerhill in 1921 as an attempt to provide an education free of the authoritarian overtones he found even in the other new schools: central to his objectives was the view he derived from Freud that 'emotions are more important than intellect', and that there was a need for 'freedom to allow the emotions to mature before you force too much into the mind'.[81]

Methods designed to encourage self-regulated activity and responsibility among children were not confined, however, to independent experimental schools. The Dalton plan found support in elementary schools. In a book on *Educational Experiments in England* in 1920 Alice Woods described efforts to introduce 'community government' at, for instance, an institute for Jewish destitute and delinquent girls in Stamford Hill, girls' elementary schools in northern England, various private and industrial schools, and socialist Sunday schools.[82] The approach which influenced many of these schools (and Summerhill very directly) was that of Homer Lane. Lane, founder of a reformatory in Detroit where he gave the boys a large measure of self-government, established a 'Little Commonwealth' in Dorset in 1913 for delinquent boys and girls. Self-government was again the central feature, and the 'citizens' were paid for their work by the community (which also imposed fines). Only the experience of responsibility, in Lane's view, could remedy anti-social conduct. There were 'no rules and regulations except those made by the boys and girls themselves . . . All the citizens of the Commonwealth attend courts and the highest judicial authority is the referendum. Disputed points as between the citizen judge and an offender are decided by public opinion by means of the roll-call.'[83] Nunn publicized the experiment. A master at Rugby was moved to experiment with classroom discipline by the boys themselves. Many secondary-school teachers were said in 1923 to be 'seeking for methods of organization which will give scope for the social capacity of boys and girls without undermining the sense of discipline no less necessary to development'.[84]

There were also developments more in line with the tradition of Abbotsholme. The most famous, Gordonstoun, was created by a refugee from Nazism in 1934. Kurt Hahn's emphasis at Gordonstoun, as at its German predecessor, Salem, was on a tough, almost spartan, training, combined with a sense of justice and social service. The stern programme (beginning with cold showers and a run at 6.30 a.m.) and the objective of self-discipline were to culminate early in the war years in the establishment of the first Outward Bound school, in Wales. This movement was to spread in the 1950s particularly, providing short courses of training in fitness, mountain and sea rescue, and self-discipline.[85]

Underlying many of the new approaches to education in the 1920s and 1930s was the growing interest in child psychology. By the mid-twenties the concept of sequential mental growth in children was strongly influencing approaches to many aspects of education, particularly work with younger children. It influenced nursery and play-way developments, and the Hadow Committee's search for a curriculum not tied to subjects, 'with a view to relating the curriculum more closely to the natural movement of the children's minds'.[86] Experiments with infant grouping after the First World War and the Dalton plan (which came to England in 1920) were related to it. There were widespread, more or less arbitrary, attempts to describe the phases of mental, physical and emotional growth. Homer Lane, for example, described the 'age of imagination' (two or three to seven), the 'age of self-assertion' (seven to eleven), and the 'age of loyalty' (a stage of transition from eleven to fourteen) and then the stage of adolescence to about seventeen.[87] Jean Piaget's *Language and Thought of the Child*, first published in English in 1926, was a major new departure in what Piaget called 'child logic'. Piaget's was to be the first systematic study of children's language and understanding, and the rate of growth of their ability to deal with concepts of different kinds. The dominant influences in this field in the 1920s and 1930s remained, however, the English and American educationists concerned with child study, notably Susan Isaacs whose books on *Intellectual Growth in Young Children* and *Social Development of Young Children* appeared at the beginning of the 1930s.

Other things contributed to 'progressive' educational thought – most notably psychoanalysis, and particularly the Freudian view of the unconscious and the nature of repression. These ideas were embodied in other aspects of the treatment of children. The first local authority child guidance clinic, for example, was opened in Birmingham in 1932: there were twenty-two wholly or partly maintained by LEAs in 1939, and seventy-nine in 1945.[88] The Children Act of 1948, establishing a child-care service, was to be one of the post-war developments that owed something to this tradition of concern for the individual child.

In the 1920s and 1930s the 'progressive' tradition was restricted to a relatively small circle of independent schools, but gained steady influence on elementary education. The new methods were attractive to inspectors, teachers and parents concerned about the education of young children; educational methods based on creative effort, self-regulated learning and a variety of informal techniques seemed more and more to fit both the well-publicized theories of the psychologists and the possibilities of the elementary school. They were resisted at the level of secondary education, which was more firmly wedded to academic courses, formal teaching and examination requirements.

University, technical and adult education

Between the university charters granted in 1900–6 and the Second World War charters were granted to Bristol and Reading Universities. Southampton was founded as a university college in 1902, and University College, Swansea, was founded in 1920 as part of the University of Wales. A movement to create a university in Leicester as a war memorial laid the basis of the opening of its university college in 1921. Out of the Royal Albert Memorial College in Exeter, which had been doing some university-level work from the beginning of the twentieth century, the University College of the South-West was created in 1922. Hull University College was founded in 1927. Imperial College, London, was formed in 1907 by the combination of the Royal College of Science, the Royal School of Mines and City and Guilds College. An Act of 1926 gave London University a new administrative structure, and in the following year it acquired its Bloomsbury site for a central university building.

The trend in university teaching and organization was

towards specialization. At University College, London, for example, in the period up to the First World War a separate chair in organic chemistry and a department of applied statistics were created, the chair in geology was made a full-time appointment and a number of departments were reorganized. The department of botany grew in size and became 'much more complex and highly specialized'. Engineering was separated from the faculty of science in 1908. After the war a chair of chemical engineering and a department of the history and method of science were created.[89] At Cambridge, to take a different kind of example, English literature had been part of the Medieval and Modern Languages Tripos since 1883. Only in 1917 did Senate agree to its establishment as a separate tripos, and then against opposition. In 1910 an opponent of the endowment of a chair in English believed that 'it would be a Professorship of English fiction, and that of a light and comic character . . . the Professorship of English was a Professorship unworthy of this University'. Seven years later the same opponent thought 'the teaching of foreign languages was futile' and of English unnecessary: 'the Englishman was English all his life; he needed no teaching in English'.[90] Elsewhere, university interest in various forms of professional training was growing, again not without opposition. Liverpool founded its school of social science in 1904 in order to train social workers. A school of sociology created in London for the same purpose in 1903 amalgamated with the London School of Economics and became its department of social science and administration in 1912.[91]

As with the individual grammar school, the social composition of the individual university or college was changing. A system of state scholarships began to operate in 1920, under which 200 scholarships (22 of them reserved for Wales) were awarded; the number was 360 in 1936. Competition for the scholarships was fierce, with only one candidate in every fourteen to eighteen being successful in the 1930s. Local authorities were also assisting university students, and by 1937–8 (not counting students in teacher training departments) over 5,000 were being so aided in the universities and university colleges of England and Wales. The proportion of full-time students being assisted in 1937–8 varied from 26 per cent at London University (because of the high proportion of medical students, who were less able than other students to obtain assistance) to an average of 45 per cent at other universities. The figure for the universities of England was 39 per cent, Scotland 46 per cent, and Wales 59 per cent – the last figure indicating Wales's 'all-round generosity to education'[92] (a tradition that was to be continued by Wales's position as the provider of the largest proportion of grammar-school places).

The number of students in the universities of Great Britain as a whole was some 20,000 in 1900 and 50,000 in 1938, although university numbers remained more or less static in the 1930s.

Girls at Oxford, 1936

The percentage from working-class homes was fairly constant, at somewhat under 25 per cent. In general terms 'rather less than one-half of undergraduates attended the State primary school at some time in their careers'.[93] A majority of undergraduates, certainly in the early decades of the century, were intending teachers.[94] Women were admitted to degrees at Oxford in 1920, and at Cambridge to 'titular' degrees the following year; they were not admitted to Cambridge degrees as equals until 1948 (nationally, the vote was acquired by women over thirty in 1918, and on equal terms with men ten years later).

The scale and organization of the universities changed substantially, therefore, in the decades up to the Second World War. The role of the state also changed. Public aid to the universities was mounting and an Advisory Committee on Grants to University Colleges was set up in 1906, to advise the Treasury. The University Grants Committee was created in 1919 as a permanent body to administer government aid to the universities (Oxford and Cambridge were not formally included in their ambit until 1922); treasury grants to British universities in 1919–20 totalled over a million pounds.[95] As a body under the Treasury, not the Board of Education, it gave the universities a direct but unique relationship with the state. The state acquired a different economic interest in higher education through the Department of Scientific and Industrial Research, set up under the pressures of wartime, among other things to finance university scientific research. The total number of postgraduate research students in science in England and Wales on the eve of the First World War was probably under 300.[96]

An important feature of the period up to the Second World War was the growth of the universities' involvement in extramural activities, and the expansion of adult education in general. The new universities began to take part in extramural work, especially after the First World War. The Workers' Educational Association, founded in 1903, was intended to bring the university extension work and the working-class movement closer together; by the Second World War its own courses were attracting over 60,000 students a year (and by 1947–8 over 100,000 a year). The WEA had enthusiastic support; its branches often had local trade union and co-operative organizations, working men's clubs, university bodies and teachers' organizations affiliated to them. The WEA was generally more successful than the universities in attracting working people to its classes (usually of one term's or one year's duration), but worked successfully with the university extramural departments in launching classes for which the universities either supplied tutors or accepted responsibility. In the winter of 1906–7, for example, Birmingham University collaborated with the WEA in arranging a special evening course of 'social study' for workpeople, consisting of: (1) the social ideal, (2) social economics, (3) industrial organization, (4) local administration, and (5) public health and housing. There were twenty-five lectures altogether, and the large audiences consisted almost entirely of trade unionists and members of adult schools. Students of Oxford University's tutorial class at Longton, in Staffordshire, helped to carry adult education into the more isolated villages near the Potteries, and created, in 1911, the North Staffordshire Miners' Higher Education Movement.[97]

Local branches of the WEA often found it difficult to define their objectives and produce programmes and teaching methods acceptable to their diverse body of students. The latter included not only manual workers but also housewives and professional people, obviously with a wide disparity of previous educational experience. A report in 1919 found that the main demand in WEA branches had been for economics and social studies, with a change in emphasis during the First World War to modern history, geography and international politics.[98] Political science, economics and history remained the staple, but the movement was also concerned with wider cultural subjects – which brought the organization into competition with other agencies, including the local authorities. In many areas, rural and urban, joint committees of various kinds were established to co-ordinate the provision of adult educational facilities: in Bradford, for instance, a Federation of Educational Societies had existed since 1913, including the WEA, YMCA, YWCA, and local historical, geographical and musical societies, as well as the local authority. The collaboration was particularly important in the scattered rural areas, to which the WEA attached particular importance, and for which in some cases it appointed resident tutors. A specifically trade union development took place after the First World War with the development of the Workers' Educational Trade Union Committee (to which thirteen trade unions were affiliated in 1931 and thirty-one in 1942). The unions involved contributed to the education of their own members, either under their own sponsorship or by financing their members to attend educational activities promoted by other bodies, mainly the WEA. Summer schools, weekend and one-day schools, as well as correspondence courses in co-operation with Ruskin College, were the main features of this development, as of the rival, more radical National Council of Labour Colleges.[99]

Some local authorities gave support to activities such as those of the WEA, at the same time as increasing their own evening classes and recreational activities. The range of classes available through local authorities, the WEA and the universities included, by the 1920s and 1930s, the directly recreational, the elementary and the advanced, the short course and the three-year tutorial course, the course which led to an external degree of London University and vocational courses in technical and commercial subjects. By 1911 the technical colleges of England and Wales had over 750,000 evening-class enrolments, and by 1937 over a million.[100] Local authority evening institutes concentrated on recreational activities. Such organizations as the Women's Institutes were expanding their activities. Cambridgeshire, in the 1930s, inaugurated its scheme for village colleges, which would house not only primary and secondary schools, but also library, recreational and evening-class facilities.

Older institutions, such as the adult-school movement in some northern areas, flourished at the end of the nineteenth century and in the first decade of the twentieth. The adult schools, often under Quaker sponsorship, held evening and weekend meetings, and in 1910 reached a peak membership of some 100,000 students.[101] The range of voluntary agencies providing part-time education in these early decades of the century was wide, but their work overlapped more and more with that of the official agencies, and the nature of their specific contribution was constantly under discussion. Part of the dilemma of such bodies as Co-operative Education Committees, for example, was the desire to stimulate education among their members in subjects which were often better provided elsewhere. Co-operative Education Committees, it was suggested in 1910, would have to keep in touch 'with the local university and the local education authority . . . Ultimately, it will mean the merging of the education committee of the co-operative society into that of the municipality.'[102] This was not, in fact, what happened, but such bodies found it necessary to concentrate their activities in those directions most relevant to their movement and the lives of its members.

The organs of the labour movement were also involved, alongside philanthropic individuals, in the establishment and support of full-time residential colleges for adults. Ruskin College, Oxford, was founded in 1899, and was dependent for financial assistance on the trade unions in particular, including for scholarships to support their members as students. Disagreements about how far Ruskin College should be committed to a socialist bias in its teaching led to internal difficulties (and a leftwing breakaway to form a Central Labour College in 1909). The 'Ruskin idea' won wide support. Other residential colleges were founded, including Fircroft at Birmingham in 1909 by George Cadbury, the Catholic Workers' College in 1921 and Coleg Harlech in Wales in 1927. In 1928–9 Harlech had students who had been 'shop-assistants, miners, steel-workers, quarrymen, lodging-house keepers, weavers, and clerks'; they studied 'history, philosophy, psychology, economics, political science, Welsh and English literature. . . .'[103] These 'second chance' colleges were designed primarily, as the founder of Coleg Harlech wrote, 'to enable people to have a year's education that would not only enrich their lives but also deepen their social consciences and help them to bring their developed talents to the service of less fortunate citizens'.[104] This development arose naturally out of the expansion of part-time 'second chance' education. It was not always easy, however, for students to return with their developed talents to their former backgrounds and occupations; they were torn between duty to the communities from which they had come and the movement which had supported them, on the one hand, and the wish, on the other hand, to take further steps into higher education.

If education, through formal and informal channels, was being driven slowly to recognize its role in 'the development of human personality', it was also coming slowly to tackle the other purpose that the Crowther Report later explained as belonging to education in a technological age: 'to set young people on the road to acquiring the bewildering variety of qualifications they will need to earn their living'.[105] Secondary education had been remoulded at the beginning of the century on the basis of equivocal attitudes towards scientific and technical subjects – subjects which only slowly made their positions secure. In the early 1930s only 100 or so junior technical schools were in operation; in 1937 they had nearly 30,000 pupils, most of them recruited at thirteen from the elementary schools. The day release of apprentices from industry occurred on only a small scale before the Second World War. The need for an expansion of technical and further education was felt in some educational and industrial circles in the 1920s and 1930s, and efforts were made by the

Board of Education to stimulate the necessary co-operation. The Yorkshire Council for Further Education, formed in 1928, was the most serious attempt at regional co-ordination. An HMI in the technical branch wrote in 1933, however, that 'regional co-operation is only in its early stages'. If the authorities would recognize the need, then 'we may hope that they will either co-operate voluntarily and fully for the improvement of technical education or that they will welcome legislation defining their several functions in a single scheme'.[106] This hope had not been fulfilled when the Second World War began.

The most important development in technical education in this period was the establishment of the ordinary and higher national certificates as new routes to professional qualifications in industry, and to a lesser extent in commerce. The first of these certificates, in mechanical engineering, was agreed between the Board of Education and the Institute of Mechanical Engineers in 1921, and similar schemes were subsequently adopted with other engineering institutes. Ordinary-level certificates were awarded at the end of a three-year part-time course at a technical college, and higher certificates after a further two-year course (candidates suitably qualified to begin the courses had to be at least sixteen). Ordinary and higher national diplomas were also introduced, on the basis of full-time study at the colleges, for two and three years respectively. The number of students acquiring these qualifications grew quickly. The total number of ordinary and higher national certificates awarded in 1931 was 2,792; in 1939 it was 5,330. In the latter year the subject in which the largest number of ordinary certificates was awarded was mechanical engineering (1,833), followed by electrical engineering (1,133) and building (533).[107]

In technical education, as in the reorganization of elementary education, the thirties was a period of expressed need and unsystematic effort. The parallel is a close one, since in both cases the Board of Education prodded and encouraged, but in neither case was the state able or willing to implement a national scheme of organization. Neither the provision of secondary education for all nor the establishment of a complete pattern of technical education at its various levels was within reach of accomplishment when war came in 1939.

Notes

1 MINISTRY OF EDUCATION, *15 to 18* (London, 1959), p. 53.
2 ALFRED RUSSEL WALLACE, *The Wonderful Century* (London, 1898), pp. 380–1.
3 R. H. TAWNEY (ed.), *Secondary Education for All* (London, undated [1922]), pp. 11, 72–3.
4 BERNARD REYNOLDS, 'Church schools and religious education', in MAGNUS (ed.), *National Education*, pp. 50–1.
5 BRYCE COMMISSION, I, p. 257.
6 *The Education of the People and the Bill of 1902* (National Education Association, London, undated), p. 13.
7 PETER GOSDEN, 'Technical instruction committees', in *Studies in the Government and Control of Education since 1860* (History of Education Society, London, 1970), p. 39.
8 MARY AGNES HAMILTON, *Sidney and Beatrice Webb* (London, undated), pp. 121–2; see also ROBERT DUDLEY HOWLAND, 'Fabian thought and social change in England from 1884 to 1914' (PhD thesis, University of London, 1942), p. 369.
9 HAMILTON, *Sidney and Beatrice Webb*, pp. 127–8; A. V. JUDGES, 'The educational influence of the Webbs', *British Journal of Educational Studies*, X (1961), p. 44. For Webb, the Fabians and the 1902 Act see A. M. MCBRIAR, *Fabian Socialism and English Politics 1884–1918* (London, 1962), pp. 206–22; also BRIAN SIMON, *Education and the Labour Movement 1870–1920*, chapters 6–7.
10 DAVIS, *The British Trades Union Congress*, II, p. 223; JOHN CLIFFORD, quoted in K. M. HUGHES, 'A political party and education', *British Journal of Educational Studies*, VII (1960), p. 120.
11 A. J. MUNDELLA, *Democracy and Education* (5th edition, undated), pp. 5, 12.
12 NATIONAL EDUCATION ASSOCIATION, *Education of the People*, pp. 14, 26–7.
13 KNOX, *Chairman's Annual Address*, p. 10.
14 BRADFORD INDEPENDENT LABOUR PARTY, *Report of the Commission on Education*, IV (Bradford, undated 1928–31), p. 13.
15 For details of the Act see GREENOUGH, *The Evolution of the Elementary Schools of Great Britain*, pp. 192–223.
16 MAGNUS, *Educational Aims and Efforts*, p. 217.
17 KEKEWICH, *The Education Department and After*, p. 228.
18 E. J. R. EAGLESHAM, 'The centenary of Sir Robert Morant', *British Journal of Educational Studies*, XII (1963–4), p. 5.
19 See BANKS, *Parity and Prestige*, chapters 3 and 5.
20 ERIC EAGLESHAM, *From School Board to Local Authority* (London, 1956), p. 190.
21 E. J. R. EAGLESHAM, *The Foundations of Twentieth-century Education in England* (London, 1967), p. 39.

22 BOARD OF EDUCATION, *Secondary Education* (Spens Report) (London, 1938), p. 66.

23 Quoted in JOHN GRAVES, *Policy and Progress in Secondary Education 1902–1942* (London, 1943), p. 62.

24 See BANKS, *Parity and Prestige*, chapters 3 and 6; *Secondary Education* (Spens Report) pp. 66–7, 72–3.

25 For statistics, 1910s–1930s, see ibid., chapter 2.

26 CAMPBELL, *Eleven-plus and All That*, pp. 9–10.

27 R. J. W. SELLECK, *The New Education 1870–1914* (London, 1968), p. 289.

28 T. PERCY NUNN, 'Science', in JOHN ADAMS (ed.), *The New Teaching* (London, 1918; 1919 edition), pp. 180–1.

29 Committee to inquire into the position of natural science in the educational system of Great Britain (THOMSON COMMITTEE), *Report* (London, 1918), pp. 7, 10.

30 NUNN, 'Science', pp. 155–7.

31 BOARD OF EDUCATION, *The Primary School* (London, 1931), p. 17.

32 BOARD OF EDUCATION, *The Education of the Adolescent* (London, 1927; 1953 edition), p. 35.

33 RUPERT WILKINSON, *The Prefects* (London, 1964), pp. 87–90.

34 See MACK, *Public Schools . . . since 1860*, especially chapter 10.

35 MINISTRY OF EDUCATION, *Report of the Committee on Maladjusted Children* (London, 1955; 1958 edition), p. 8.

36 See, for example, FABIAN SOCIETY, *The Workers' School Board Program*, p. 10. For the earlier interest of the labour movement in meals and welfare, see MCCANN, 'Trade unionism, co-operative and socialist organisations', *passim*, but especially pp. 249–52.

37 DAVID LLOYD GEORGE, *The People's Insurance* (London, 1912), p. 31.

38 *Report of the Eighty-Third Meeting of the British Association for the Advancement of Science, 1913* (London, 1914), pp. 726–8.

39 EAGLESHAM, *Foundations of Twentieth-century Education*, pp. 51–3.

40 St Mark's boys' school, Kennington, logbook 1895–1905 (12–16 November 1900).

41 St Mark's girls' school, Kennington, logbook 1899–1913.

42 See LANCE G. E. JONES, *The Training of Teachers in England and Wales* (London, 1924), pp. 28, 400–2.

43 JAMES A. PETCH, *Fifty Years of Examining* (London, 1953), p. 51.

44 ROBERT J. MONTGOMERY, *Examinations* (London, 1965), p. 108; CAMPBELL, *Eleven-plus and All That*, pp. 46, 81–5.

45 J. J. FINDLAY, *The School* (London, 1911), pp. 134–7.

46 KEKEWICH, *The Education Department and After*, p. 306.

47 Quoted in GRACE M. PATON, *The Child and the Nation* (London, 1915), p. 34.

48 Quoted in GRAVES, *Policy and Progress*, p. 110.

49 KEKEWICH, *The Education Department and After*, p. 307.

50 See J. A. R. PIMLOTT, *Recreations* (London, 1968), chapter 5.
51 BOARD OF EDUCATION, *Handbook of Suggestions* (London, 1905; 1937 edition, reprinted 1947), p. 6.
52 *The Primary School*, p. 93.
53 See R. D. BRAMWELL, *Elementary School Work 1900–1925* (Durham, 1961), *passim*.
54 The report contains a useful 'historical retrospect' and an introduction which analyses the status of English as a subject in English schools at this period.
55 See *The Primary School*, pp. 91–104.
56 See C. G. STILLMAN and R. CASTLE CLEARY, *The Modern School* (London, 1949), chapter I.
57 JONES, *The Training of Teachers*, pp. 447–8.
58 From ibid., pp. 414–15; see above p. 289.
59 *Secondary Education*, pp. 91, 94–5, 99, 256–7; for details of candidates for school certificate and higher school certificate examinations 1919–1950 see PETCH, *Fifty Years of Examining*, pp. 84, 121.
60 COMMITTEE ON NATURAL SCIENCE, *Report*, pp. 21–2.
61 *Secondary Education*, pp. 146–7, 219.
62 TAWNEY (ed.), *Secondary Education for All*, pp. 25–6, 37, 62, 77.
63 BRADFORD INDEPENDENT LABOUR PARTY, *Report*, IV, p. 3.
64 M. O'BRIEN HARRIS, lecture (undated) reprinted in M. E. SADLER (ed.), *Continuation Schools in England and Elsewhere* (Manchester, 1907), pp. 393–4.
65 See BOARD OF EDUCATION, *The New Prospect in Education* (London, 1928), chapters 1 and 2.
66 F. H. SPENCER, *Education for the People* (London, 1941), pp. 292–3. For the Bradford reorganization see F. J. ADAMS *et al.*, *Education in Bradford since 1870* (Bradford, 1970), pp. 103–7.
67 R. H. TAWNEY, 'Keep the workers' children in their place', in *The Radical Tradition* (London, 1964; Penguin edition 1966), pp. 50–2.
68 J. H. GARRETT, *Mass Education in England* (London, 1928), pp. 10, 115, 121–2.
69 MUMFORD, *Manchester Grammar School*, p. 427.
70 CAMPBELL, *Eleven-plus and All That*, p. 78.
71 R. H. TAWNEY, introduction to LEYBOURNE and WHITE, *Education and the Birth-rate*, p. 12.
72 KENNETH LINDSAY, *Social Progress and Educational Waste* (London, 1926), pp. 8–9, 15, 23.
73 CROSS COMMISSION, I, p. 131; *The Education of the Adolescent*, p. xix; *Secondary Education*, p. 123.
74 BOARD OF EDUCATION, *Memorandum on Examinations for Scholarships and Free Places in Secondary Schools* (London, 1928), pp. 16, 54–5; *Supplementary Memorandum on Examinations for Scholarships and Special Places* (London, 1936), p. 7.
75 *Secondary Education*, pp. 124–5, 376.

76 HOLMES, *What Is and What Might Be* (these are the headings of the two parts of the book).

77 B. H. MONTGOMERY and AUDREY PAUL-JONES, 'King Alfred co-educational day school from 4 to 18', in H. A. T. CHILD, *The Independent Progressive School* (London, 1962), p. 86.

78 See DEWEY, *Democracy and Education*, especially chapters 4–6, 15; *The School and Society* (Chicago, 1900), chapter 1.

79 See MONTESSORI, *The Montessori Method*, chapter 7.

80 See HELEN PARKHURST, *Education on the Dalton Plan* (London, 1922), p. 16.

81 DONALD MCLEAN, 'A. S. Neill looks back', interview in *The Times Educational Supplement* (16 August 1963), p. 191.

82 WOODS, *Educational Experiments*, pp. 106–76.

83 HOMER LANE, *Talks to Parents and Teachers* (London, 1928; 1954 edition), pp. 188–93.

84 J. J. FINDLAY, *The Children of England* (London, 1923), p. 197. The Rugby master, J. H. Simpson, described his experience at the school in *An Adventure in Education* (1916).

85 See H. RÖHRS and H. TUNSTALL-BEHRENS (eds.), *Kurt Hahn* (London, 1970), especially HERMANN RÖHRS, 'The educational thought of Kurt Hahn', and SPENCER SUMMERS, 'The Outward Bound Movement'.

86 *The Primary School*, p. xxii.

87 LANE, *Talks to Parents*, chapters 2–4.

88 *Report of the Committee on Maladjusted Children*, pp. 10–12.

89 BELLOT, *University College*, pp. 403–4.

90 Quoted in F. L. LUCAS, 'English literature', in HAROLD WRIGHT (ed.), *University Studies Cambridge 1933* (London, 1933), p. 259.

91 MARJORIE J. SMITH, *Professional Education for Social Work* (London, 1953; 1965 edition), pp. 35, 56–9.

92 LEYBOURNE and WHITE, *Education and the Birth-rate*, pp. 253–4, 259–60, 270.

93 Ibid., p. 275. The committee on higher education (ROBBINS COMMITTEE) gives the figure of 23 per cent for men and women undergraduates with fathers in manual occupations (*Higher Education*, II (B) (London, 1963), p. 5).

94 See D. S. L. CARDWELL, *The Organisation of Science in England* (London, 1957), pp. 164–6.

95 ROBERT O. BERDAHL, *British Universities and the State* (Berkeley, 1959), p. 201.

96 CARDWELL, *The Organisation of Science*, p. 165.

97 SADLER (ed.), *Continuation Schools*, pp. 101–2; R. A. LOWE, 'The North Staffordshire Miners' Higher Education Movement', *Educational Review*, XXII (1970), pp. 263–77.

98 MINISTRY OF RECONSTRUCTION, ADULT EDUCATION COMMITTEE, *Final Report* (London, 1919), p. 216; WORKERS' EDUCA-

TIONAL ASSOCIATION, *Adult Education after the War* (London, undated), p. 3.

99 Ibid., pp. 4–5; BOARD OF EDUCATION, ADULT EDUCATION COMMITTEE, *Adult Education and the Local Education Authority* (London, 1933), p. 25, and *passim* for the WEA's rural scheme.

100 STEPHEN F. COTGROVE, *Technical Education and Social Change* (London, 1958), p. 69.

101 KELLY, *History of Adult Education* (Liverpool, 1962), p. 260.

102 M. O'BRIEN HARRIS, *The Education of the Citizen* (Manchester, 1910), p. 18.

103 FLEXNER, *Universities, American, English, German*, quoted in HAROLD SILVER, 'Coleg Harlech', *Technical Education and Industrial Training*, X (1968), p. 182.

104 THOMAS JONES, quoted in ibid., p. 183.

105 See above p. 365.

106 A. ABBOTT, *Education for Industry and Commerce in England* (London, 1933), pp. 221–2.

107 MINISTRY OF EDUCATION, *Education 1900–1950* (London, 1951; 1966 edition), p. 50.

Further Reading

OLIVE BANKS, *Parity and Prestige in English Education* (London, 1955).

GERALD BERNBAUM, *Social Change and the Schools 1918–1944* (London, 1967).

R. D. BRAMWELL, *Elementary School Work 1900–1925* (Durham, 1961).

FLANN CAMPBELL, *Eleven-plus and All That: the grammar school in a changing society* (London, 1956).

E. J. R. EAGLESHAM, *The Foundations of Twentieth Century Education in England* (London, 1967).

A. D. EDWARDS, *The Changing Sixth Form in the Twentieth Century* (London, 1970), chapters 1–3.

DAVID V. GLASS, 'Education', in MORRIS GINSBERG (ed.), *Law and Opinion in the 20th Century* (London, 1959).

JOHN GRAVES, *Policy and Progress in Secondary Education 1902–1942* (London, 1943).

LANCE G. E. JONES, *The Training of Teachers in England and Wales* (London, 1924).

KENNETH LINDSAY, *Social Progress and Educational Waste: being a study of the 'free-place' and scholarship system* (London, 1926).

G. A. N. LOWNDES, *The Silent Social Revolution: an account of public education in England and Wales 1895–1935* (London, 1937).

MINISTRY OF EDUCATION, *Education 1900–1950* (London, 1951).

JAMES A. PETCH, *Fifty Years of Examining* (London, 1953).

MICHAEL PARKINSON, *The Labour Party and the Organization of Secondary Education 1918–65* (London, 1970), chapter 2.

R. J. W. SELLECK, *English Primary Education and the Progressives 1914–1939* (London, 1972).

BRIAN SIMON, 'Classification and streaming: a study of grouping in English schools, 1860–1960', in *Intelligence, Psychology and Education* (London, 1971).

W. A. C. STEWART, *The Educational Innovators: the progressive schools 1881–1967* (London, 1968).

See also pp. 473–5.

CHAPTER XI

Education and social ideals
1939–1972[1]

The war and after

The sense of solidarity in a nation under duress, the dislocations and destruction of the war, and heightened awareness of the weaknesses in the educational system, produced a widely expressed demand that what had been half done before the war should be completed, and a radical reappraisal of educational needs be made. Education and welfare assumed pivotal roles in thinking about post-war society. There was profound agreement on the need to finish remodelling post-primary education, to raise the school leaving age to fifteen (and eventually to sixteen), to implement a system of continued part-time education beyond the leaving age, and to provide adequate health and welfare services for schoolchildren. There was considerable wartime debate concerning the purposes of education; new books about education abounded, and political and educational organizations tried to define objectives for education after the war. One wartime committee, the McNair Committee on the supply of teachers, described in 1944 how 'the nation as a whole has woken up to the deficiencies of its public educational system . . . we are witnessing one of the most widespread and insistent of popular demands for its reform'. Another committee, the Norwood Committee on the secondary-school curriculum, found it necessary in 1943 to warn against 'a tendency to assume that because a thing existed before the war it must be changed after the war'.[2]

The outbreak of war seriously disrupted educational services. Some 750,000 children were evacuated from centres vulnerable to air attack, though within six months more than half had drifted back to the towns, and the scheme was described in 1940 as having 'now frittered away'.[3] Heavy bombing in that year raised the number of evacuees to over 600,000, but early in 1941 the number again began to fall. Education in areas to which and from which children were evacuated was in a chaotic state in the early part of the war. Many urban schools closed and children who were not evacuated were often without schooling. Schools which were evacuated frequently shared premises with host schools on a half-time basis. Evacuation was a revelation to hundreds of thousands of people; to urban children from poor families the countryside and the homes to which they were sent lay totally outside their experience, and to many of those receiving the children their physical condition, behaviour, standards of speech and cleanliness were often a disappointment or a shock. At the beginning, the teachers who accompanied the children were more involved with social problems than education. A teacher evacuated to Brighton wrote that 'the first week of evacuation was unbearable. The rumours of lousy, dirty, ill-behaved children bandied about Brighton were exasperating. We knew that 90% of the children were well behaved and happy. But the only stories regaled to me were of the horrors of the wild London children.' There were reports (some accurate, some exaggerated) of evacuees wrecking flower beds and furniture, and not knowing how to wash or what a nightgown was for.[4] Although by 1942 almost all children were on school registers there was a serious problem of attendance.

Attention was devoted in wartime more than ever before to the health of children; the school meals service, for example, grew enormously (some 1½ million children were taking school dinners before the war ended − three times the pre-war figure). Determination to prevent a return to pre-war social conditions and related problems of nutrition and health was the main factor behind the Labour victory in the elections of 1945 and post-war efforts to construct a 'welfare state'. Educationists during the war clearly expressed the state of public opinion. In 1944 Sir Richard Livingstone described 'the chief uses' of the existing system of elementary education as being 'to enable a minority to proceed to further education, and the rest to read the cheap press'. The curriculum had become 'a mass of uncoordinated subjects, a chaos instead of a cosmos'. In 1940 Sir Fred Clarke, in a powerful book entitled *Education and Social Change*, asked whether grammar-school resistance to 'multilateral' education was not 'some tradition-born . . . suspicion that the Ark of the Covenant may be handled by the unclean Gentile'.[5] To both Livingstone and Clarke the renewal of education and of society could only come from the reaffirmation of Christian faith. During the war the voices calling for an explicit Christian commitment in education became more insistent than at any time before in the twentieth century. The Norwood Report of 1943 talked of 'the present genuine demand that there shall be an opportunity for religious education in all schools': of the agencies of Christian education, the home 'has very generally ceased to be the place of religious instruction', the churches were often 'very scantily attended', and only the schools could supply the deficiency. The NUT accepted that the overwhelming majority of the people of this country and of the members of the teaching profession wished religious instruction to be given in state schools.[6]

A memorandum of the Board of Education (the 'Green Book') was circulated confidentially to a variety of organizations in 1941, in order to canvass opinions about educational reforms. A Conservative Party subcommittee reported in 1942 on post-war educational aims. In the same year Mr R. A. Butler became president of the Board of Education, and work was begun on the education bill which came before Parliament for its first reading in December 1943 and received the royal assent in August 1944.

The most important provision of the 1944 Act[7] was that which proclaimed that 'public education shall be organized in three progressive stages to be known as primary education, secondary education, and further education'. Local authorities were now required to provide secondary education, and schools would 'not be deemed to be sufficient unless they are sufficient in number, character, and equipment to afford for all pupils opportunities for education offering such variety of instruction and training as may be desirable in view of their different ages, abilities and aptitudes'. The school leaving age was to be raised to fifteen from 1945 (subsequently postponed for two years), and to sixteen at a later date. The scheme for county colleges was revived, providing for compulsory part-time education up to eighteen (in the event this was again not implemented). The Board of Education was turned into a ministry, and part III

authorities were abolished (though county authorities could dele-
gate powers in education to 'divisional executives'). Local
authorities were to provide school meals and free milk, regular
medical inspection and, in special schools or otherwise, 'education
by special methods' for children suffering from mental or physical
handicaps classified in eleven categories, including the maladjusted and the educationally subnormal. Only the severely subnormal, considered ineducable, were excluded from these
provisions and remained under the Ministry of Health, until an
Act of 1970 brought them under the education service.

All privately owned schools were henceforward to be registered
and inspected, and a new settlement was reached with the voluntary schools, given their inability to cope with the costs of
reorganization. At the outbreak of war over 60 per cent of
children in the relevant age group in local authority schools had
been in senior schools or departments, but only 16 per cent in the
case of voluntary schools. Schools were now given the choice of
accepting 'controlled' status, under which the local authority
would meet all the school's expenses, or 'aided' status, under
which the authority would pay for the running of the school and
half the capital cost of adapting the school to meet the requirements of the Act. In 1959 the support in the latter case was
increased from 50 to 75 per cent, and the same proportion was
made available for building new voluntary secondary schools.
Although Church of England schools were willing, when necessary, to accept the limited degree of independence involved in
controlled status, Roman Catholic schools were not willing to do
so. Of over 9,000 voluntary schools in 1970, more than 5,000
were aided and nearly 4,000 controlled. More than two-thirds of
the children in voluntary schools in the 1960s were in primary
schools. All-age schools, still a prominent feature of pre-war
schooling, were now scheduled to disappear, though progress
was to depend on economics and buildings as well as on good
intentions (by the 1960s they had virtually disappeared – there
were 133 left in 1966).

In all voluntary and 'county' schools, as the local authorities'
own schools were now called, it was made a requirement that
there should be religious instruction and a daily act of collective
worship. There was to be an 'agreed syllabus' (that is, agreed
between the local authorities and the religious bodies) for
religious instruction in county schools. The religious clauses in

the Act have been described as 'an investment of the hopes for religious education of many Christians in the early forties. . . . What battles are ended in the word "agreed", what a laying down of weapons in such abandoning of denominational particularism.'[8] Weapons were being laid down in the 1940s also between opponents of religious instruction and its supporters: neither in Parliament nor in the country was there serious opposition to its provision or to the settlement with the voluntary schools. From 1944, paradoxically, religious instruction was to retain a firm basis in schools, in a society that was predominantly secular. The nature of religious instruction itself was to be the subject of constant discussion; very often it came to be barely distinguishable from civics or general or social studies.

Three official reports published in 1943 and 1944 examined aspects of education likely to prove important in the post-war situation – secondary-school curricula and examinations (the Norwood Report), the supply and training of teachers (the McNair Report) and the public schools (the Fleming Report). The McNair Report insisted that 'nothing but drastic reforms involving the expenditure of considerable additional sums of public money will secure what the schools need and what children and young people deserve'. It proposed the establishment of a central body to supervise the training of teachers (and this was, in fact, created). The committee had divided views on the local machinery to co-ordinate training; all the members agreed that it required co-operation between the training colleges (as they continued to be called until the 1960s) and the universities, but disagreed about the extent and nature of the universities' role. The subsequent establishment of university institutes of education followed most closely the views of those members (including the general secretary of the NUT) who wished the universities to play a strong supervisory role. The committee was anxious to raise the status of the profession: it acknowledged that teachers were often 'said to lead a narrow life', and saw improvements in their status and job satisfaction as bound up with improvements in buildings, the size of classes and conditions of service.[9]

To meet post-war needs, a scheme for the emergency training of teachers was introduced at the end of the war and over a period of six years some 35,000 prospective teachers attended one-year crash courses, some of them in colleges opened specially for the purpose. To enable ex-service men and women whose education had been interrupted by the war to obtain university and further education a Further Education and Training Scheme was also introduced; some 85,000 grants had been made under it by 1950, when it was drawing to a close.

The position of the public schools was an important feature of wartime discussion about the future of education, though there was no consensus of opinion. The political left was generally in favour of abolishing or in some way absorbing these schools, as strongholds of privilege. For R. H. Tawney in 1943, for instance, it was a question of whether 'the existence of a group of schools reserved for the children of the comparatively prosperous . . . is or is not, as the world is today, in the best interests of the nation. It cannot be decided by the venerable device of describing privileges as liberties.' The Workers' Educational Association told the Fleming Committee that 'the position of the Public Schools is anomalous in a modern democratic society' and recommended their inclusion, 'if suitable', in the public system of education. For the Conservative Party in 1942, on the other hand, the contribution of the schools was 'too valuable to be jeopardised', and the aim should be 'to increase the value of their special contribution'.[10] Many organizations sought some form of integration which would preserve the character of the schools but bring them into a relationship with the state sector. It was this last course that was recommended by the Fleming Report on the public schools in 1944. Its proposals included two different forms of association with the maintained schools; the most ambitious scheme was for independent schools to reserve at least 25 per cent of their places for children from grant-aided primary schools, who would be supported out of public funds.[11] The Labour Party took little interest in the proposals, no national policy was adopted, and local authorities made only occasional smallscale arrangements along the lines of the Fleming Report. Among the public schools themselves, unsure of their post-war position, the report caused some controversy when it appeared. At Rugby one member of the governing body circulated a memorandum arguing that 'if we accept the Report the Public schools are doomed'; another argued that 'acceptance is a policy of appeasement to an outcry of political origin'. The school decided, however, that it 'would welcome a scheme which secured the admission to Rugby School of a substantial number of boys from grant-aided Primary Schools, who intellectually or otherwise would be likely to benefit'. In the end it provided two places a year for boys from Hertfordshire.[12] The public schools settled down to an undisturbed, prolonged period of prosperity.

When the 1944 Act was implemented the system of direct grant schools was retained, with modifications. Of the 231 existing schools, 160 retained direct grant status, 36 were rejected and 35 became independent. Four LEA grammar schools were accepted onto the list (another 27 applied and were rejected). Direct grant schools had to reserve at least a quarter of their places for non-fee-paying children from local authority primary schools. Some took more: Bristol grammar school, for example, in addition to its 25 per cent of free places had another 25 per cent of 'reserved places' if the local LEAs wished to take advantage of them; at King Edward's school, Birmingham, the LEA paid the fees of half of the boys.[13] In 1950 nearly 83,000 children (more than half of them girls) were attending direct grant schools, the social composition of which had since their creation come increasingly to resemble that of the public schools.[14]

The educational reforms which were to take effect from 1945 were intended to remove some of the stigmas attached to lower-class education, provide a new pattern of opportunity, and set education in a framework of improved welfare and social justice. On the basis of the Beveridge Report on *Social Insurance and Allied Services*, published in 1942, the new dispensation in welfare was enacted immediately after the war. National insurance, family allowances, national health, improvements in old age pensions – all these were in being by 1948. The Children Act of 1948 created a new child-care service. B. Seebohm Rowntree and G. R. Lavers set out in 1950 to conduct a survey of York in order 'to throw light on the question of how far the various welfare measures which have come into force since 1936 have succeeded in reducing poverty'. Rowntree's previous surveys of York in 1900 and 1936 provided a comparative yardstick for measuring poverty in the city in 1950. Using similar, but updated criteria of need they came to the conclusion that those 'living in poverty' had been reduced from 31·1 per cent in 1936 to 2·77 per cent in 1950, and that the latter figure would have been 22·18 per cent had it not been for welfare legislation after the war.[15] Welfare provision had made a striking contribution to the reduction of the most profound, or what Rowntree called 'primary', poverty.

Although poverty had by no means been eliminated, in sections of the community where it had existed, important changes were taking place. To G. D. H. Cole in 1956 the improvement, even if it had disappointed 'larger hopes', had meant 'immense improvements in the welfare of the people – above all in that of the poorer sections'. As long as the new welfare dispensation remained associated with full employment, poverty as it affected children was considerably mitigated. 'Those who knew the schools twenty years ago', said the Crowther Report in 1959, 'can see the revolution in the faces of the children.'[16]

Secondary education and sociologists

Like the pre-war Spens Report, the Norwood Committee reported in 1943 in favour of different types of secondary schools for different children. It even used the language of the 'progressive' educationist to make its main recommendation – that, 'in accordance with the principle of child-centred education the definition of "secondary education" should be enlarged so as to embrace three broad types of education'. It asserted that English education had 'in practice recognised the pupil who is interested in learning for its own sake . . . the pupil whose interests and abilities lie markedly in the field of applied science or applied art', and thirdly the pupil who 'deals more easily with concrete things than with ideas'.[17] The Spens Committee, in 1938, may have had to rely on overconfident psychological evidence; the Norwood Report of 1943 was concerned not with evidence but with assertion. It had less of a basis in discriminating analysis and concern for data than any other modern report on education; it was produced by a narrow committee and, it has been said, the circumstances in which it was published were 'a perfect example of that departmental procedure which to the uninitiated seems like official chicanery'. The report contained 'obscurities and inconsistencies, perhaps not quite unintentional'.[18]

In spite of the report's poor reception Labour ministers of education after 1945 accepted the tripartite argument and interpreted the 1944 Act in the light of it. A pamphlet on *The Nation's Schools* issued by the Ministry of Education in 1945 was withdrawn after protests about its tripartite assumptions. *The New Secondary Education*, issued by the ministry in 1947, followed the same lines, however. 'Different types of secondary

Kidbrooke Comprehensive School, 1954

education will be needed', it affirmed, 'to meet the differences
that exist between children' and it reproduced the description of
three different kinds of children who could be identified for three
different types of schools. A ministry pamphlet on school-building
asserted, in 1957 under a Conservative minister, that 'we now
hold that there should be different kinds of schools to provide for
variety in the ages, aptitudes and abilities of children themselves
and to suit local circumstances'. Labour leaders continued,
throughout the 1950s, to defend the retention of the grammar
school.[19]

At the end of the war the organization of secondary schooling
on comprehensive lines had only sporadic support. The 'multilateral' or 'bilateral' concepts of separate types of education
within the same building (or in separate schools on the same
campus, as favoured by the Liberal Party) competed with the concept of comprehensive schools which took children of all abilities
in the area. The London county council decided in 1944 on a
scheme of partial comprehensive organization, and issued a
London School Plan in 1947 – although the first purposebuilt
comprehensive school was not opened in London until 1954.

Anglesey had a complete comprehensive system of secondary education by 1953. The main impetus for comprehensive re-organization began in the mid-1950s, after a decade of strong opposition, and of reluctance among even Labour-controlled local authorities. The headmaster of Watford grammar school in 1956 voiced the concern of the opponents of comprehensive schools: 'the whole process can be seen at work in the area ad-ministered by the LCC, which marches blindly forward under the Comprehensive banner, undeterred by criticism from the pro-fession or by the anguish of parents'. He was afraid of 'death by drowning in the deep waters of the Comprehensive School'.[20] There was a widely held view that the grammar schools could and should have an enhanced contribution to make, and were too pro-foundly rooted in history and experience to be sacrificed to a new and partisan idea. There was also a view that the secondary modern schools which had replaced the senior classes of the elementary system could make, with essentially non-academic children, a new sort of contribution to the pattern of secondary-school life. These assumptions were challenged in the 1950s in three ways: the experience of the existing comprehensive schools was being collated (notably by Robin Pedley), doubt was growing about the part of intelligence tests in educational selection, and sociologists began to play an influential part in educational thinking.

The main criticism of intelligence testing was based on its claim, firmly accepted in the 1930s and 1940s, to be able to measure intelligence divorced from social determinants. Un-certainty about the relationship between intelligence and environ-mental factors was being voiced in the late 1940s, and in 1953 Brian Simon in *Intelligence Testing and the Comprehensive School* built on some of the early doubts of psychologists and others about the accuracy and validity of the instrument they had evolved. By the following year sociologists and social psycho-logists investigating social mobility were publishing results which accepted that 'there is suggestive evidence that working-class children do relatively less well on the tests of attainment which comprise 66 per cent of the selection examination'.[21] By 1957 the argument about the validity of tests and the arguments about the desirability of selection had become difficult to disentangle. The margins of error in the 11-plus were wide enough to allow of the wrong allocation of considerable numbers of children. Innate or general intelligence was admitted to be less easy to define or measure than had previously been thought. Intelligence quotients were demonstrated to be affected by coaching, and were not unrelated to previous social and educational experience. Professor P. E. Vernon, an important figure in the history of intelligence testing, himself helped to throw doubt on their use as a mechanism of selection. By the early 1960s it was possible for the Robbins Committee to pass a historical verdict:

> Years ago, performance in 'general intelligence tests' was thought to be relatively independent of earlier experience. It is now known that in fact it is dependent upon previous experience to a degree sufficiently large to be of. great relevance. And once one passes beyond tests of this kind and examines for specific knowledge or aptitudes, the influence of education and environment becomes more and more important.[22]

It was from the 1950s that sociologists began seriously to investigate the relationship between 'previous experience' and the distribution of educational opportunity. When the Central Advisory Council reported in 1954 on *Early Leaving* it found that in its grammar-school sample there would have been 927 children from unskilled workers' homes if the proportion had been the same as in the population as a whole; there were in fact 436. Of these, two-thirds left without as many as three passes at ordinary-level GCE (which had begun to operate three years earlier); only one in twenty entered for two or more advanced-level subjects, representing 1·4 per cent of the total number taking advanced-level courses. In seeking explanations the council felt itself to be 'in territory that had so far been little explored; and it is probable that many economic, social and perhaps biological factors have escaped us'.[23] Sociologists were, in fact, already exploring this territory. Jean Floud, A. H. Halsey and others began to publish research data on the differential access of children from the two main social classes to grammar schools. In 1956 Floud, Halsey and Martin published *Social Class and Educational Opportunity*, demonstrating how class affected chances of a grammar-school education. What the research of the 1950s showed was that post-war educational expansion

> benefited the children of all social classes – not just those of the less prosperous groups . . . The widening of educational

provisions does not by itself reduce social inequalities in educational opportunity . . . no less than nine in every ten of the lowest social group were still deprived of a grammar school education in the 1950's; the proportion so deprived was barely a tenth smaller than thirty or forty years before.[24]

If *Early Leaving* was the first report of an official committee on education to ask mainly sociological questions, the Central Advisory Council's 1959 report on education, *15 to 18* (the Crowther Report), was the first to look for systematic sociological answers. It set out to explore the implications of economic and social change for the education, full-time and part-time, of young people in this age range. Problems of population and family, and changes in teenage employment and interests, for example, were of central importance to it. It was concerned with the school's role in preparation for family life and adulthood. It looked at the earlier age of marriage among girls, and suggested that this required a new approach to the education of girls of seventeen and eighteen still in full-time education. It considered aspects of increased economic prosperity ('the community is about one-third richer in material wealth than it was in 1938') and believed that the effects of prosperity had been beneficial to education, though educational expenditure had in the previous twenty years 'been doing little more than keep up with the general expansion of the national income'.[25] It reiterated the need to raise the school leaving age to sixteen, and to implement the agreed policy on county colleges. The report was not directly concerned with the problems of selection for secondary education which had preoccupied the sociologists in the 1950s, but it was, as a leading sociologist described it, 'the most up-to-date account available of the social distribution of educational opportunity for boys in Britain, and a valuable analysis of some of the major social influences of educability'.[26]

Expansion and the 'affluent society'

The economic and social trends of the 1950s were of immediate relevance to education. Full employment, social security and economic growth had all contributed to generally higher standards, in what became labelled at the end of the 1950s 'the affluent society'. It was also to an increasing extent a consumer society, at all levels. One of the implications was that 'as a good in itself, education is felt to add to the interest and grace of life; and when people get richer they seek more of it, just as they buy more novels or hi-fi sets . . . But people also want education as a way to better-paid jobs.'[27] A direct outcome was the increase in the number of children staying on at school after the leaving age. The proportion of grammar-school children, for example, staying to the age of seventeen increased by more than half between 1953 and 1960, and the percentage increase was growing annually. There were important differences by geographical region, social class and type of school, but the overall trend was unmistakable. This was of particular importance, given the rising level of affluence among young people, and the prospects of economic independence and fuller participation in the youth consumer culture when they left school. 'While the economic compulsion to leave school as early as possible has diminished', said the Crowther Report, 'the economic attraction of doing so has increased.'[28]

Although investigations in the 1960s were to upset some of the complacency about the affluent society, the predominant view of society in the 1950s was moulded by memories of the pre-war world. Among teachers, however, as in other professions, there was also an unease at the outpacing of salaries by prices, and at the relative downgrading of teachers' salaries compared to manual workers' wages, which were increasing more rapidly. Whatever teachers gained from the affluent society, they were

> comparing their lives with those of the working class around them and expressing resentment at their continuing lower-middle-class 'poverty' in contrast with the new working-class 'affluence'. It is possible that this feeling of resentment was strengthened by the changing class background of teachers, as the members of the profession have been drawn increasingly from the lower middle class rather than from the working class.[29]

Between 1954 and 1956 the teachers fought a battle to try to prevent the government raising their superannuation benefits (and in effect cutting salaries), and at the same time began a prolonged series of salary negotiations and struggles. A new level of teachers' militancy dates from these middle years of the 1950s.

From the late 1940s to the early 1960s the statistics of education reflect considerable changes. In the 1950s the population of England and Wales increased by some 2·5 million, reaching 46 million by 1961 (it was to increase by a similar figure in the following decade). Post-war population trends are marked by the increased birth rate at and after the end of the war, reaching a peak in 1947; this was followed by a fall in births and a further rise from 1957. The post-war 'bulge' and the raising of the school leaving age in 1947 increased the number of children in grant-aided schools in England and Wales from just over 5 million in 1946 to some 7 million in the early 1960s (the increase beyond that date, to 8 million in 1970, is also partly accounted for by the trend towards a longer school life). The early 1950s and early 1960s both saw an influx of larger numbers into the primary schools, though the impact of the first 'bulge' was the most dramatic; much of the planning for educational developments in the 1950s had to take account of the increased numbers that would be entering secondary and higher education.

Together with the increased numbers of pupils and a crash programme of temporary and permanent school-building, the number of teachers also rose. From 196,000 teachers in grant-aided schools in England and Wales before the war the number rose to nearly 216,000 in 1950 and 269,000 in 1961. One of the main features of the expansion of education in the 1950s and 1960s was, in fact, the transformation of the training colleges. The local authorities, which had run twenty-two training colleges in 1922, had twenty-nine in 1944, sixty-three in 1954 and seventy-seven in 1962 (by which date there were forty-seven voluntary colleges, three fewer than in 1922). The dramatic increase in the size of the individual colleges was to come in the mid-1960s; between 1954 and 1963, however, the total number of students in the colleges doubled, to approximately 48,000 (the number of students on postgraduate courses of teacher training, approaching 2,000 before the war, was 2,700 in 1957–8). A decision was also taken in 1960 to lengthen college courses of teacher training from two to three years.

From the end of the war economic pressures for educational expansion were further evident in efforts to ensure an adequate supply of trained manpower, especially at the level of the professional scientist and technologist. The Percy Report on higher technological education, published in 1945, proposed the development of university-level courses in selected technical colleges, with a national body to supervise appropriate awards. From these proposals came the development of advanced work in some technical colleges, under the auspices of the National Council for Technological Awards from 1955. The Diploma in Technology, whose standards it supervised, was intended to be a degree equivalent, though industry was not always ready to accept it as such. It was based on a 'sandwich' principle, under which students spent part of their four-year course in industry. The Barlow Committee, which reported in 1946, was concerned with forecasting scientific manpower needs – the first attempt at such official prediction. It recommended the immediate doubling of the output of scientific manpower, and helped to influence developments in university and further education towards the production of such trained manpower. Although there was resistance to a major expansion in university science the number of graduate scientists being produced trebled in the fifteen years after the end of the war. Only in the mid-1950s did it become clear that the sights had been set too low, and that in many disciplines, primarily technology, the numbers of trained personnel were insufficient. The teaching of science and mathematics was to suffer from this shortfall, but the problem had been masked in the decade after the war by a swing towards science in the schools – a swing that was not to be sustained. Even the government's 1956 white paper on *Technical Education*, which signalled the onset of a new sense of urgency, could talk sanguinely about school science and attitudes towards technical education among school leavers: 'Here the prospects are good. The romance of science is catching on as can be seen even in the toy shops.'[30] International technological competition, however, led to a greater awareness of the need for an expansion of higher technological and scientific education. The 1956 white paper proposed the concentration of advanced technological courses at a number of 'colleges of advanced technology'. Ten of these were duly designated, and from 1962 received grants direct from the Ministry of Education instead of from the local authorities.

A general increase was also taking place in the 1950s and early 1960s in the numbers of full-time and part-time students at institutions of further education, including technical and art colleges and colleges of commerce. From 1954 to 1962 the number of full-time day students of all kinds at these colleges in

England and Wales increased from 36,000 to 114,000, and the number of part-time students from 251,000 to 454,000. The proportion of boys released by industry for part-time courses varied in the mid-1950s from 90 per cent in engineering to 10 per cent in textiles and 5 per cent or less in the distributive trades and agriculture. Whereas in 1954, in all industries, 27 per cent of boys under eighteen were being so released, the parallel figure for girls was only 7 per cent.[31] By 1950 the numbers attending part-time evening classes at further education establishments, including evening institutes, was over 2 million. From the publication of the 1956 white paper a new interest was shown in the nature of courses offered at all levels of technical education, from Diploma in Technology courses to the day release classes for apprentices. The white paper stressed that 'a place must always be found in technical studies for liberal education . . . We cannot afford either to fall behind in technical accomplishments or to neglect spiritual and human values.' The Ministry of Education issued a circular the following year on *Liberal Education in Technical Colleges* to 'stress the importance of introducing a liberal element into technical education'.[32] A feature of technical education from this point was the rapid expansion of liberal studies departments in the colleges, and the broadening of courses to include such studies.

The 1950s saw important beginnings to the process of university change and expansion. The number of university students in Great Britain as a whole doubled to over 100,000 between 1945 and the end of the 1950s. The number of grants awarded by local authorities increased at the same time, but, as the Robbins Committee was to emphasize, the proportion of students from working-class backgrounds had remained unaltered since the 1920s (at about 25 per cent).[33] From the beginning of the 1960s local authorities were required to make awards to suitably qualified students accepted for university first-degree courses. All the remaining university colleges achieved independent university status in the 1950s, and the University College of North Staffs., at Keele, received its first students in 1950. Keele was created out of a tradition of adult education, with a four-year pattern of studies intended to be appropriate to its location and the times; it was able from the beginning to award its own degrees and was sponsored initially, not by London University, but by the universities of Oxford, Birmingham and Manchester.

The educational problems of the 1950s clustered around questions of numbers, manpower and objectives. The numbers of pupils and students were reflected in a great increase in public expenditure on education, from some £400 million in 1952 to over £900 million ten years later. By the beginning of the 1960s the total school population contained some 4 million in maintained primary and 3 million in maintained secondary schools. There were over 50,000 children in special schools, well over 100,000 in direct grant schools, over 300,000 in independent schools 'recognized as efficient', and 200,000 in other independent schools. Important new departures were taking place in school architecture (including the trend towards the multipurpose use of space), and the pace of the movement towards comprehensive schools was accelerating. Some of these developments were the outcome of the educational planning at the end of the war; some were the outcome of new movements of opinion or the problems of the technological age. In all of them there was an uneasy search for educational objectives which could respond to the widespread and profound changes taking place in society. At the beginning of the 1960s an analysis of 'rebellious youth in the welfare state' came to the conclusion that education was now the most crucial instrument of social policy and needed to change in order to be able to give

> the seventy to eighty per cent majority of British boys and girls who are early school leavers a more appropriate and modern education than many of them are getting today. Indeed, it may well be the most important task of social reform facing the country ... the material advance of British working-class youth should be accompanied by an equivalent cultural advance.[34]

The 1960s: inequalities and opportunities

An important feature of education in the 1960s was the increased role of the central government in developments of many kinds. The debate about educational principles and practice dominated the reports of the national committees. Outstanding reports of the sixties covered the universities, less able children, primary and public schools, the youth service and the recruitment of scientists.

The reports reflected in general the growing concern about evidence of underprivilege and the problems of manpower. The Crowther Committee's concern with sociological analysis and the definition of educational objectives was repeated in the reports of the 1960s. They also showed a concern, implicit or explicit, with national economic needs, with the rights and requirements of the individual, the distribution of resources and acceptable philosophies for educational processes. Out of such reports came developments which strengthened the role of the state in education: the Ministry of Education was reconstituted, a national Schools Council was created, a government scheme for a system of higher education to run parallel with the universities was implemented, educational priority areas were designated, and ministers played a more intimate part in decisions on comprehensive-school schemes and the pay of university and school teachers.

Two reports which were to be of profound importance for educational development appeared in 1963 – the Newsom Report, *Half our Future*, on children of average and less than average ability, and the Robbins Report on *Higher Education*. Both accepted and reinforced the premise that social factors had deprived poor children of adequate educational opportunities. The fact had been obscured by the processes of selection: the belief, said Robbins, 'that there exists some easy method of ascertaining an intelligence factor unaffected by education or background is outmoded'. Tests, said Newsom, were measurements of 'largely an acquired characteristic'. Educational opportunities were not equal. 'There is little doubt', said Newsom, 'that among our children there are reserves of ability which can be tapped.' There was no risk within twenty years, thought Robbins, that 'the growth in the proportion of young people with qualifications and aptitudes suitable for entry to higher education will be restrained by a shortage of potential ability'. The Robbins Report carried further the sociological analysis of the influence of class on access to the higher levels of education. The Newsom Committee was impressed by the evidence from the secondary modern schools of 'the discovery of unexpected reserves of talent'. In the House of Lords, Lord Robbins, defending his committee's proposals against charges of lowering university standards, underlined one of the main findings: 45 per cent of children from higher professional families were entering higher education, but only 4 per cent from skilled manual families. The tables in the report, he insisted, showed inescapably 'that the reserves of untapped ability are extensive'. If the Robbins and Newsom reports voiced humane and principled arguments for the extension of educational opportunity, both were also aware that these humane appeals for expansion were at the same time proposals to the exchequer. However, reserves of ability which could be 'tapped' were, in the mood of the 1960s, a compelling argument: 'in the national economic interest', said the Newsom Report, 'we cannot afford to go on waiting.'[35]

The process of university expansion was already under way at the beginning of the 1960s, with a wave of new university foundations. The universities of Sussex, Kent, Essex, East Anglia, York, Warwick and Lancaster (and Stirling, in Scotland) were founded between 1961 and 1965, and Newcastle became an independent university. The new universities made deliberate efforts to produce diversified and often unconventional courses of study. The University Grants Committee itself, reporting in 1963, explained its support for the new foundations: there was a need for more places, but also 'for more experiment in the structure of degree courses, in the content of curricula, in methods of teaching and in university organisation . . . we felt . . . that new

Lining up for afternoon school

universities might achieve these aims more easily and more rapidly than the existing ones'.[36] The new universities did more than increase total numbers and diversify courses, they also modified the hierarchy of university popularity. Oxford and Cambridge, which featured so prominently in earlier chapters, had by the mid-twentieth century become part of a broad pattern of universities and university colleges, but despite the competition and their own internal changes had retained a pre-eminent social and academic position. Up to the 1960s Oxford and Cambridge stood out in English esteem as unrivalled centres of social prestige and academic excellence, and the highest aspiration of future university students. The centuries of Oxbridge tradition began in the 1960s, however, to meet competition from the new architecture, the new styles of life, the innovatory atmosphere and the rapidly established academic reputations of some of the new universities. The older provincial universities were affected by the same challenge. The standards of university learning and the criteria of university popularity were being defined at this point as much by the University of Sussex as by the ancient universities. The special attractions of Oxford and Cambridge and their reputations remained, but other and challenging reputations were being established.

With the process of expansion under way, the need for it to be carried further was realized. A study group of the Labour Party reported in 1962 in favour of a total of about seventy universities in England and Wales and ten in Scotland, within twenty years.[37] The Robbins Committee, appointed in 1961, looked at likely future demand in higher education (embracing the universities, training colleges and advanced work in the colleges of further education); on the basis of the trend in qualified school leavers it deduced that the total of 216,000 students in Great Britain in 1962 should increase to over 390,000 in 1973 and nearly 560,000 in 1980. Of the 1973 figure 219,000 should be in universities, 122,000 in colleges of education, and 51,000 in further education. It was soon pointed out that even the Robbins figures, accepted and acted upon by the government, were conservative estimates; they failed to take full account of other social trends, discussed by the report itself, which would mean not a continuation but an acceleration of the trend of the early 1960s. The Robbins projections for Great Britain began to be outstripped in the second half of the 1960s; by 1967 there were over 100,000 students in colleges of education, the further education estimate of 51,000 was reached in 1965, and the universities had some 228,000 students in 1970.[38] Official estimates of the need for places in higher education in Britain in 1980 were revised upwards to an expectation of over 800,000 students in higher education by 1980; there were signs at the beginning of the 1970s, however, that the level of demand for places (notably for the universities) might not be maintained.

The government, in accepting the implications of the Robbins forecasts, also accepted the committee's proposal to give university status to the colleges of advanced technology. The commitment of the Conservative government in 1963 to a more active national policy for higher education was carried further by the Labour government which came to power the following year. The Conservative government had decided against the Robbins proposal for two separate ministries, one for the schools and one for higher education and science, and in 1964 created a single Department of Education and Science, under a secretary of state, assisted by two ministers. The Labour government finally rejected the Robbins proposal to transfer the colleges of education away from local authority to university control.

In 1966 the Labour government also produced a *Plan for Polytechnics* which would create an alternative system of higher education controlled by the local authorities. This 'binary' system began to be implemented the following year; and the designation of twenty-one polytechnics had been agreed by the end of 1968. The degrees were awarded by the Council for National Academic Awards, a body proposed by the Robbins Committee to replace the National Council for Technological Awards; the new body had been given a charter in 1964 specifically to award degrees in approved colleges outside the university system. The intention was, with the polytechnics, to create a sector of higher education oriented to courses of a more applied nature, and more directly amenable to public influence than the traditional universities. The latter lost another feature of their old independence by becoming financially accountable to the government, and university teachers found their salaries being negotiated within the machinery of national economic planning. The cost of university expansion led, in the late sixties, to a serious government interest in possible economies, including the possibility of student loans rather than grants. The development of higher education had brought it into a close relationship with the ups and downs of national economics.

The education of teachers was undergoing important changes in the 1960s. Following a recommendation of the Robbins Committee the first awards of a new Bachelor of Education degree were made in 1968. By the end of the 1960s there were twenty-eight university departments of education, taking some 5,000 students, and over 2,000 graduates were attending courses at colleges of education, whose incursion into graduate training was one of the growth points in education at the end of the 1960s. Socially, the most important change in the colleges of education in the sixties was the breakdown in their traditional single-sex structure. Even in the five years from 1958, the Robbins Committee discovered, the number of all-male colleges had decreased by five, and the number of all-female colleges by twenty-two. Opportunity in teacher training, however, was not only a question of initial training for school leavers and recent graduates; it also became one of efforts to recruit married women to teacher training (or to bring trained women teachers back into employment), in the situation of teacher shortage in the 1960s. Trained women teachers were being lost to teaching when they had their families (most noticeable when the birth rate began to rise in the late 1950s), but might be interested in returning to teaching. A survey published in 1963 showed that a high percentage of women teachers with young families wished to return to employment when their children were old enough, but that more part-time posts were urgently needed.[39] A campaign had already been launched in 1961 to bring married women back into teaching, to be trained or to be retrained. As in all professions, the pattern of women's employment was profoundly changing with earlier marriage. But the pattern of training was also changing. In 1967 20 per cent of all non-graduates entering teacher training were aged twenty-five or over. Special colleges and courses for mature women students with families were now being opened.

There remained, it is important to note, considerable differences in the pattern of further, higher and professional training for men and women. The percentage of 17-year-olds still at school rose, in the case of boys, from 6·2 to 11·1 per cent between 1947 and 1958; the parallel figures for girls were 4·8 and 8·8 per cent. In the early 1960s the percentage of boys in the relevant age group going to university was over twice that of girls (5·6 and

2·5 per cent respectively). The proportion of girls with two or more A-levels who went on to university in 1967 was 44 per cent; in the case of boys the figure was 67 per cent. In full-time and part-time further education the percentage of boys far outstripped that of girls, and only in the colleges of education was the percentage of women higher than that of men. The fact that only a quarter of students in British universities were women was a factor in the Robbins Committee's assessment of the likely future expansion of higher education; the rising professional standards of some occupations taken up by girls was likely, the committee believed, to lead to more girls entering them via full-time courses of higher education. By the beginning of the 1970s, however, these differentials in higher education were still marked.[40]

In terms of opportunities for adults the Open University was the most important development of the 1960s. The Labour Party's study group on higher education which reported to the party in 1962 proposed that 'as an experiment, the BBC sound radio and television and the ITA should be required to co-operate in organising a "University of the Air" for serious planned adult education'.[41] The proposal was supported by Harold Wilson in a speech in 1963, and subsequently by the Labour government; an advisory committee was set up, and the Open University received its charter in 1969. Twenty-five thousand students were enrolled for the first session in 1971, for courses which included correspondence assignments, television and radio programmes, weekend or short courses and a regionally organized system of tutorials. Developments in education since the war had not lessened the demand for adult education; the pressure for places in residential adult colleges, for example, was increasing, with a greater proportion of students receiving local authority grants and going on from the colleges to full-time higher education. Demand was strong for all kinds of correspondence courses and university extramural courses, especially from women seeking preliminary qualifications. The demand for adult education coincided also with the growing demand for books. The number of titles published annually was increasing, and a rapidly rising percentage of book sales was of paperbacks. The public library service, which had been expanding throughout the century, was more fully co-ordinated under a Public Libraries and Museums Act of 1964. The pattern of library provision included the National Central

Library (created as the Central Library for Students in 1916 and becoming the NCL in 1930) as an agent of inter-library loans and the National Lending Library for Science and Technology (created in 1961); it included the large public library, with its reading and reference rooms, the small branch library and the travelling van. It also included the university and college library, the substantial school library and the reading corner. Since the Second World War libraries in general had been conceived of increasingly as an educational service, and the important role of the library within the educational system had been defined more explicitly.

At the same time as these developments, part-time education for employees below the age of eighteen was also growing; under an Industrial Training Act in 1964 industrial training boards were created for different industries to develop industrial training, and the proportion of young employees on day release rose in the late 1960s. One of the salient features of English education in the 1960s was, in fact, the enormous increase in further education; the number of full-time teachers in this sector in England and Wales rose from just over 15,000 in 1958 to some 50,000 in 1970.

The 1960s: secondary education

Questions of educational opportunity had their most strident public discussion in the 1960s in terms of secondary education, and specifically of comprehensive schools. Of the 3 million or so pupils in maintained secondary schools in the early 1960s some quarter of a million were in non-selective schools. In 1962 there were 106 comprehensive schools, maintained by 23 local education authorities (more than 100 authorities had none). 'England as a whole', wrote Robin Pedley in that year, 'has barely scratched the surface of this problem.'[42] Leicestershire's scheme of re-organization, which began to be implemented in parts of the county in 1957, was attracting attention as a relatively simple way of adapting existing schools to a new comprehensive pattern: all children in an area attended a junior high school from eleven to fourteen, and then either stayed at the school until the leaving age or transferred to the senior grammar school, according to the parents' choice. Great interest centred on Leicestershire's two-tier scheme, and on London's all-through comprehensive schools, which in the mid-1960s ranged in size from under 700 to nearly 2,000 pupils.

The Labour Party nationally was won over to the idea of comprehensive schools in the mid-1960s. In 1965 the Labour government announced plans 'to end selection at eleven plus and to eliminate separatism in secondary education'; local education authorities which had not done so were to submit plans 'for reorganizing secondary education in their areas on comprehensive lines'. Circular 10/65 in which the Department of Education and Science issued their instructions described six main forms of comprehensive organization and left it to local authorities to select their preferred pattern (the six included schools for 11- to 18-year-olds, two-tier schemes, and schemes which used 'middle schools' or sixth-form colleges). During the lifetime of the Labour government the majority of local authorities adopted reorganization schemes of one kind or another, in some areas against a background of pronounced controversy, disputes between parents and local councils, and marches and protests. Support for the comprehensive idea was also increasing in the Conservative Party; the Conservative government elected in 1970 withdrew circular 10/65, but the movement towards reorganization was not halted. By 1970 115 authorities had had reorganiza-

Sixth-form discussion

tion plans approved for all or most of their areas (those of thirteen authorities had been rejected, and ten authorities had so far refused to respond to the requirements under 10/65). By 1970 even authorities which had embarked reluctantly on reorganization found it inexpedient to turn back.

Support for an opposition to complete comprehensive reorganization had continued along established lines. Its opponents argued that by removing the choice of schools comprehensive education undermined freedom, and by eliminating the grammar school it did away with a known tradition of academic excellence; that it substituted schools which tended to be too large, and in which brighter children were penalized; and that secondary modern schools had not yet been given a fair chance. Quintin Hogg said in Parliament, for example, that

> If Labour members would go and study what was being done in good secondary modern schools they would not find a lot of pupils biting their nails in frustration because they had failed the 11-plus. The pleasant noise of the banging of metal and the sawing of wood would greet their ears. The smell of a cooking meal, produced with expensive equipment, would come out of the front door to greet them. They would find that boys and girls were getting an education tailor-made for their bents and requirements.[43]

The supporters of comprehensive education argued in general that it undermined privilege and inequality, and that comprehensive schools could provide broader and more flexible courses and opportunities, including for the more able pupils. The record of the comprehensive schools in GCE examinations and university entrance began to come under close scrutiny.

Some local authorities opted for modified versions of the Leicestershire scheme, with a choice of school at thirteen or fourteen. The development of middle schools, with transfer at nine and thirteen, was an important innovation in English education. Bradford, for example, developed the concept with new approaches to school organization and timetables. The design for Delf Hill School, Bradford, assumed that children would be in groups of 100 or so (with a number of teachers) for their home 'base', where they could 'meet together, keep their clothes and belongings, and display their work. Throughout the day, however, it is expected that the pupils will be working partly in their own centres, partly elsewhere.' There would be a changing pattern of groups, and children would spend approximate percentages of time in different broad areas of activity.[44] The middle schools, it was evident, would be able to combine some of the features of the more open primary schools (flexible architecture and curricula and activity methods) with new approaches to subjects in the curriculum (there were mathematics and science projects, for example, which fitted into such schemes).

In 1971 there were some 1,300 comprehensive schools in England and Wales taking about 35 per cent of the secondary age group: the greatest increase in numbers had come some two to four years after circular 10/65. The percentage of new comprehensive schools of an all-through type (from eleven or twelve to eighteen) fell from the early 1960s, although these still formed the main block of comprehensive schools – in 1968 well over half were of this kind.[45] The pattern of comprehensive organization was changing markedly from that of the large, pioneer all-through schools – of London, for example. More than half of the comprehensive schools were at this point in time, however, coexisting and competing with grammar schools for their intake. 'Genuine comprehensive schools', it was being pointed out, 'are hard to organize where coexistence or creaming takes place.' The problem was most acute in urban areas which retained grammar schools, a policy which 'inevitably forces certain comprehensive schools into a second-class rôle'.[46]

One of the most important educational problems highlighted by the comprehensive schools was streaming. In the early comprehensive schools it was used explicitly to reflect within the school the situation in the selective system: the Anglesey schools arranged 'internal tests for the newly-arrived pupils . . . to grade the pupils in order of ability', and the early comprehensive schools in London 'all used the external selection test to assist them in classifying incoming pupils'.[47] The case against streaming – in the junior school as well as the comprehensive school – began to be expressed most strongly from 1955, and by 1963 it could be said that 'there was now universal interest in the question, if not universal agreement about it'.[48] In many comprehensive schools in the 1960s the tendency was to provide common courses for the first two years and postpone the streaming process. 'Setting' and the redistribution of children in a variety of ways for different subjects and activities was a common feature of the schools. Non-streaming in the junior school became an important campaign in the late 1960s. Streaming, its opponents generally argued, was as socially determined as selection; a sociological study at the end of the 1960s indicated that in a situation of streaming there was 'no *evidence* that comprehensive education contributes to the breaking down of the barriers of social class which still divide adults and children alike'.[49]

Comprehensive schools were one of the factors which stimulated the demand for education beyond the school leaving age in the 1960s. By 1970, for example, over 15 per cent of 17-year-olds were at school, by comparison with 12 per cent in 1962. In this as in other aspects of education there were regional differences which reflected different levels of prosperity and opportunity: of children who were thirteen in 1960, in the northern region 8·5 per cent were still at school at the age of seventeen, whereas in the south-eastern region the figure was 13·8. Sixth forms were growing steadily. Although there were some local plans to separate off sixth formers in sixth-form colleges (including a plan at Croydon in the mid-1950s), only a few had materialized by the end of the 1960s. Sixth forms were more widely being provided with separate facilities of a new kind: sixth-form club rooms and other facilities in some schools made the prospect of staying on more attractive, and indicated a new approach to the education of the older adolescent. It is important to remember, however, that the percentage of 17-year-olds still at school varied enormously at the beginning of the 1970s from region to region (most of the boroughs with the highest percentages were in London, and with the lowest percentages in the north).

The recasting of the pattern of secondary education involved radical new approaches to the curriculum, associated, for example, with the Nuffield Foundation and the Newsom Report. The Nuffield Science Teaching Project, launched in 1962, resulted in O- and A-level materials of a new kind. The science projects for junior and secondary schools were intended, through greater practical investigation, to improve the approach to school science. 'What we've tried to do', said the organizer of the 5–13 Mathematics Project, 'is to produce, not bibles, texts or package deals, but guides.'[50] This was true of the science materials, produced after extensive consultation with and trials by practising teachers. The materials included in some cases films, background readers and guides to apparatus, and the projects led to negotiations with examining boards for a new type of examination.

The Newsom Report also pressed in 1963 for new approaches to courses for children who would not be taking GCE. More broadly based courses for less able children, a search for 'outgoing' approaches, inquiry methods which took starting points in the modern world and the children's experience, and the need to review the studies (including vocational ones) of the older children, especially when the school leaving age was raised to sixteen – all these were Newsom demands.[51] Curriculum developments which followed in this spirit included a Nuffield project in secondary science for non-GCE children, using inquiry methods in association with a series of relevant themes, such as the 'interdependence of living things' and 'harnessing energy'.

Curriculum developments ran parallel with a new departure in secondary-school examinations. The General Certificate of Education had been introduced in 1951 and became established as an external examination run by the different examining boards (there had been hopes that it would gradually became an internal, teacher-controlled examination). When the secondary modern schools began to find their 'reserves of ability' they also turned to existing examinations, including the GCE. The Beloe Committee, set up in 1958 to look at secondary-school examinations other than the GCE, reported two years later in favour of a new examination for candidates 'of a reasonably high competence and ability at a level somewhat below that of GCE'. Basic to its recommendations was that 'the teachers in the schools using the examinations must have a major role in operating them and shaping their policy'.[52] It was on this basis that the Certificate of Secondary Education was introduced in 1965, offering schools three different 'modes' of examining: an examination based on a syllabus prepared by the subject panel of the regional board; an external examination based on a school's own syllabus; an internal examination (externally moderated) based on a school's own syllabus. Although mode three of the CSE gave the teachers greatest control over the examination, in all three cases they had a new role to play. Each of the fourteen regional boards (and their respective examination committees and subject panels) was under the control of serving teachers from the schools taking part. From the outset pressures began to be exerted to extend this type of examining and do away with the

GCE. *The Times Educational Supplement*, however, explained why it thought further change undesirable:

> The whole tradition of the grammar school is towards a formal examination, academic in content and arranged on established lines. This is in keeping with the functions of the grammar school . . . the grammar schools have no great reputation for reform. They are essentially conservative institutions . . . We need therefore to reaffirm at this time that the Certificate of Secondary Education is meant essentially for the secondary modern schools and is to be planned for them alone.[53]

New approaches to examinations and the curriculum gave rise to the Schools Council for the Curriculum and Examinations. The creation of the Schools Council (the first initiative for which was taken by the Ministry of Education in the form of a curriculum study group in 1962) was an outstanding event in English education in the 1960s. From 1964 it brought together representatives of teachers, all branches of higher education, the inspectorate and the local education authorities; it took over the functions of the existing Secondary School Examinations Council and set out to 'secure a happier marriage than in the past between the actual work of the schools . . . and the examinations which . . . can all too easily stand in the way of necessary innovation'.[54] It initiated new schemes of work connected with, for example, the future raising of the school leaving age; it continued the momentum of curriculum development inaugurated by the Nuffield Foundation, and launched new development projects jointly with it – for example, a humanities project, begun in 1967. In 1971 one of its examinations bulletins (No 23) put forward the case for a common system of examining at 16-plus by 1975, ending the separate GCE and CSE examinations. The establishment of the Schools Council as a basis for a wide range of educational initiatives was, thought Sir William Alexander, secretary of the Association of Education Committees, the most important development in education in his lifetime.[55]

Out of the curriculum developments, especially in mathematics and junior science, grew teachers' centres (nearly 500 by 1971) where teachers could, often for the first time, meet locally to discuss developments in the teaching of their subjects; a new pattern of professional relationships was inaugurated. Consultations over the CSE had the same effect. In the classroom teachers were also being involved in changes. New teaching techniques were being rapidly evolved in the sixties, in part on the basis of research by experimental psychologists. Such work as that of E. S. Thorndike in the United States at the turn of the century had its major practical repercussions only after the Second World War; this and other work on 'positive reinforcement' in stimulus-response (S-R) learning situations, especially by B. F. Skinner at Harvard in the 1950s, led to the development of teaching machines. Programmed learning was to become a serious development in the 1960s, though only a tiny percentage of British schools were as yet using it. More widespread in the sixties were language laboratories; introduced for the first time in 1962, there were some 1,500 in British schools by the end of the 1960s. Overhead, closed-loop and slide projectors, record players, tape recorders, television sets (including closed circuit television) and other learning resources became considerably more widespread in schools in the sixties. Educational programmes on radio and television became more widely used in schools. Some secondary schools were acquiring computer terminals. The importance of the new techniques, as of the new curriculum developments, lay in the challenge they presented to teachers, either to justify existing practices or to adopt or modify new ones.

Educational innovation had taken on a new shape. Once a question primarily of the individual innovator outside publicly financed education, it was now also an institutionalized process with established procedures, but also with opportunities in some – though by no means all – cases for teachers in state schools to take part in national, local or individual innovatory schemes. The tradition of 'progressive' independent schools remained, but there were marked differences between the innovations in progressive schools, based on precise theories of human personality and behaviour and conducted in a closed community, and those in the state system, having to respond to a profoundly different range of internal and external pressures and problems. There were limits to the extent of experimentation possible in maintained schools, but the traditions of the progressive educators were being taken up in some parts of the state system more extensively in the sixties than ever before.

Educational opportunity in the 1960s was being seen in terms of the quality and suitability of education as well as the structure of the system. It was being assessed in relation to the likelihood of a child's staying on at school beyond the age of fifteen, and the differences in academic performance and access to higher education that were attributable to social class and regional differences. Like the Robbins Report, sociologists continued in the sixties to point to the absence 'of sufficient informed and persistent action to compensate for built-in inequalities of conditions, attitudes and behaviour'. They emphasized the likelihood that children living in poor housing conditions would attend schools with a poor record of, for example, 11-plus successes, and would find themselves 'allocated to the lower streams at school and their school performance will tend to conform accordingly. In general they are less likely to receive encouragement from their parents. Between the ages of 8 and 11 years, the working class and middle class children will thus tend to grow further apart in operational ability.'[56] The survey on the basis of which these comments were made went on to look at the same children when they reached secondary schools. It came to the conclusion (in 1968) that 'the social class differences in educational opportunity which were considerable at the primary school stage have increased at the secondary and extend now to pupils of high ability. Thus nearly half the lower manual working class pupils of high ability have left school before they are sixteen and a half years.'[57] It was the attempt not just to describe but to explain the difficulties of working-class children in 'operational ability' that gave prominence to the work of Basil Bernstein from the late 1950s. Bernstein analysed these difficulties in terms of the social determinants of forms of language available to children in different social contexts:

> What is the most important single factor in a boy's history, which generates this consistency of emotional and intellectual behaviour in the learning situation? . . . How does the boy become like this and what is the main agency through which this becoming is facilitated and reinforced? I suggest that forms of spoken language induce in their learning orientations to particular orders of learning, and condition different dimensions of relevance.[58]

Bernstein's emphasis on the different language codes of children from different backgrounds gave sociology in the 1960s an interest in the child's relationship with his teachers, in his total educational behaviour, which could be analysed within the classroom and the family, and could help to explain the functioning of interconnected educational and social processes.

At the same time as the instruments for improving educational opportunities were being developed in and for schools, the sociologists were explaining why and how important sections of the population were unable to take full advantage of them.

Educational priorities

Change has always to be kept in perspective. In very many schools the developments of the 1950s and 1960s made little or no impression. Newly trained teachers had to trim enthusiasms to established situations. There were still primary schools without indoor lavatories, teachers without equipment, and schools of all kinds in old and unsuitable buildings. Attitudes do not change uniformly or overnight. A book which in 1968 traced the background of 'children in distress' described those schools where children 'seem to shed their distress the moment they cross the threshold', but others 'where it is still possible for a visitor to be told in a voice audible to the whole class, "These are our 11 + failures" ', and which take the view that 'a child's social background is not their concern'.[59]

Social priorities are established in the framework of economic possibility and the state of political and public opinion. The uncertainties of the British economy in the 1960s were accompanied by heightened public controversy about educational and social policy. Political and social ideals were being re-examined under new pressures. The political radicalisms and protest movements of the late 1950s and 1960s were based not only on grievances connected with foreign policy, but also on concerns about social priorities, child poverty, neglect of the aged, antiquated hospitals, and the continued underprivilege of low-income and immigrant groups in the affluent society. The evidence of underprivilege went alongside the evidence of its distribution. Regional differences in education had been shown up persistently in the statistics but attracted little attention. They were most forcefully analysed in 1969 by Taylor and Ayres in a discussion of divergent standards of living and educational opportunity between regions. The 'two nations' of the nineteenth century, it was suggested, still existed in terms of educational opportunities in the second half of the twentieth century:

> One is of children living in new or expanding areas with favourable environments, attending well equipped and well staffed schools. The other nation consists of generations of children conditioned by obsolete and inefficient schools; they are children who come from homes whose standards and environment are as deplorable as those of their schools . . . What is significant and alarming for the future of our society is the concentration in large areas, principally located in the three northern regions, of children so handicapped in comparison with more fortunate children elsewhere that the majority will fail to achieve their potential intellectual and aesthetic development. It cannot be doubted that the marked regional differentiation in the provision of new schools is increasing the gap between the two nations.

In spite of great efforts by the local authorities in the northern region (Cumberland, Durham, Northumberland and the North Riding of Yorkshire), and increased government support in the late 1960s, the region remained disadvantaged in its school provision. The region was still, it was reported in 1970, 'suffering from the aftermath of the 1920s and 1930s, when Public Assistance expenditure imposed such heavy demands on the very limited resources available . . . the end of the last war found these authorities starting the task of reconstruction from a base-line well behind many other parts of the country'.[60]

Just as educational deprivation measured in terms of social class was a major feature of educational discussion in the late 1950s and 1960s, so its measurement in terms of regional differences became a major issue in the late 1960s and early 1970s. The Plowden Report and the establishment of educational priority areas led, as we shall see, to an increasing interest in the nature of regional deprivation. Proposals for local government reform in the early 1970s included the creation in some regions of relatively small educational authorities; as Sir Alec Clegg pointed out, the north would under the new arrangements have all but four of the twenty smallest districts and all but two of the twenty poorest. Such a distribution he attributed

> either to crass and unpardonable ignorance or to political malevolence of a high order . . . It is as if those in high places had

said: 'We know exactly which social conditions do the most educational harm. Let us make certain that, in the future, the authorities into which these conditions are most densely concentrated are both small and poor.'[61]

These areas tended to be those with the highest proportion of children having free meals, the highest unemployment levels, the poorest housing conditions. Small educational authorities in these areas could not, it was argued by the critics, deploy specialist staff and resources as well as wealthier or larger authorities could do; they could not build or improve schools or try out new ideas to the same extent.[62] Echoing the words of those most involved in the analysis, even newspapers like the *Guardian* could declare that 'there are two nations within schools', two nations which had a geographical as well as a social class profile.[63] The chances of a child still being at school at seventeen, his educational and social life chances in general, were still considerably affected by his home and the region in which he lived.

Although radical politics in many of its forms were concerned with these aspects of educational and social deprivation, youth militancy in the 1960s was concerned less with these than with the values of youth itself and of authority. The youth culture, which in one form was concerned with fashionable clothing, gramophone records and motorcycles, was in another form concerned to reject middle-class or adult or authoritarian values. In terms of education Sir Edward Boyle forecast in 1966 that

> we are moving into a period when the student body is going to become increasingly . . . an estate of the university realm. As 'shadow' Secretary of State for Education I have been struck by the very large number of official or semi-official representations which have been made to me by student organisations. They are going to 'ask the reason why' increasingly often, and will demand to be given proper answers.[64]

Protest and conflict, from the London School of Economics to the new universities, from the polytechnics to the schools of art, were concerned in the late 1960s with such questions as student representation on the organs of government, the nature of courses and examinations, library facilities and the appointment of principals. The strike, the sit-in and the demonstration reached a crescendo in 1967–8 as students, and in some cases schoolchildren, publicly 'asked the reason why'.

The schools themselves were being increasingly seen as an instrument for tackling social problems causing concern. Attempts were being made at the end of the sixties to strengthen the role of the school in relation to such problems as sexual morality and race relations, smoking and drugs. There was a sentiment, strongly expressed by English teachers, for example, and in the Crowther Report and in humanities and social studies projects, that the schools should act as a countervailing force to the mass media.

Throughout the history of education, as we have seen, the nature and distribution of reading material have been clues to the extent and use of literacy. The growth of the popular press has been an important adjunct to the story of education. The expansion of the cinema and radio in the twenties and thirties were further relevant developments. The rapid spread of television in the fifties and sixties, however, while continuing the development of the mass media, was quite new in its direct importance to education. Not only did it offer a new tool and technology which could be, and was, adapted to educational purposes, it affected the consciousness of children and the situation in the classroom in a way which no other medium of mass culture had done. Television was in these decades becoming a ubiquitous experience for schoolchildren, helping to mould their musical tastes, their heroes, their aspirations and their language. It was an experience which children brought with them into the classroom, and of which teachers were made persistently aware. It was something in the children's culture to which education was finding it necessary to respond. The impact of television, new popular publications for young teenagers, popular music and all-pervasive advertising was felt in the classroom to an extent that had not been true of comics or the radio in the 1930s.

If the priorities of the 1950s and early 1960s were mainly those of secondary and higher education, from the late 1960s increasing priority was attached to primary education. The traditions of progressive methods in English primary schools had been strengthened after the war, with the construction of imaginative primary buildings in some areas, and the evolution of new methods and emphases in reading, movement and even, from the early 1960s, the teaching of modern languages. At the end of the 1950s Sir James Pitman and others launched the Initial Teaching Alphabet, which in the 1960s gained support among many infant

Student demonstration at LSE, 1970

Primary class of forty-one children

teachers.[65] From the late 1950s a new range of equipment and techniques began to come into the primary schools, especially for mathematics teaching. From the 1950s the interest in children's creative writing spread widely in schools. New approaches to the primary school timetable, open-plan school designs, experiments with family grouping, the increasing abandonment of fixed rows of desks, the conception of rooms as workrooms rather than classrooms – all of these were growing features of primary education in the 1950s and 1960s.

In the 1960s there were over 4 million children in primary schools, the largest number in schools with junior and infant departments, and somewhat smaller numbers in separate infant and junior schools. One of the main struggles in post-war primary education was to reduce the size of classes. Classes with fifty or more children were common after the war (there were still over 1,500 of them in 1950). The target of a maximum of forty children in a primary class was being more widely achieved, but the proportion of classes with more than forty pupils was nearly 10 per cent for most of the 1960s. A sharp improvement in the last two years of the decade, however, brought the figure down to just over 3 per cent – one of the most important gains in primary education in recent decades. Pressure to set a target of thirty for primary as well as secondary-school classes began to mount, notably from the National Union of Teachers. The very concept of a 'class' was at the same time, it must be remembered, being challenged from some directions: flexibility was becoming as important as size, and open-plan design and new approaches to activity and grouping in the primary school altered the framework within which the class size had traditionally been discussed. At the heart of the discussion remained, however, the ability of schools to achieve more generous standards of staffing.

A stimulus for further change in primary schools was given by the publication in 1967 of the Plowden Report on *Children and their Primary Schools*. The basic philosophy of the report was one of controlled progressivism, and was influenced by research into child development, including that of Piaget. It favoured a balance of individual and class work, and preferred a transfer age of twelve or thirteen to that of eleven, thus encouraging the growth of interest in middle schools. The committee's most far-reaching contribution was in connection with the relationship between the primary school and the home and social background. It recalled that the Crowther, Robbins and other reports had 'produced evidence that shows how closely associated are social circumstances and academic achievement. We have been able to set on foot research which has suggested that the most vital factor in a child's home is the attitude to school, and all that goes on there, of his mother and father.' The committee put forward a programme for stronger contacts between schools and parents: 'it has long been recognised that education is concerned with the whole man; henceforth it must be concerned with the whole family.' Influencing the child to learn and the family to lend support was obviously closely related to problems of social circumstances. The report was concerned in detail with those areas which 'have for generations been starved of new schools, new houses and new investment of every kind'. The educational priority areas, as the committee called them, were deprived areas whose main educational need was 'perfectly normal, good primary schools alive with experience from which children of all kinds can benefit'. What was needed to solve this problem was 'a new distribution of educational resources'.[66]

An educational priority area school, wrote the director of the

EPA project in Liverpool, was characteristically an old school: schools in these areas

> stand as crumbling monuments to the mid-nineteenth century era of grants-in-aid to Church schools; many celebrate all too fittingly the centenary of the 1870 Education Act. Despite great efforts by teachers and local authorities alike, too many of these schools are bleak, unwelcoming, gaunt and unserviceable, that is, in architectural and technical terms. The teachers work in conditions that would drive the most inoffensive and mild-mannered clerk to militancy for returns that a lot of self-respecting dockers would scoff at.[67]

Areas which qualified for EPA status were given special financial aid (£16 million for a special building programme in 1968, for example). One of the aims was to develop ways of establishing closer links, along Plowden lines, between school, home and community. 'Community school' projects in Liverpool and Deptford, for example, sought to bring the parent ('borne down by the strenuous pressures of a grim urban existence, desperately wondering what he can possibly do to help his children')[68] into active association with the life of the school. Attempts were made to mould the teaching schemes in such schools to the realities of urban life, to local conditions, to the social life of the children and their families.

Educational priorities were also affected in the 1960s by the problem in some areas of large numbers of immigrant children. Although the annual number of immigrants rose from a few thousand at the beginning of the 1950s to 42,000 in 1955, it was in the early 1960s that the inflow of immigrants had its main impact on education. There were some 46,000 immigrant children in primary schools in 1961, and over 100,000 in 1966 (the respective numbers in secondary schools were 33,000 and 49,000). It was from about 1961 that primary schools in the areas of main immigrant concentration had to face most seriously the problems of classes with a substantial number of immigrant children, and the most serious need in areas with non-English-speaking immigrants was to provide special facilities for learning English. Between 1966 and 1970 the total number of immigrant children in all schools of England and Wales doubled, to over 250,000, but the proportion with 'serious inadequacies of English' declined from 25 to 16 per cent.[69] The allocation of priorities in the

1960s had to take account of the problems of the concentration in some towns and regions of groups of immigrant children, with different backgrounds, cultures and languages. By the beginning of the 1970s authorities with immigrant populations had been able to acquire more than 3,000 additional teachers, financed under an Act of 1966 which supported extra staff to meet the needs of immigrant pupils.

The search to define educational priorities, influenced by economic fortunes and more directly than ever before by changes of dominant political ideology, ranged more widely in the 1960s than these areas of comprehensive organization, primary-school buildings, deprived areas and immigrant populations. It also embraced, for example, the public and direct grant schools, science teaching at school and university, questions of health, the school leaving age and the training of teachers. Competition for resources was intense, and likely to become more so whenever economic difficulties coincided with developments which involved new buildings, expensive re-equipment or other capital expenditure. Educational technology, for example, was particularly vulnerable to such constraints at a time when, in the 1960s, it had important new contributions to offer.

The Labour Party's long-standing uncertainties about the future of the independent schools led the Labour government to set up a Public Schools Commission, whose first report appeared in 1968 (a second report, on independent day schools and direct grant schools, appeared two years later). The committee pointed to post-war changes in the public schools, including their greater commitment to academic success. In recent years, the committee explained

> public schools have been changing their assumptions and aims, diversifying and opening up their culture. The change of emphasis to academic achievement, a decline in the importance of team games, a greater concern for the arts, and some dismantling of the complex disciplinary machine, are all, in many schools, conspicuous. Nevertheless . . . their activities are based on the assumptions and aspirations of the British middle class, from which their pupils come and upon which their fees depend.

About the continued relationship between the public schools and social privilege there was no doubt. A list compiled in 1964, for example, showed the percentage of posts filled by people with a public-school education; they included:[70]

	per cent
Conservative cabinet (1964)	87
judges (1956)	76
Conservative MPs (1964)	76
ambassadors (1953)	70
lieutenants general and above (1953)	70
bishops (1953)	66
chief executives in 100 largest firms (1963)	64
civil servants above assistant secretary (1950)	59
all city directors (1958)	47
Labour cabinet (1964)	35

The Public Schools Commission, like the earlier Fleming Committee, wished to see the schools integrated with the public system, but recommended that considerably more than 25 per cent of the schools' places should be available to children supported by public funds: 'they should be there in large numbers if they came at all'. A radical new departure in the commission's proposals was its definition of 'boarding need' – the criterion by which children should be selected for this kind of education. 'Need' could be either social or academic: in the former category were children 'of adverse home or family conditions', and in the latter were children who, for one reason or another, could not obtain locally an education suited to their needs. The arrangements (to be worked out school by school) should enable children to be admitted at an ability level 'corresponding with that required for courses leading to the Certificate of Secondary Education', or even below this level: 'very few children with boarding need should be excluded from the opportunity of a place at an integrated school on grounds of low academic ability'. A basic aim of the commission was to end the 'divisive influence' of the independent schools by making more than half of their places available not merely to pupils from maintained schools, but to pupils who were either socially and educationally deprived or from difficult home backgrounds.

The commission's second report recommended that direct grant and independent day schools should become comprehensive schools of one kind or another, financed through a School Grants Committee, while retaining essentially the same form of government; those schools which did not wish to participate should become independent.[71] No action was taken to implement either of the reports. In 1971 the Conservative government increased grants to direct grant schools to enable them to reduce fees (and at the same time made it easier for parents to qualify for remission of fees). The quality of education at these schools, said the secretary of state for education and science, was excellent, and 'we should concentrate on keeping what is good and not destroying it'.[72] The previous Labour government had, in fact, reduced the grant to direct grant schools; in the allocation of resources for this purpose, and more clearly, as we shall see, in the case of school milk and meals, the impact of political priorities on education was at its most obvious.

Considerable attention was given in the late 1960s to the position of science in schools. The Federation of British Industries was worried in the mid-sixties by the inability of industry to recruit science and technology students in the same proportion as were their competitors (in 1962 the figure was 36 per cent for Britain, 68 per cent for West Germany and 49 per cent for the United States). After the implementation of the Robbins proposals just over a third of the extra university places were in science and technology – instead of the two-thirds proposed; at the same time a large number of the places in science and technology were unfilled.[73] The Dainton Committee, set up in 1965, produced three years later its *Enquiry into the Flow of Candidates in Science and Technology into Higher Education*, which analysed the so-called swing from science in the schools and its implications. Its main concern was with the factors which influenced the choice for or against science, a major one of which was the structure of school courses. The report proposed the broadening of sixth-form studies so as to postpone 'irreversible decisions for or against science, engineering and technology . . . as late as possible'. It recommended that all pupils should normally study mathematics till they left school, and stressed the 'urgent need more rapidly to infuse breadth, humanity, and up-to-dateness into the science curriculum and its teaching'.[74] There were indications by the end of the decade that support for science in schools and universities was beginning to increase; greater support was being lent by bodies such as the Schools Council, the Royal Society and research foundations, to investigating and publicizing possible improvements in the teaching of science at all levels. The swing

back to science was reflected in an increased percentage of O-
and A-level candidates with a science bias at the end of the
1960s.

Among priorities still to be implemented at the beginning of
the 1970s there were some that had been agreed upon decades
previously. The school leaving age of sixteen, for example, had
been acknowledged in 1938 by the Spens Committee as inevitable, accepted for implementation by the 1944 Act when practicable, re-emphasized as a major priority by the Crowther Report,
finally fixed for 1970–1 by a Labour government and then postponed to 1972 by the same government for economic reasons. A
long-standing demand for an all-trained teaching profession had
been reaffirmed by the Newsom Report in 1963, which proposed
that 'a training requirement for graduates should be introduced
at the earliest practicable moment'.[75] It was decided in 1969
that no one graduating after January 1970 would be accepted as a
teacher in a maintained primary school without a course of professional training, and the same would apply in secondary schools
after January 1974; this decision was part of a pattern of developments in teacher education from the mid-1960s, which included
the increasing number of students taking the BEd degree (there
were some 1,500 candidates in 1969 and 3,000 in 1971), the
institution by a number of universities of four-year concurrent
courses leading to a degree and a teaching qualification, and
widespread anxiety about the structure and content of courses of
teacher education. The future pattern of teacher education was
one of the most prominent problems in education at the beginning of the 1970s, and after an attempt by the Labour government to investigate it through the existing machinery, the James
Committee was appointed by its successor in 1971 to conduct an
inquiry. Its report on *Teacher Education and Training* the following year, in recommending a restructuring of the pattern of
general education and professional training for the future teacher,
proposed a system whereby all entrants to the profession would be
graduates. It proposed new regional organization for the education of teachers, an initial two-year diploma course of a general
nature for all students in colleges of education, and a course of
professional training which would incorporate what had previously been the probationary year, and which would now be
carried out in association with an appropriate professional centre.
The report for the first time built into a set of proposals about the

training of teachers a much-emphasized proposal for regular in-service training to be seen as an integral part of a teacher's continuing education. The search for educational expansion and the proper distribution of educational priorities had by the beginning of the 1970s given greater weight to the problems of improving the quality of teacher education and of ensuring constant contact between the serving teacher and innovation and advance in his academic and professional spheres of interest. A government white paper, *Education: a framework for expansion*, issued at the end of 1972, included among its proposals support for three-year BEd degrees and an all-graduate profession, and substantial advances in in-service training, including during the new 'induction' year. This period ended, therefore, with a programme for important advances in teacher education, including a commitment to a transition to an all-graduate profession – a commitment cemented in 1972 by the James Committee and the white paper.

Another long-agreed field of action was nursery education. Nursery school expansion had been slow since the beginning of the century, when Margaret McMillan in particular had campaigned for it, and since local authorities were empowered to provide it under the 1918 Act. Some authorities made generous provision, others made none. Economic difficulties held back progress with nursery schools more than with schools for children of compulsory school age, and the percentage of children under five in schools and nurseries barely increased between the 1930s and 1960s. From 1960 local authorities were, in fact, officially discouraged from increasing their expenditure on nursery education. Demands for wider nursery provision came in the 1960s from married women workers with young families (notably teachers) and from the educational priority areas. Under an urban aid programme inaugurated in 1968, local authorities with the greatest need were allocated special grants to provide nursery classes in underprivileged areas. The first phase of the urban aid programme was concerned exclusively with improving amenities for very young children. Although nursery-school provision was improved, it remained fragmentary. The possibility of a coherent development of pre-school provision took shape, however, in 1972. The Conservative government's white paper on education at the end of 1972 contained as its most radical proposal the systematic development of preschool education for the children of all parents wishing to make use of it. This commitment was the result of a long campaign, a growing demand from working mothers, and the experience of the educational priority areas. The hesitant approach to nursery education seemed at this point to have given way to an official endorsement of growth.

The search for educational priorities at the beginning of the 1970s involved the still acutely controversial questions of comprehensive schools. These included not only the question of secondary organization in general, but also that of finance for new buildings, and that of the internal organization of schools – mainly streaming, but also such matters as houses and year groups, and the organization of sixth-form studies. The defeat in 1970 of a Labour government committed to eventual complete comprehensive reorganization did not, as we have seen, entirely halt the process. Even some Conservative-controlled authorities subsequently made decisions to go comprehensive (the London borough of Sutton, for example, in January 1972). A small number of authorities reversed previous decisions and decided to retain their grammar schools, and the secretary for education and science intervened in some cases to prevent the amalgamation of grammar schools into comprehensive schemes – even, as in the instance of Surrey, against the pro-comprehensive decision of a Conservative-controlled local authority.

Child health and welfare re-established themselves as issues of educational politics and priorities, mainly in 1970, when the new Conservative government decided both to increase charges for school meals and to withdraw free milk (with exceptions) in primary schools the following year. The proportion of children staying for school dinners fell in 1970 after charges were raised by the government (the percentage had been steadily rising in the 1960s, from an average of 52 per cent in 1960 to 70 per cent in 1969). The percentage of free dinners (to children of poorer families) had risen in the 1960s, from 6·7 per cent in 1961 to 12·3 per cent at the end of the decade. The rise in the price of school meals from 9p to 12p in 1971 coincided with a marked rise in unemployment; as a result the numbers of children staying for school dinners fell, and the numbers having free meals rose from 575,000 in the autumn of 1970 to 733,000 a year later.

The government also withdrew milk from 1971 except for children under eight or in special schools or for whom it was recommended on medical grounds. The improvement in child

health in the twentieth century had made such a decision argu-
able, but the wisdom of the decision was widely challenged,
including by the NUT; some local authorities defied the government and refused to discontinue free milk. The government's
'blind ideological approach', as *The Times Educational Supplement*
described it,[76] was particularly resisted in the most disadvantaged areas (Merthyr Tydfil waged one of the most active
campaigns to continue free milk). Many boroughs sought to
frustrate the Education (Milk) Act by making it easier for
children to gain exemption on medical grounds, or by distributing
free or cheap alternatives (such as soup or hot chocolate).

Free milk and school meals (together with other welfare provisions) had undoubtedly contributed in preceding decades to
improved health among children, especially in the most deprived
areas. In pointing out the advantages that had accrued from this
public policy an analysis of the situation in the 1960s had concluded that school meals and milk 'are here to stay . . . It is now
firmly accepted that the child has a *right* to milk and a midday
meal at school.'[77] At the beginning of the following decade this
'right' was challenged in a search for a different allocation of
resources and priorities, under a different political light. The
government which took this decision also launched a five-year
building programme for primary schools to begin in 1972, and
intended to replace or bring up to date some 500 schools, mostly
built in the nineteenth century. Since primary education had been
less favoured than other sectors in the Labour government's
allocation of resources, and since the completion of comprehensive schemes was in many instances dependent on resources which
were not available, a different set of educational priorities was
clearly being established in this connection also. The decision on
a primary-school building programme was accompanied by a resistance to allocations for secondary-school building. A plan by the
Inner London education authority, for example, to build six new
secondary schools to replace Victorian schools in depressed areas
was vetoed by the secretary for education and science in 1971.

In the field of medical care a move towards the concentration
of resources was evident in the 1960s, with the trend towards
selective medical examinations, because, in the words of an
official comment, 'in the prevailing social circumstances the
devotion of so much time to the examination of a large number of
healthy children could not be justified when so many other

children needed help'. Between 1966 and 1968 school entrants and leavers continued to be medically examined, but half the local authorities had 'adopted a selective system during the pupil's time at school'.[78] The education of mentally and physically handicapped children was also conditioned by the availability of economic resources. To discuss in terms of an either/or situation the education of such children in special schools or under special guidance in ordinary schools, it was suggested in 1971, was unrealistic: 'both are needed . . . more children could be educated in ordinary schools if special classes were well organized, staffed with specially trained teachers and well supported by health, psychological and advisory services'.[79]

Within this whole context of the need properly to correlate research, resources and effort the social services themselves were being reorganized at the end of the 1960s, as a result of the recommendations of the Seebohm Report on *Local Authority and Allied Personal Social Services*. The reorganization proposed by this committee and embodied in legislation involved the creation of unified social service departments 'to provide better services for those in need because it will ensure a more co-ordinated and comprehensive approach to the problems of individuals and families and the community . . . it should attract more resources and use them more efficiently'.[80] Questions of the overall organization of educational and social services, the relationship between national and local government in decision-making processes, the methods of adjusting financial and social priorities, were of importance in the 1960s and on the agenda of public debate at the beginning of the 1970s. The reorganization of local government, for example, was being discussed from the late 1960s and incorporated in different forms in Labour and Conservative government proposals. Government proposals in 1971 for establishing large county authorities also split the new northern metropolitan counties into small educational districts. The new organization of local government was, as we have seen, highlighting the problems of the northern urban areas in particular.

Education, as we have seen, was becoming in many respects more exposed to the pressures of economic and political policy. It was directly affected by family size and population distribution. Social problems of many kinds were also resulting in a new involvement of students, parents and the public generally in educational controversy. In connection with new teaching methods, the reorganization of schools and educational politics, parents had become involved as never before in informal and organized activity relating to education. Closer relationships between parents and schools had been fostered since the war by parent–teacher associations and other ways of bringing parents into the life of schools (though resistance to such developments was still very great in many schools). Parents had themselves been responsible for setting up preschool play groups. Through the Confederation for the Advancement of State Education and other national and local bodies parents were playing a larger part in educational pressure groups (and CASE, for example, was pressing in the early 1970s for greater parent participation on school governing bodies and on education committees). Parents were more ready to respond to decisions affecting school organization, and to demonstrate on the streets for or against comprehensive-school plans. The expansion of education had impinged not only on national politics and economics, pupils and students, teachers and local authorities, but also on the aspirations of parents. Educational problems were woven more firmly than ever into the fabric of social life. Education was being interpreted more and more precisely as an agent of social mobility.

Continuities

In the second half of the twentieth century there were educational issues which demonstrated clearly the continuities from earlier decades and centuries – for example in the relationship between education and population, between education and dominant social values and objectives, education and social background and social status. Controversies about grammar-school standards or the comprehensive school were new versions of old conflicts, as were those around the position of the public school or the expansion of nursery education. Earlier traditions were present in campaigns for more open schools, more flexible school and timetable design, more integrated curricula and more humane approaches to teaching and learning. The versions of educational radicalism which we have seen in Robert Owen's *A New View of Society* or in Edmond Holmes's *What is and what might be*, in the work of Henry Armstrong or in the progressive-school movement, were present in new forms in fresh challenges to established school organization, established curricula and established educational objectives. They were present in attempts to establish 'free schools' or even to 'deschool' society. The continuities in education are ones not only of institutions and curriculum content, but also of the discussion of innovations and radical alternatives.

The discontinuities, of course, are also great, though any study of the process of change inevitably exaggerates their magnitude. Some themes which we have discussed at one point and abandoned at another have not necessarily ceased altogether to be of importance. Even the question of the extent and quality of literacy, which had ceased to be a major educational issue from the end of the nineteenth century, did not entirely disappear. In 1945, for instance, Cyril Burt conducted tests among adults to estimate the number of illiterates and semi-illiterates (the former being totally unable to read or write, and the latter able to make no effective use of these skills). His calculation was that the former numbered some 1·5–2 per cent of all adults, and the latter 15–20 per cent. Other tests at the end of the 1940s suggested 1 per cent for the former and under 4 per cent for the latter. The Newsom Report in the early 1960s said it had been 'particularly struck by the steady growth in the standards of literacy' since the war as measured in reading tests.[81] There was still controversy at the end of the 1960s about the increase or otherwise in reading ability, a debate which related at one end to the efficiency of different teaching and learning procedures, and at the other end to the impact of the mass media. There were still, however, in the early 1970s, agencies in some areas educating illiterate adults.

Examples of this kind illustrate merely the continuity of some educational problems, even if their dimensions and social context change profoundly. Other old institutions were in the second half of the twentieth century either disappearing or being transformed beyond recognition – the all-age school, the village school and the grammar school were some of these. The Department of Education and Science, summarizing developments in education in the 1960s, pointed to 'the unprecedented growth of public expenditure on education . . . the share of national resources devoted to the education service was five and a half per cent in 1967–68 compared with three and a half per cent of considerably smaller resources a decade earlier'.[82] The percentage was 6·2

London schoolchildren

in 1968–9. The annual percentage increase in educational
expenditure in the 1960s was about 10 per cent (and rose faster
than inflation). 'Ask any economist about Britain's last ten years',
commented one writer on this increase in 1971, 'and it's a sad
story. Ask someone with a professional interest in education, and
the answer is rather different.'[83] What the improvements had
failed to do was radically to alter the distribution of privilege
and underprivilege. 'The solution to the problem of the inner city
child eludes us', said Lady Plowden five years after the publication of her committee's report, 'and his failure to benefit from
what is provided by our educational system still remains.' The
problems were not just those of education: developments like the
educational priority areas had tried to face up to urban social
realities but, she pointed out, the problems were 'outstripping our
knowledge of how to deal with them' in EPA areas:

It is not the fault of the children that they fail to profit from their education. It is their family background and history, the environment in which that family lives, and the schools which often fail to give them a setting, and an education within that setting, in which they can succeed . . . The EPA parents are, like many of their children, frightened, angry, bewildered, and bored. They move in, to them, uncharted seas of officialdom, not understanding how the system works, what they can get if only they know how, not understanding what goes on in school, buffeted by forces completely outside their control: unemployment, slum clearance, housing policy, the economic condition of the country, regional inequality. . . . It is not only a problem of education. It is an economic problem, a town planning and housing and social problem . . . The contribution which the schools can make, and which must be made by the secondary as well as the primary schools, is to see that, in the name of education, they do not unjustly make failures of their pupils. To do this, they must be given the necessary resources, leadership, and vision. We still have a long way to go.[84]

The changes in the 1960s, and generally since the war, had certainly been unprecedented and substantial. It is unlikely that they will be seen to have been enough.

Notes

1 Statistics used in this chapter are not in general acknowledged separately. They are mostly taken from publications of the Ministry of Education and the Department of Education and Science – *Statistics of Education, Reports on Education* and annual reports, and also from the main committee and commission reports discussed in the text.

2 BOARD OF EDUCATION, *Curriculum and Examinations in Secondary Schools* (London, 1943; 1962 edition), p. viii.

3 MASS OBSERVATION, *War Begins at Home* (London, 1940), p. 296. For evacuation see also H. C. DENT, *Education in Transition* (London, 1944), chapters 1–2, and JOHN GRAVES, *Policy and Progress in Secondary Education* (London, 1943), chapter 23.

4 MASS OBSERVATION, *War Begins at Home*, pp. 305–11.

5 RICHARD LIVINGSTONE, *The Future in Education* (Cambridge, 1944), pp. 3, 126; F. CLARKE, *Education and Social Change* (London, 1940), p. 20.

6 *Curriculum and Examinations*, pp. 84–5; Staples' 'Reconstruction' Digests, III, *The Spens Report and After* (London, 1943), pp. 40–1.

7 For details see H. C. DENT, *The Education Act, 1944* (London, 1944).

8 W. ROY NIBLETT, 'The religious education clauses of the 1944 Act', in A. G. WEDDERSPOON (ed.), *Religious Education 1944–1984* (London, 1966), pp. 17–22.

9 BOARD OF EDUCATION, *Teachers and Youth Leaders* (London, 1944), pp. 8, 47–61.

10 TAWNEY, 'The problem of the public schools', in *The Radical Tradition*, p. 72; WORKERS' EDUCATIONAL ASSOCIATION, *The Public Schools and the Educational System* (London, 1943), pp. 2, 18; *The Spens Report and After*, p. 22.

11 BOARD OF EDUCATION, *The Public Schools and the General Educational System* (London, 1944), pp. 100–4.

12 J. B. HOPE SIMPSON, *Rugby Since Arnold* (London, 1967), pp. 231–2.

13 HILL, *Bristol Grammar School*, pp. 216–17; HUTTON, *King Edward's School, Birmingham*, p. 210.

14 For the social composition of the direct grant schools, 1905–50, see CAMPBELL, *Eleven-plus and All That*, p. 51.

15 B. SEEBOHM ROWNTREE and G. R. LAVERS, *Poverty and the Welfare State* (London, 1951), pp. 39–41.

16 G. D. H. COLE, *The Post-war Condition of Britain* (London, 1956; 1957 edition), p. 438; *15 to 18*, I, p. 46.

17 *Curriculum and Examinations*, pp. 2–3, 139.

18 PETCH, *Fifty Years of Examining*, p. 165–8.

19 MINISTRY OF EDUCATION, *The New Secondary Education* (London, 1947; 1954 edition), pp. 13, 22–3; MINISTRY OF EDUCATION, *The Story of Post-war School Building* (London, 1957); MICHAEL PARKINSON, *The Labour Party and the Organization of Secondary Education 1918–65* (London, 1970), pp. 84–5.

20 H. A. RÉE, *The Essential Grammar School* (London, 1956), pp. 11, 21.

21 H. T. HIMMELWEIT, 'Social status and secondary education since the 1944 Act: some data for London', in D. V. GLASS (ed.), *Social Mobility in Britain* (London, 1954; 1963 edition), p. 158.

22 *Higher Education*, Report, p. 49.

23 MINISTRY OF EDUCATION, *Early Leaving* (London, 1954; 1966 edition), pp. 34–5.

24 ALAN LITTLE and JOHN WESTERGAARD, 'The trend of class differentials in educational opportunity in England and Wales', *British Journal of Sociology*, XV (1964), pp. 308–10.

25 *15 to 18*, pp. 33, 449–50.

26 JEAN FLOUD, 'Reserves of ability', *Forum*, III (1961), p. 66.

27 RICHARD LAYARD, JOHN KING and CLAUS MOSER, *Impact of Robbins* (Harmondsworth, 1969), p. 16.

28 *15 to 18*, pp. 46–7.
29 RONALD A. MANZER, *Teachers and Politics* (Manchester, 1970), p. 141.
30 *Technical Education* (London, 1956), p. 5.
31 Ibid., p. 18.
32 Ibid., p. 5.
33 *Higher Education*, Appendix 2 (B), pp. 4–5.
34 T. R. FYVEL, *The Insecure Offenders* (London, 1961; 1963 edition), p. 238.
35 *Higher Education*, Report, pp. 49–54; MINISTRY OF EDUCATION, *Half Our Future* (London, 1963), pp. 6–7, 34; *Times Educational Supplement* (13 December 1963), p. 881 (percentages of young people entering higher education are from *Higher Education*, Appendix 1, p. 40: the figure for semi-skilled and unskilled workers' children was 2 per cent).
36 UNIVERSITY GRANTS COMMITTEE, *University Development 1957–1962* (London, 1964), p. 104.
37 LABOUR PARTY, *The Years of Crisis* (London, undated), p. 26.
38 *Higher Education*, Report, chapters 6 and 9; JEAN FLOUD, 'Are the Robbins estimates conservative?', *Forum*, VI (1964), pp. 79–82; LAYARD, KING and MOSER, *Impact of Robbins*, p. 23.
39 R. K. KELSALL, *Women in Teaching* (London, 1963), pp. 19–22.
40 *Higher Education*, Report, pp. 16–17, 62–3; ibid., Appendix 2 (A), pp. 24–6; LAYARD, KING and MOSER, *Impact of Robbins*, pp. 42–3; *15 to 18*, I, p. 228.
41 *The Years of Crisis*, p. 34.
42 ROBIN PEDLEY, 'The comprehensive school: England', *Forum*, V (1962), p. 4.
43 Reported in *The Times Educational Supplement* (29 January 1965), p. 272.
44 DEPARTMENT OF EDUCATION AND SCIENCE, *New Problems in School Design: Middle Schools* (London, 1966), pp. 137–9. See also ADAMS et al., *Education in Bradford*, pp. 262–7.
45 CAROLINE BENN, *Survey of Comprehensive Reorganization Plans* (London, 1971), p. iii; CAROLINE BENN and BRIAN SIMON, *Half Way There* (London, 1970), pp. 57–8, 70–1, 372.
46 Ibid., pp. 307–8.
47 ROBIN PEDLEY et al., *Comprehensive Schools To-day* (London, undated), p. 2.
48 J. C. DANIELS, reported in *Forum*, V (1963), pp. 39–40; for an early commentary on this debate see ALFRED YATES and D. A. PIDGEON, 'The effects of streaming', *Educational Research*, II (1959), pp. 65–9.
49 JULIENNE FORD, *Social Class and the Comprehensive School* (London, 1969), pp. 129–30.
50 G. MATTHEWS, 'Mathematics in the middle years', in SCHOOLS COUNCIL, *The Middle Years of Schooling from 8 to 13* (London, 1969), p. 64.
51 *Half Our Future*, chapters 5, 14, 16–19.

52 DEPARTMENT OF EDUCATION AND SCIENCE, *Secondary School Examinations Other than the GCE* (London, 1960: 1965 edition), pp. 7, 31.

53 *The Times Educational Supplement* (19 July 1963), p. 93.

54 SCHOOLS COUNCIL, *Change and Response* (London, 1965), p. 21.

55 Reported in *The Times Educational Supplement* (19 November 1965), p. 1093.

56 D. V. GLASS, Introduction to J. W. B. DOUGLAS, *The Home and the School* (London, 1964), p. xix.

57 J. W. B. DOUGLAS, J. M. ROSS and H. R. SIMPSON, *All our Future* (London, 1968), p. 186.

58 BASIL BERNSTEIN, 'Social structure, language, and learning', in JOHN P. DE CECCO, *The Psychology of Language, Thought and Instruction* (New York, 1967; 1969 edition), p. 91.

59 ALEC CLEGG and BARBARA MEGSON, *Children in Distress* (Harmondsworth, 1968), pp. 40–1.

60 GEORGE TAYLOR and N. AYRES, *Born and Bred Unequal* (London, 1969), p. 79; NORTHERN ECONOMIC PLANNING COUNCIL, *Report on Education*, part 1 (1970), p. 1.

61 Quoted in the *Guardian* (4 January 1972).

62 See GEORGE TAYLOR, *The Threat to Northern Education* (Cambridge, 1971).

63 The *Guardian* (19 November 1971).

64 EDWARD BOYLE in *Twentieth Century*, CLXXIV (1966), p. 44.

65 For the story of this development see SIR JAMES PITMAN, 'The purpose, planning and future of i.t.a.', in BRIAN ROSE (ed.), *Modern Trends in Education* (London, 1971).

66 DEPARTMENT OF EDUCATION AND SCIENCE, *Children and their Primary Schools*, I, pp. 48, 51, 55, 461.

67 ERIC MIDWINTER, *Education: a priority area* (London, undated), p. 2. For an account of the Liverpool project see the same author's *Projections* (London, 1972).

68 ERIC MIDWINTER, quoted in *The Times Educational Supplement* (10 September 1971), p. 13.

69 GORDON BOWKER, *The Education of Coloured Immigrants* (London, 1968), pp. 58–60; TREVOR BURGIN and PATRICIA EDSON, *Spring Grove: the Education of Immigrant Children* (London, 1967), pp. 32–4.

70 HOWARD GLENNERSTER and RICHARD PRYKE, *The Public Schools* (London, 1964), p. 17.

71 PUBLIC SCHOOLS COMMISSION, *First Report* (1968), I, pp. 18, 21, 30; *Second Report* (1970), I, pp. 11–16.

72 Quoted in *The Times Educational Supplement* (12 November 1971), p. 12.

73 FEDERATION OF BRITISH INDUSTRIES, *Industry and the Schools* (London, 1965), pp. 1–3; LAYARD, KING and MOSER, *Impact of Robbins*, p. 47.

74 COUNCIL FOR SCIENTIFIC POLICY, *Enquiry into the Flow of Candi-*

dates in Science and Technology into Higher Education (London, 1968), pp. 87–90; for the discussion of student choice see chapters 6–7.

75 *Half Our Future*, p. 108.

76 *The Times Educational Supplement* (17 December 1971), p. 1.

77 DENNIS PIRRIE and A. J. DALZELL WARD, *A Textbook of Health Education* (London, 1962; 1966 edition), p. 133.

78 DEPARTMENT OF EDUCATION AND SCIENCE, Reports on Education, LXI, *Health at School* (London, 1970), p. 1.

79 R. GULLIFORD, *Special Educational Needs* (London, 1971), pp. 11–12.

80 *Report of the Committee on Local Authority and Allied Personal Social Services* (London, 1968), p. 44.

81 M. M. LEWIS, *The Importance of Illiteracy* (London, 1953), pp. 76–7; *Half Our Future*, pp. xiv, 119.

82 DEPARTMENT OF EDUCATION AND SCIENCE, *Education and Science in 1968* (London, 1969), p. 9.

83 ANNE CORBETT in *New Society* (30 December 1971), p. 1291.

84 Speech to North of England Education Conference, quoted in the *Guardian* (5 January 1972).

Further Reading

GORDON BOWKER, *The Education of Coloured Immigrants* (London, 1968).

H. C. DENT, *Education in Transition: a sociological study of the impact of war on English education 1939–1943* (London, 1944).

H. C. DENT, *Growth in English Education 1946–1952* (London, 1954).

A. D. EDWARDS, *The Changing Sixth Form in the Twentieth Century* (London, 1970), chapters 4–6.

A. H. HALSEY (ed.), *Educational Priority, I: E.P.A. Problems and Policies* (London, 1972), chapters 1–4.

RICHARD LAYARD, JOHN KING and CLAUS MOSER, *The Impact of Robbins* (Harmondsworth, 1969).

RONALD A. MANZER, *Teachers and Politics: the role of the National Union of Teachers in the making of national educational policy in England and Wales since 1944* (Manchester, 1970).

MINISTRY OF EDUCATION, *Education 1900–1950* (London, 1950).

MINISTRY OF EDUCATION, *15 to 18*, I (Report) (London, 1959).

JAMES MOUNTFORD, *Keele: an historical critique* (London, 1972).

MICHAEL PARKINSON, *The Labour Party and the Organization of Secondary Education 1918–65* (London, 1970), chapters 3–6.

DAVID RUBINSTEIN and BRIAN SIMON, *The Evolution of the Comprehensive School 1926–1966* (London, 1965).

Staples 'Reconstruction' Digests, *Education, Part I: The Spens Report and After* (London, 1943).

See also pp. 473–4.

General bibliography

The following works are relevant to a large number or all of the chapters of this book, and are supplementary to the lists of suggested reading at the end of each chapter. Given the relatively large amount of literature dealing specifically with the nineteenth and twentieth centuries, a separate list of recommended reading is given for this period.

I *English social history*

SIR JOHN CLAPHAM, *A Concise Economic History of Britain . . . to 1750* (Cambridge, 1949).

CHRISTOPHER HILL, *Reformation to Industrial Revolution*, Pelican Economic History of Britain, II (Harmondsworth, 1969).

E. J. HOBSBAWM, *Industry and Empire*, Pelican Economic History of Britain, III (Harmondsworth, 1969).

PETER LASLETT, *The World we have lost* (London, 1965).

PETER MATHIAS, *The First Industrial Nation: an economic history of Britain 1700–1914* (London, 1969).

JUDITH RYDER and HAROLD SILVER, *Modern English Society: history and structure 1850–1970* (London, 1970).

II *Education: general*

PHILIPPE ARIES (trans. R. Baldick), *Centuries of Childhood* (London, 1962).

S. H. ATKINS, *A Select Check-list of Printed Material on Education . . . to 1800* (Hull, 1970).

BOARD OF EDUCATION, *The Public Schools and the General Educational System* (London, 1944), chapters 1–2, historical sketch of the public schools.

BOARD OF EDUCATION, *Secondary Education with Special Reference to Grammar Schools and Technical High Schools* (London, 1938), chapter I, history of secondary-school curriculum.

NICHOLAS CARLISLE, *A Concise Description of the Endowed Grammar Schools of England* (2 volumes, London, 1818).

CARLO M. CIPOLLA, *Literacy and Development in the West* (Harmondsworth, 1969).

J. E. G. DE MONTMORENCY, *State Intervention in English Education* (Cambridge, 1902).

O. J. DUNLOP and RICHARD D. DENMAN, *English Apprenticeship and Child Labour* (London, 1912).

LESLIE WYNNE EVANS, *Education in Industrial Wales 1700–1900* (Cardiff, 1971).

DOROTHY GARDINER, *English Girlhood at School* (Oxford, 1929).

C. P. HILL, *The History of Bristol Grammar School* (London, 1951).

JOSEPHINE KAMM, *Hope Deferred: girls' education in English history* (London, 1965).

THOMAS KELLY, *A History of Adult Education in Great Britain* (Liverpool, 1962).

JOHN LAWSON, *A Town Grammar School through Six Centuries: a history of Hull grammar school against its local background* (London, 1963).

ARTHUR F. LEACH (ed.), *Educational Charters and Documents, 598–1909* (Cambridge, 1911).

ARTHUR F. LEACH, *A History of Winchester College* (London, 1898).

H. C. MAXWELL LYTE, *A History of Eton College* (3rd edition, London, 1899).

SIR CHARLES MALLET, *A History of the University of Oxford* (3 volumes, London, 1924).

J. B. MULLINGER, *The University of Cambridge* (3 volumes, Cambridge, 1873–1911).

ALFRED A. MUMFORD, *The Manchester Grammar School 1515–*

1915: a regional study of the advancement of learning in Manchester since the Reformation (London, 1919).

P. W. MUSGRAVE (ed.), *Sociology, History and Education: a reader* (London, 1970).

J. S. PURVIS, *Educational Records* (York, 1959).

J. P. C. ROACH (ed.), *Victoria County History of Cambridge*, III (London, 1959).

H. E. SALTER and M. D. LOBEL (ed.), *Victoria County History of Oxford*, III (London, 1954).

MALCOLM SEABORNE, *The English School: its architecture and organization 1370–1870* (London, 1971).

MALCOLM SEABORNE, *Education: a visual history* (London, 1966).

BRIAN SIMON (ed.), *Education in Leicestershire 1540–1940* (Leicester, 1968).

LAWRENCE STONE, 'Literacy and education in England 1640–1900', *Past and Present*, XLII (1969).

D. W. SYLVESTER, *Educational Documents 800–1816* (London, 1970).

M. F. THWAITE, *From Primer to Pleasure: an introduction to the history of children's books in England from the invention of printing to 1900* (London, 1963).

P. J. WALLIS, *Histories of Old Schools: a revised list for England and Wales* (Newcastle, 1966).

III *Education: nineteenth and twentieth centuries*

JOHN WILLIAM ADAMSON, *English Education 1789–1902* (Cambridge, 1930).

RICHARD D. ALTICK, *The English Common Reader: a social history of the mass reading public 1800–1900* (Chicago, 1957).

R. L. ARCHER, *Secondary Education in the Nineteenth Century* (London, 1921).

W. H. G. ARMYTAGE, *Civic Universities: aspects of a British tradition* (London, 1955).

T. W. BAMFORD, *Rise of the Public Schools: a study of boys' public boarding schools in England and Wales from 1837 to the present day* (London, 1967).

H. HALE BELLOT, *University College London 1826–1926* (London, 1929).

BOARD OF EDUCATION, *The Education of the Adolescent* (London, 1927), chapter I, post-primary education 1800–1918.

BOARD OF EDUCATION, *The Primary School* (London, 1931), chapter I, primary education in the nineteenth and twentieth centuries.

RICHARD BOURNE and BRIAN MACARTHUR, *The Struggle for Education 1870–1970: a pictorial history of the National Union of Teachers* (London, 1970).

D. S. L. CARDWELL, *The Organisation of Science in England: a retrospect* (London, 1957).

STEPHEN F. COTGROVE, *Technical Education and Social Change* (London, 1958).

MARJORIE CRUIKSHANK, *Church and State in English Education 1870 to the Present Day* (London, 1964).

P. H. J. H. GOSDEN, *The Development of Educational Administration in England and Wales* (Oxford, 1966).

P. H. J. H. GOSDEN, *The Evolution of a Profession: a study of the contribution of teachers' associations to the development of school teaching as a professional occupation* (Oxford, 1972).

J. F. C. HARRISON, *Learning and Living 1790–1960: a study in the history of the English adult education movement* (London, 1961).

MARION JOHNSON, *Derbyshire Village Schools in the Nineteenth Century* (Newton Abbot, 1970).

J. STUART MACLURE, *Educational Documents England and Wales 1816–1963* (London, 1965).

J. STUART MACLURE, *One Hundred Years of London Education 1870–1970* (London, 1970).

R. J. MONTGOMERY, *Examinations: an account of their evolution as administrative devices in England* (London, 1965).

W. A. MUNFORD, *Penny-rate: aspects of British public library history 1850–1950* (London, 1951).

JAMES MURPHY, *Church, State and Schools in Britain, 1800–1970* (London, 1971).

R. W. RICH, *The Training of Teachers in England and Wales during the Nineteenth Century* (Cambridge, 1933).

G. W. RODERICK, *The Emergence of a Scientific Society in England 1800–1965* (London, 1967).

M. E. SADLER (ed.), *Continuation Schools in England and Elsewhere: their place in the educational system of an industrial and commercial state* (Manchester, 1907).

R. R. SELLMAN, *Devon Village Schools in the Nineteenth Century* (Newton Abbot, 1967).

FRANK SMITH, *A History of English Elementary Education 1760–1902* (London, 1931).

MARY STURT, *The Education of the People: a history of primary education in England and Wales in the nineteenth century* (London, 1967).

ASHER TROPP, *The School Teachers: the growth of the teaching profession in England and Wales from 1800 to the present day* (London, 1957).

See also pp. 266, 313, 362–3, 413–14, 470.

Index

Aachen, palace school at, 10
abbeys, as patrons of schools, 23
Abbotsholme school, 344, 355–6, 400
ABC schools, 70, 112, 170
Aberdare Commission, on intermediate and higher education in Wales (1881), 339
Aberystwyth University College, 348
Addison, Joseph, on charity schools, 185
adult school movement, 406
Ælfric, *scholasticus*, and later abbot, 14, 15
Æthelweard, ealdorman of Wessex, 14
Æthelwold, bishop of Winchester, 14
age: of starting school and entering university (late medieval), 49, 56; of treating children as adults by law (sixteenth–seventeenth centuries), 111; of pupils at grammar schools (seventeenth century), 118; of entering university (eighteenth century), 217
Agricola, 7
Agricultural Children Act (1873), 325–6
Albert, Prince Consort, 301, 303
Alcock, John, bishop of Ely, 49, 50, 67; tutor to Prince of Wales (Edward V), 80
Alcuin of York, 10
Aldhelm, abbot of Malmesbury, 11
Alexander, Sir William, secretary of Association of Education Committees, 444

Alfred, king of the West Saxons, 12
All Souls College, Oxford, 59, 213.
Allen, Rev. John, HMI, 272
almonry schools, 42–3, 62; at the Reformation, 95–6
Anglesey, comprehensive schools in, 424, 441
Anglo-Saxon period, 7–16
anti-clericalism, (fourteenth century), 55
Anti-Jacobin, The, and Sunday schools, 235
Applegarth, Robert, trade union leader, 294, 316, 352
apprenticeship, 12, 72–5, 122–5; to trades requiring competence in Latin, 48; charities for, 104, 123; of workhouse children, 188; in the professions (eighteenth century), 209
Aquinas, St Thomas, 49
architecture: books on, 124; education for, 209, 300
Argyll Commission on education in Scotland (1865–8), 322
Aristotle, 18, 49; study of, at universities, (early medieval) 26, 28–9, (from 1590s) 129, 130, 160, 168, (eighteenth century) 210–11
arithmetic: at monastic schools, 10; for calculating date of Easter, 11; at universities, 99; at grammar schools, 118, 196; books on, 124–5